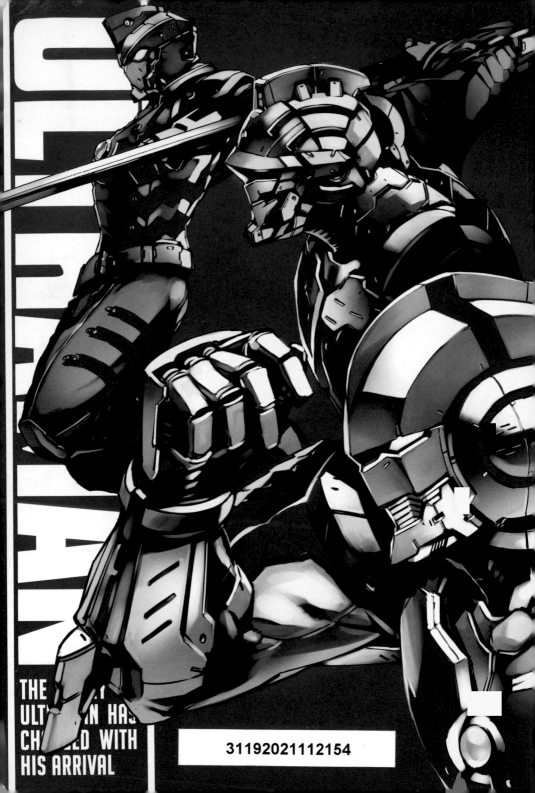

ULTRAMAN

THE ... ...
ULT...N HAS ...
CH...ED WITH
HIS ARRIVAL

31192021112154

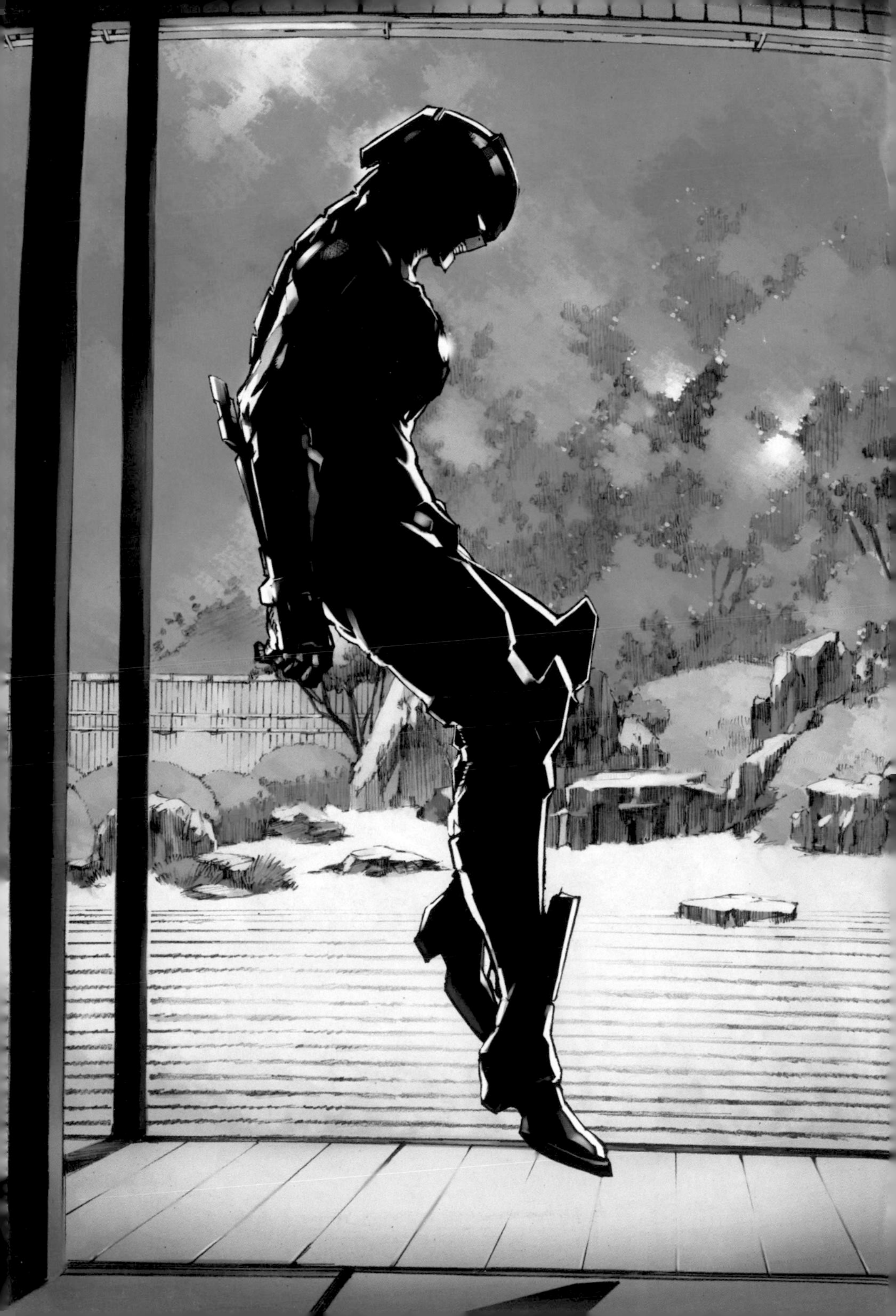

THIS IS THE BEGINNING OF A NEW AGE.

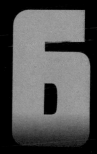

CONTENTS

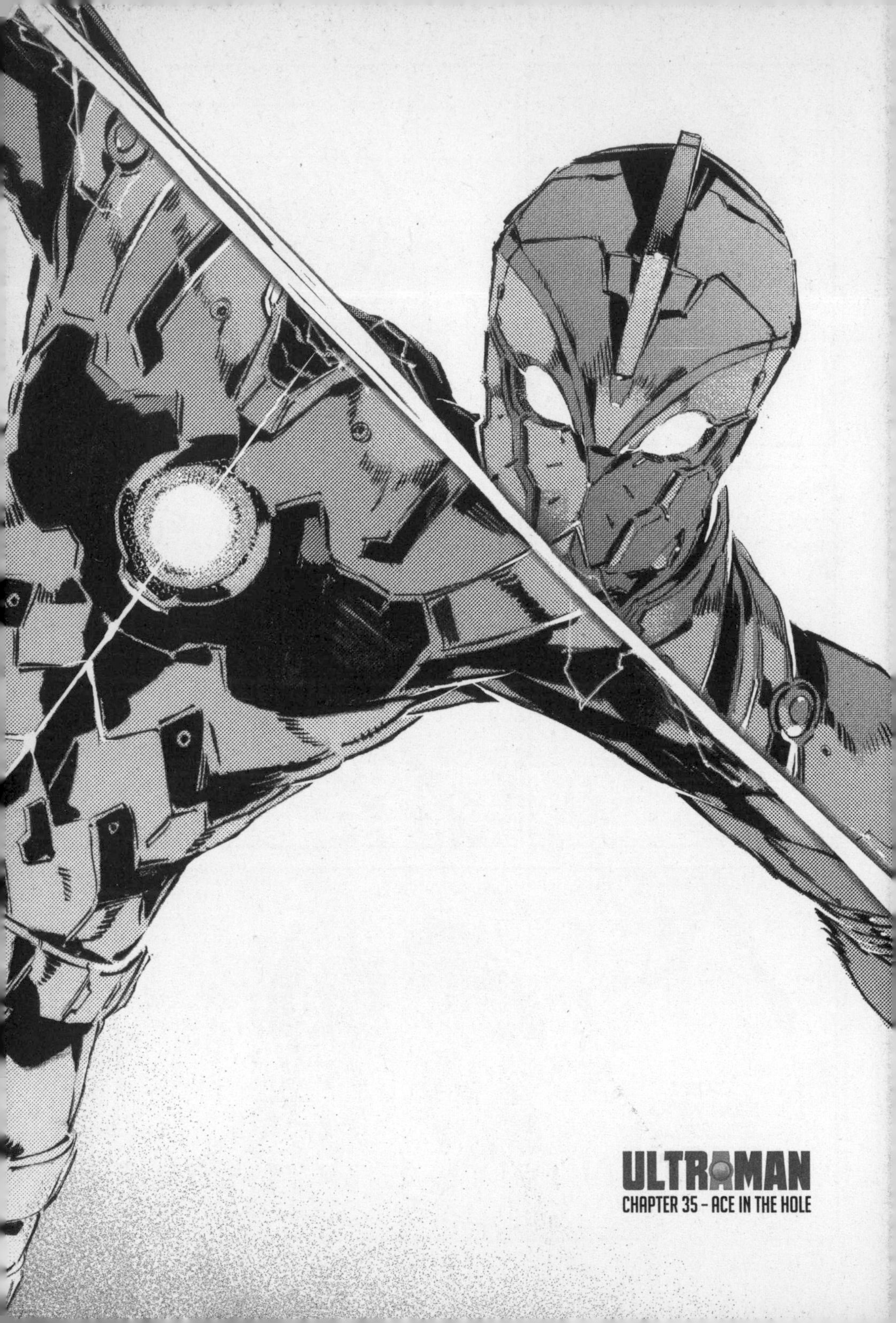

ULTRAMAN

CHAPTER 35 – ACE IN THE HOLE

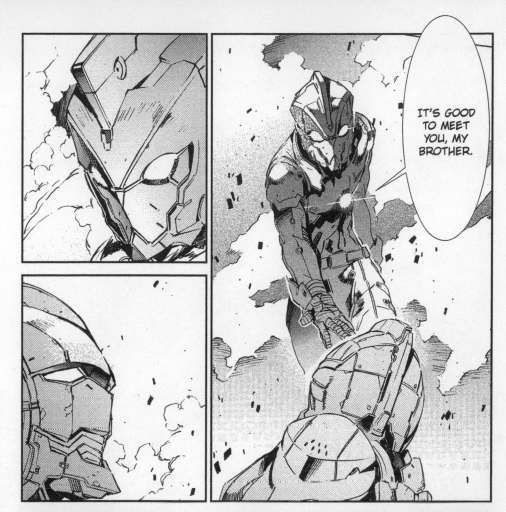

IT'S GOOD TO MEET YOU, MY BROTHER.

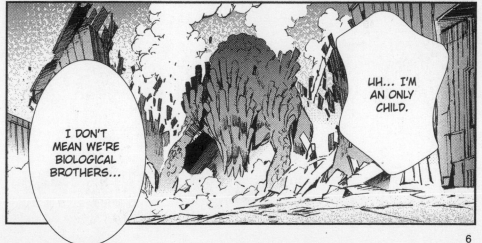

I DON'T MEAN WE'RE BIOLOGICAL BROTHERS...

UH... I'M AN ONLY CHILD.

6

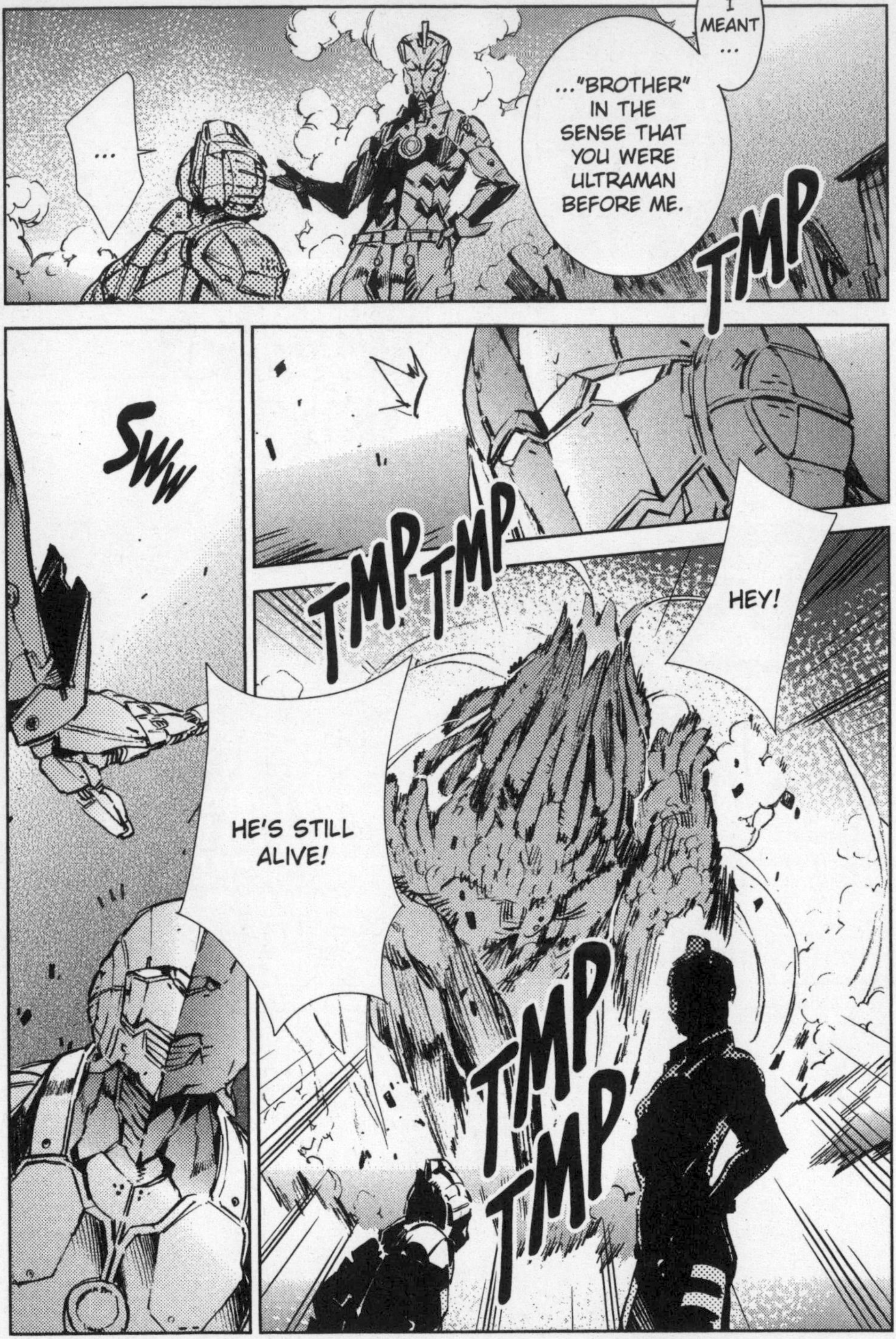
I MEANT ...
..."BROTHER" IN THE SENSE THAT YOU WERE ULTRAMAN BEFORE ME.
...
TMP
TMP TMP
HEY!
TMP TMP
SWW
HE'S STILL ALIVE!

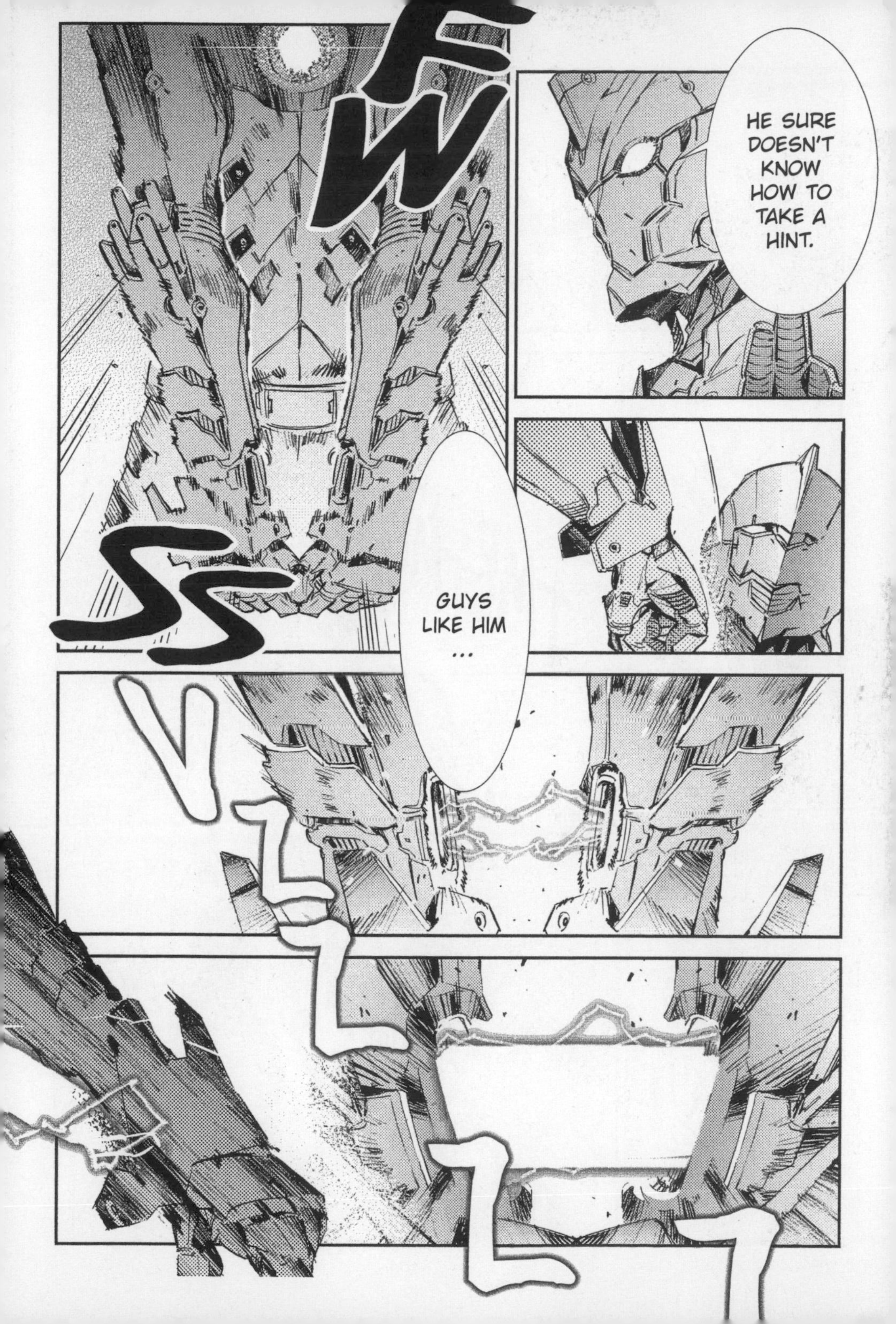
HE SURE DOESN'T KNOW HOW TO TAKE A HINT.
GUYS LIKE HIM ...
FW
SS

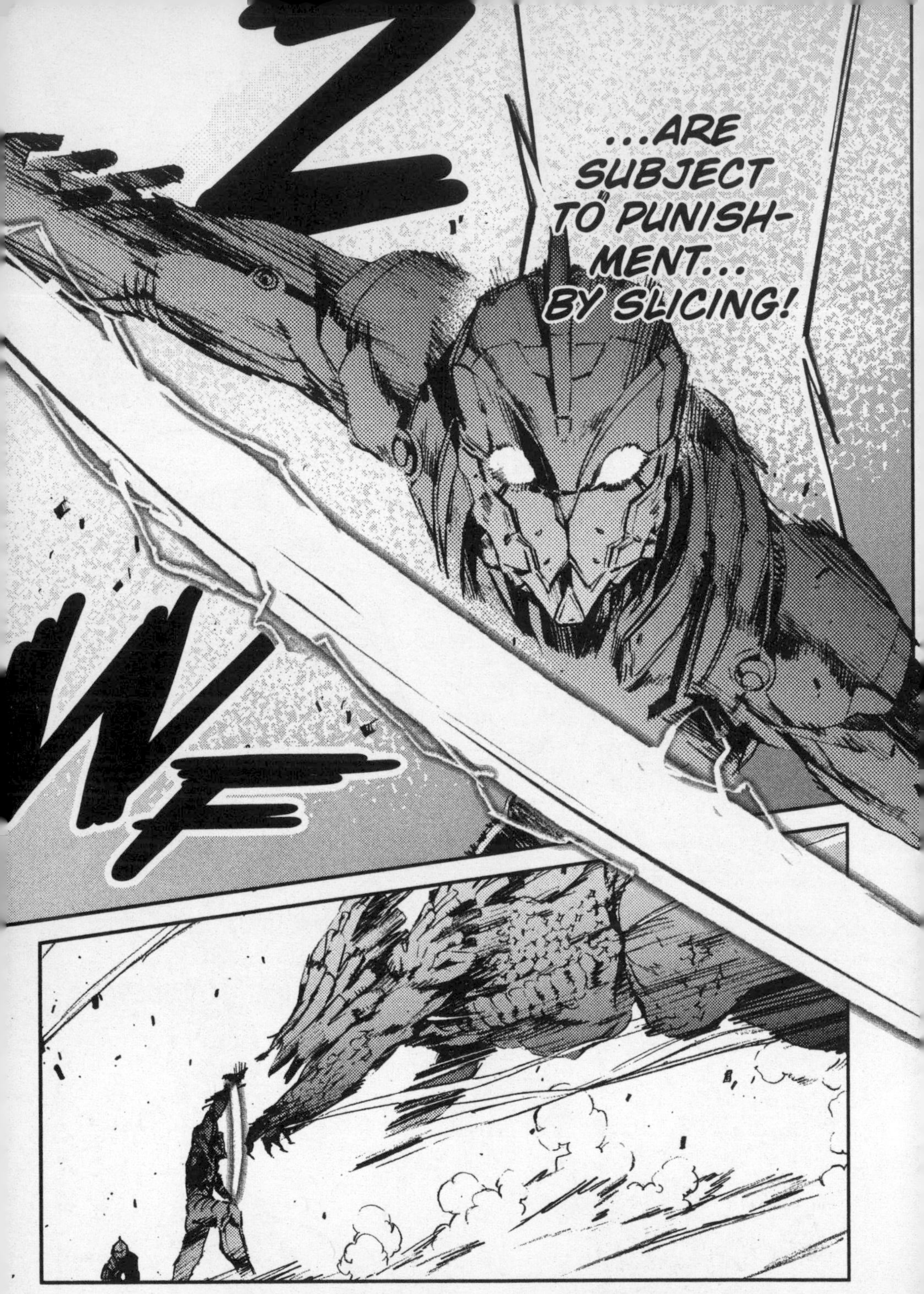
...ARE SUBJECT TO PUNISH-MENT... BY SLICING!

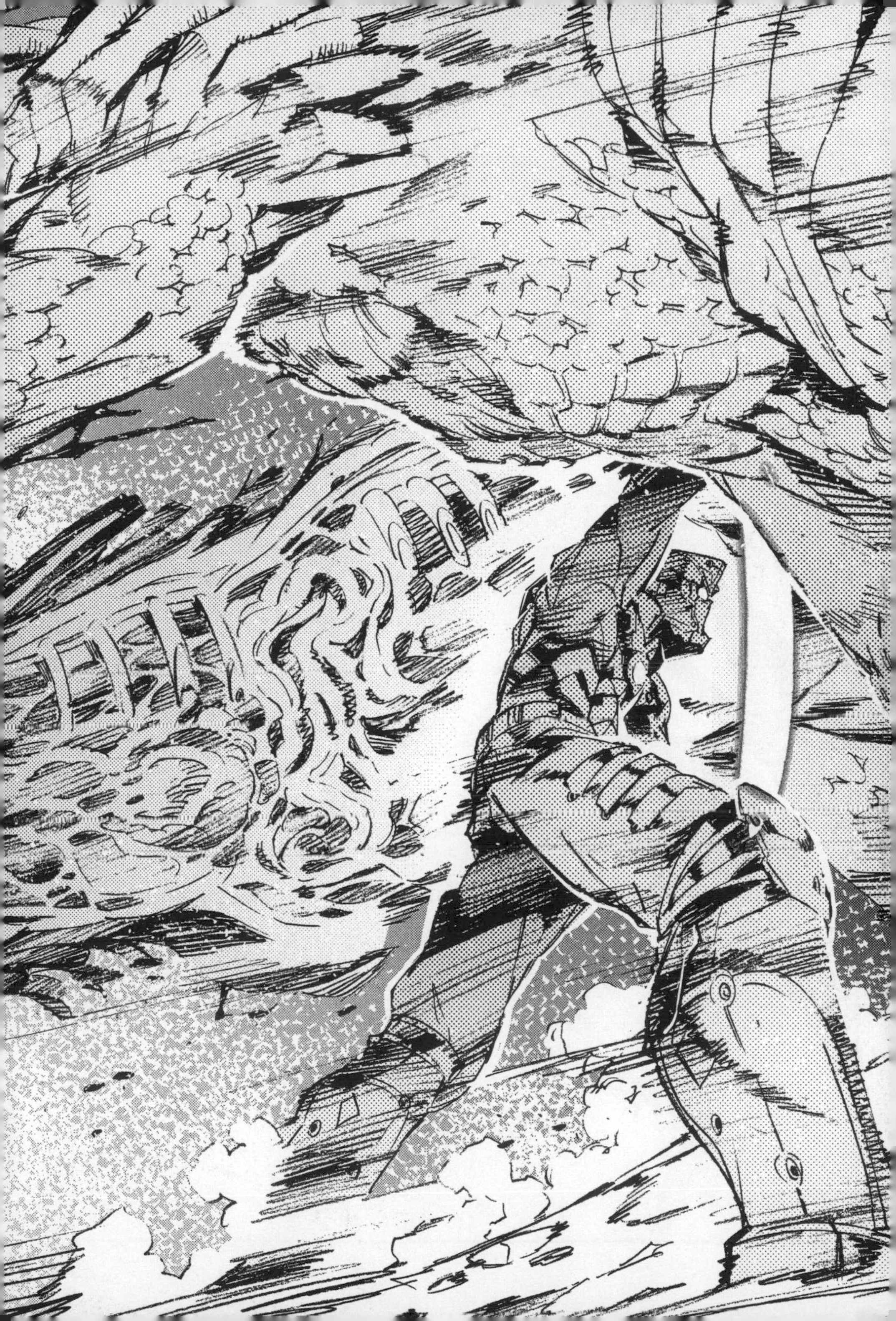

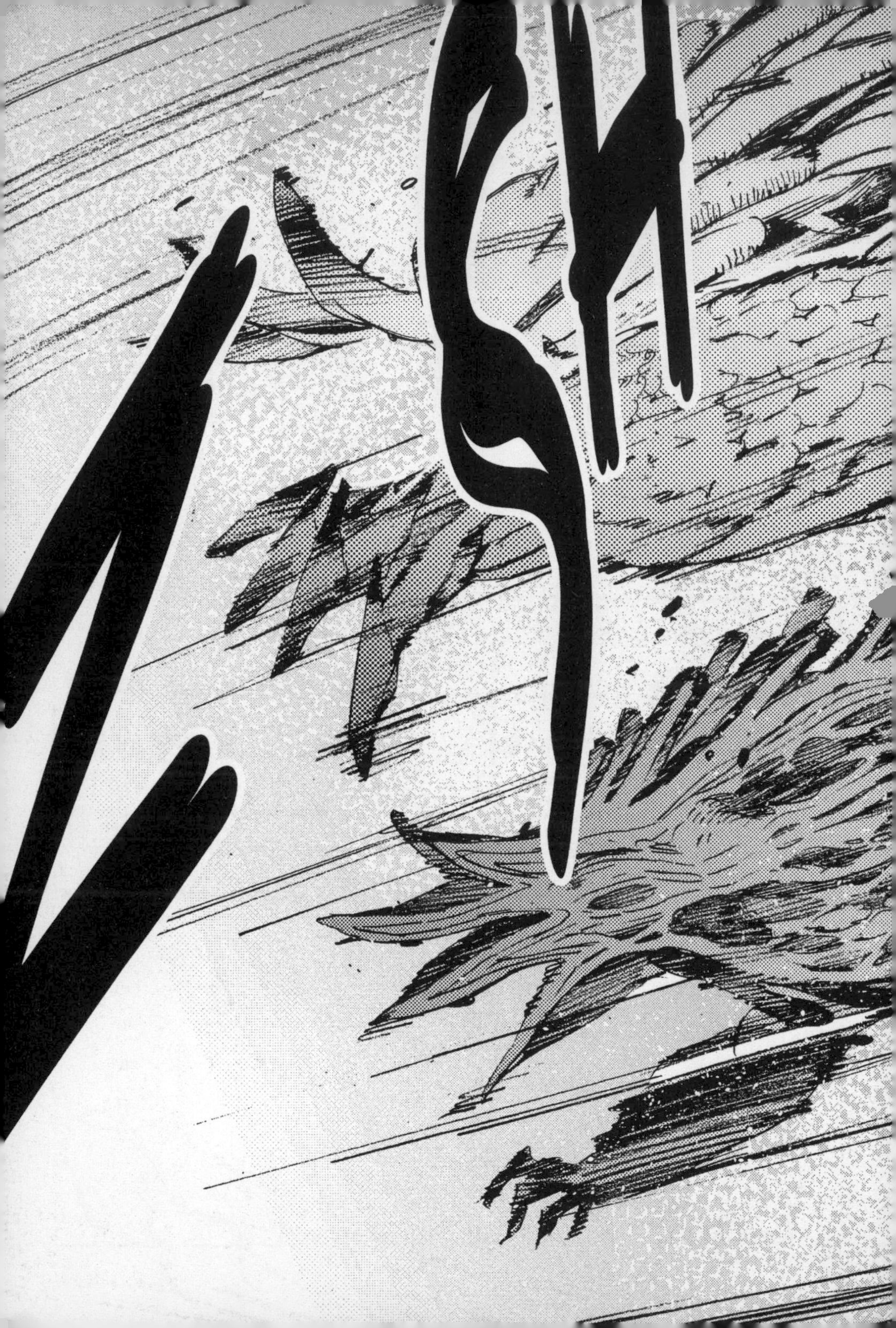

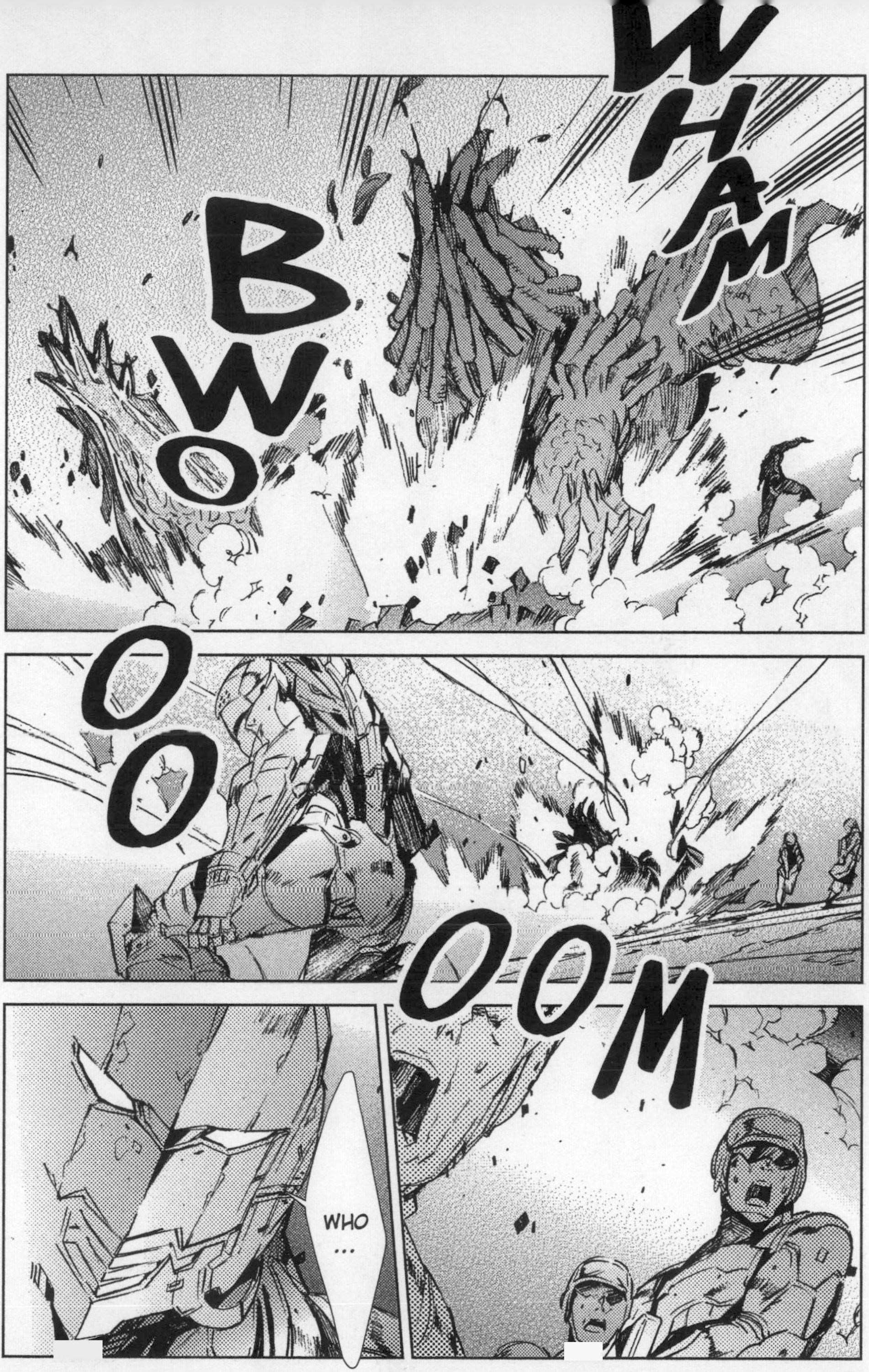
WHAM
BWOOOOOM
WHO ...

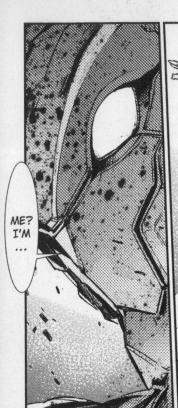

ME?
I'M
...

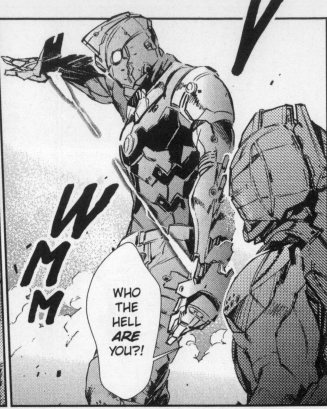

WMM

WHO
THE
HELL
ARE
YOU?!

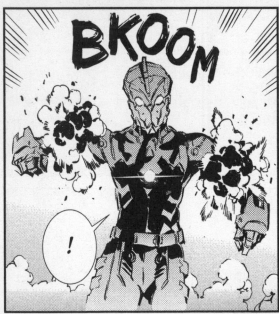

BKOOM

!

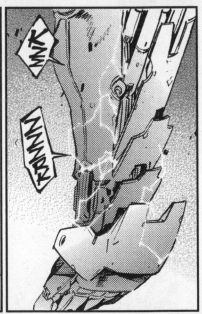

KIN

NNNRK

13

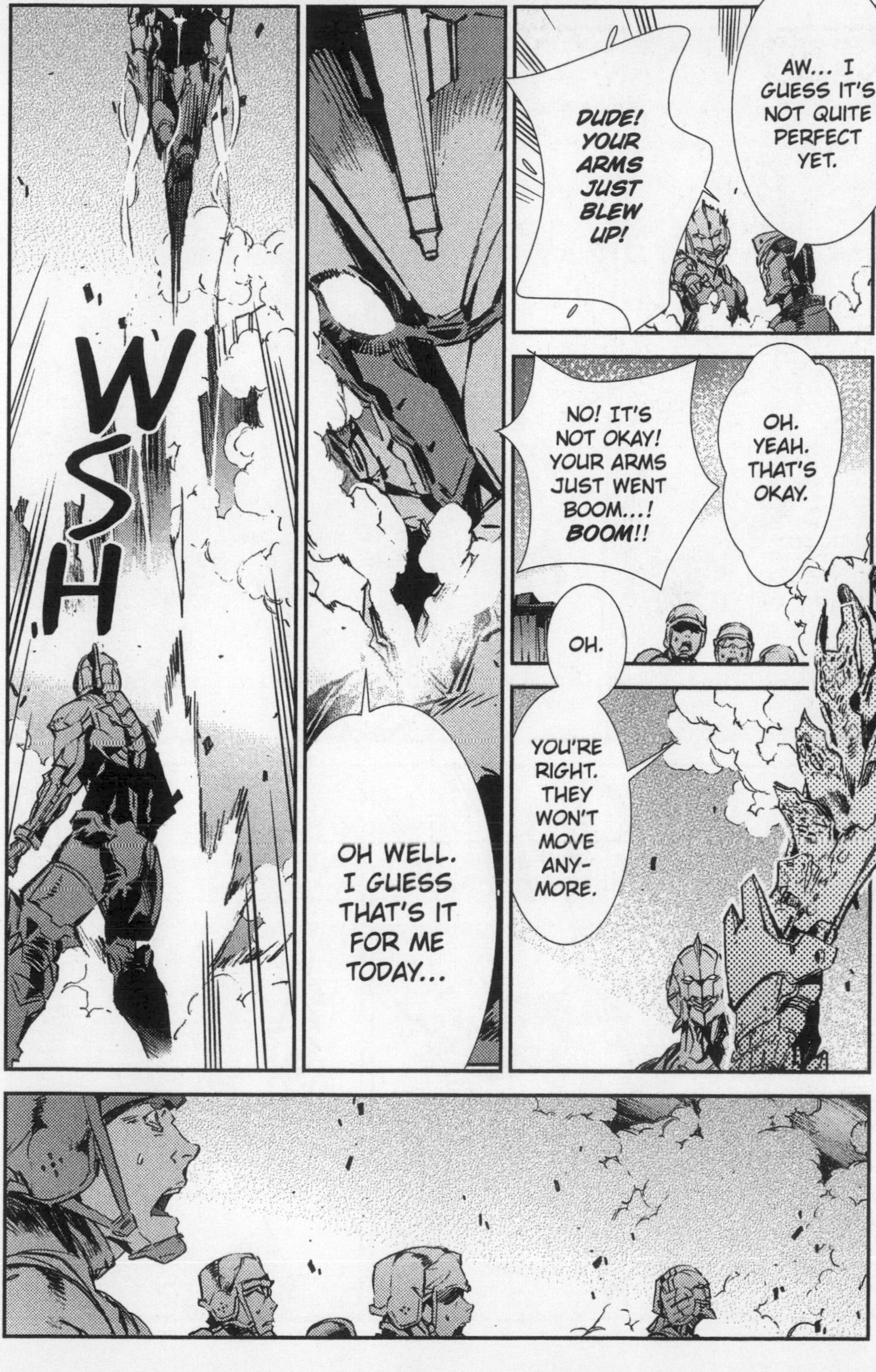
AW... I GUESS IT'S NOT QUITE PERFECT YET.
DUDE! YOUR ARMS JUST BLEW UP!
OH. YEAH. THAT'S OKAY.
NO! IT'S NOT OKAY! YOUR ARMS JUST WENT BOOM...! BOOM!!
OH.
YOU'RE RIGHT. THEY WON'T MOVE ANY-MORE.
OH WELL. I GUESS THAT'S IT FOR ME TODAY...
WSH

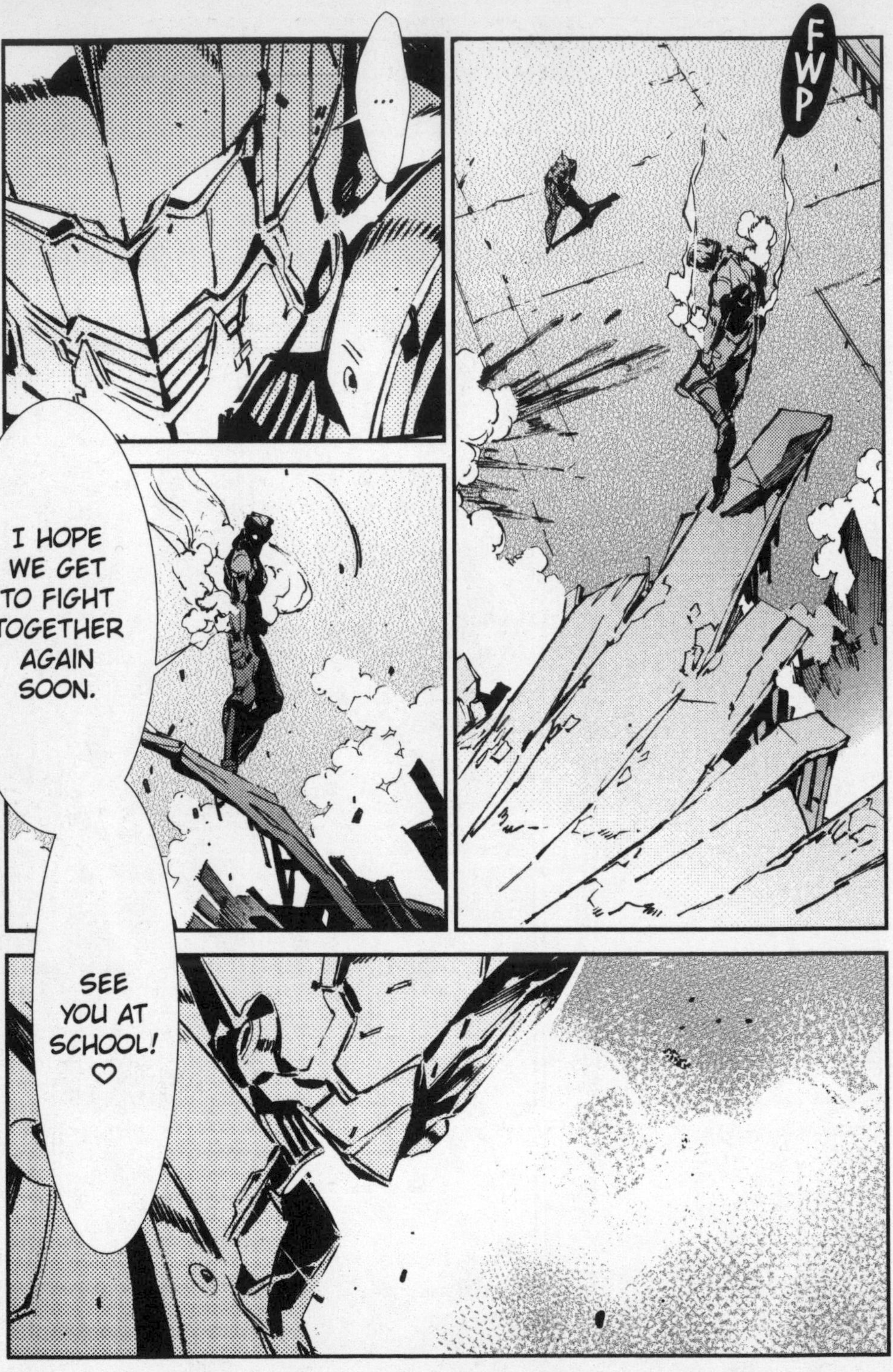
FWP
...
I HOPE WE GET TO FIGHT TOGETHER AGAIN SOON.
SEE YOU AT SCHOOL! ♡

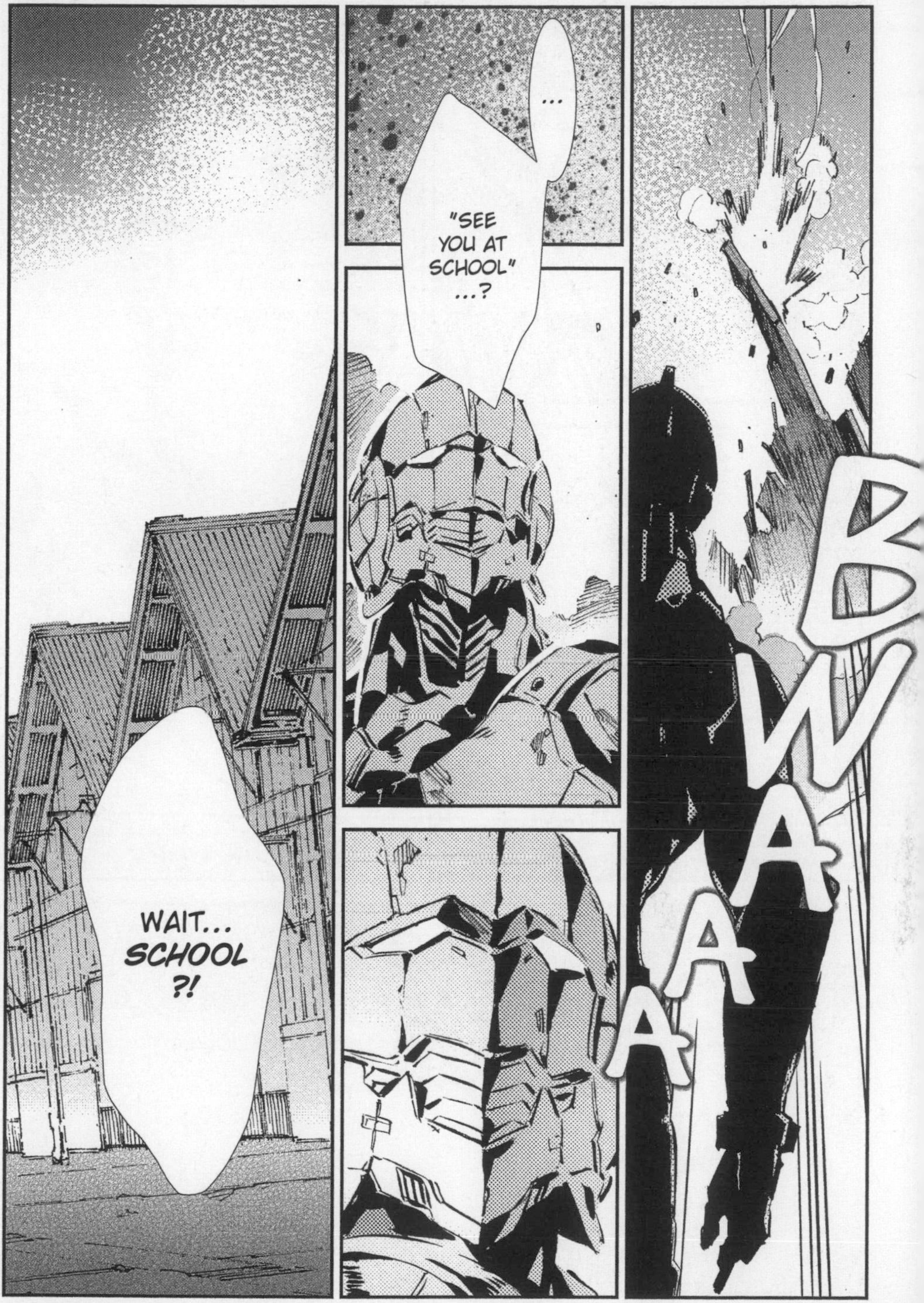
BWAAA
...
"SEE YOU AT SCHOOL" ...?
WAIT... SCHOOL ?!

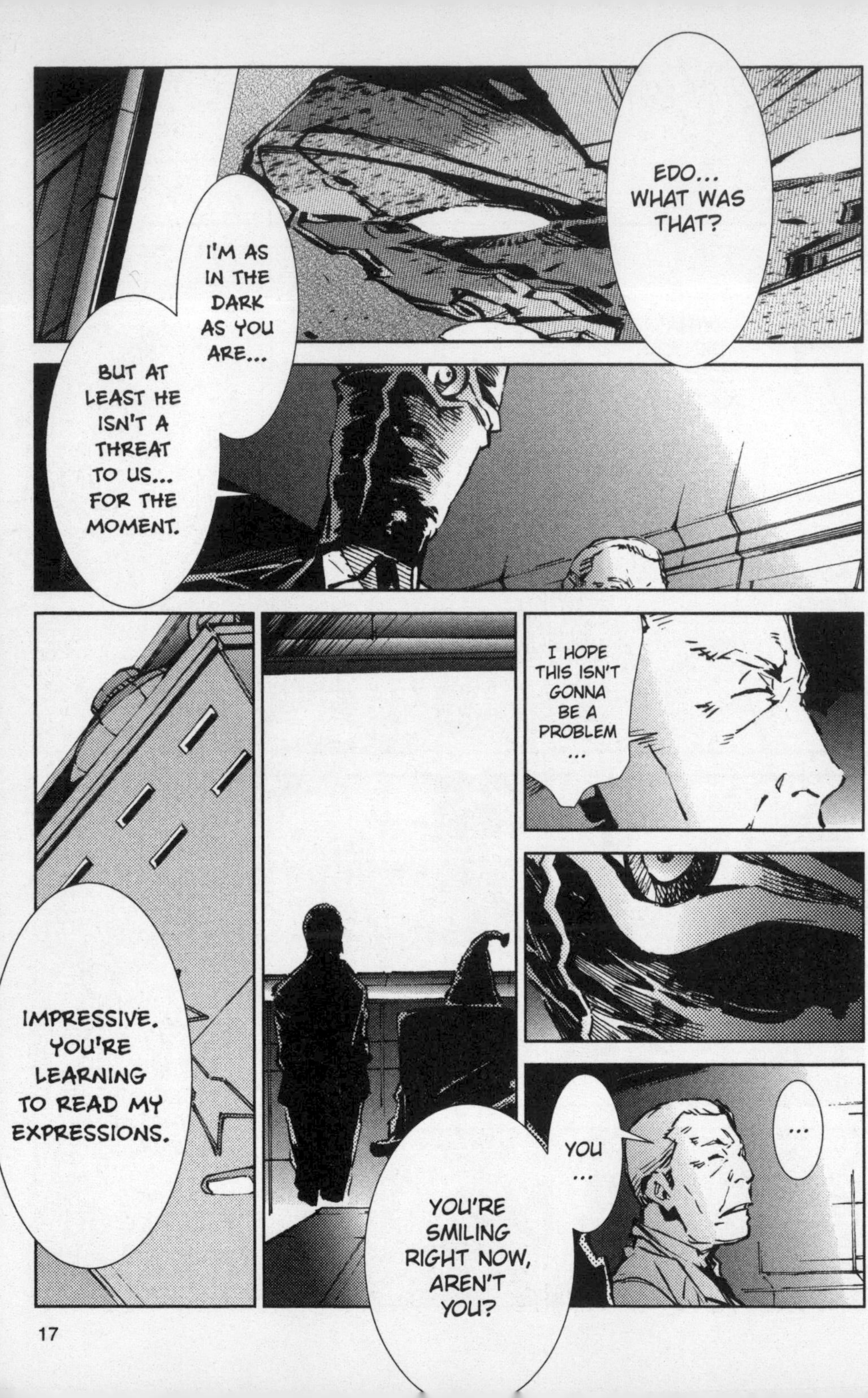
EDO... WHAT WAS THAT?
I'M AS IN THE DARK AS YOU ARE...
BUT AT LEAST HE ISN'T A THREAT TO US... FOR THE MOMENT.
I HOPE THIS ISN'T GONNA BE A PROBLEM ...
...
YOU ...
YOU'RE SMILING RIGHT NOW, AREN'T YOU?
IMPRESSIVE. YOU'RE LEARNING TO READ MY EXPRESSIONS.

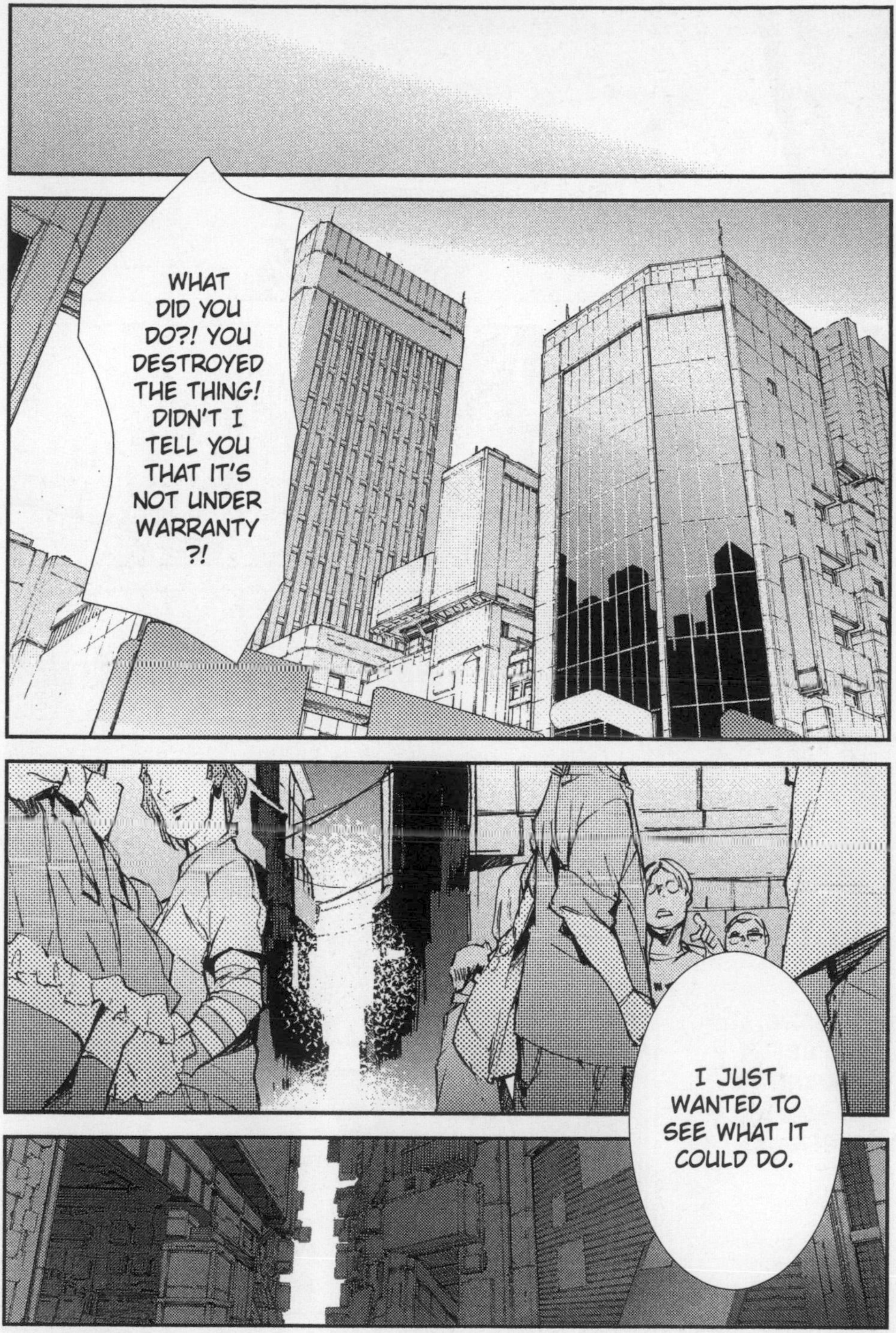
WHAT DID YOU DO?! YOU DESTROYED THE THING! DIDN'T I TELL YOU THAT IT'S NOT UNDER WARRANTY ?!
I JUST WANTED TO SEE WHAT IT COULD DO.

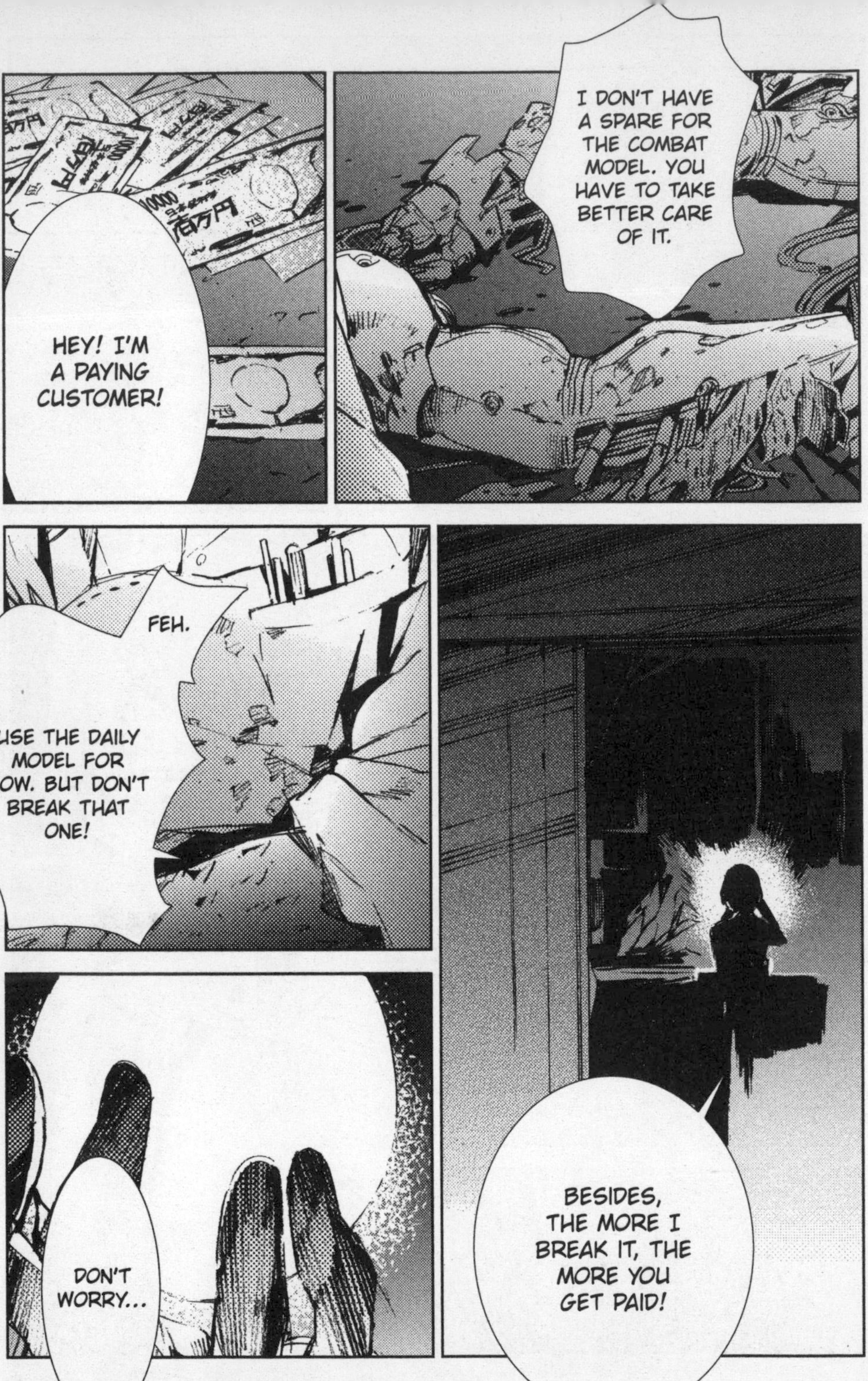
I DON'T HAVE A SPARE FOR THE COMBAT MODEL. YOU HAVE TO TAKE BETTER CARE OF IT.
HEY! I'M A PAYING CUSTOMER!
BESIDES, THE MORE I BREAK IT, THE MORE YOU GET PAID!
FEH.
USE THE DAILY MODEL FOR NOW. BUT DON'T BREAK THAT ONE!
DON'T WORRY...

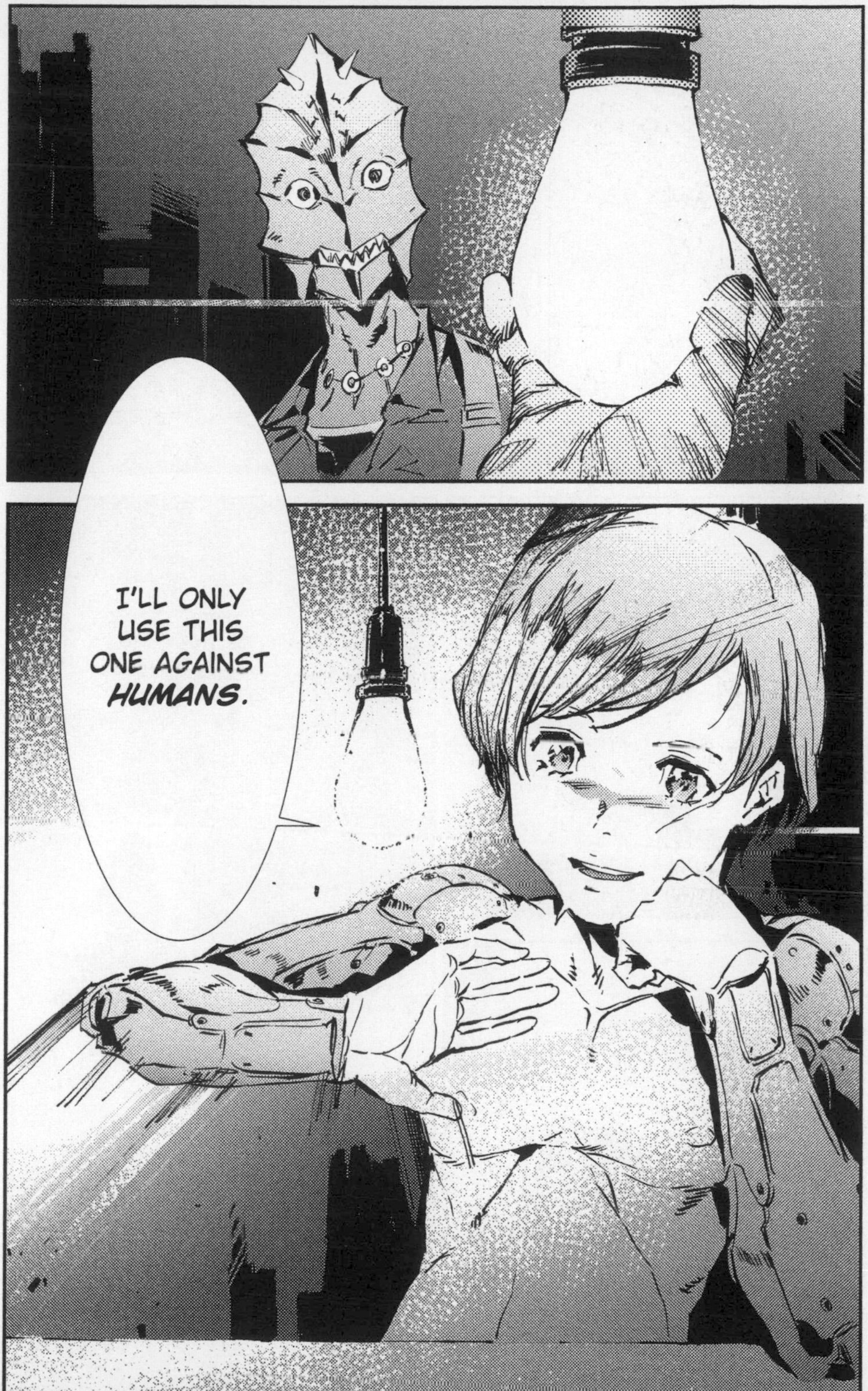
I'LL ONLY USE THIS ONE AGAINST HUMANS.

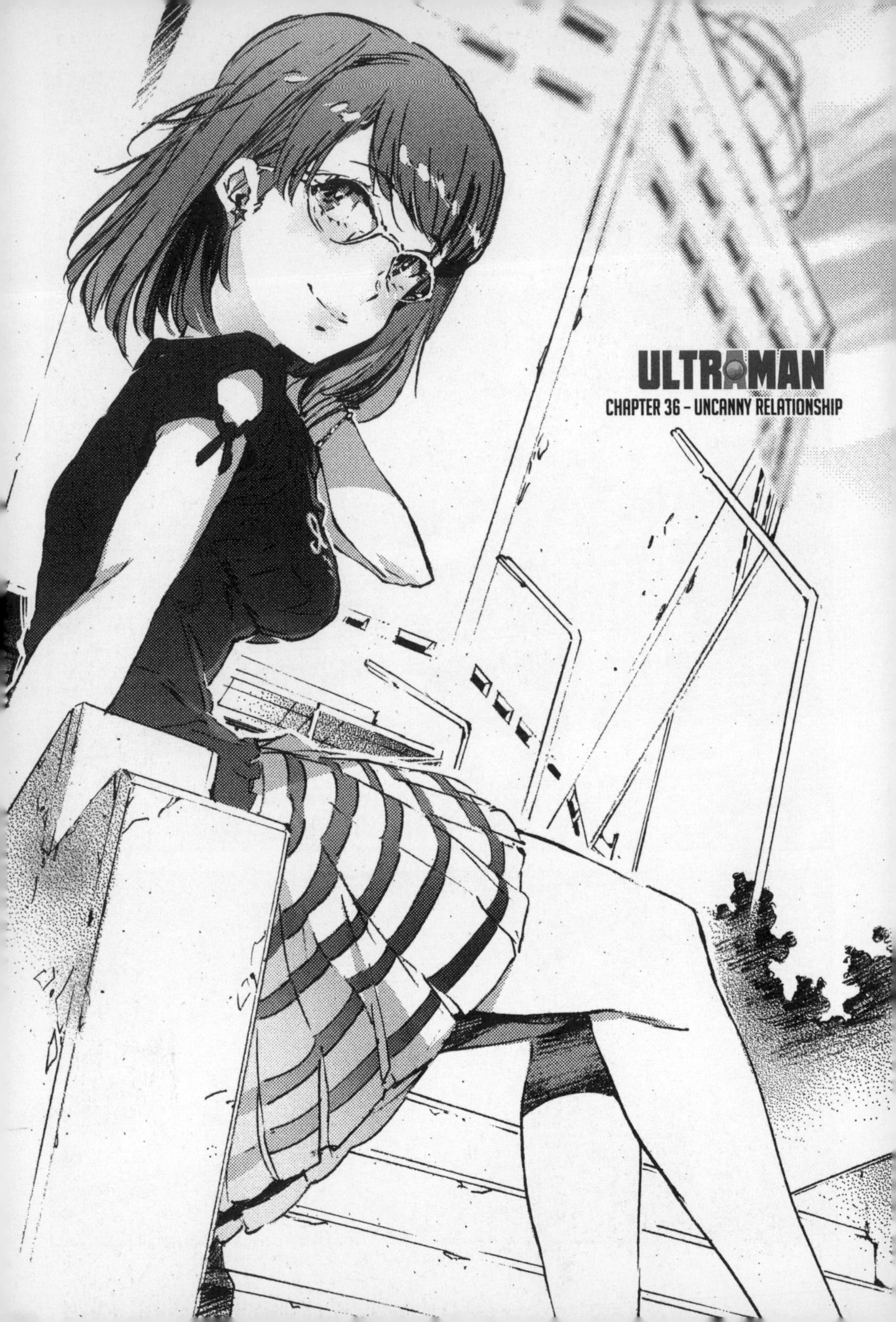
ULTRAMAN
CHAPTER 36 – UNCANNY RELATIONSHIP

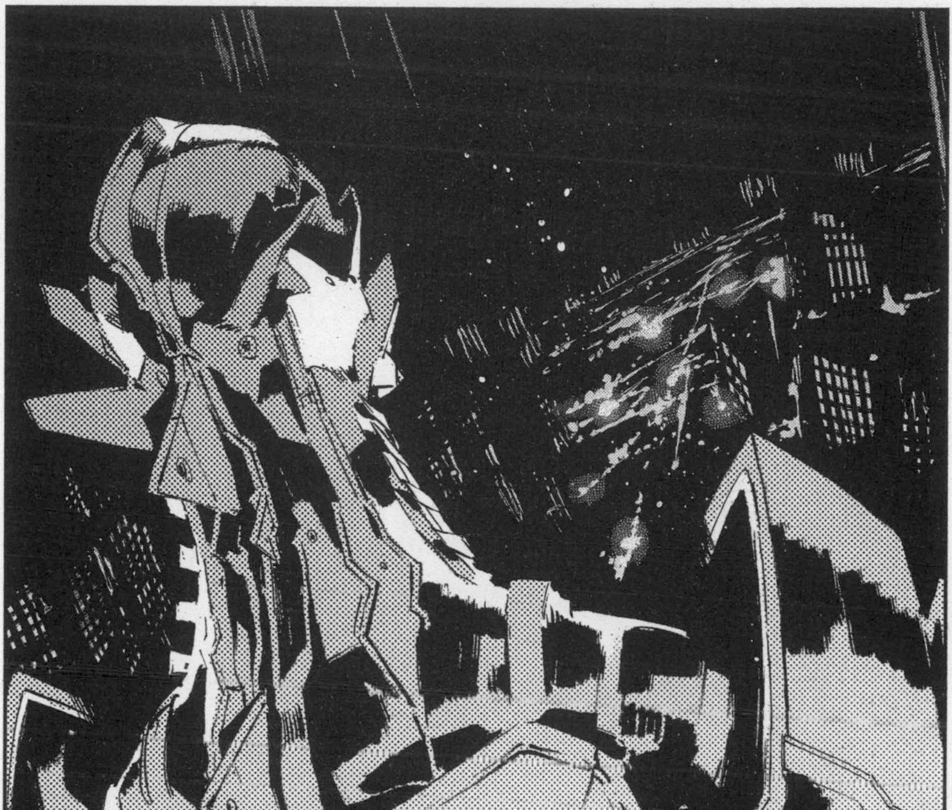
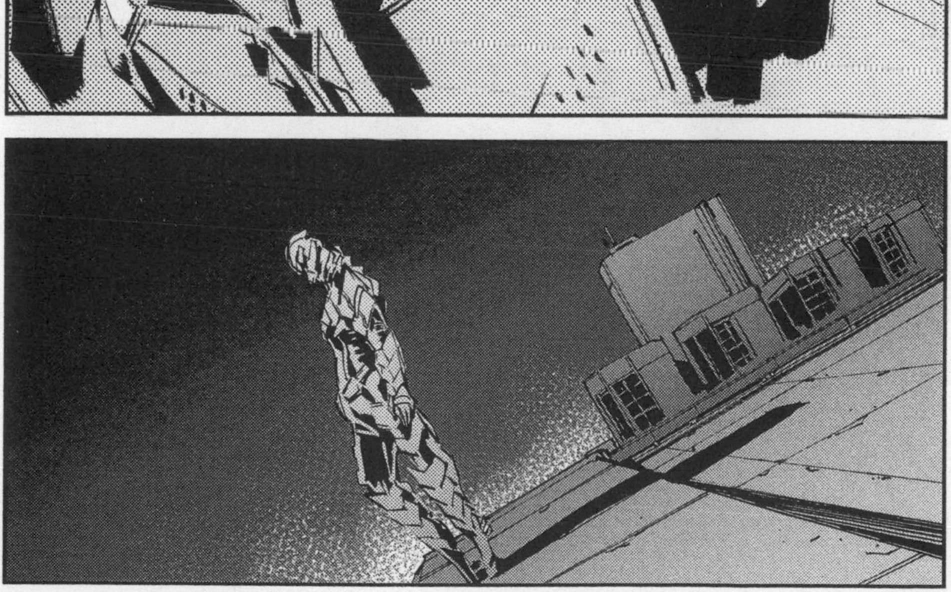

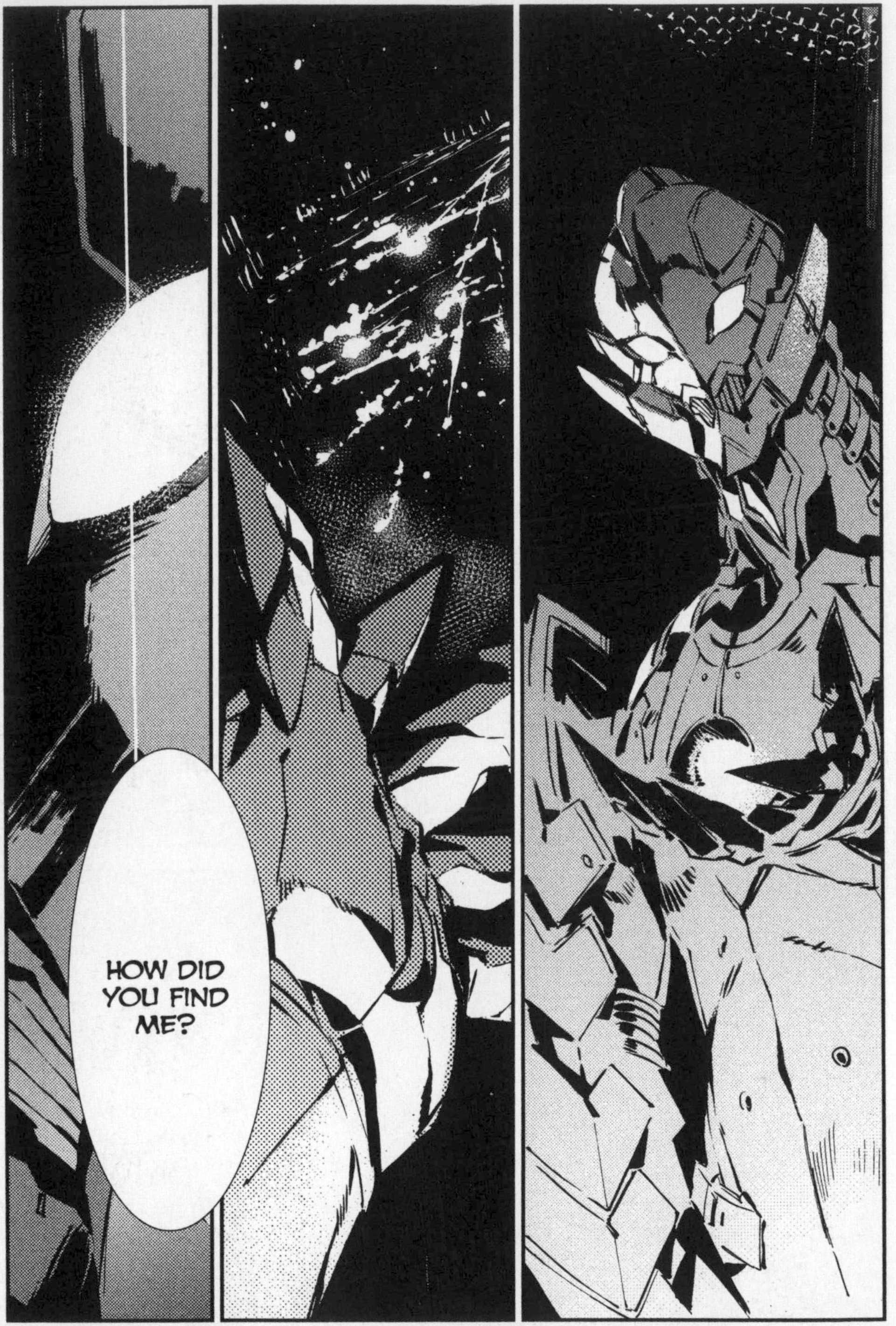
HOW DID YOU FIND ME?

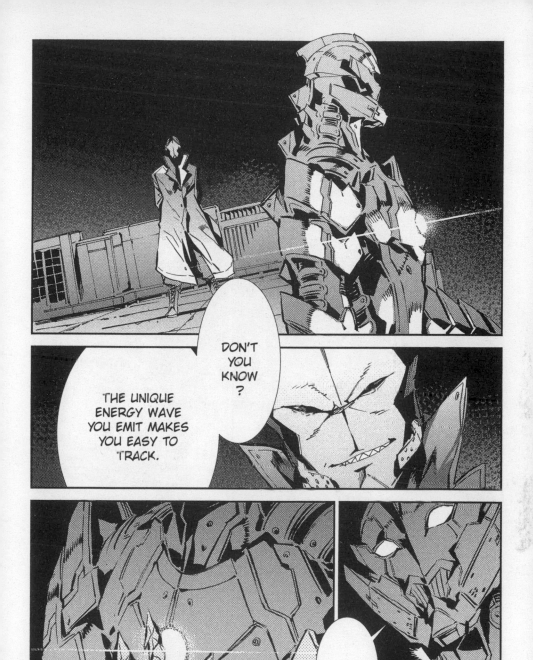

DON'T YOU KNOW ?

THE UNIQUE ENERGY WAVE YOU EMIT MAKES YOU EASY TO TRACK.

...

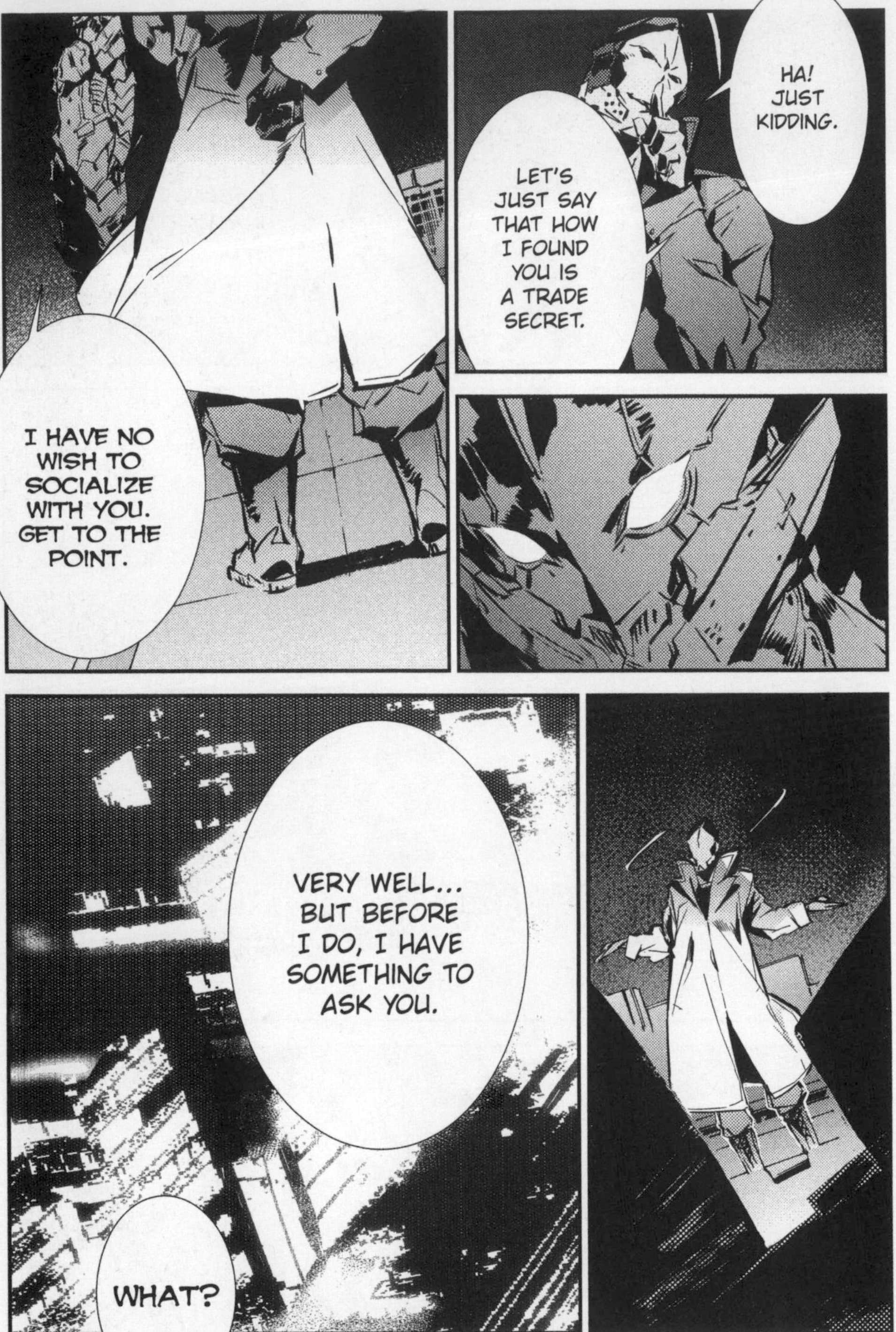
HA! JUST KIDDING.
LET'S JUST SAY THAT HOW I FOUND YOU IS A TRADE SECRET.
I HAVE NO WISH TO SOCIALIZE WITH YOU. GET TO THE POINT.
VERY WELL... BUT BEFORE I DO, I HAVE SOMETHING TO ASK YOU.
WHAT?

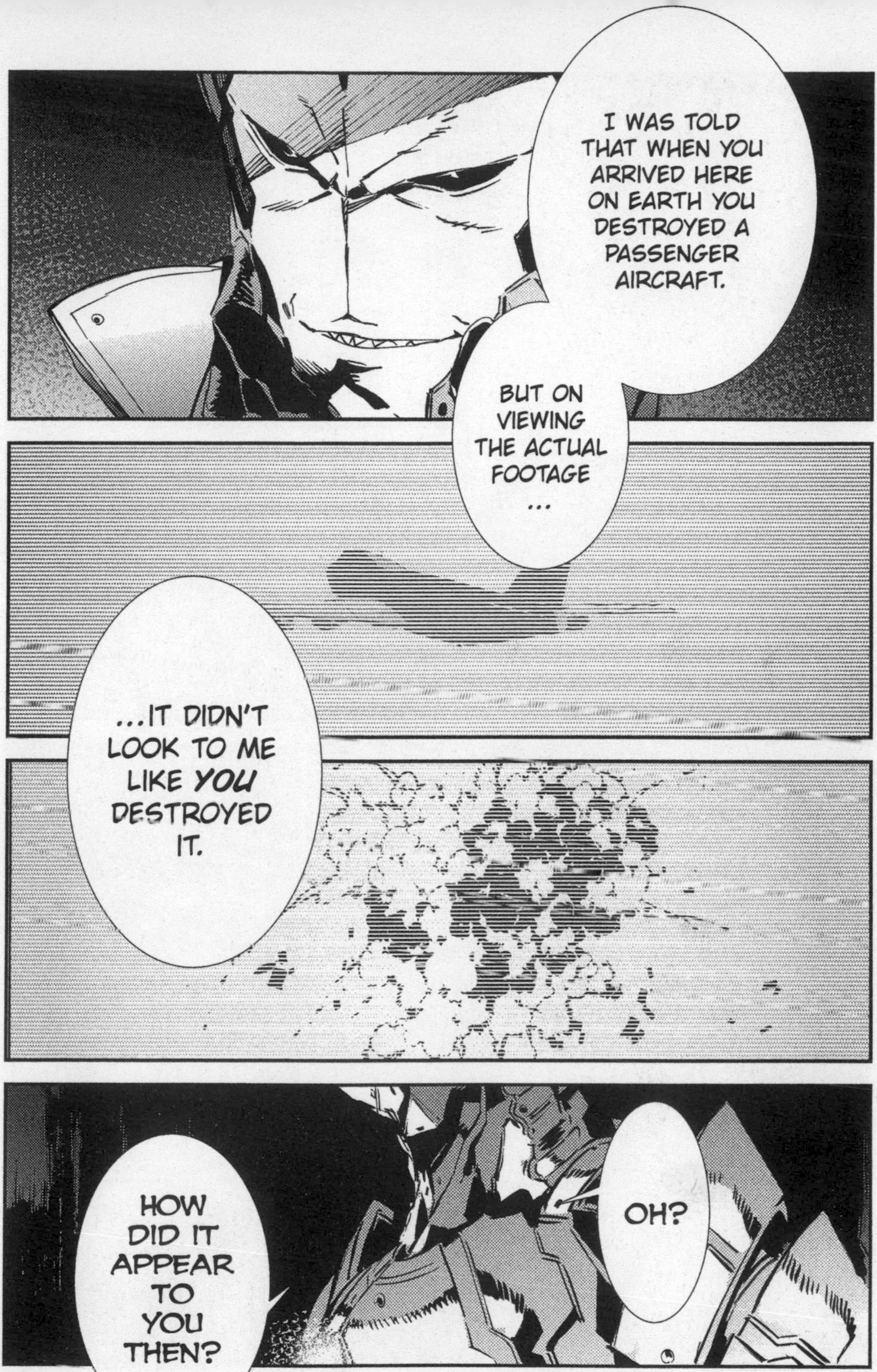
I WAS TOLD THAT WHEN YOU ARRIVED HERE ON EARTH YOU DESTROYED A PASSENGER AIRCRAFT.
BUT ON VIEWING THE ACTUAL FOOTAGE ...
...IT DIDN'T LOOK TO ME LIKE *YOU* DESTROYED IT.
OH?
HOW DID IT APPEAR TO YOU THEN?

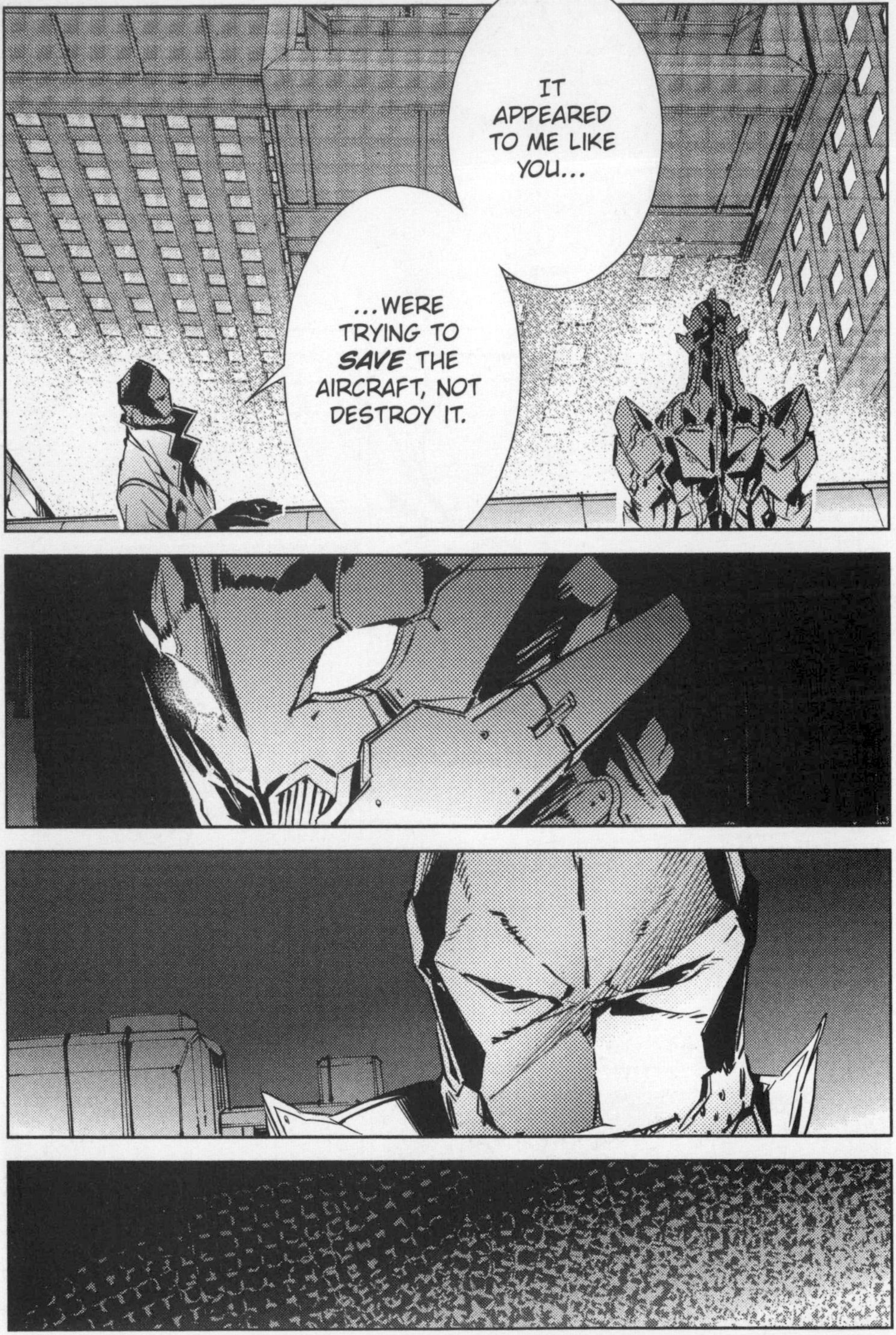
IT APPEARED TO ME LIKE YOU...
...WERE TRYING TO SAVE THE AIRCRAFT, NOT DESTROY IT.

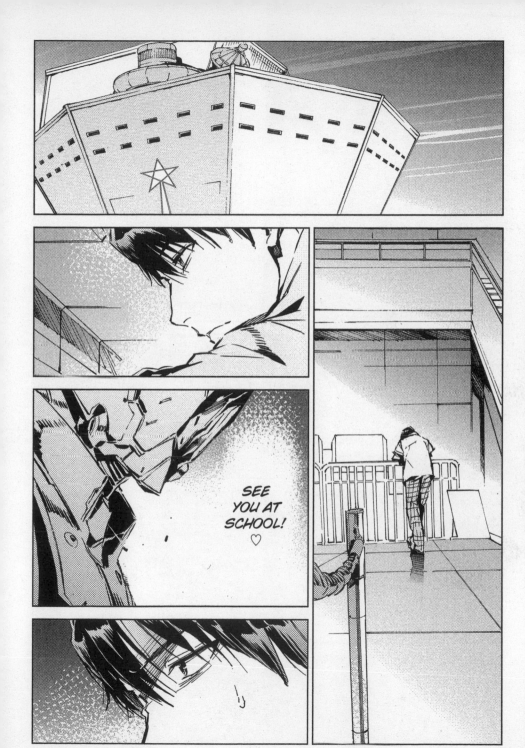

SEE
YOU AT
SCHOOL!
♡

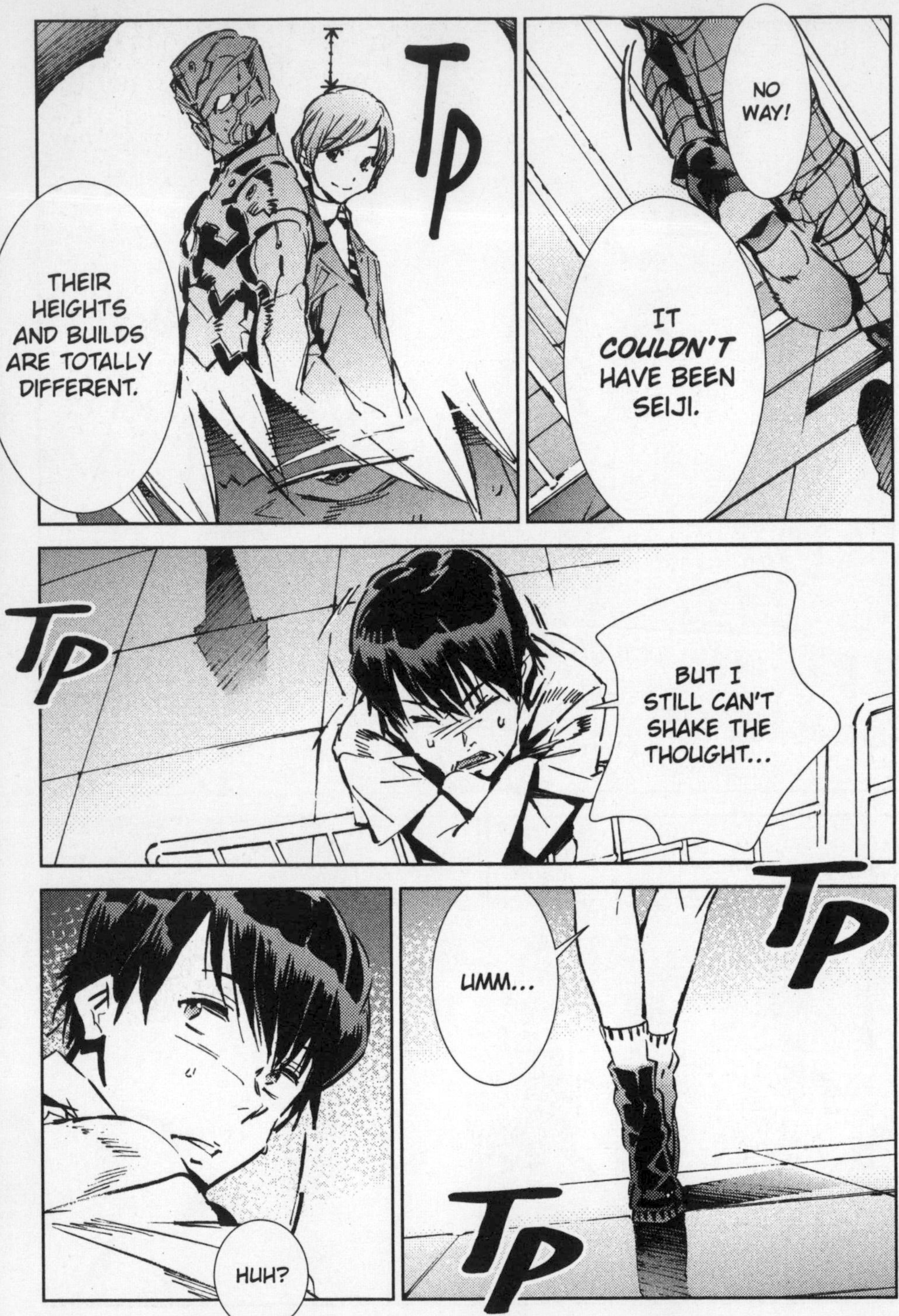
NO WAY!
IT COULDN'T HAVE BEEN SEIJI.
TP
THEIR HEIGHTS AND BUILDS ARE TOTALLY DIFFERENT.
TP
BUT I STILL CAN'T SHAKE THE THOUGHT...
TP
UMM...
TP
HUH?

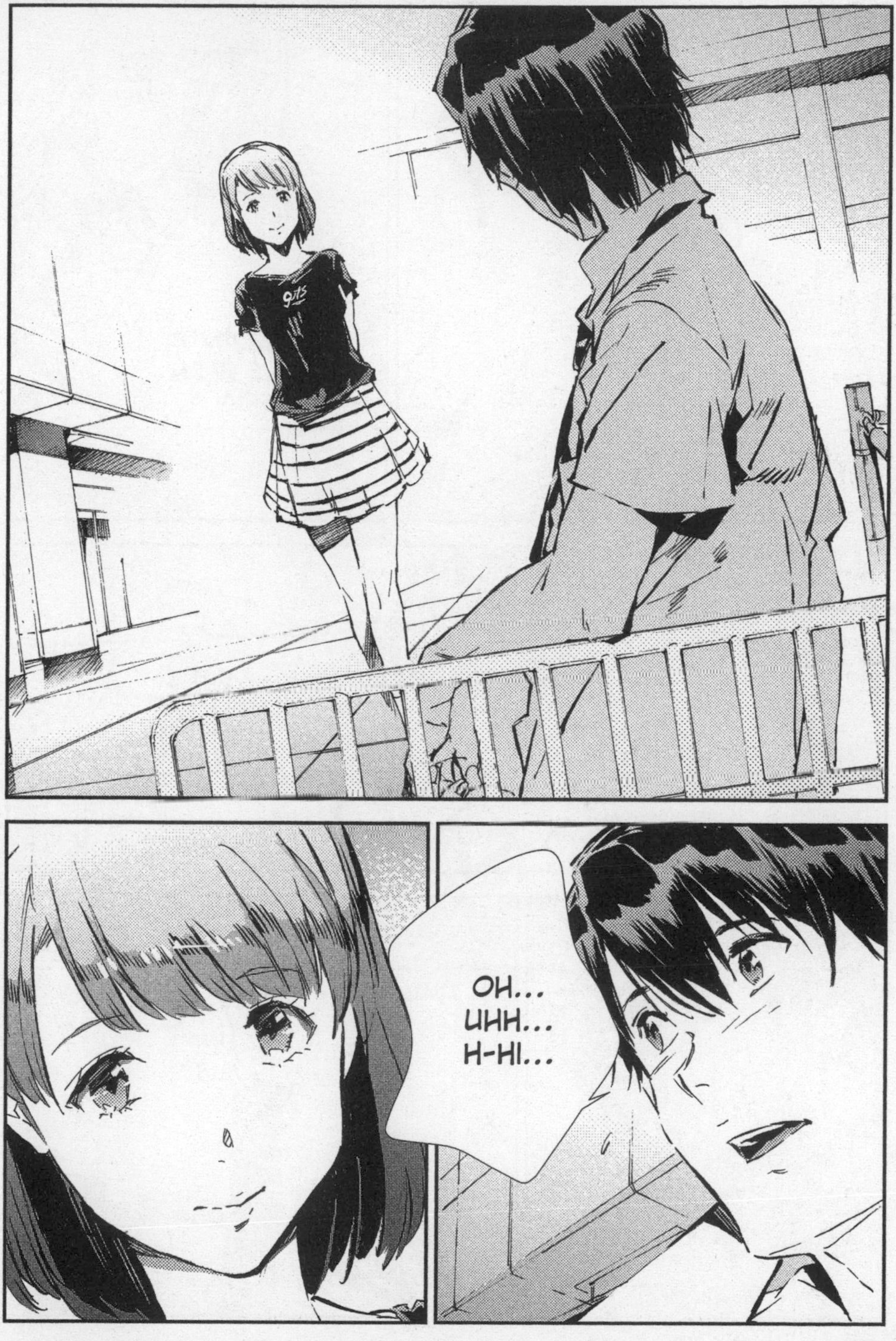
OH... UHH... H-HI...

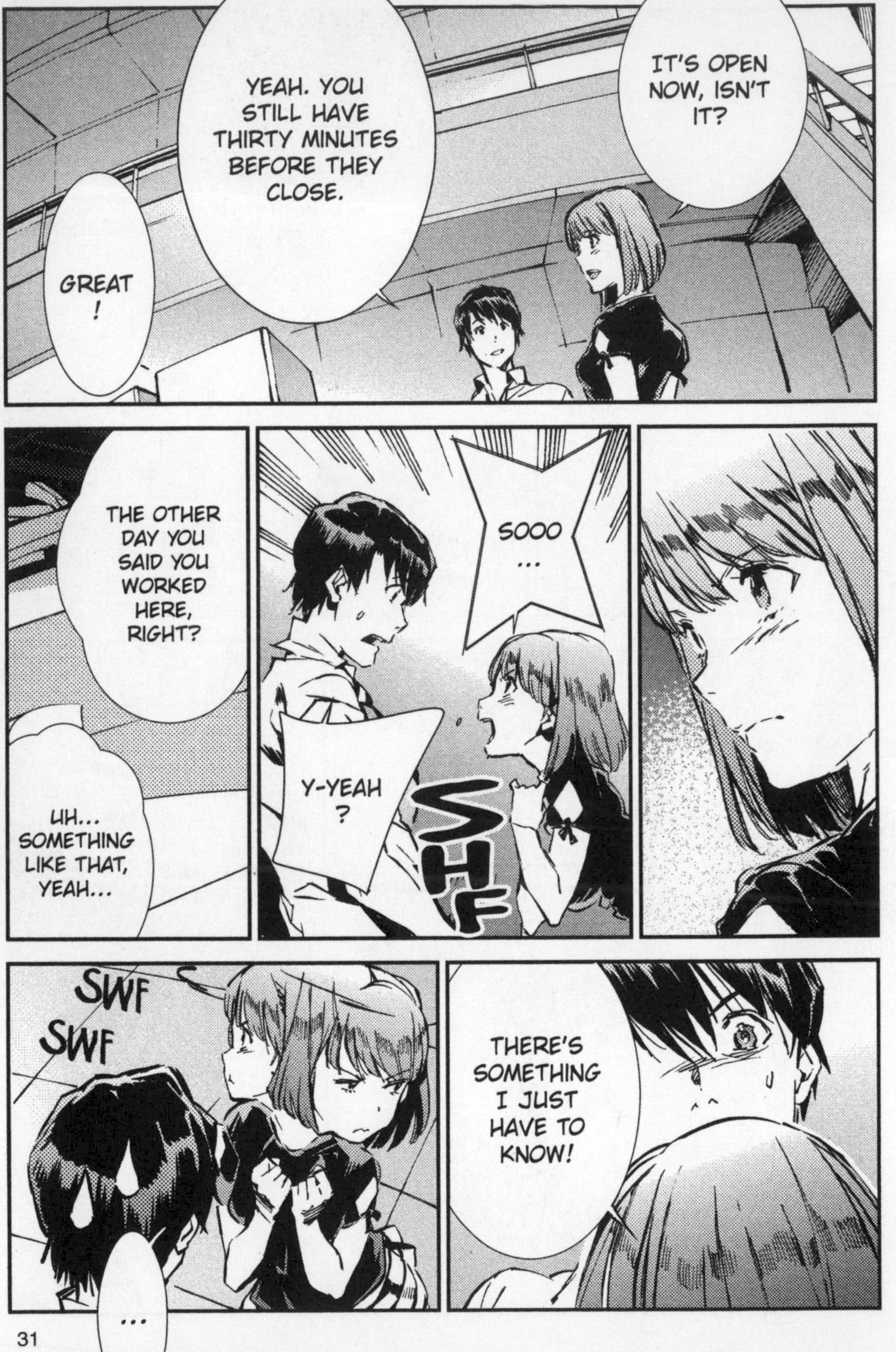
IT'S OPEN NOW, ISN'T IT?
YEAH. YOU STILL HAVE THIRTY MINUTES BEFORE THEY CLOSE.
GREAT!
SOOO...
Y-YEAH?
SHF
THE OTHER DAY YOU SAID YOU WORKED HERE, RIGHT?
UH... SOMETHING LIKE THAT, YEAH...
THERE'S SOMETHING I JUST HAVE TO KNOW!
SWF
SWF
...

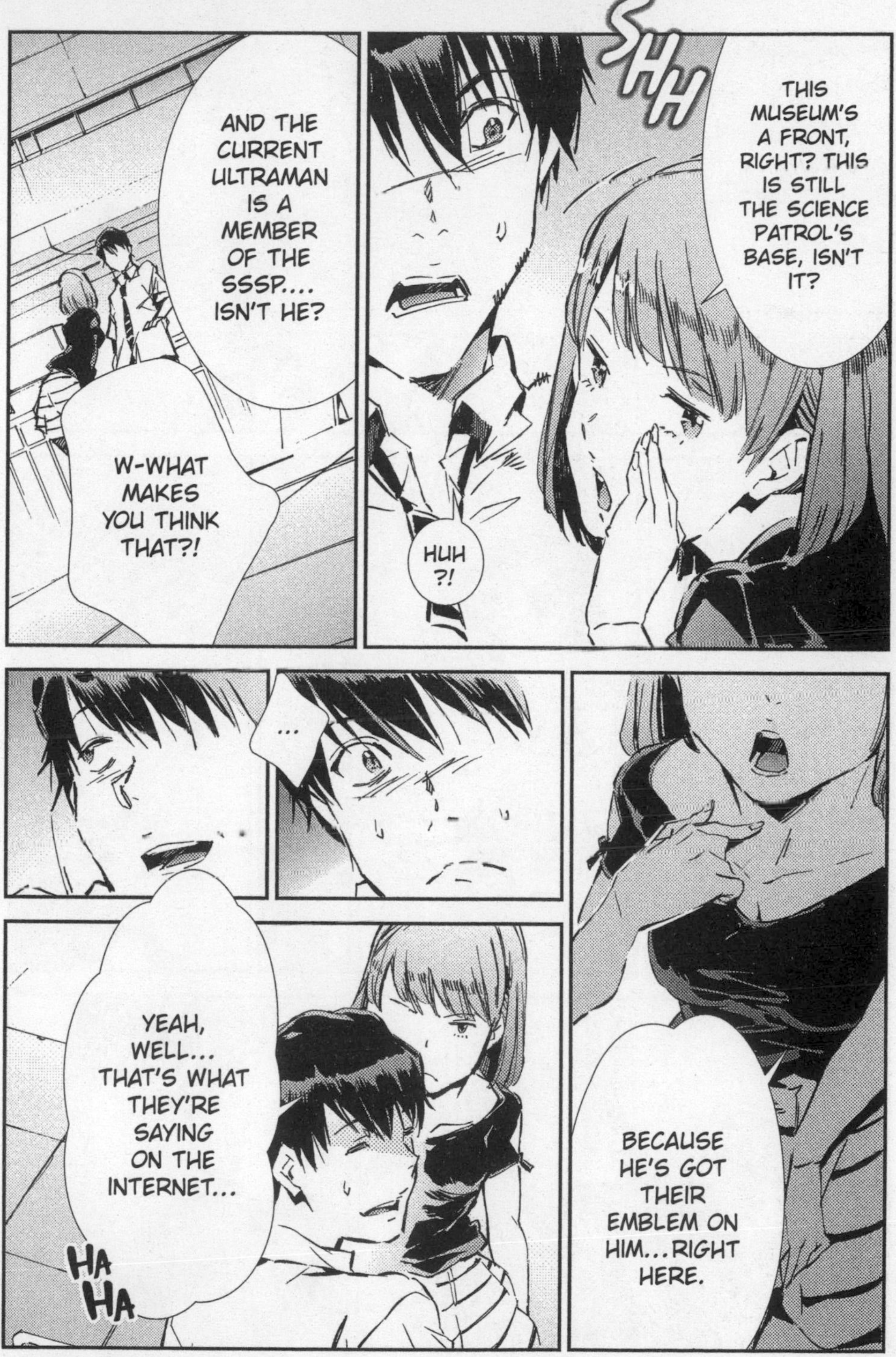
SHH
THIS MUSEUM'S A FRONT, RIGHT? THIS IS STILL THE SCIENCE PATROL'S BASE, ISN'T IT?
HUH ?!
AND THE CURRENT ULTRAMAN IS A MEMBER OF THE SSSP.... ISN'T HE?
W-WHAT MAKES YOU THINK THAT?!
BECAUSE HE'S GOT THEIR EMBLEM ON HIM...RIGHT HERE.
...
YEAH, WELL... THAT'S WHAT THEY'RE SAYING ON THE INTERNET...
HA HA

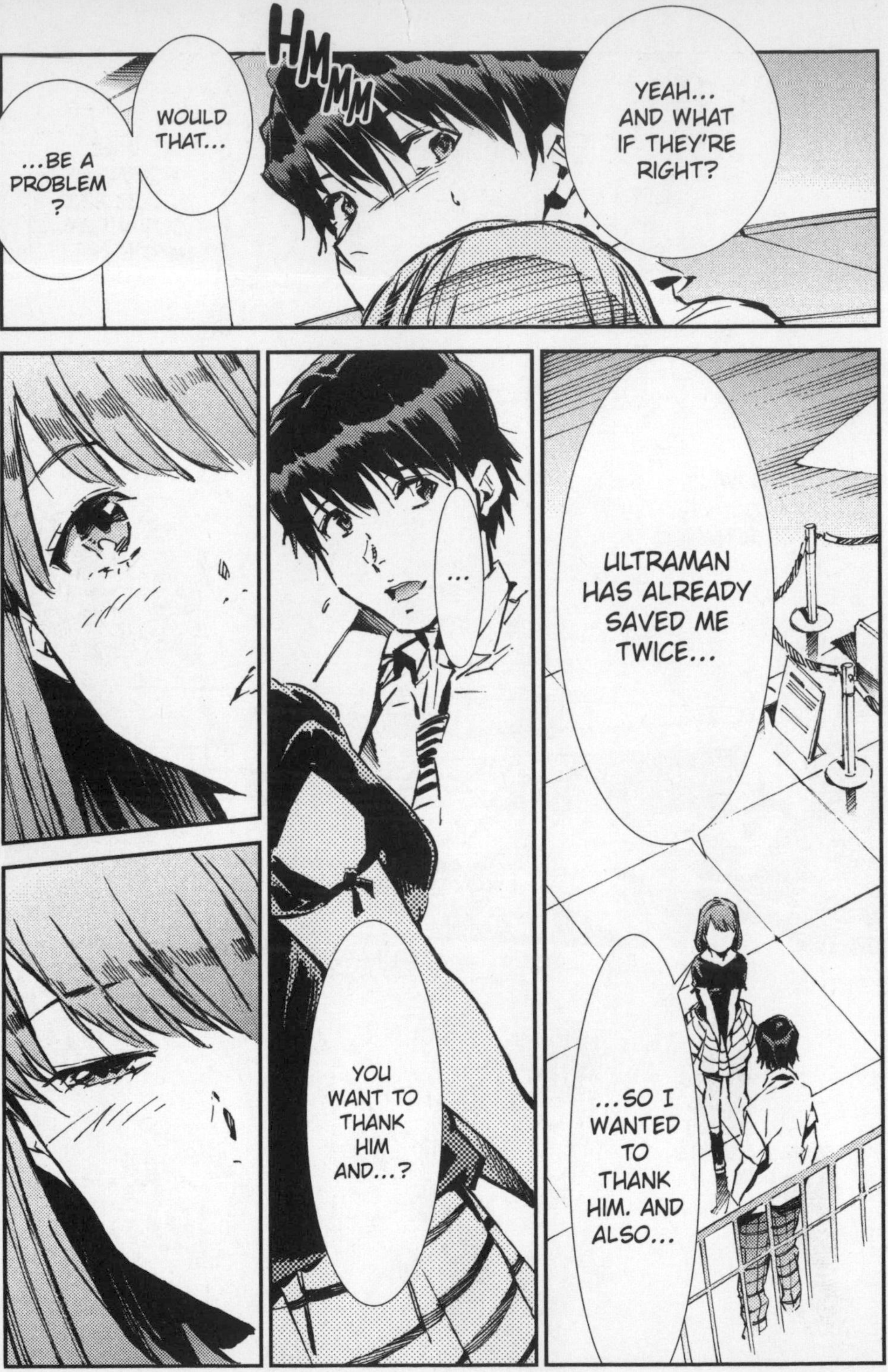
YEAH... AND WHAT IF THEY'RE RIGHT?
HMMM
WOULD THAT...
...BE A PROBLEM ?
ULTRAMAN HAS ALREADY SAVED ME TWICE...
...SO I WANTED TO THANK HIM. AND ALSO...
...
YOU WANT TO THANK HIM AND...?

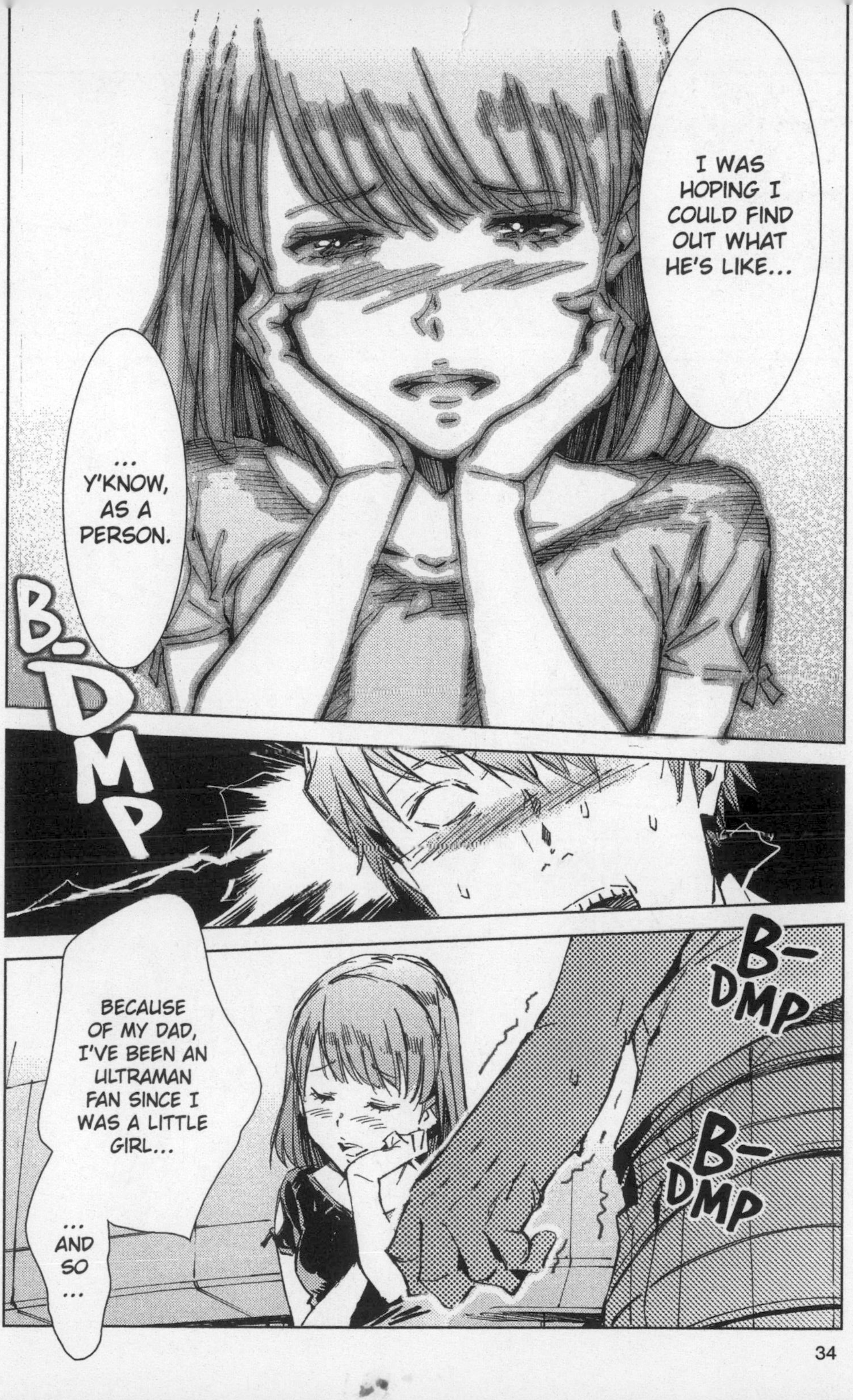
I WAS HOPING I COULD FIND OUT WHAT HE'S LIKE...
... Y'KNOW, AS A PERSON.
B-DMP
B-DMP
B-DMP
BECAUSE OF MY DAD, I'VE BEEN AN ULTRAMAN FAN SINCE I WAS A LITTLE GIRL...
... AND SO ...

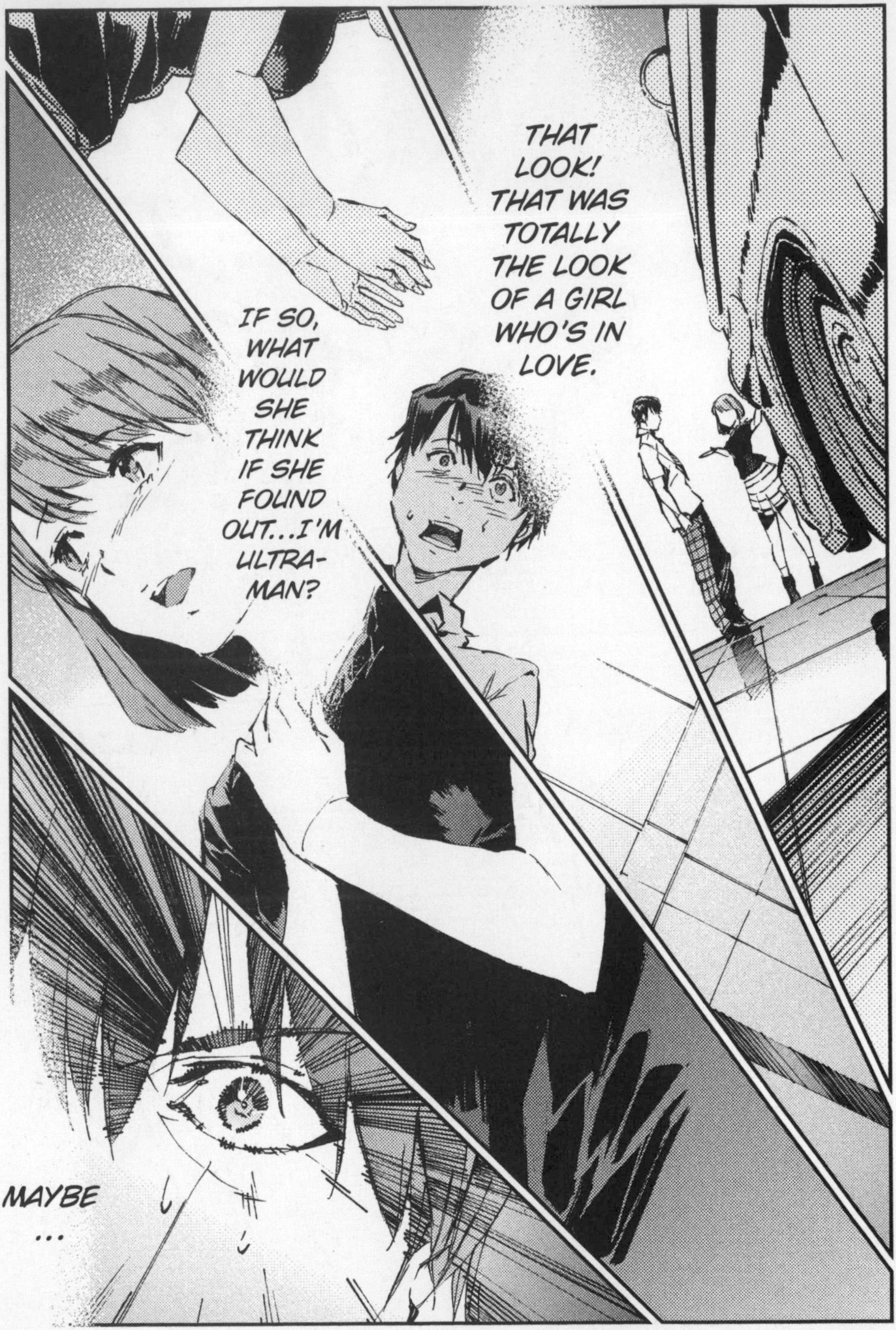
THAT LOOK! THAT WAS TOTALLY THE LOOK OF A GIRL WHO'S IN LOVE.
IF SO, WHAT WOULD SHE THINK IF SHE FOUND OUT...I'M ULTRA-MAN?
MAYBE ...

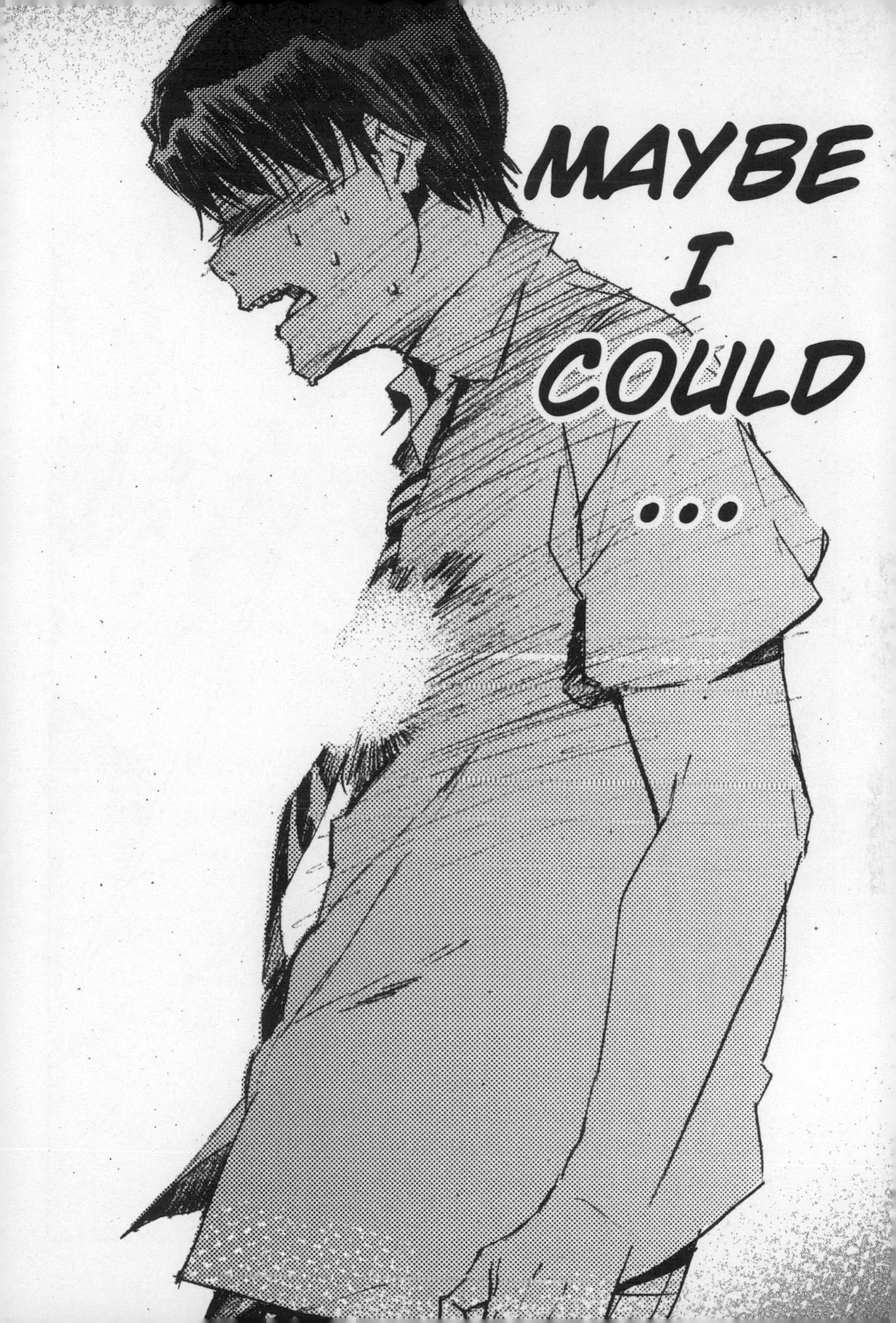
MAYBE I COULD ...

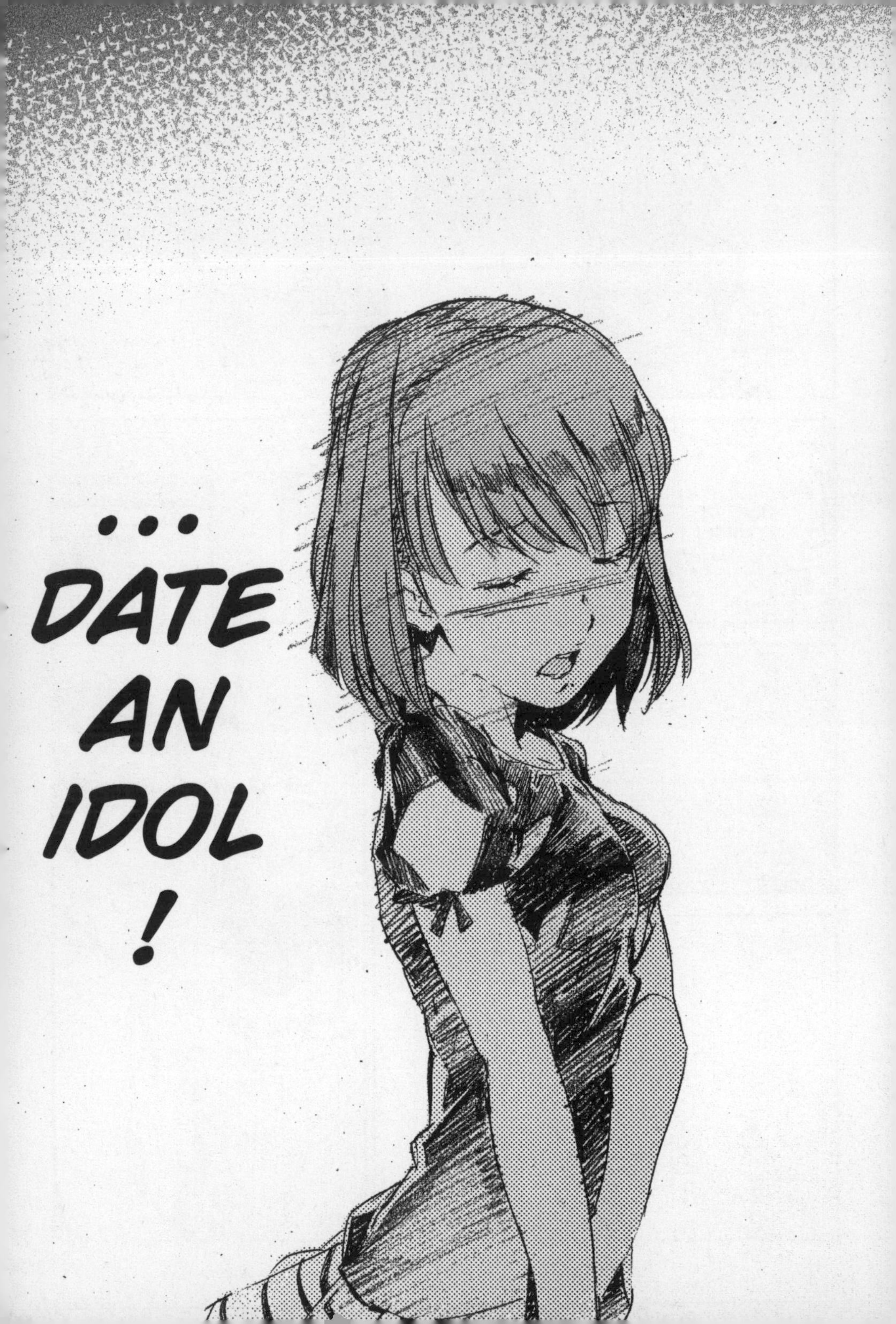
...DATE AN IDOL!

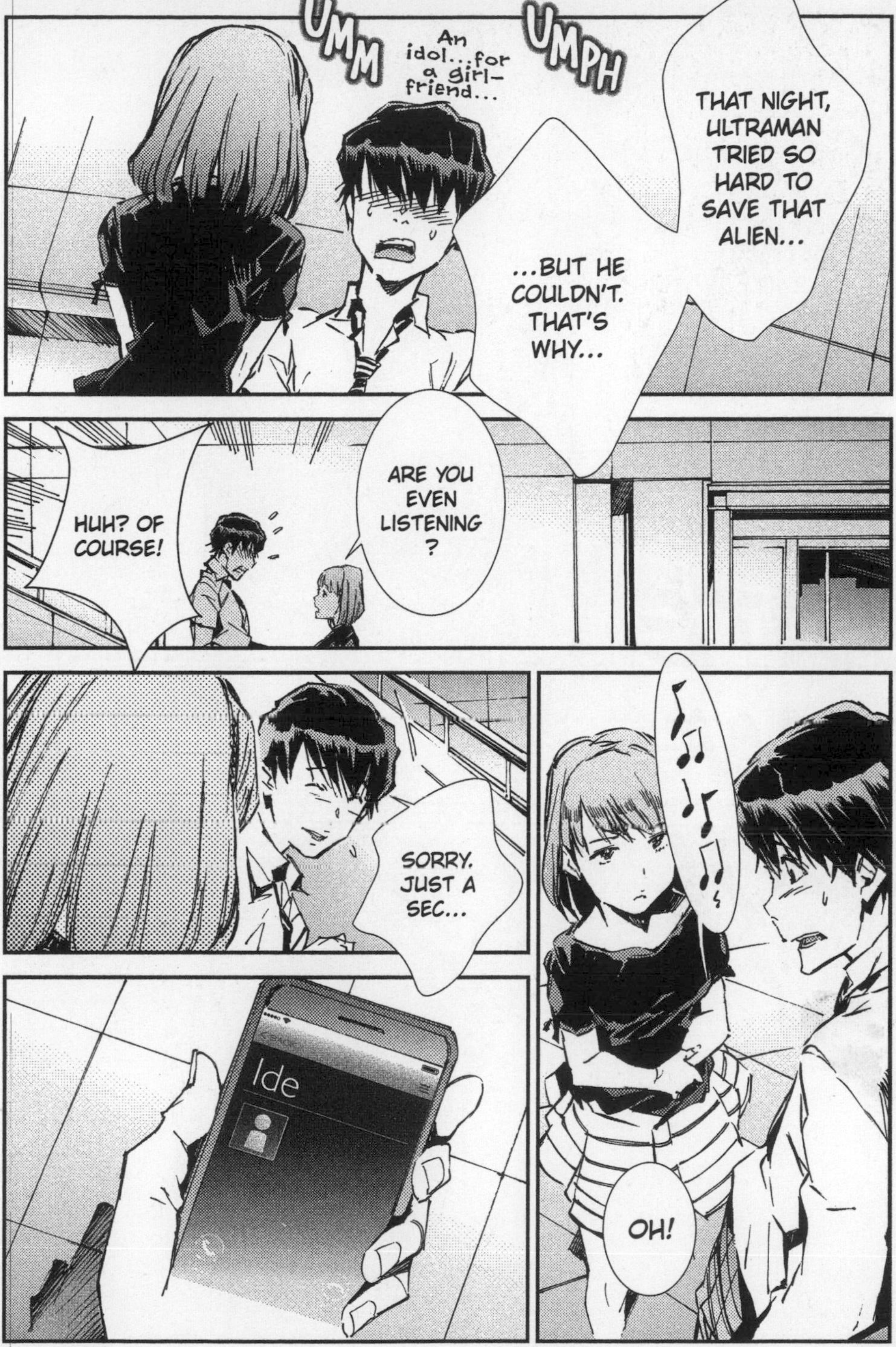

THAT NIGHT, ULTRAMAN TRIED SO HARD TO SAVE THAT ALIEN...
UMPH
...BUT HE COULDN'T. THAT'S WHY...
An idol...for a girl-friend...
UMM
ARE YOU EVEN LISTENING?
HUH? OF COURSE!
OH!
SORRY. JUST A SEC...
Ide

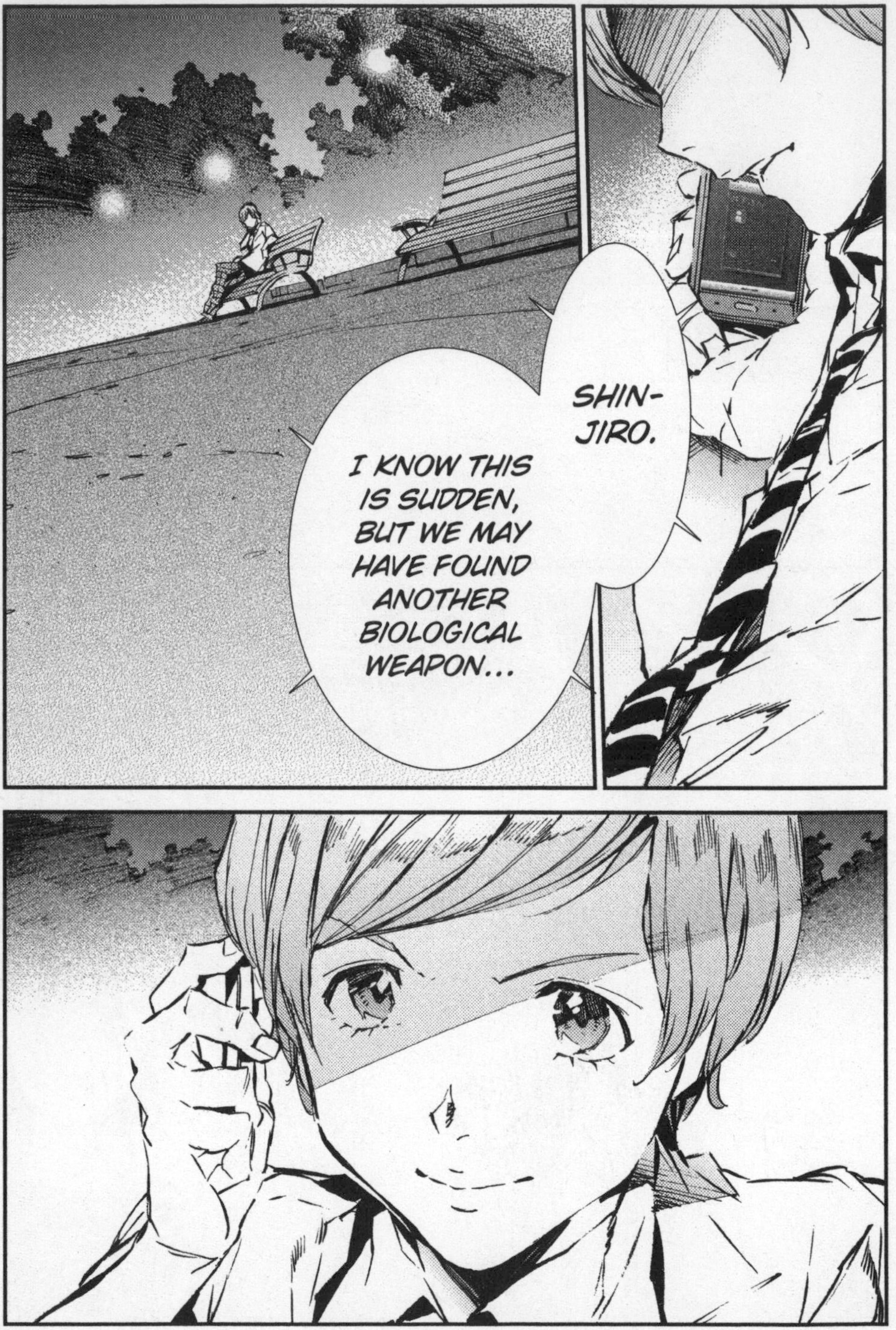
SHIN-JIRO.
I KNOW THIS IS SUDDEN, BUT WE MAY HAVE FOUND ANOTHER BIOLOGICAL WEAPON...

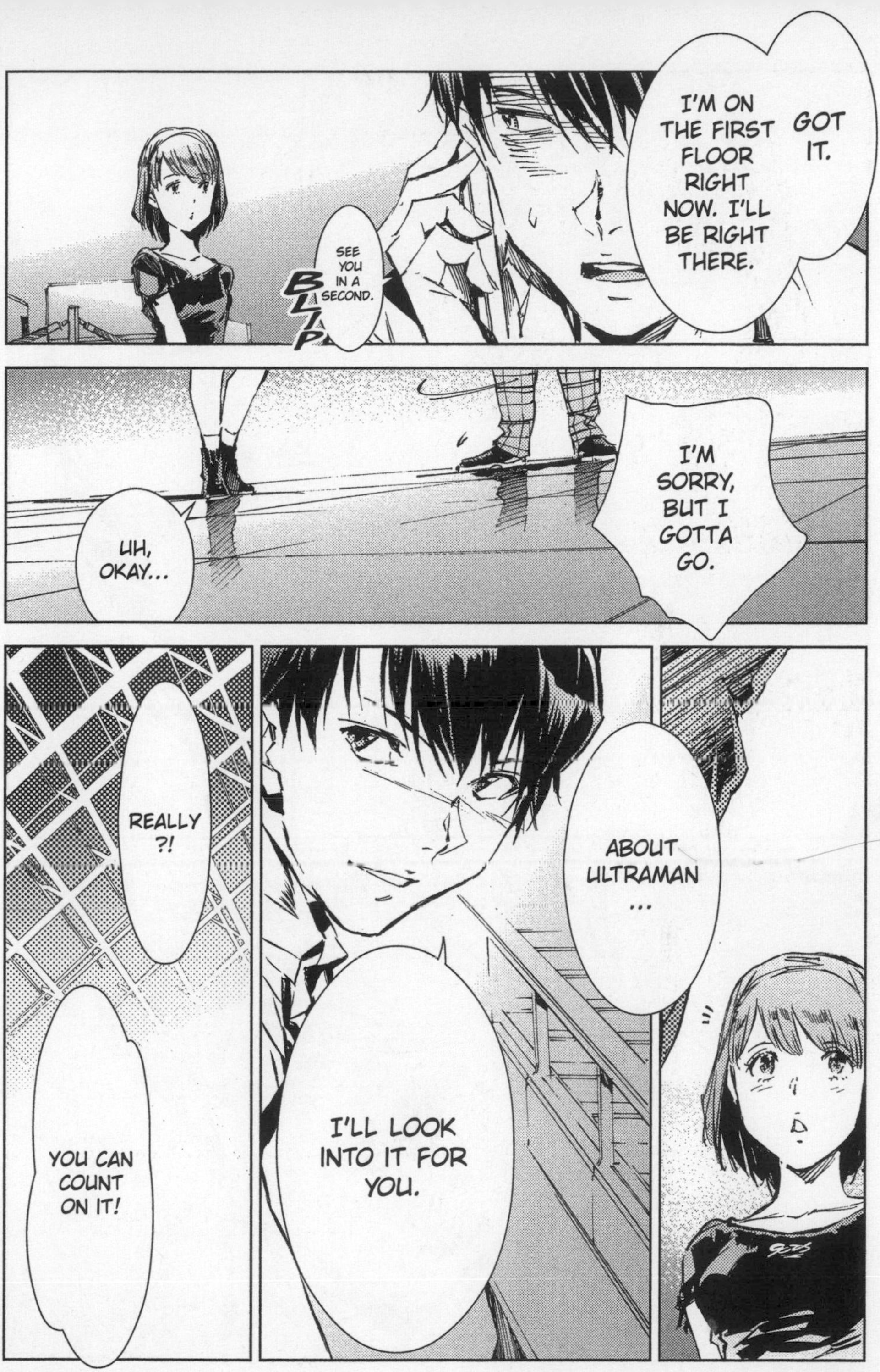
GOT IT.
I'M ON THE FIRST FLOOR RIGHT NOW. I'LL BE RIGHT THERE.
SEE YOU IN A SECOND.
BLIP
I'M SORRY, BUT I GOTTA GO.
UH, OKAY...
ABOUT ULTRAMAN ...
I'LL LOOK INTO IT FOR YOU.
REALLY ?!
YOU CAN COUNT ON IT!

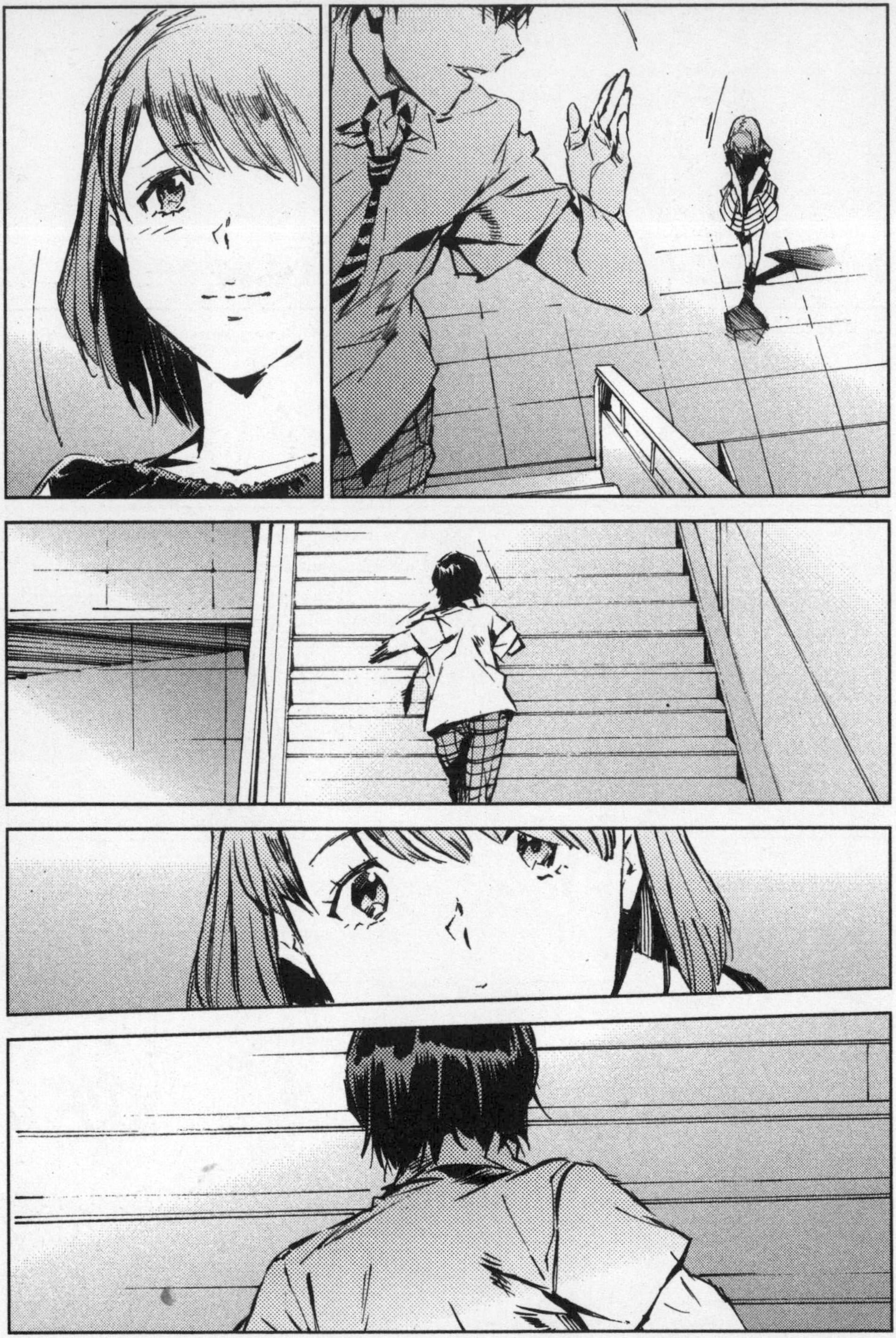

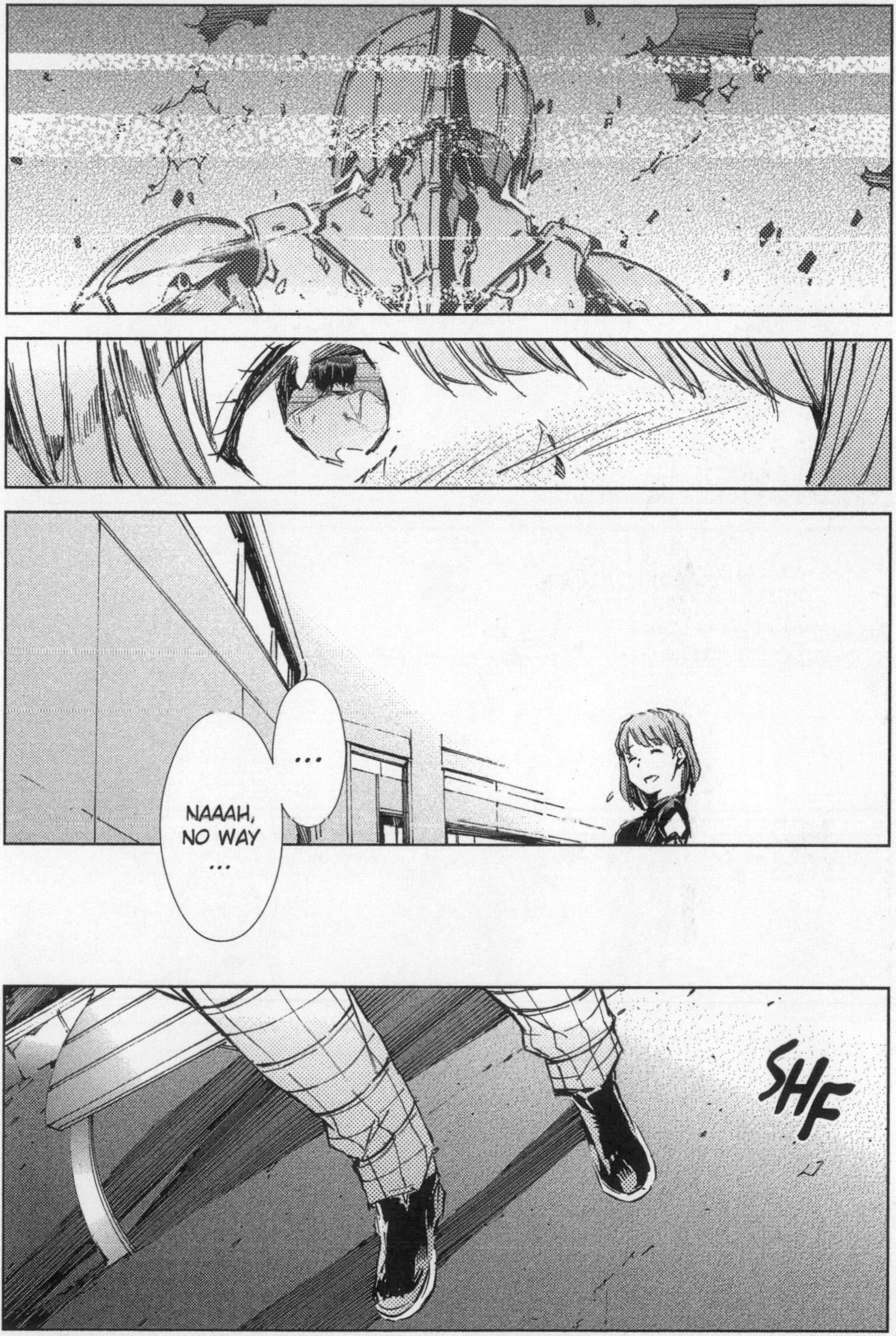
...
NAAAH, NO WAY ...
SHF

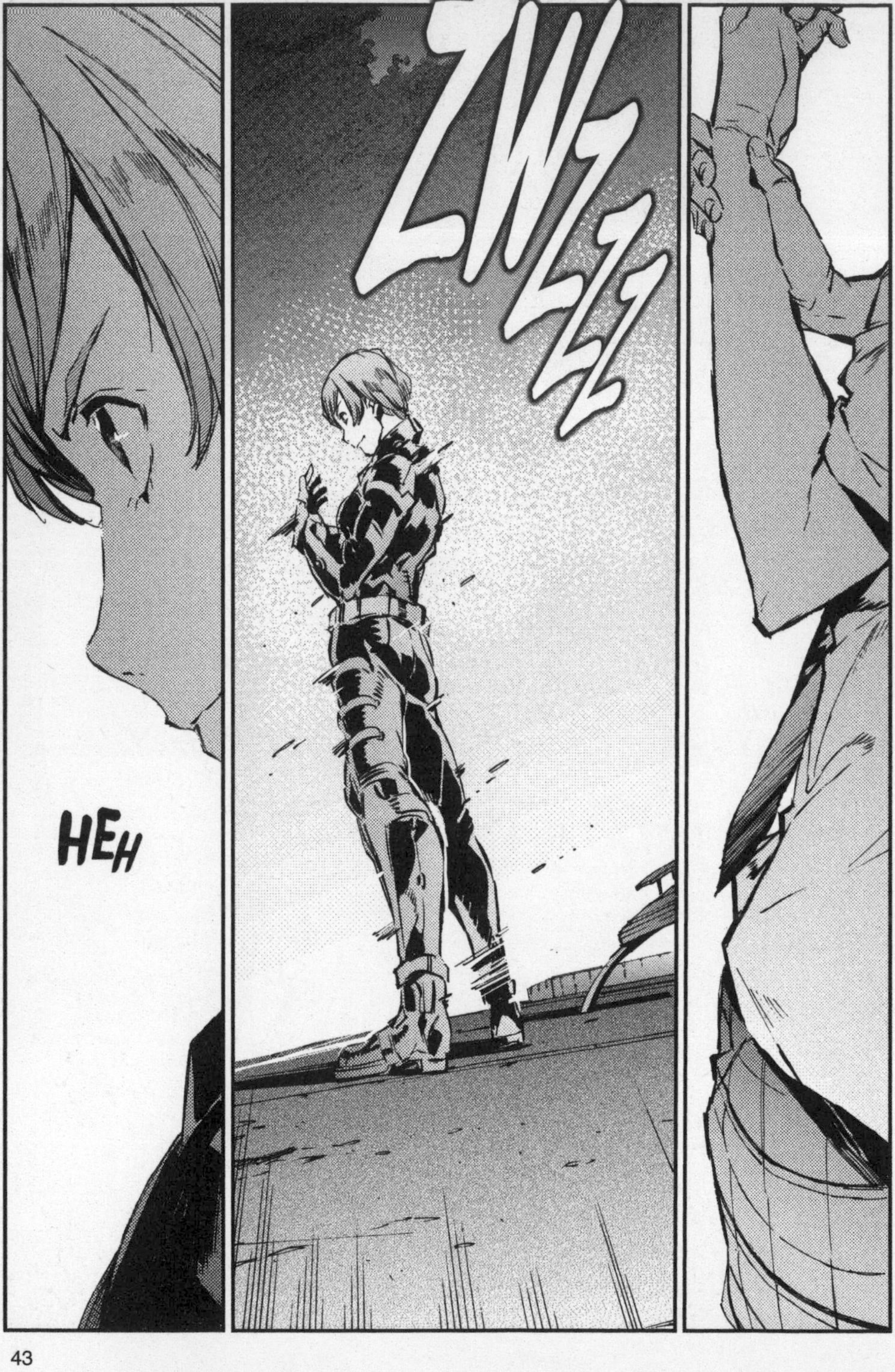
ZWZZZ
HEH

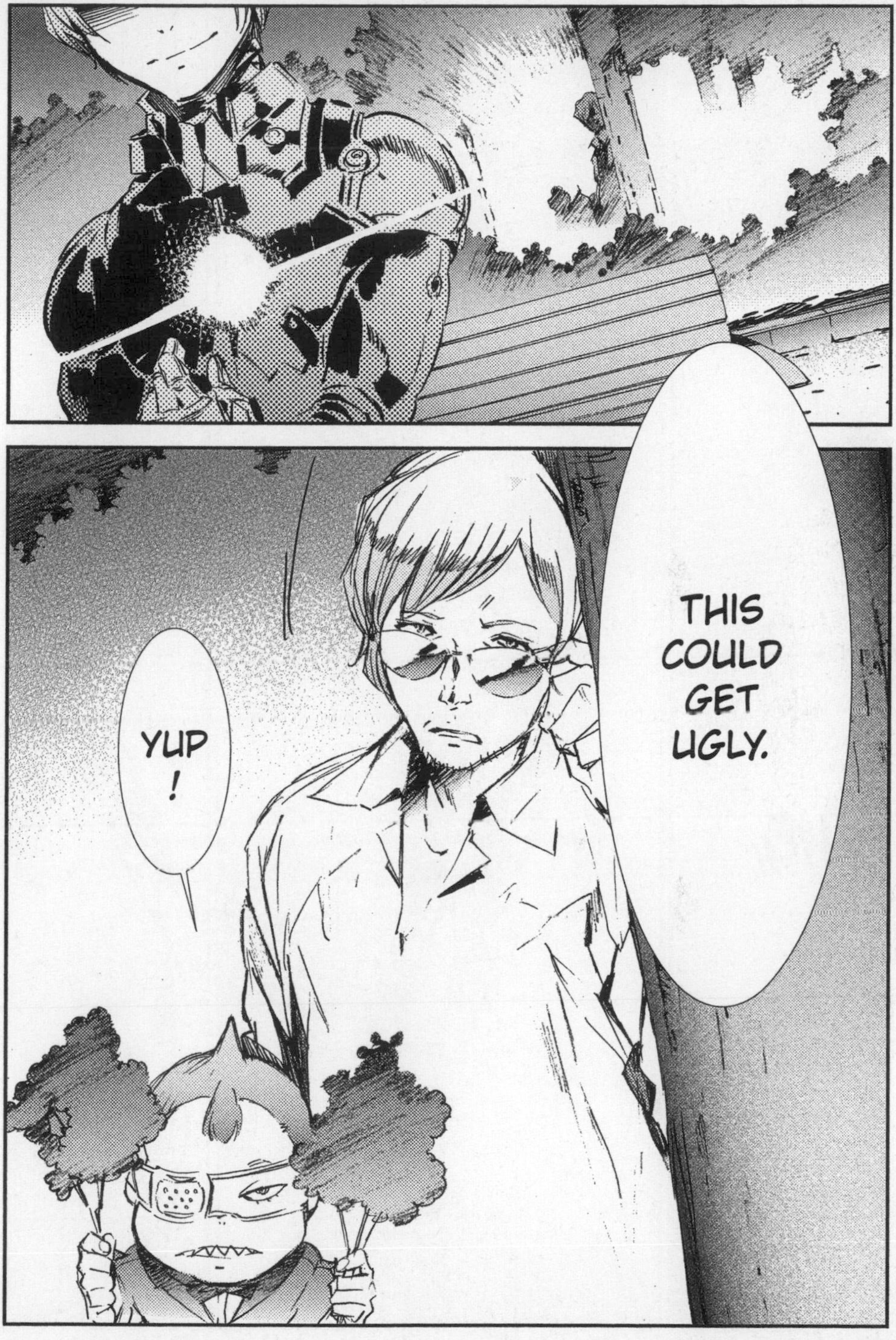
THIS COULD GET UGLY.
YUP!

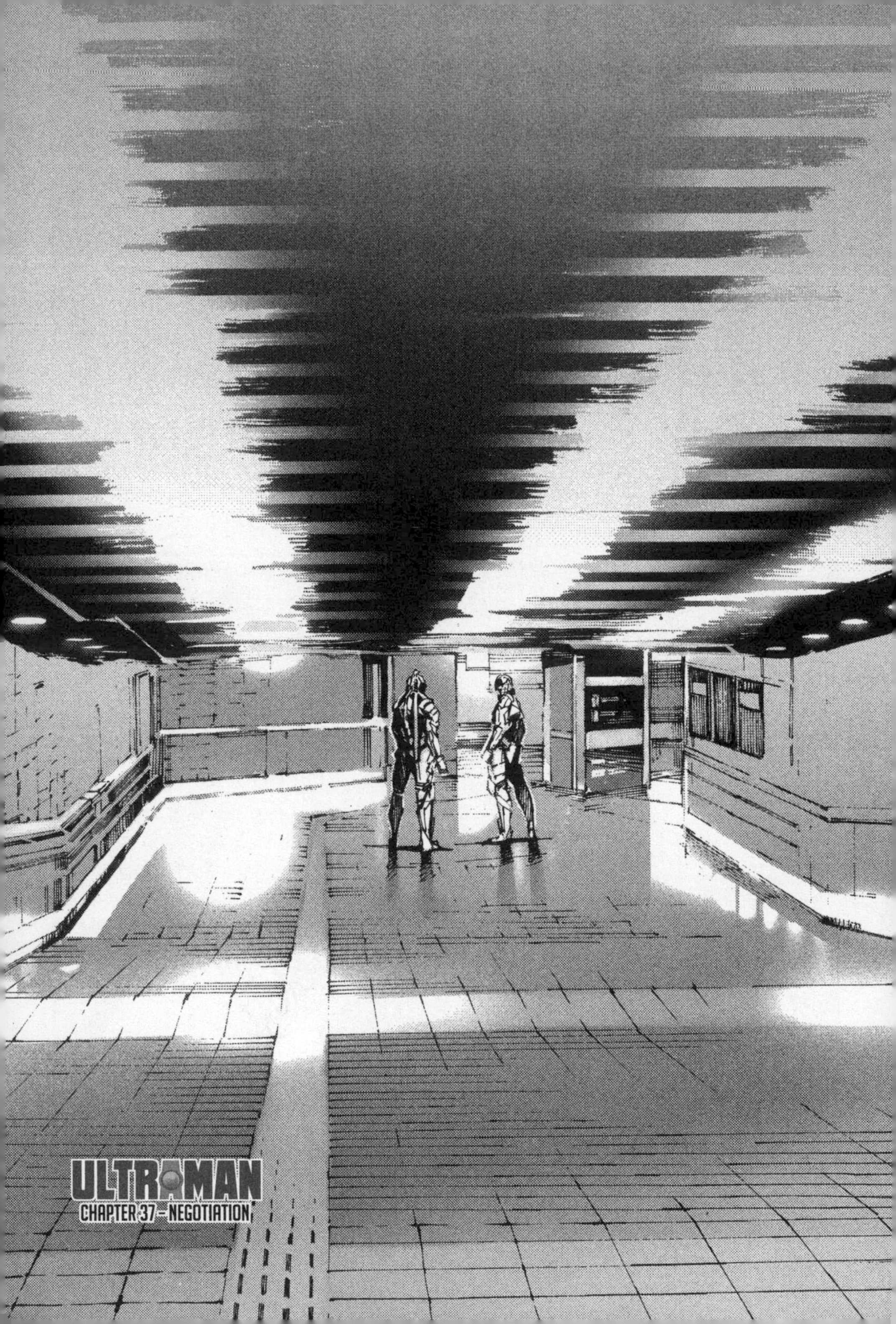
ULTRAMAN
CHAPTER 37 – NEGOTIATION

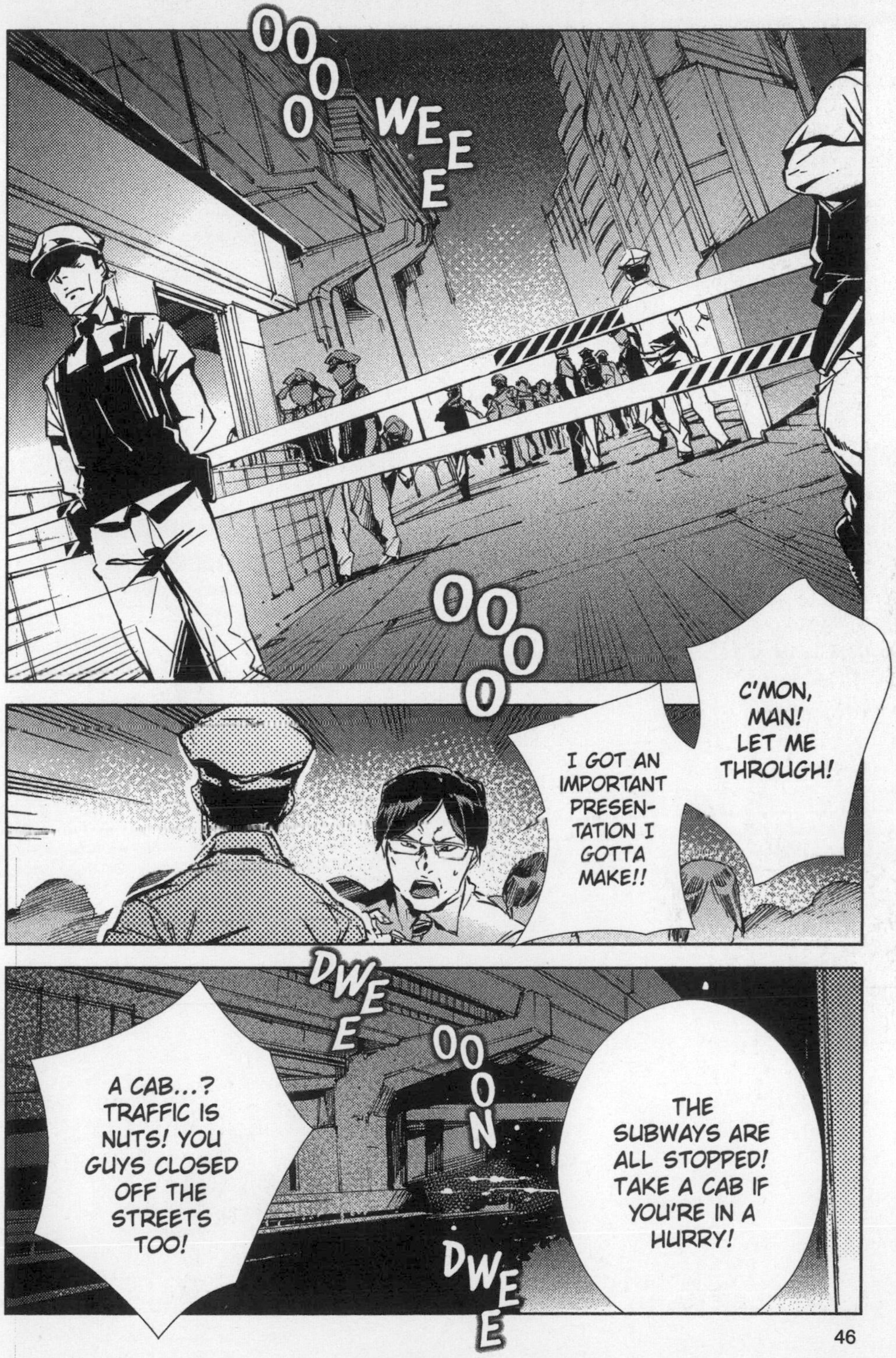
OOOO WEEE
OOOO
C'MON, MAN! LET ME THROUGH!
I GOT AN IMPORTANT PRESEN-TATION I GOTTA MAKE!!
DWEE OOON
THE SUBWAYS ARE ALL STOPPED! TAKE A CAB IF YOU'RE IN A HURRY!
A CAB...? TRAFFIC IS NUTS! YOU GUYS CLOSED OFF THE STREETS TOO!
DWEE

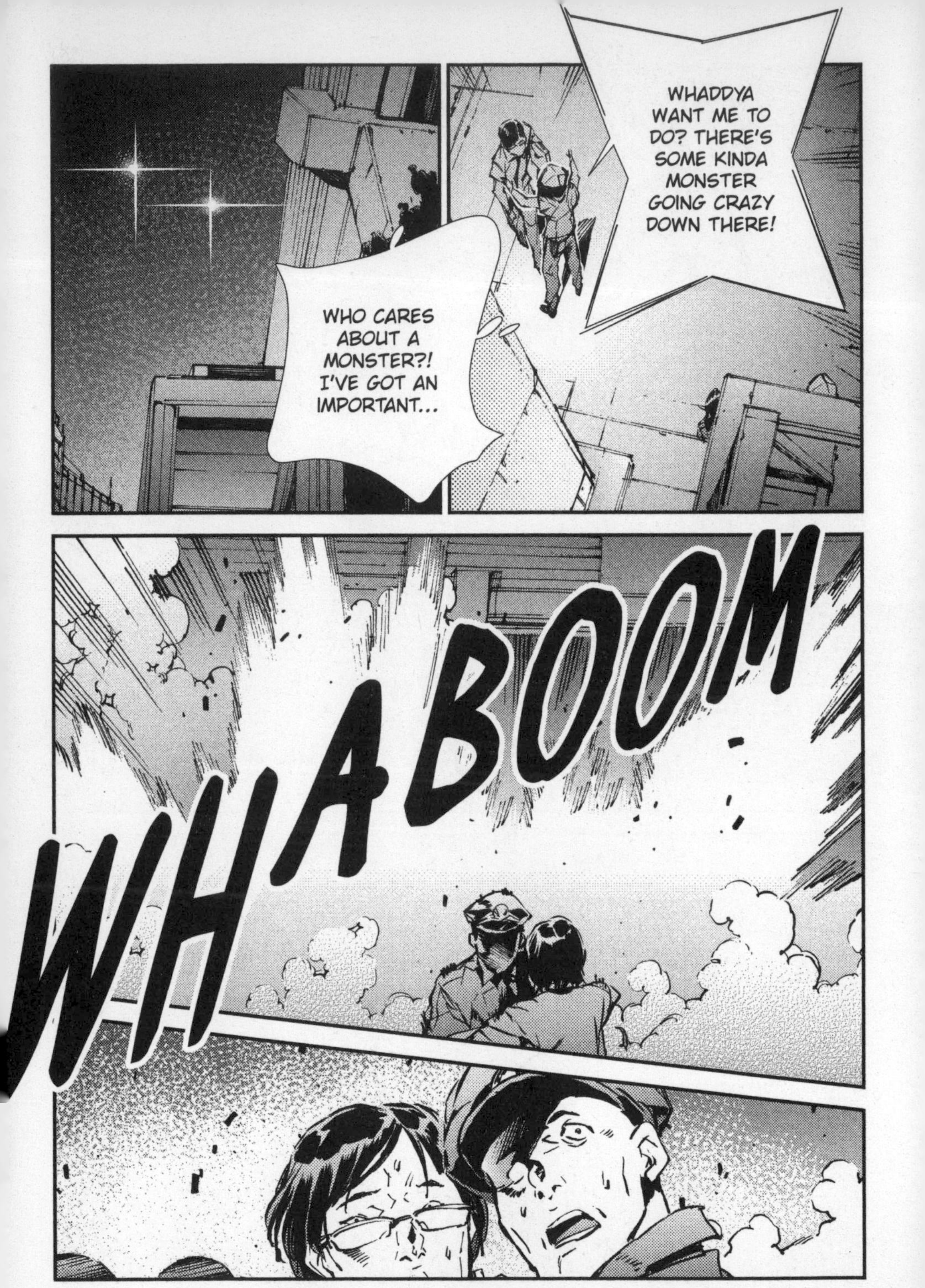
WHADDYA WANT ME TO DO? THERE'S SOME KINDA MONSTER GOING CRAZY DOWN THERE!
WHO CARES ABOUT A MONSTER?! I'VE GOT AN IMPORTANT...
WHABOOM

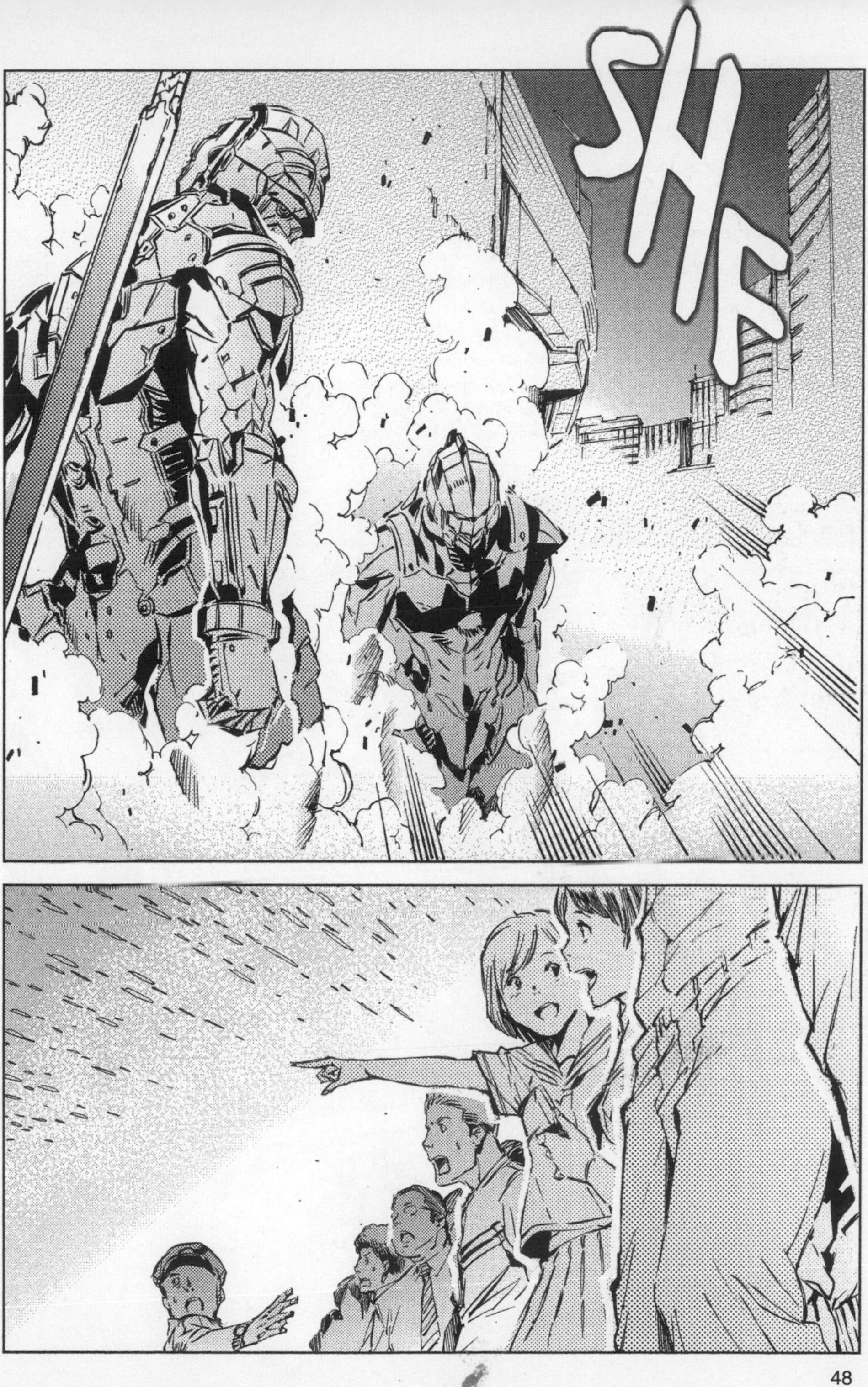
SHF

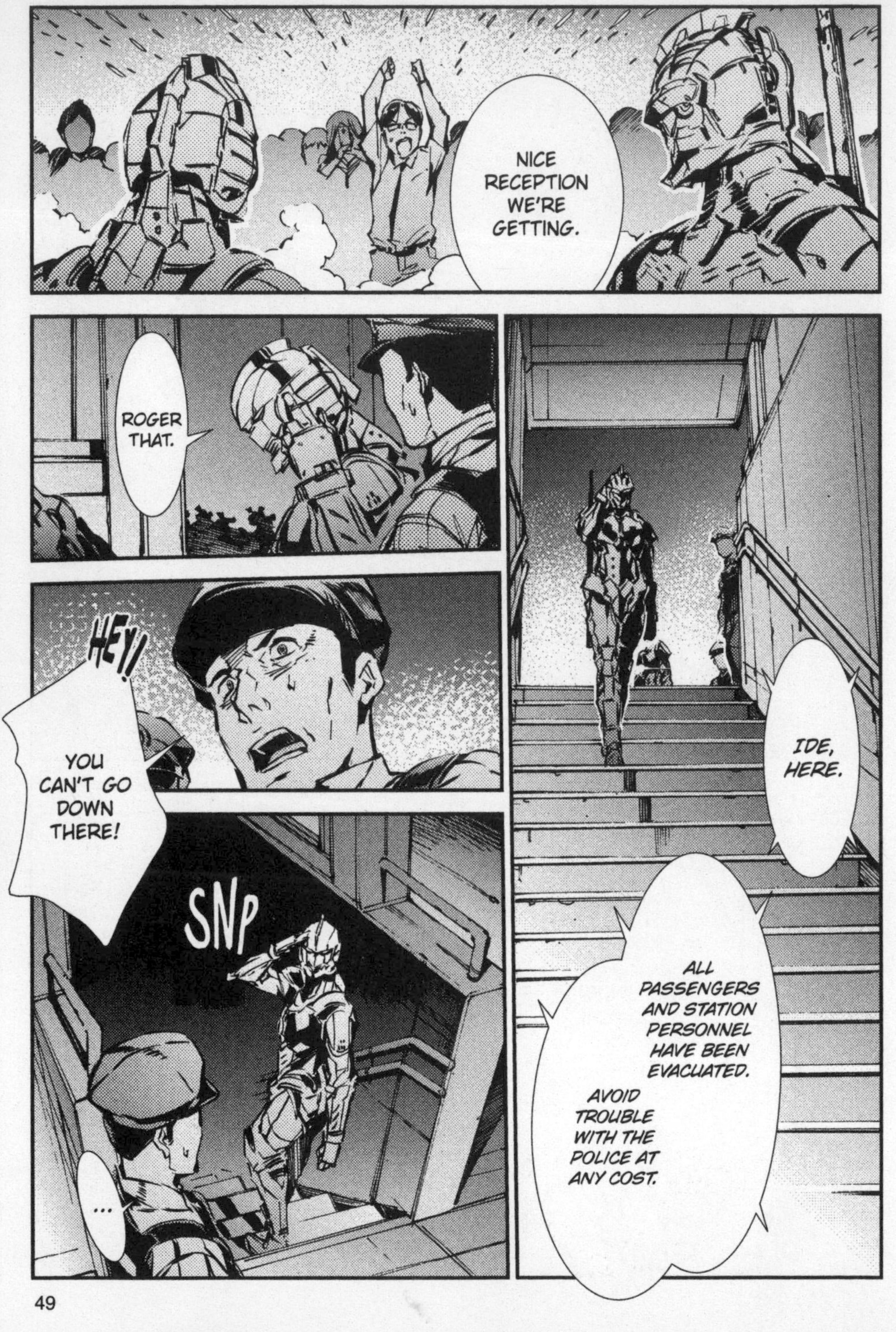
NICE RECEPTION WE'RE GETTING.
IDE, HERE.
ALL PASSENGERS AND STATION PERSONNEL HAVE BEEN EVACUATED.
AVOID TROUBLE WITH THE POLICE AT ANY COST.
ROGER THAT.
HEY!
YOU CAN'T GO DOWN THERE!
SNP
...

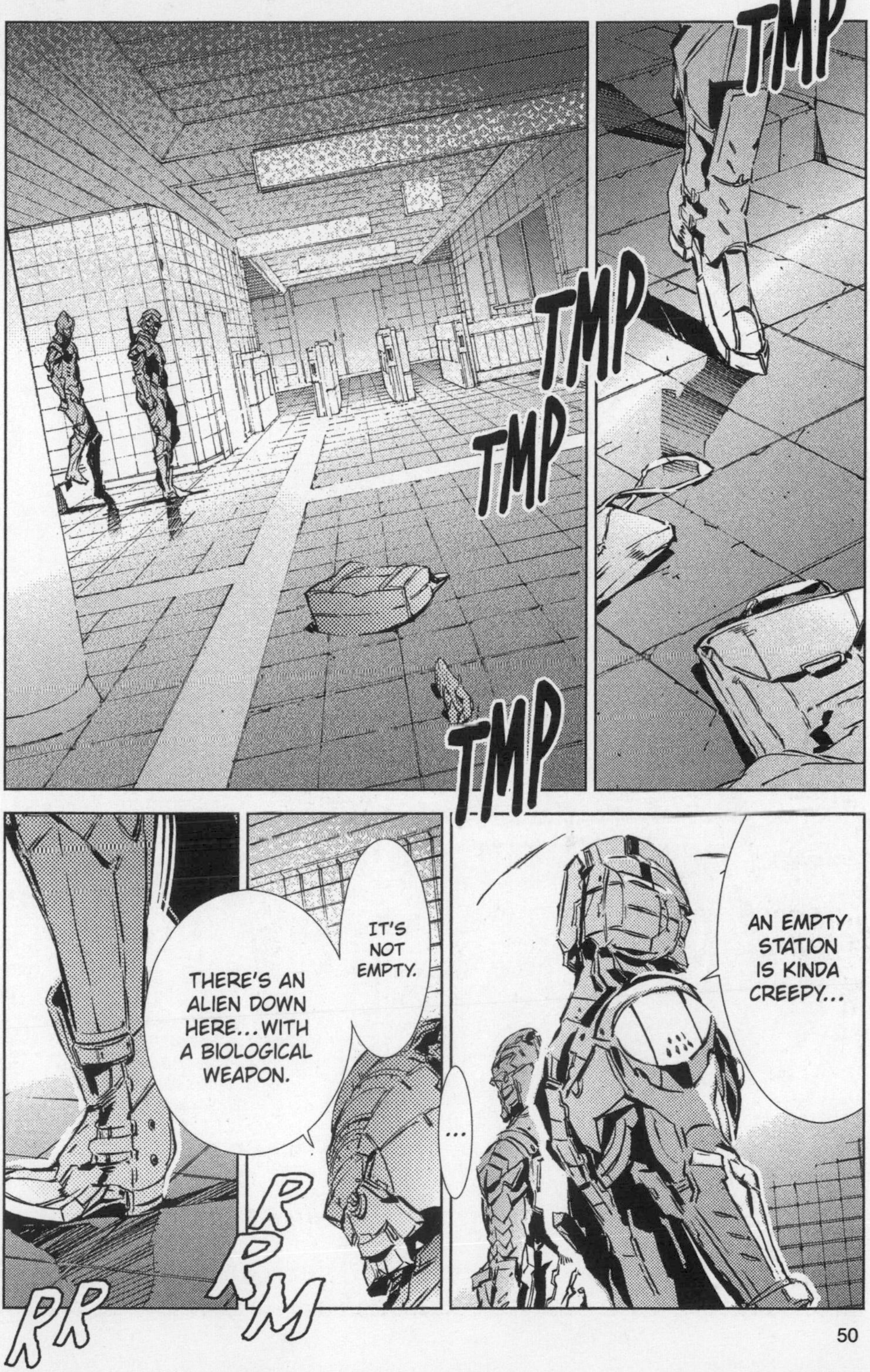
TIMP
TMP
TMP
TMP
AN EMPTY STATION IS KINDA CREEPY...
...
IT'S NOT EMPTY.
RRM
THERE'S AN ALIEN DOWN HERE...WITH A BIOLOGICAL WEAPON.
RR

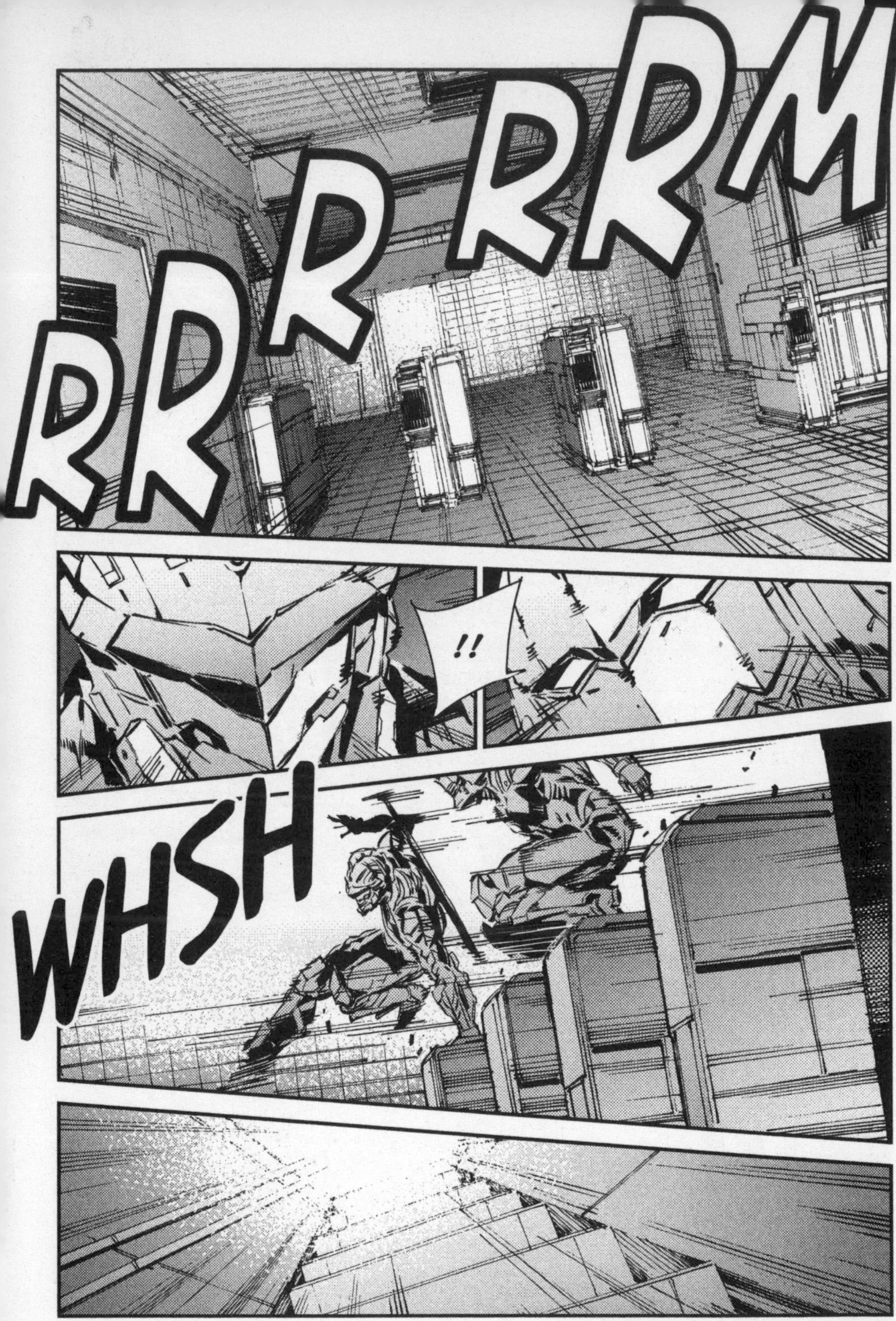
RRRRRM
!!
WHSH

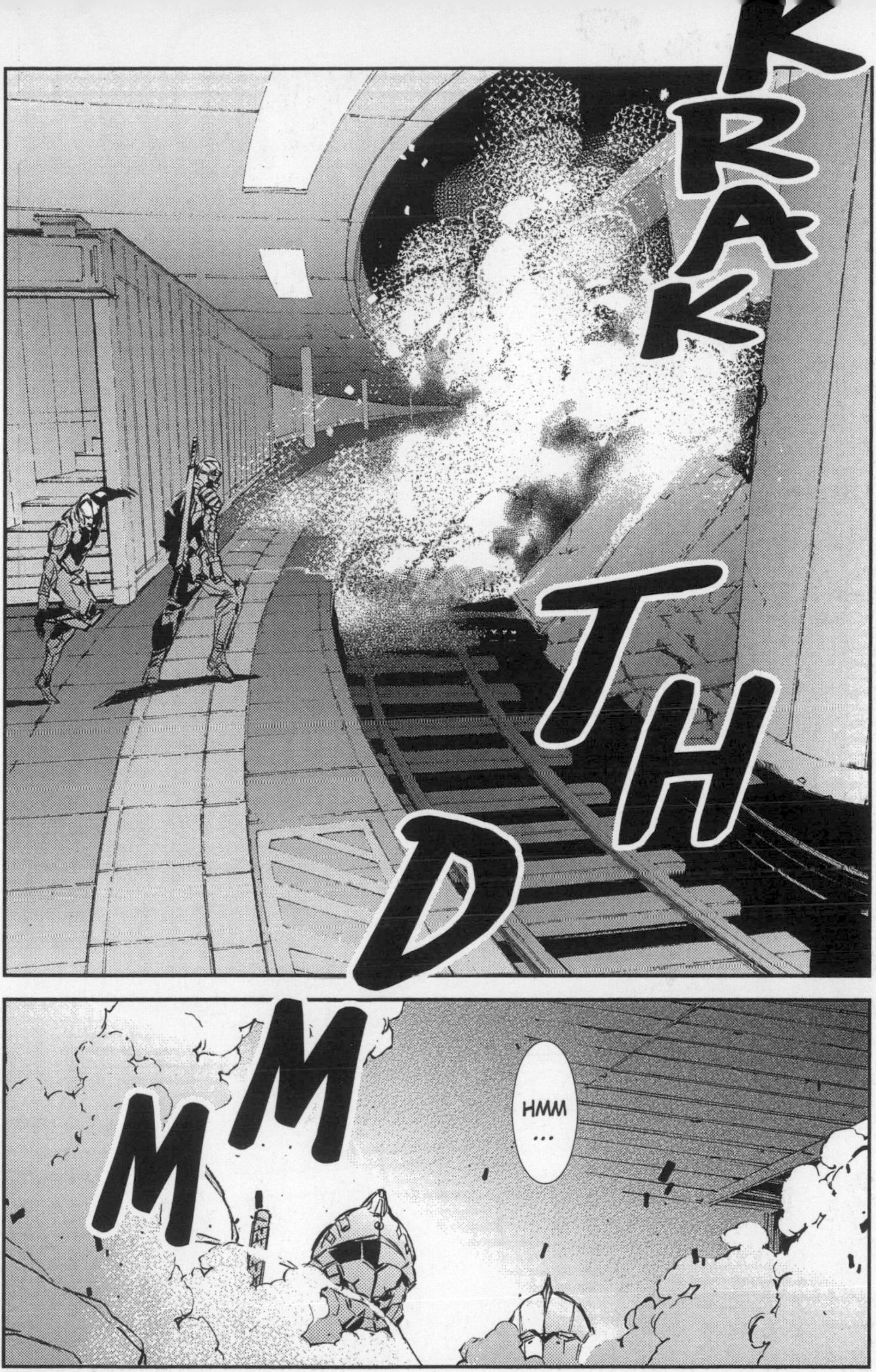
KRAK
THDMMM
HMM
...

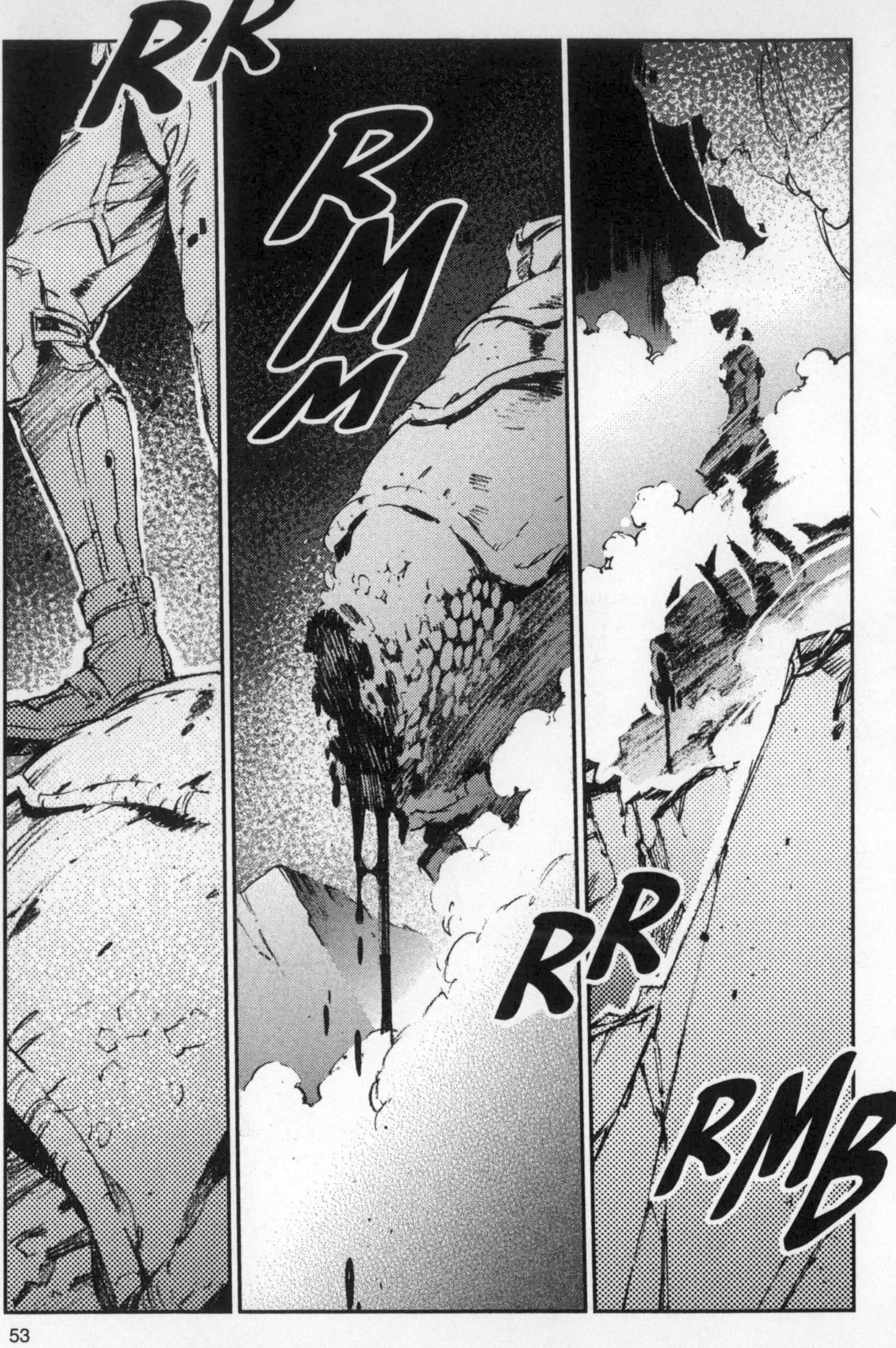
RRRMMM
RRRMB

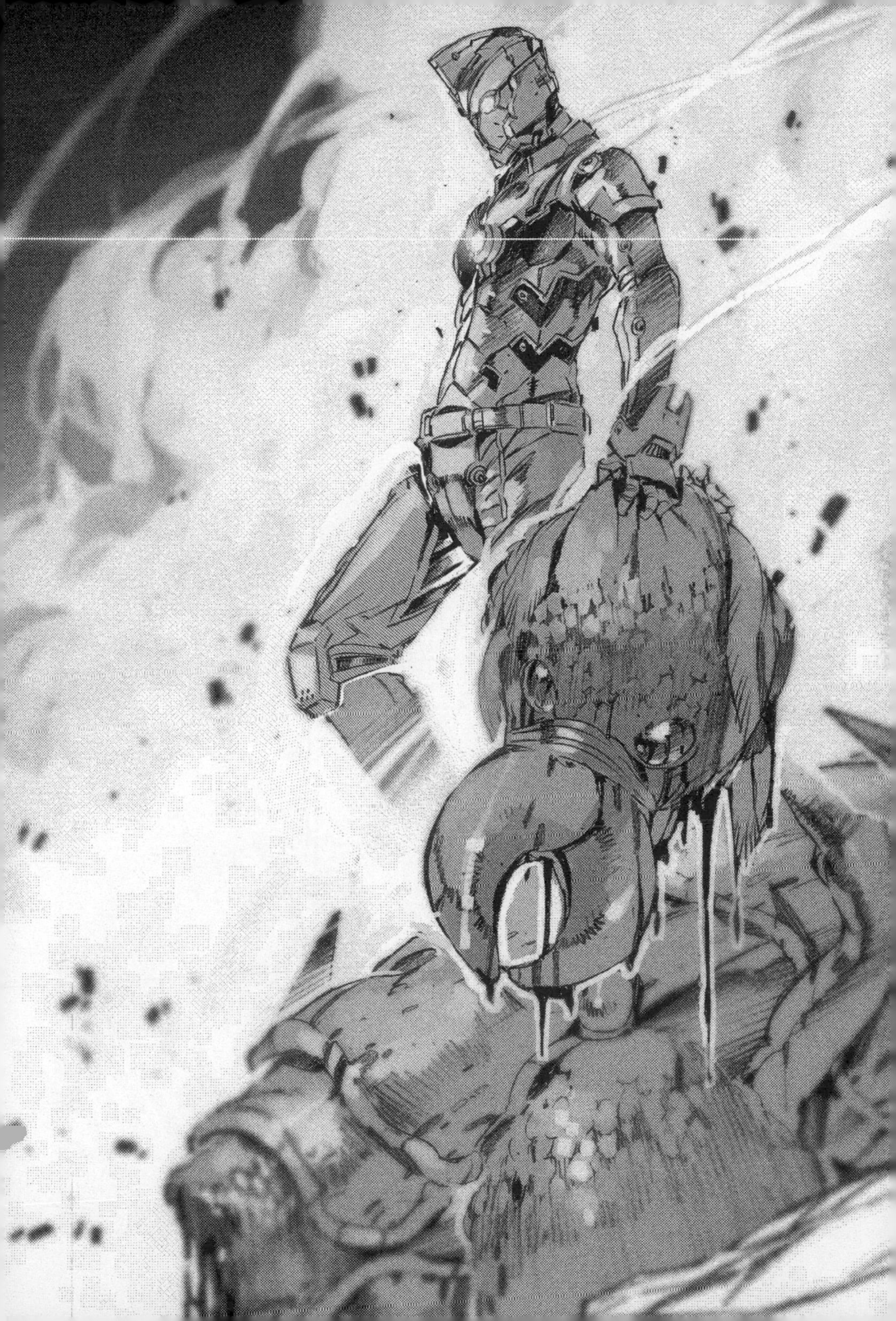

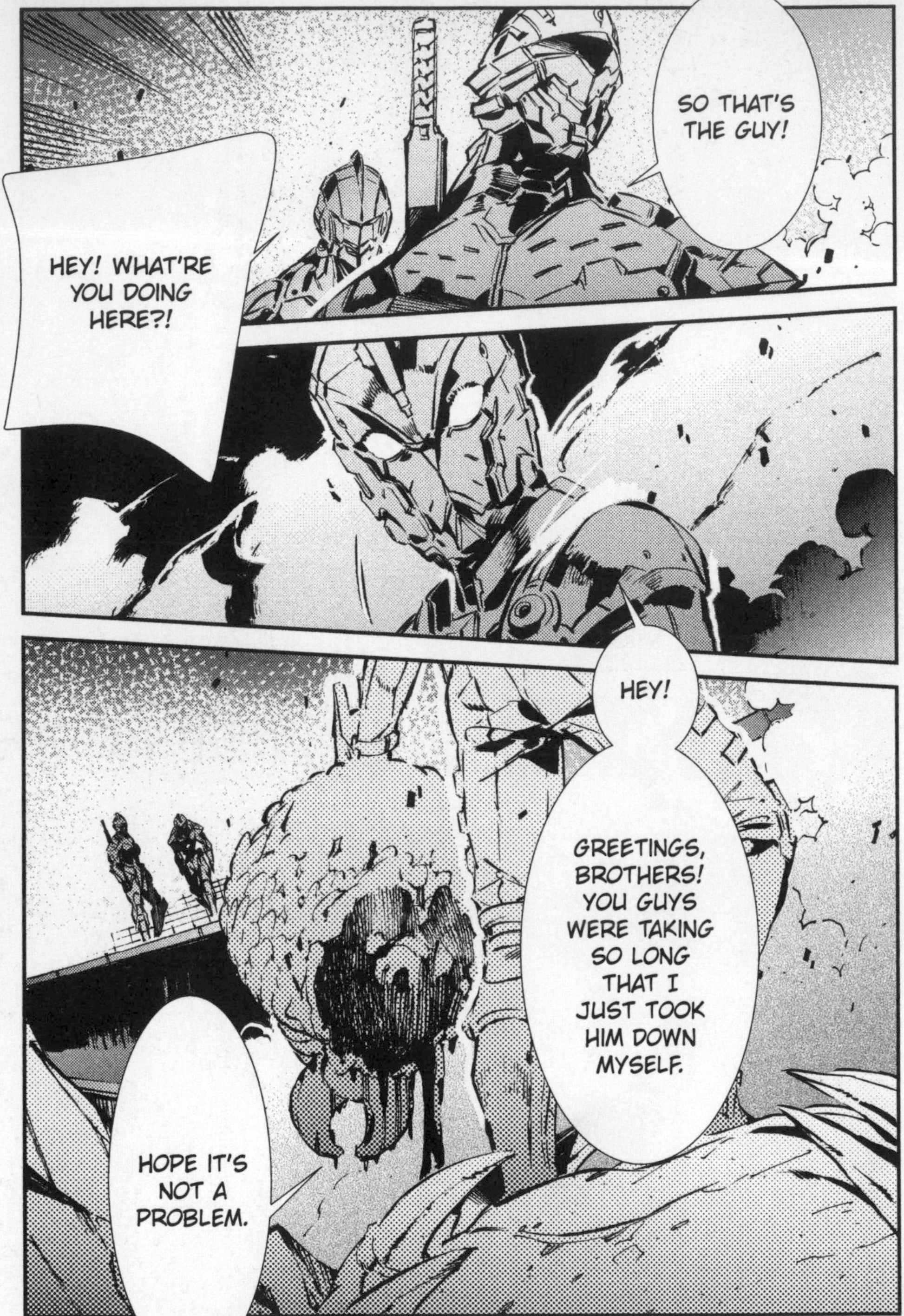
SO THAT'S THE GUY!
HEY! WHAT'RE YOU DOING HERE?!
HEY!
GREETINGS, BROTHERS! YOU GUYS WERE TAKING SO LONG THAT I JUST TOOK HIM DOWN MYSELF.
HOPE IT'S NOT A PROBLEM.

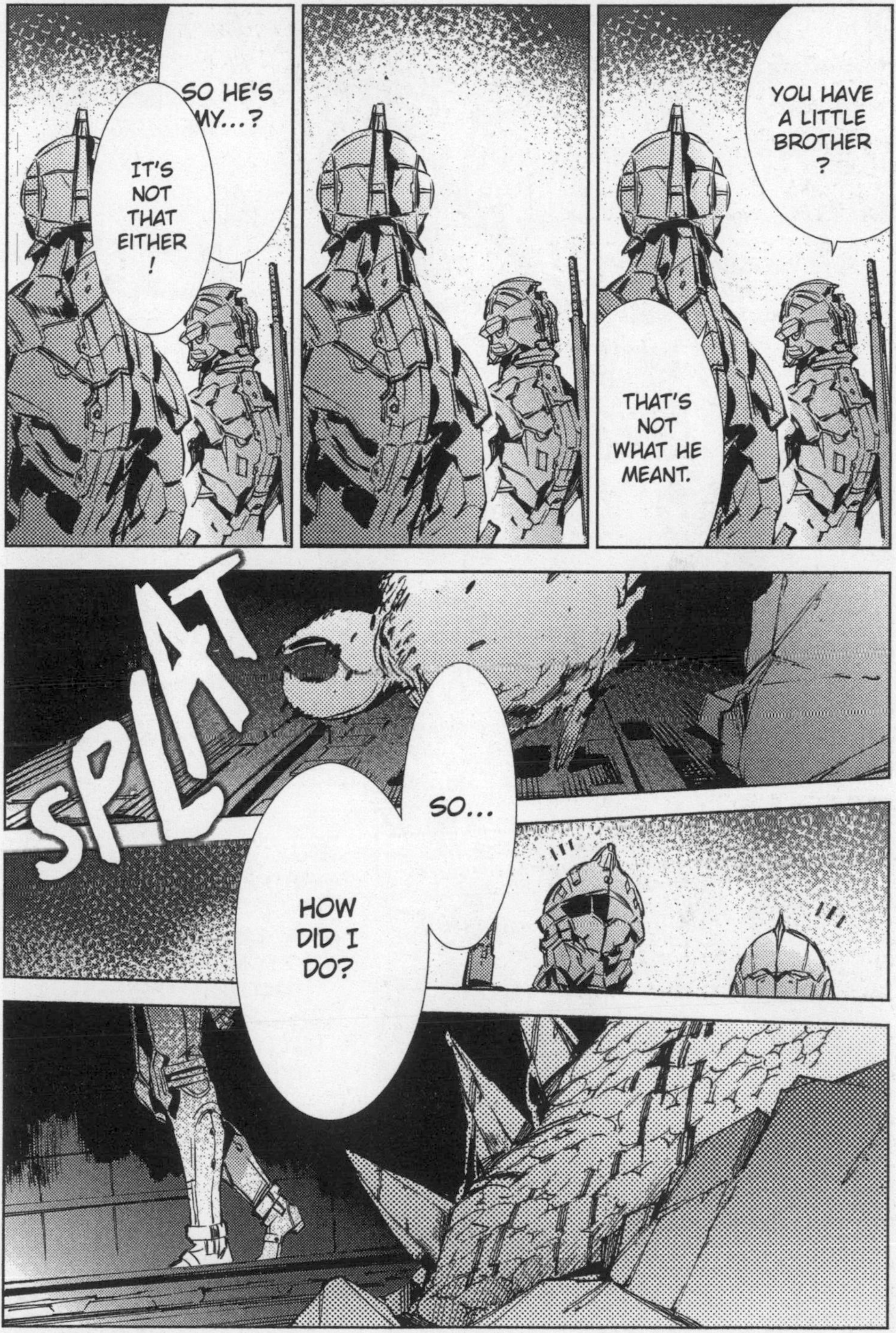
YOU HAVE A LITTLE BROTHER ?
THAT'S NOT WHAT HE MEANT.
SO HE'S MY...?
IT'S NOT THAT EITHER !
SPLAT
SO...
HOW DID I DO?

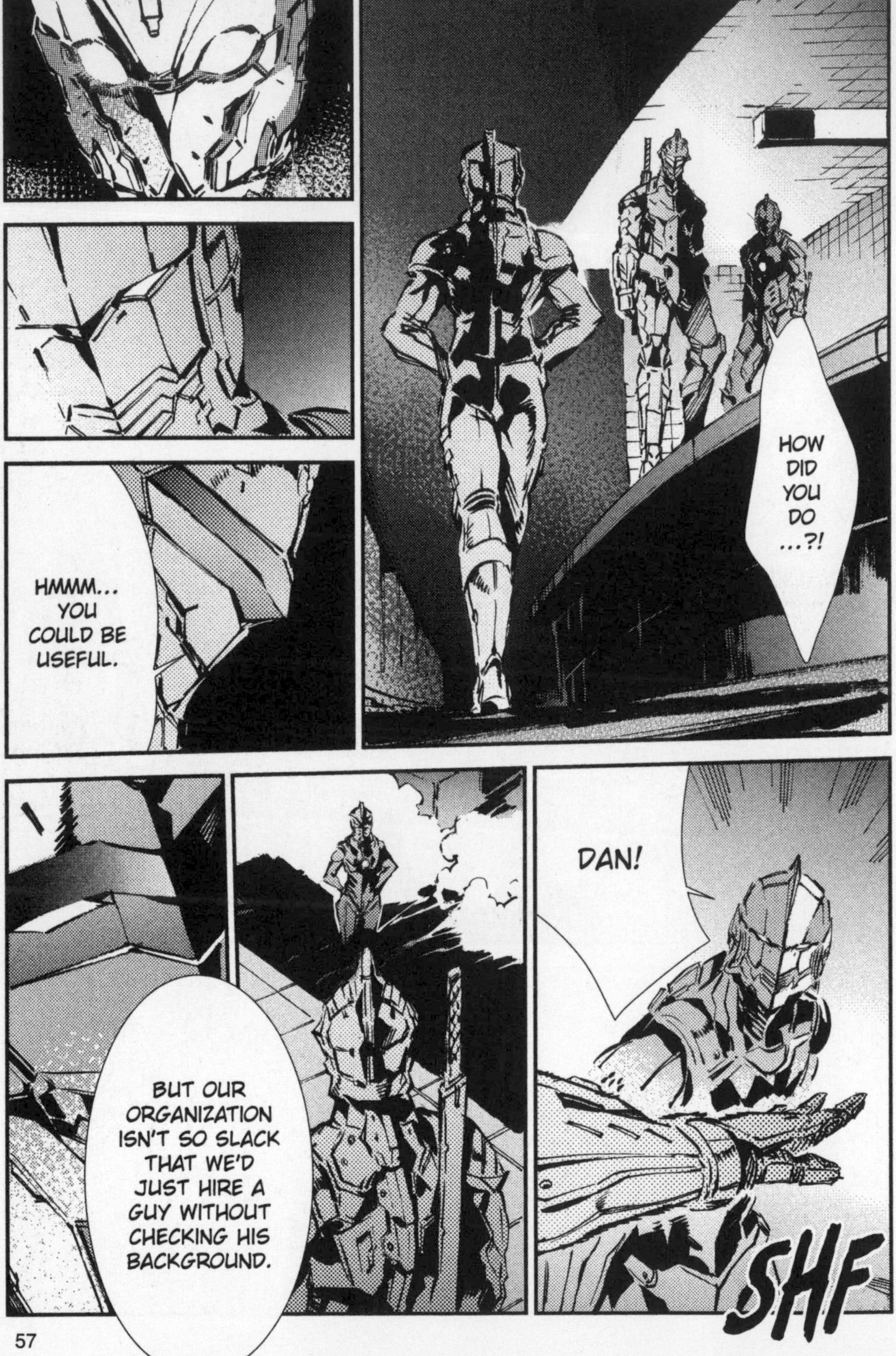
HOW DID YOU DO ...?!
HMMM... YOU COULD BE USEFUL.
DAN!
SHF
BUT OUR ORGANIZATION ISN'T SO SLACK THAT WE'D JUST HIRE A GUY WITHOUT CHECKING HIS BACKGROUND.

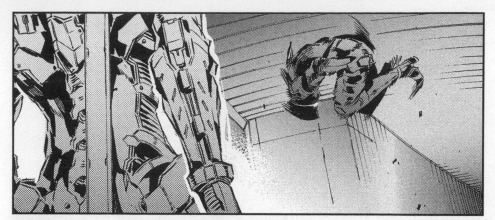

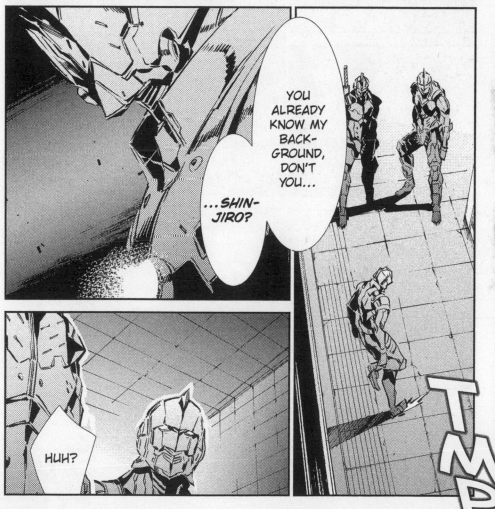

YOU ALREADY KNOW MY BACK-GROUND, DON'T YOU...

...SHIN-JIRO?

HUH?

TMP

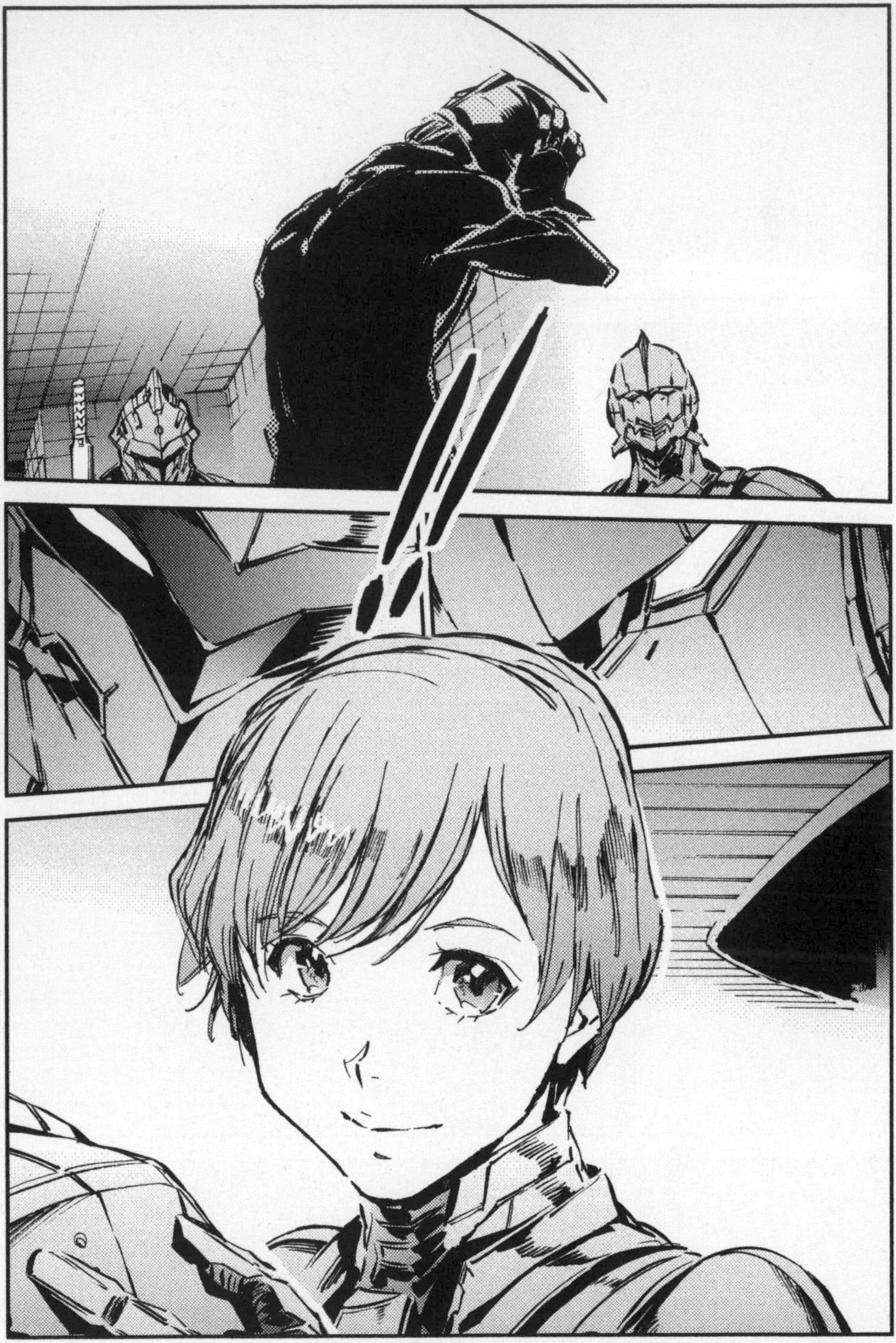

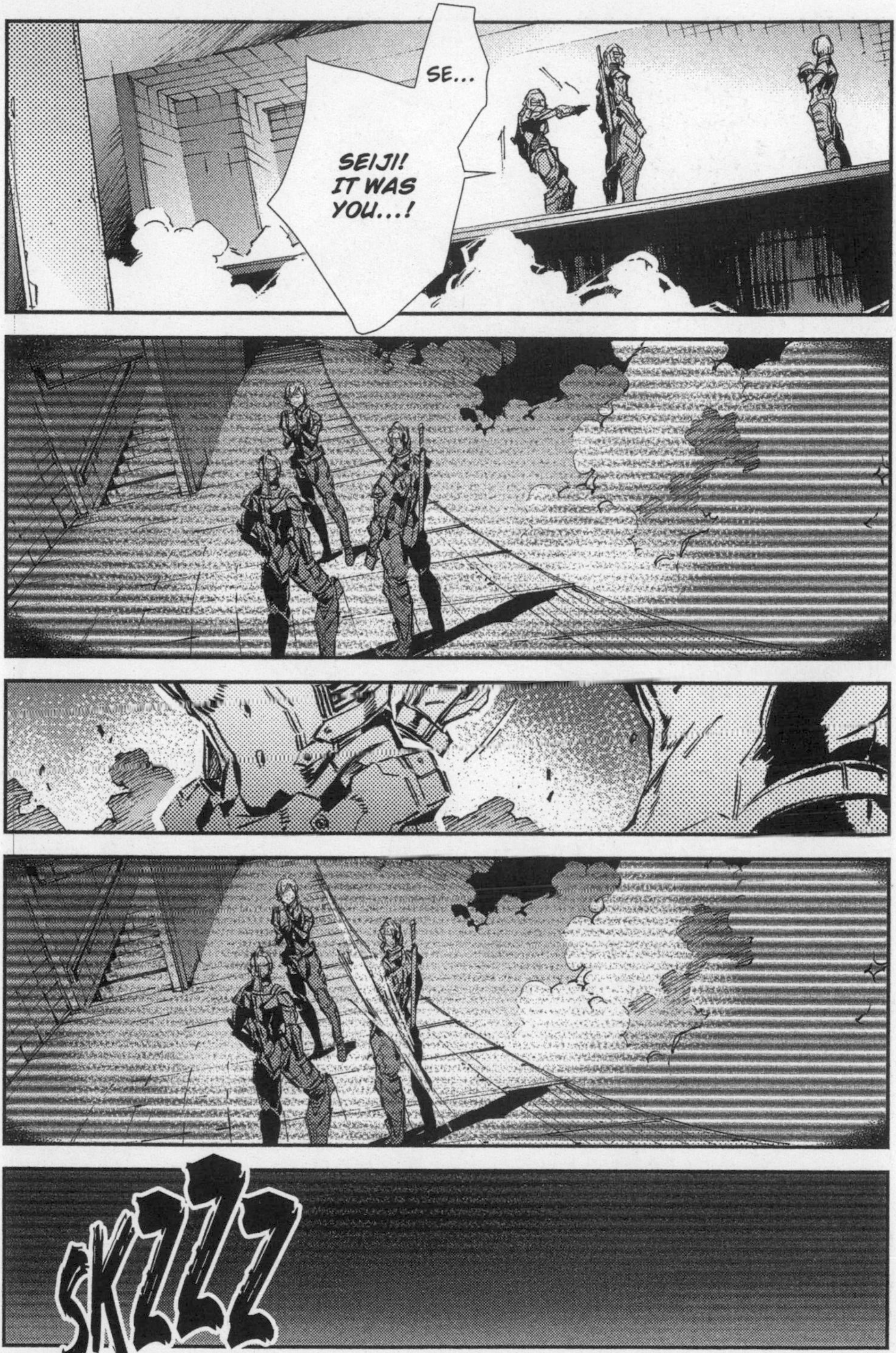
SE...
SEIJI! IT WAS YOU...!
SKZZZ

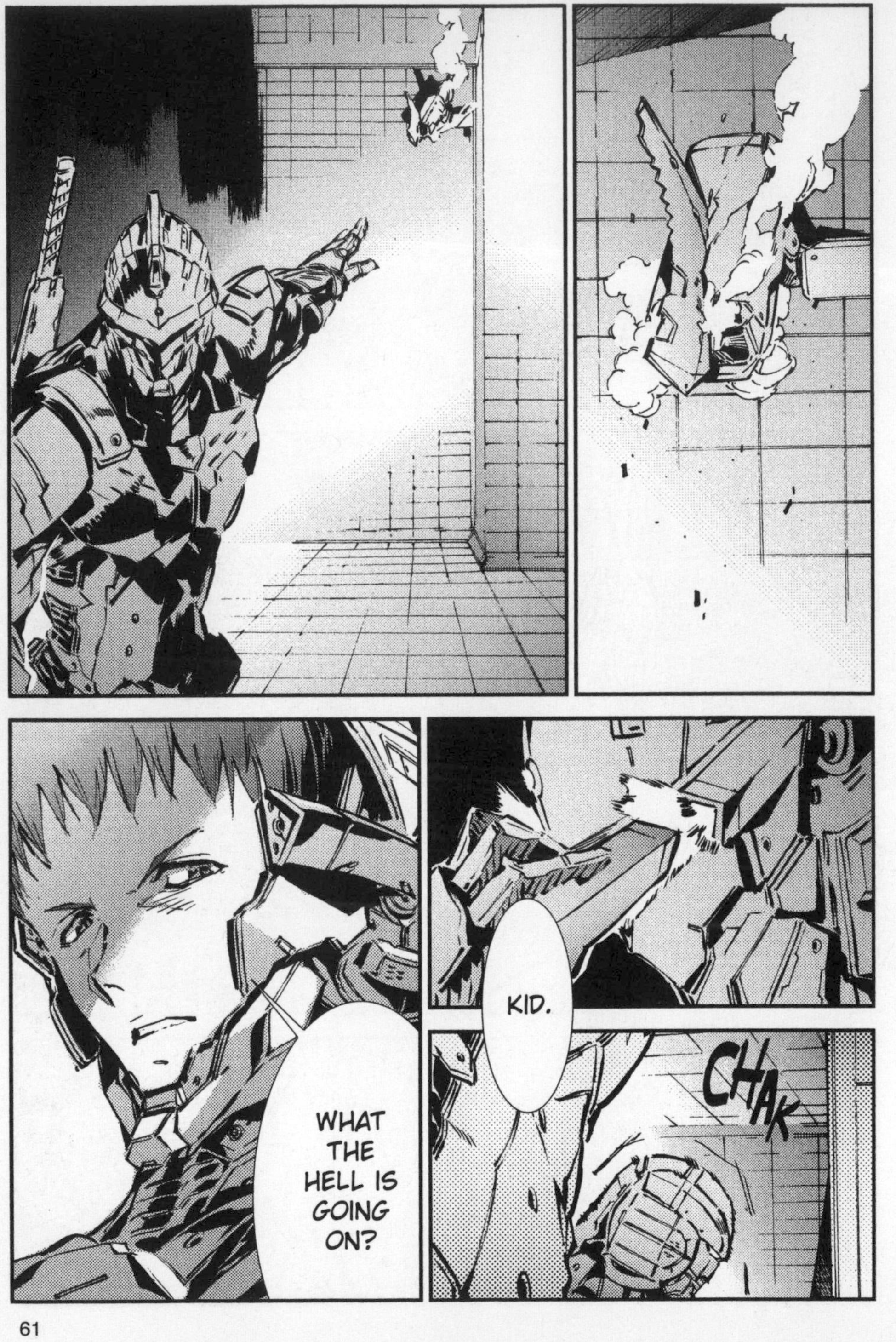
KID.
CHAK
WHAT THE HELL IS GOING ON?

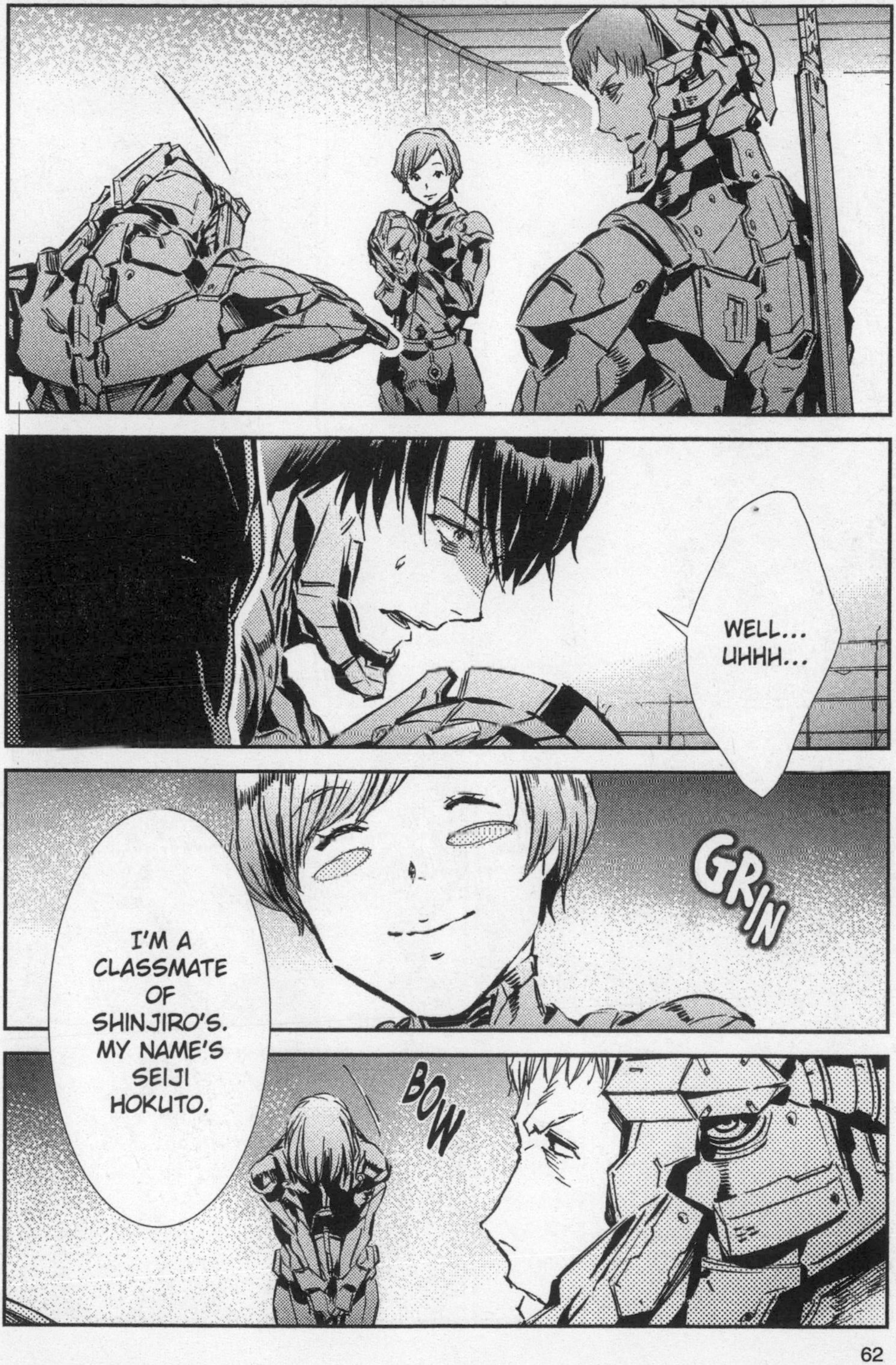
WELL... UHHH...
GRIN
I'M A CLASSMATE OF SHINJIRO'S. MY NAME'S SEIJI HOKUTO.
BOW

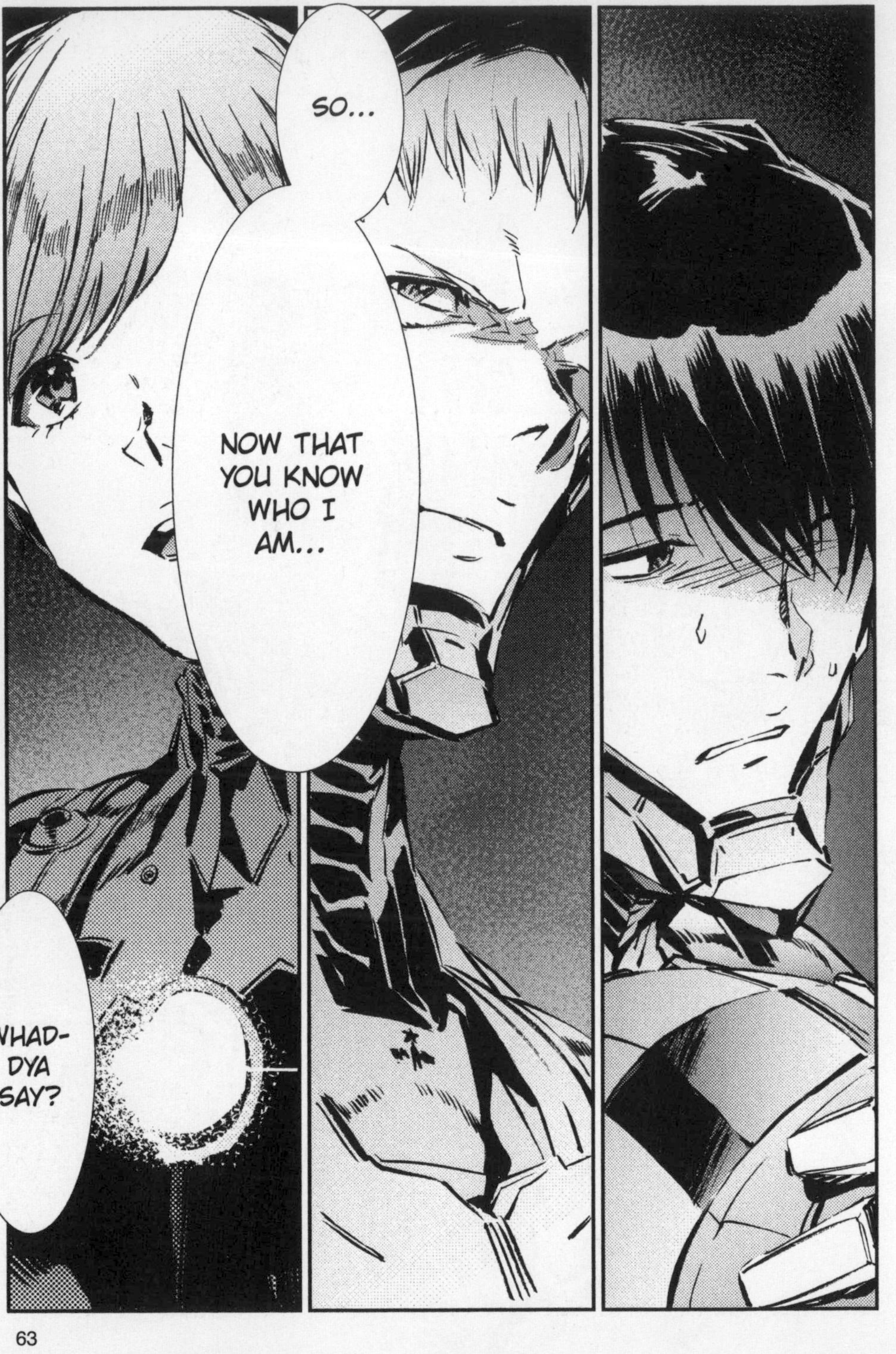
SO...
NOW THAT YOU KNOW WHO I AM...
WHAD-DYA SAY?

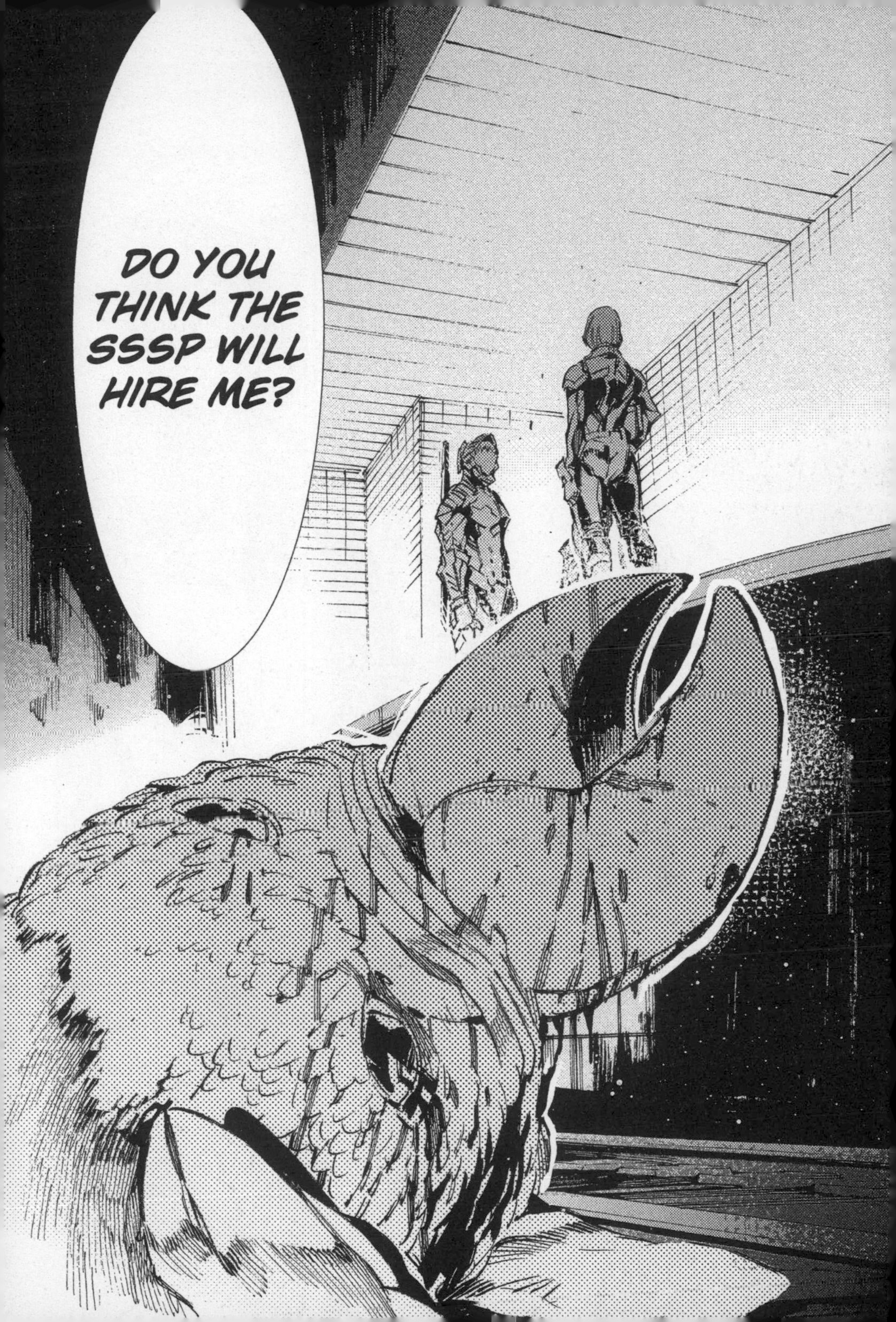
DO YOU THINK THE SSSP WILL HIRE ME?

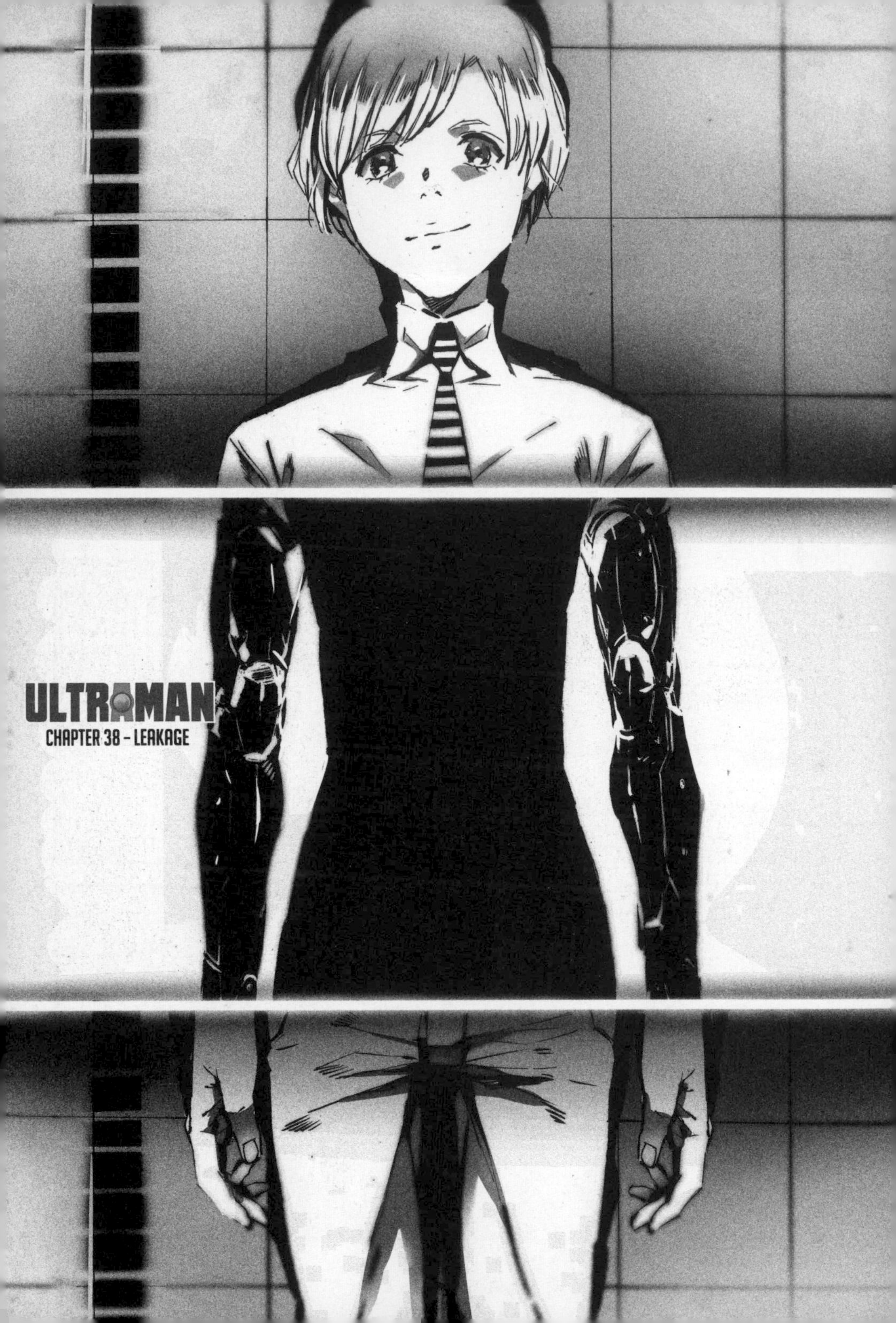
ULTRAMAN
CHAPTER 38 - LEAKAGE

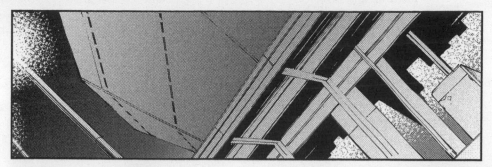

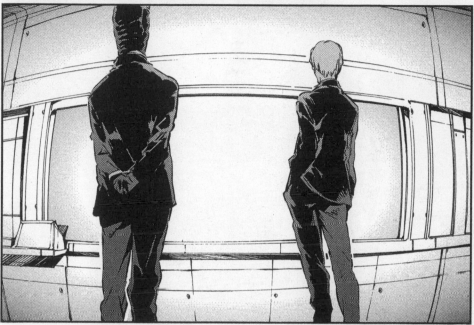

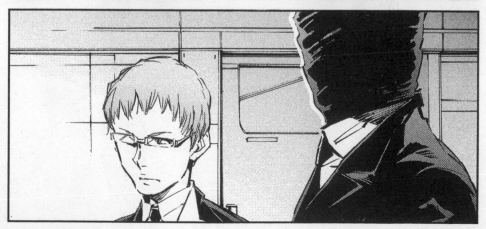

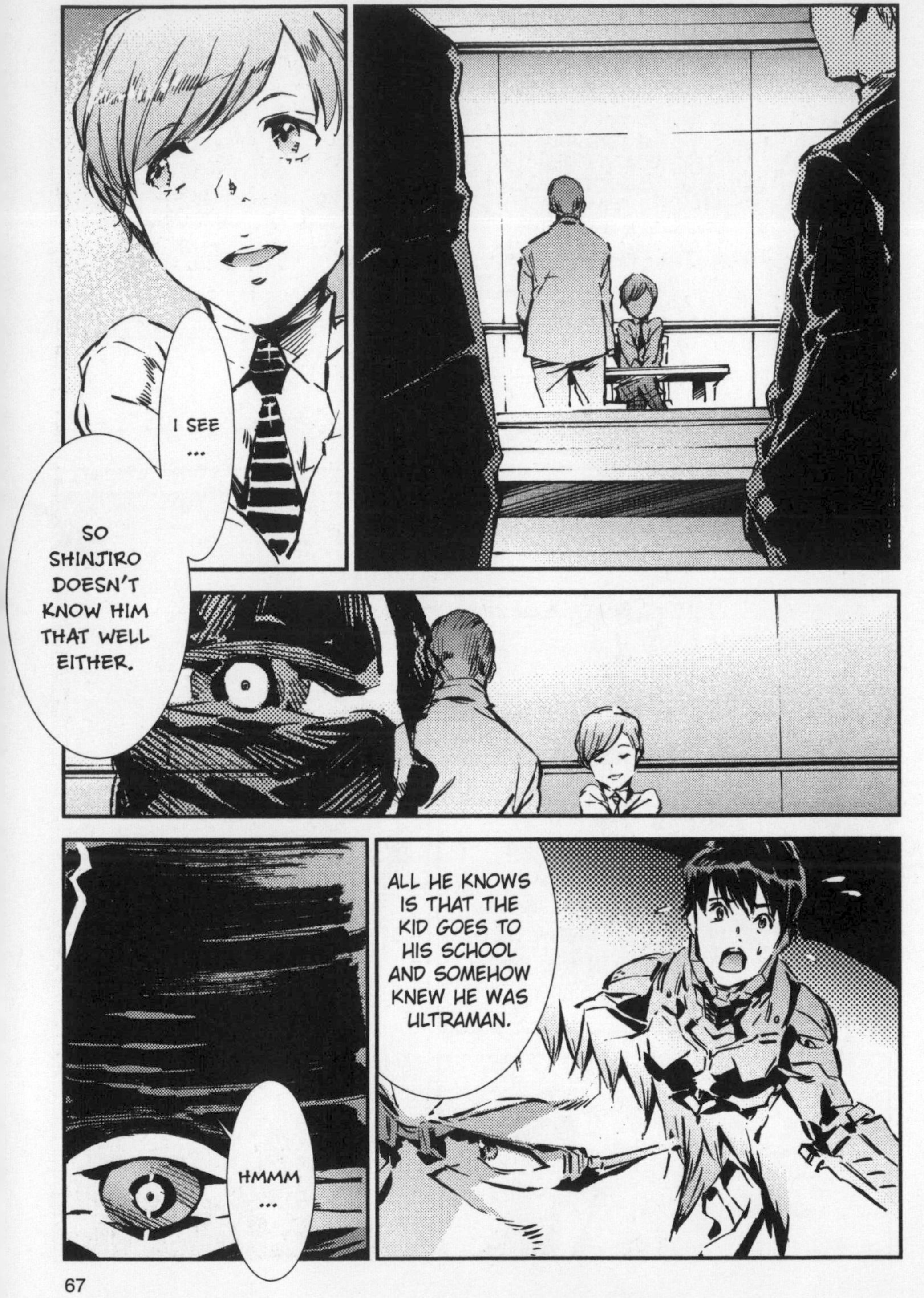
I SEE ...
SO SHINJIRO DOESN'T KNOW HIM THAT WELL EITHER.
ALL HE KNOWS IS THAT THE KID GOES TO HIS SCHOOL AND SOMEHOW KNEW HE WAS ULTRAMAN.
HMMM ...

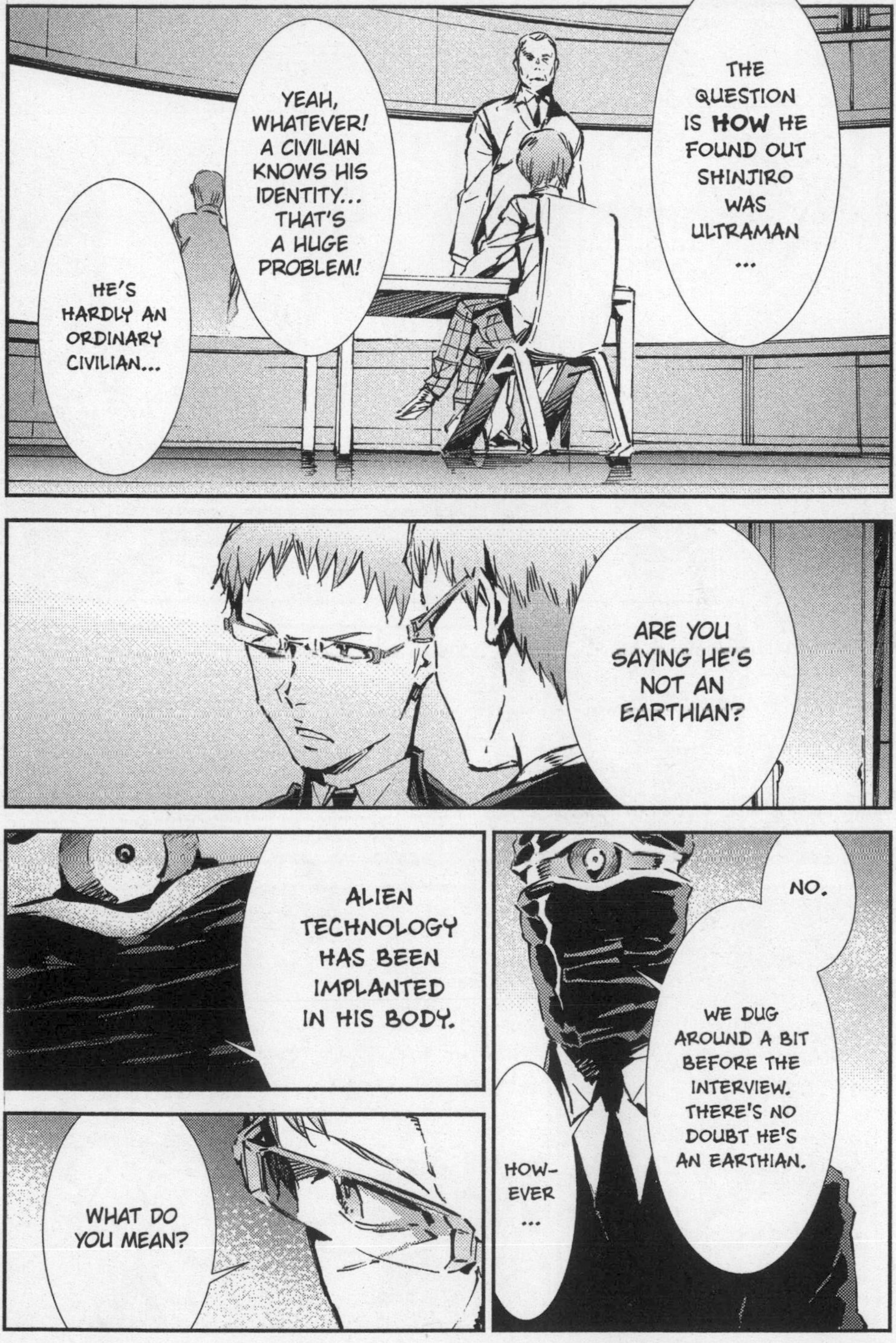
THE QUESTION IS **HOW** HE FOUND OUT SHINJIRO WAS ULTRAMAN ...
YEAH, WHATEVER! A CIVILIAN KNOWS HIS IDENTITY... THAT'S A HUGE PROBLEM!
HE'S HARDLY AN ORDINARY CIVILIAN...
ARE YOU SAYING HE'S NOT AN EARTHIAN?
NO.
WE DUG AROUND A BIT BEFORE THE INTERVIEW. THERE'S NO DOUBT HE'S AN EARTHIAN.
HOW-EVER ...
ALIEN TECHNOLOGY HAS BEEN IMPLANTED IN HIS BODY.
WHAT DO YOU MEAN?

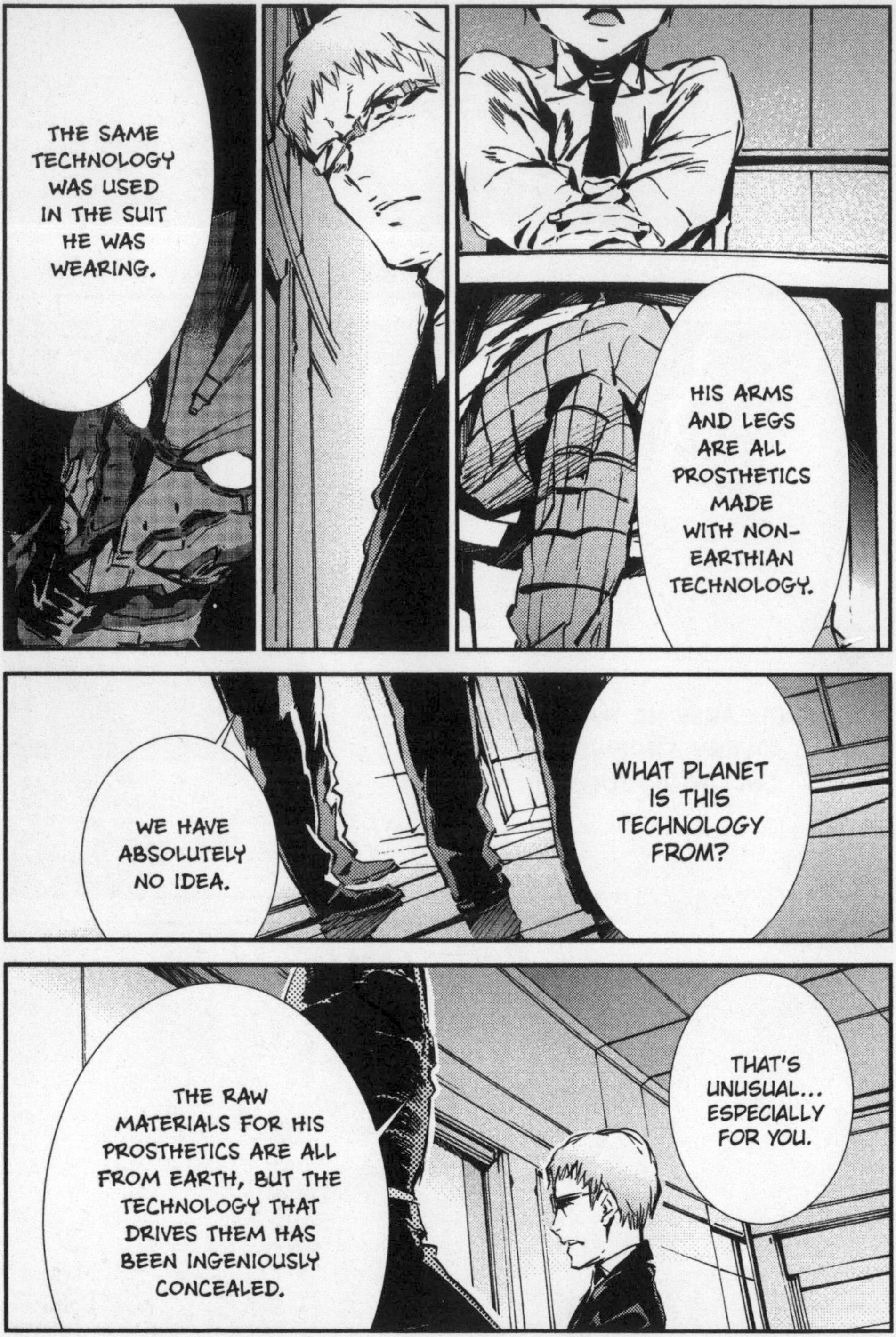
HIS ARMS AND LEGS ARE ALL PROSTHETICS MADE WITH NON-EARTHIAN TECHNOLOGY.
THE SAME TECHNOLOGY WAS USED IN THE SUIT HE WAS WEARING.
WHAT PLANET IS THIS TECHNOLOGY FROM?
WE HAVE ABSOLUTELY NO IDEA.
THAT'S UNUSUAL... ESPECIALLY FOR YOU.
THE RAW MATERIALS FOR HIS PROSTHETICS ARE ALL FROM EARTH, BUT THE TECHNOLOGY THAT DRIVES THEM HAS BEEN INGENIOUSLY CONCEALED.

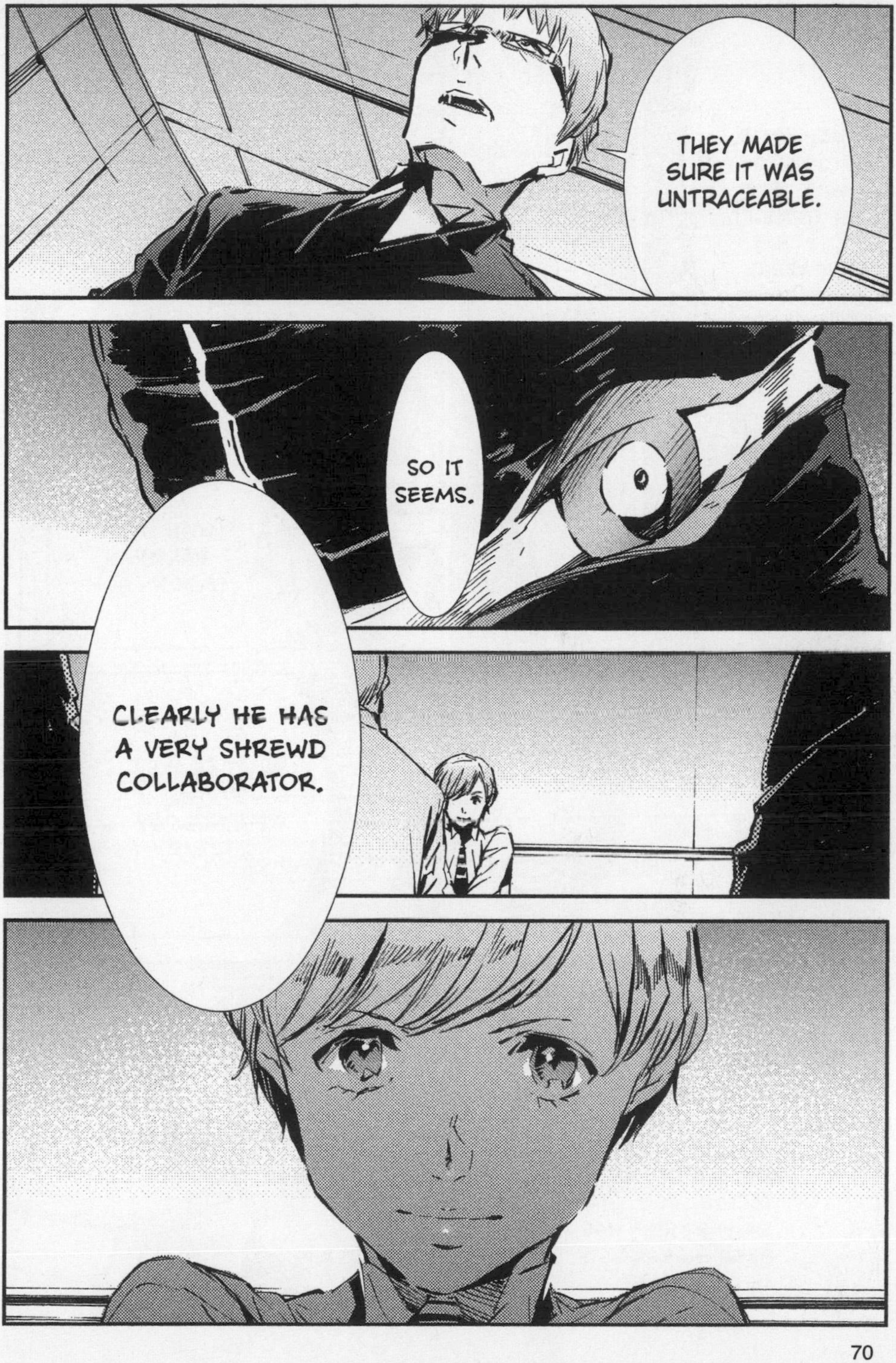
THEY MADE SURE IT WAS UNTRACEABLE.
SO IT SEEMS.
CLEARLY HE HAS A VERY SHREWD COLLABORATOR.

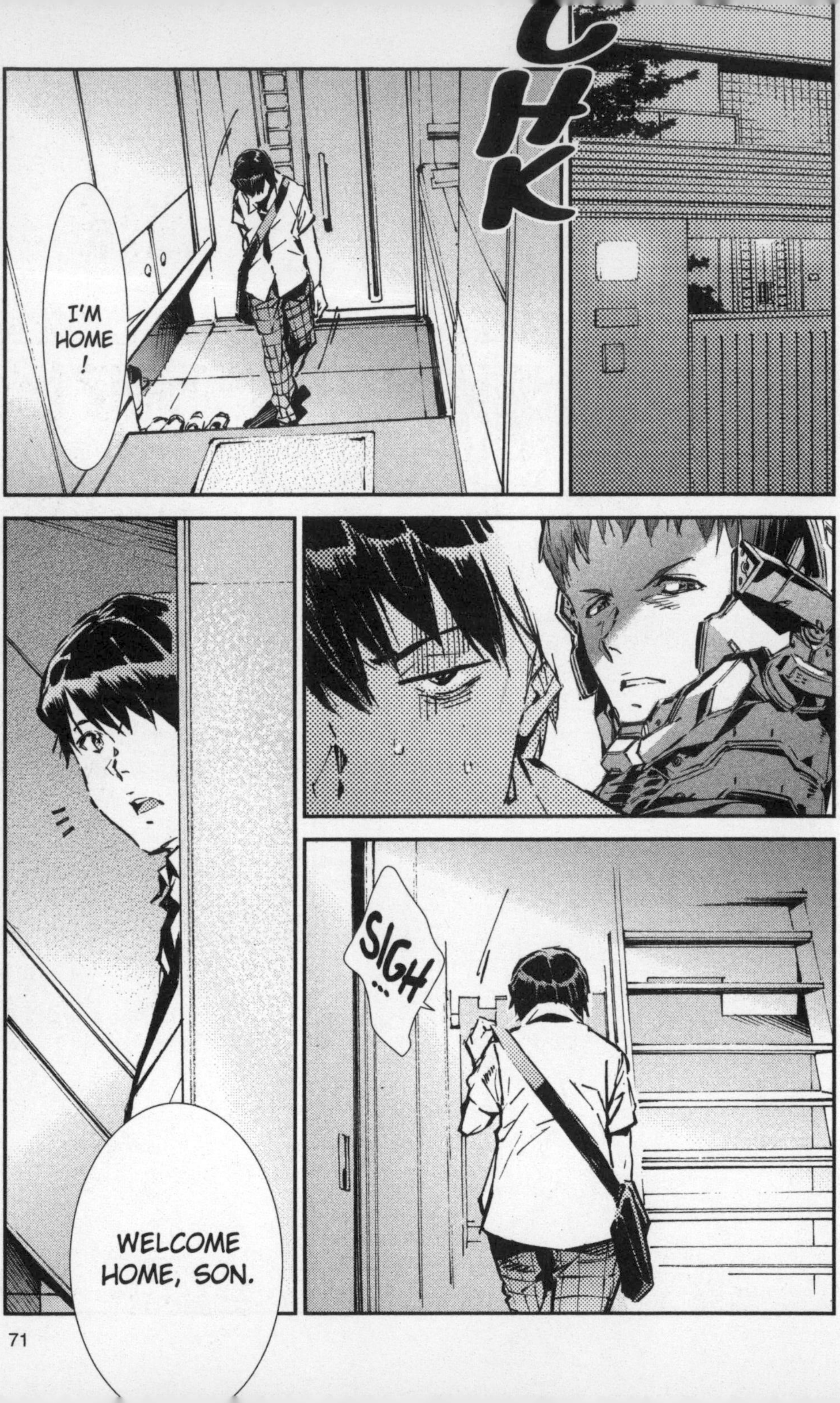
CHK
I'M HOME!
SIGH...
WELCOME HOME, SON.

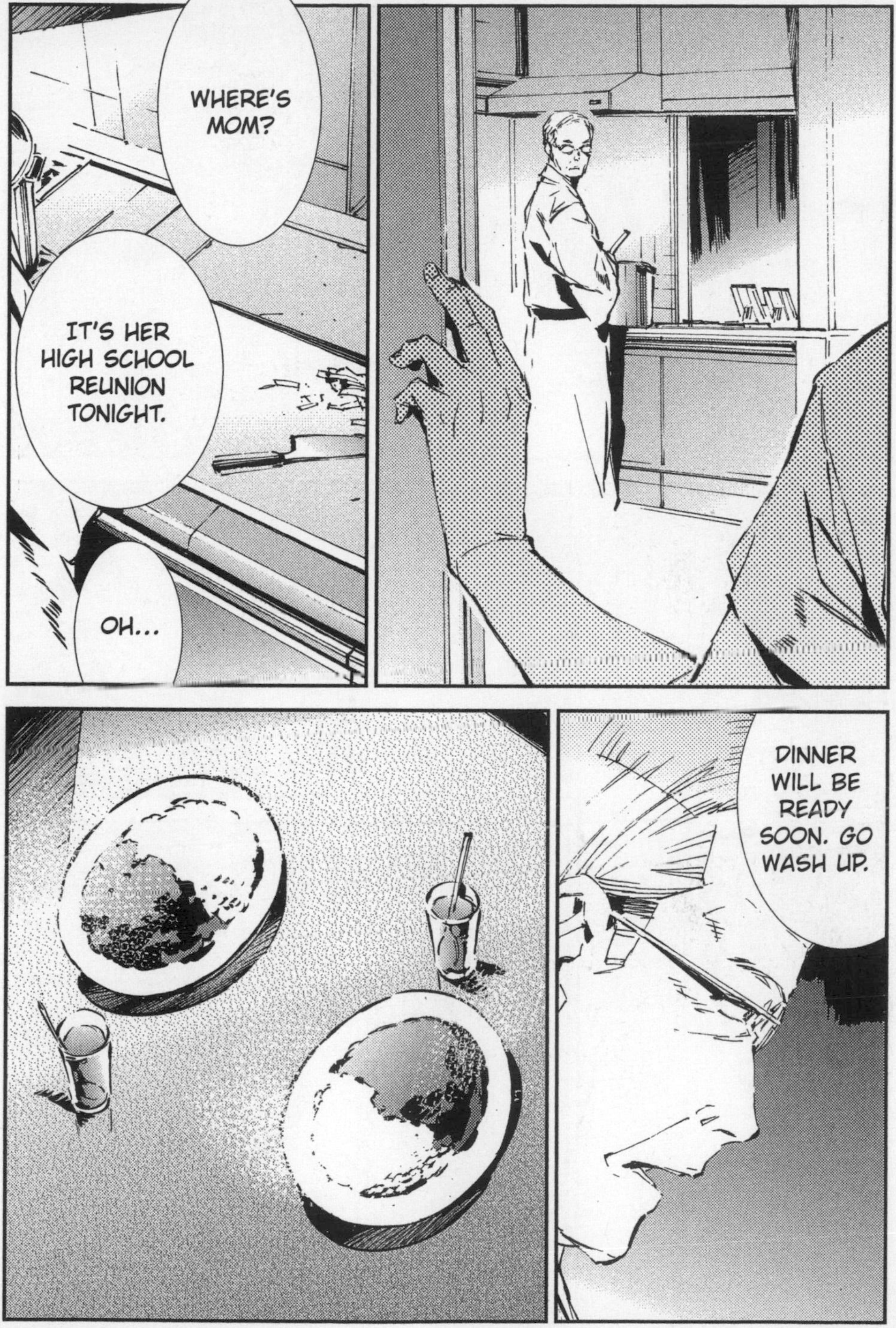
WHERE'S MOM?
IT'S HER HIGH SCHOOL REUNION TONIGHT.
OH...
DINNER WILL BE READY SOON. GO WASH UP.

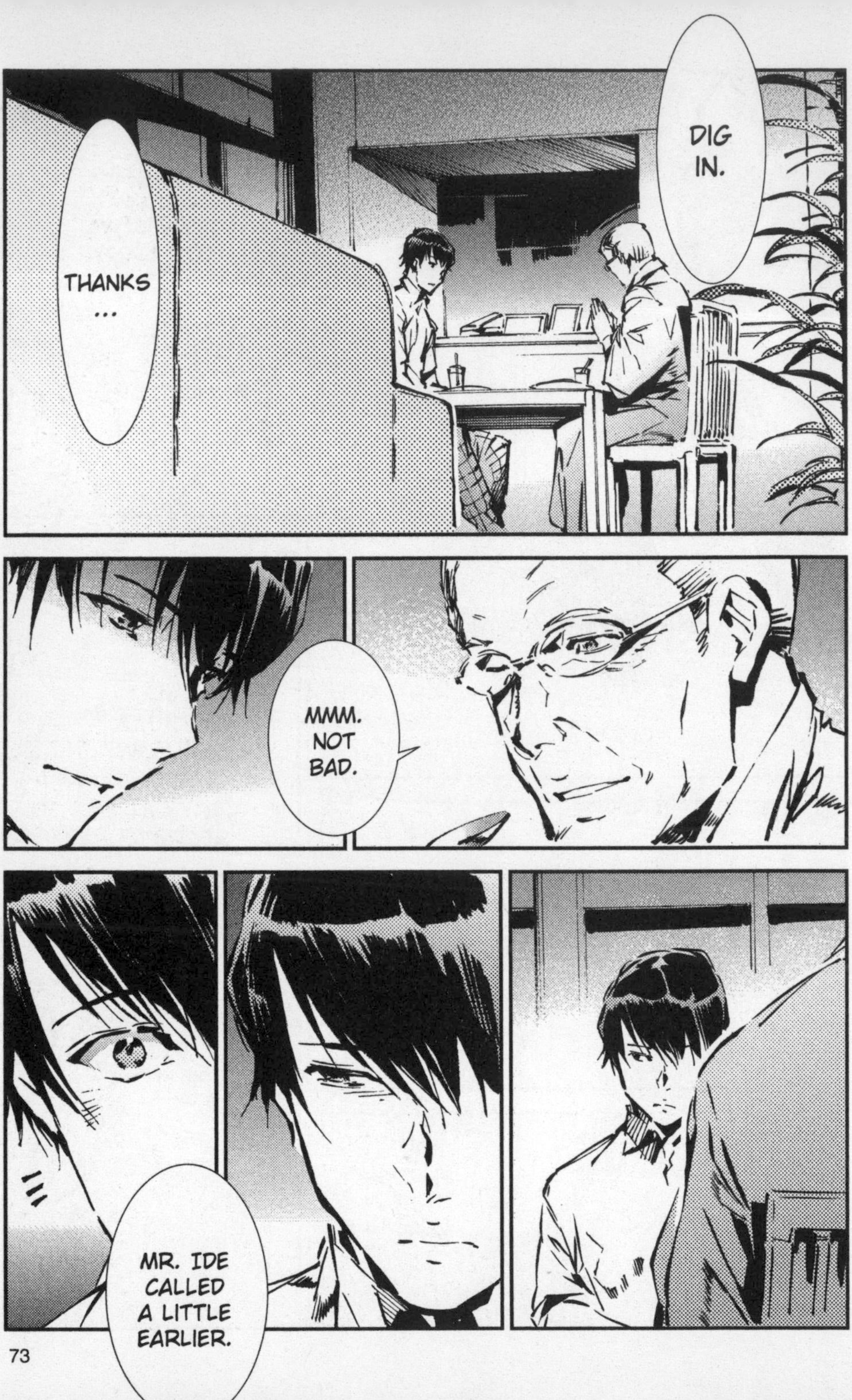

DIG IN.
THANKS ...
MMM. NOT BAD.
MR. IDE CALLED A LITTLE EARLIER.

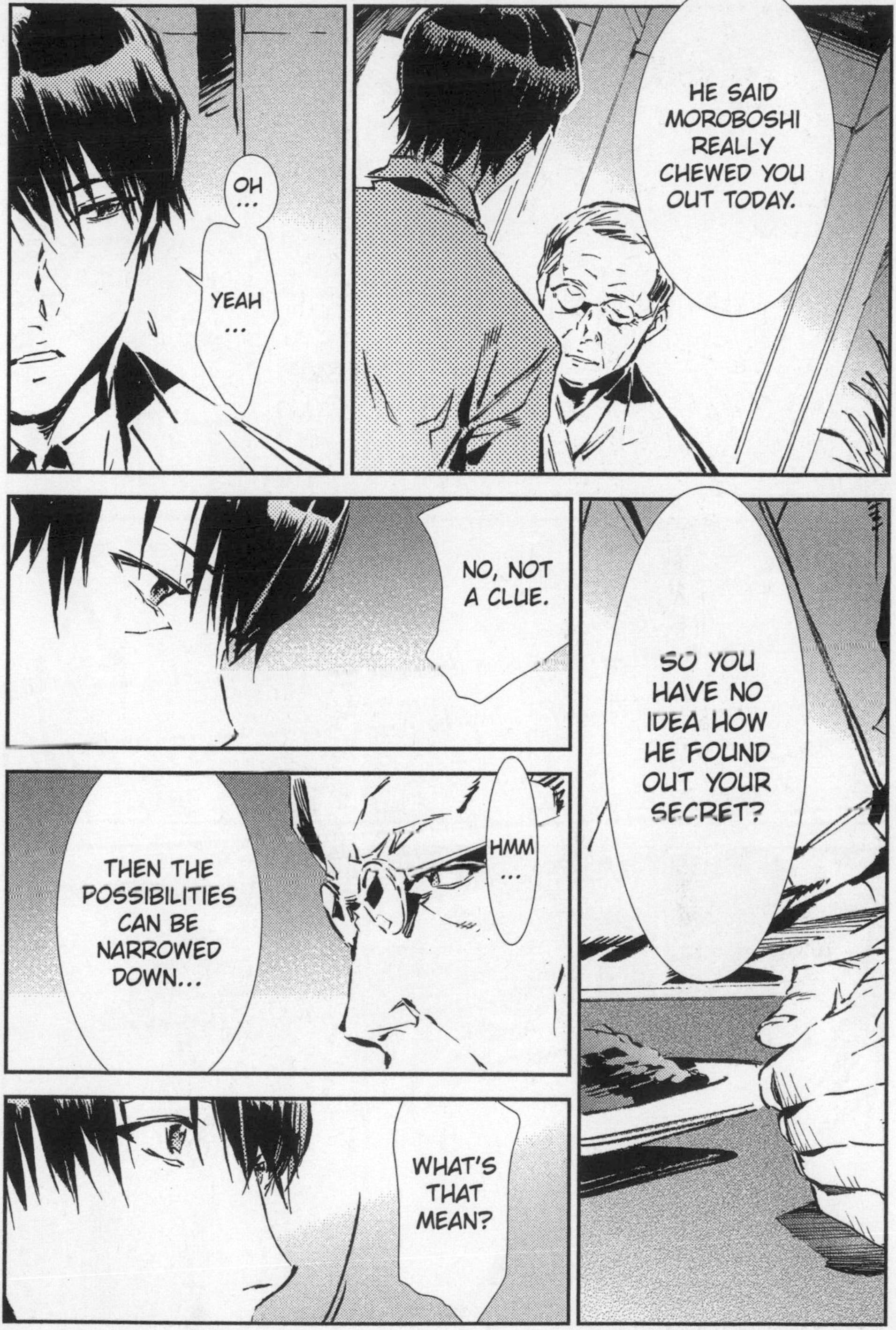
HE SAID MOROBOSHI REALLY CHEWED YOU OUT TODAY.
OH ...
YEAH ...
SO YOU HAVE NO IDEA HOW HE FOUND OUT YOUR SECRET?
NO, NOT A CLUE.
HMM ...
THEN THE POSSIBILITIES CAN BE NARROWED DOWN...
WHAT'S THAT MEAN?

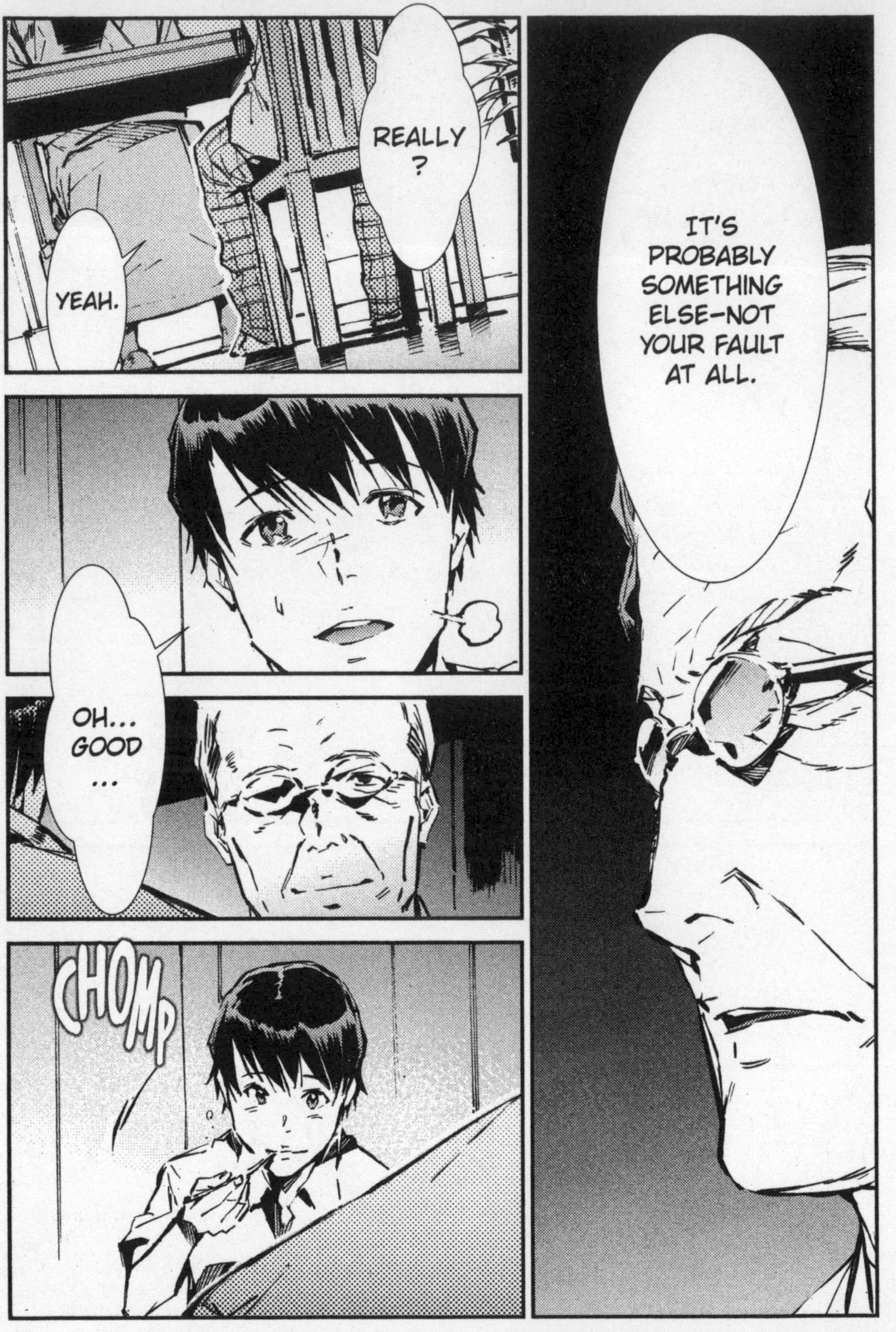
IT'S PROBABLY SOMETHING ELSE—NOT YOUR FAULT AT ALL.
REALLY?
YEAH.
OH... GOOD...
CHOMP

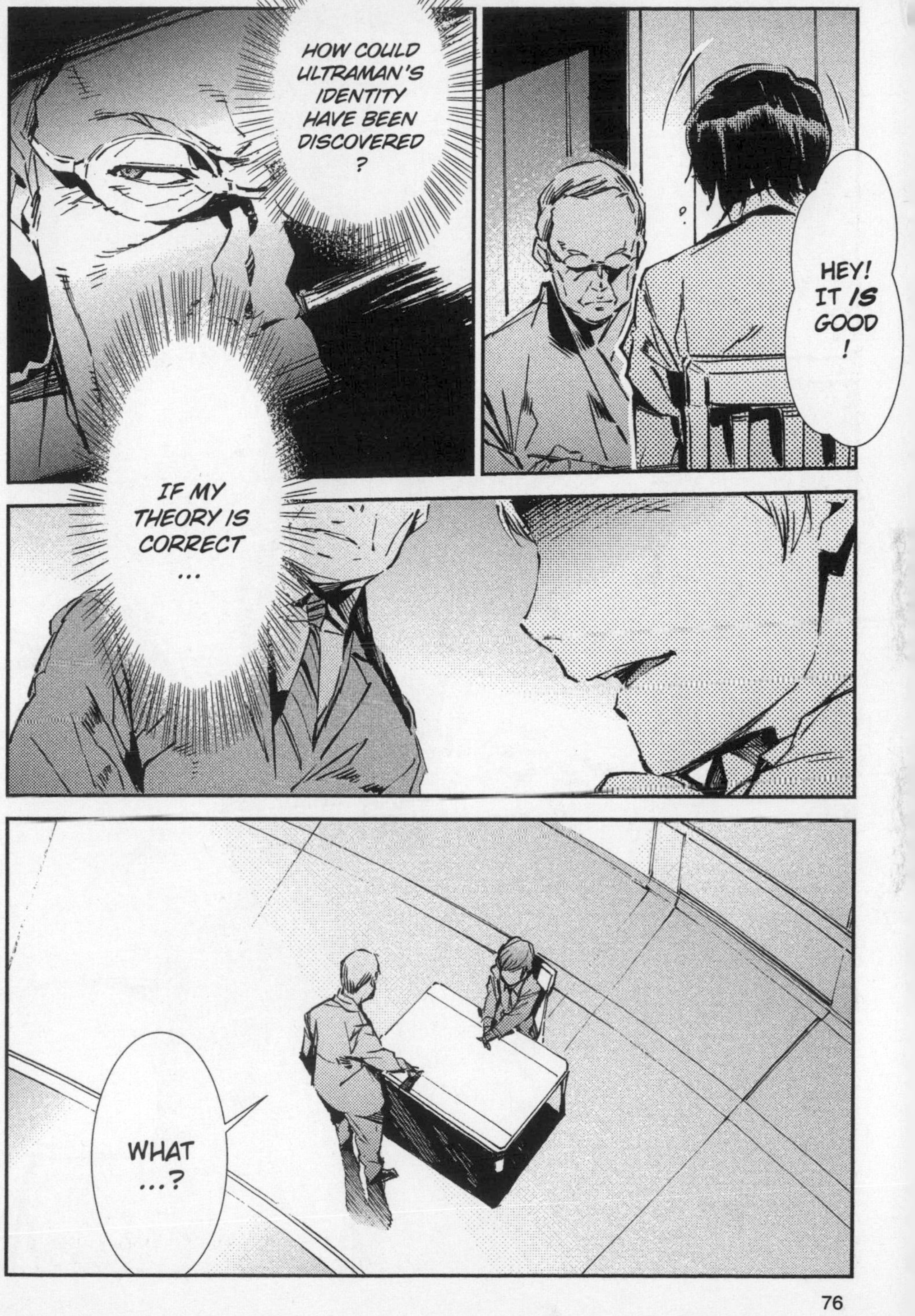
HEY! IT *IS* GOOD!
HOW COULD ULTRAMAN'S IDENTITY HAVE BEEN DISCOVERED?
IF MY THEORY IS CORRECT...
WHAT...?

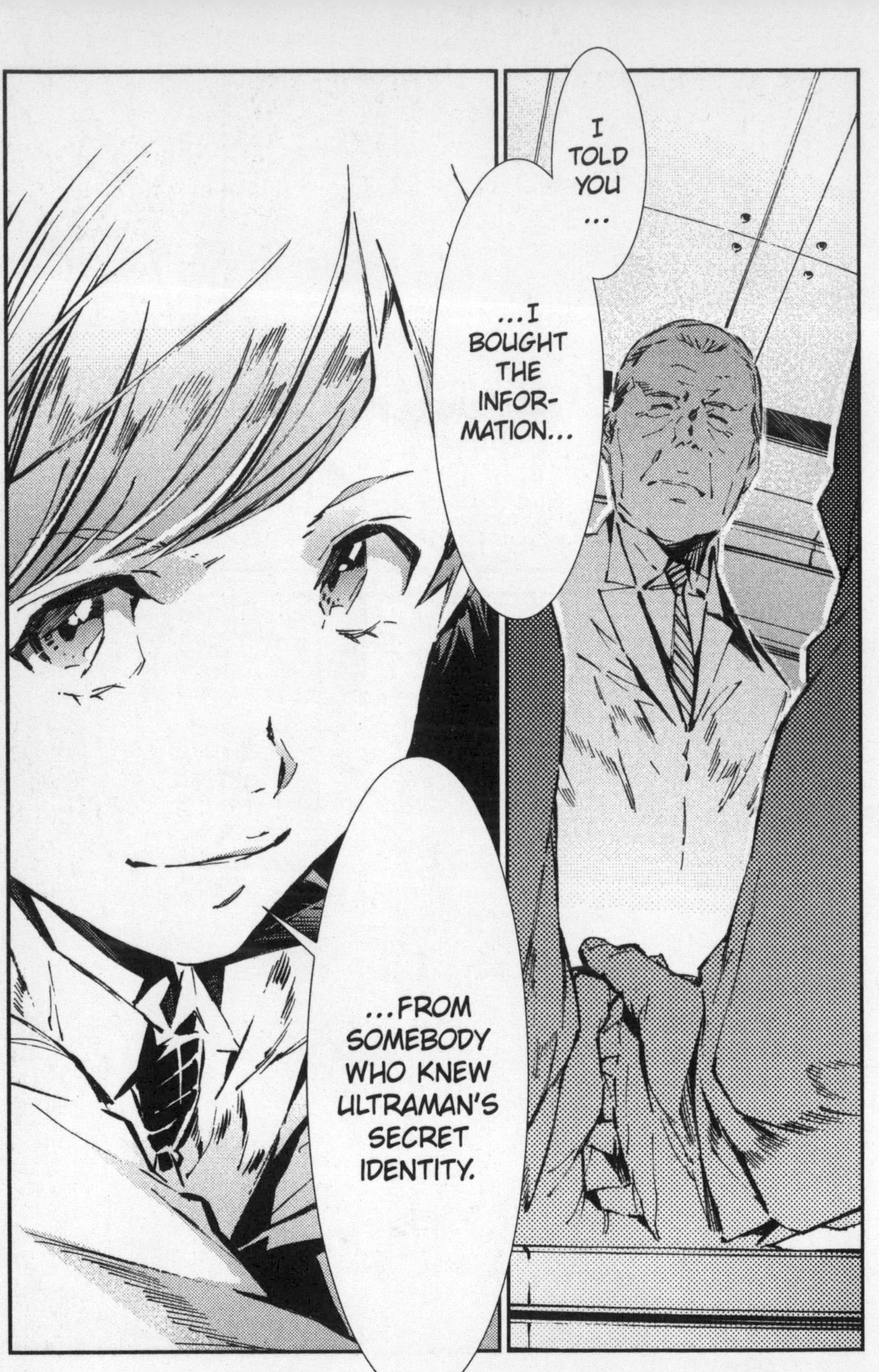
I TOLD YOU ...
...I BOUGHT THE INFORMATION...
...FROM SOMEBODY WHO KNEW ULTRAMAN'S SECRET IDENTITY.

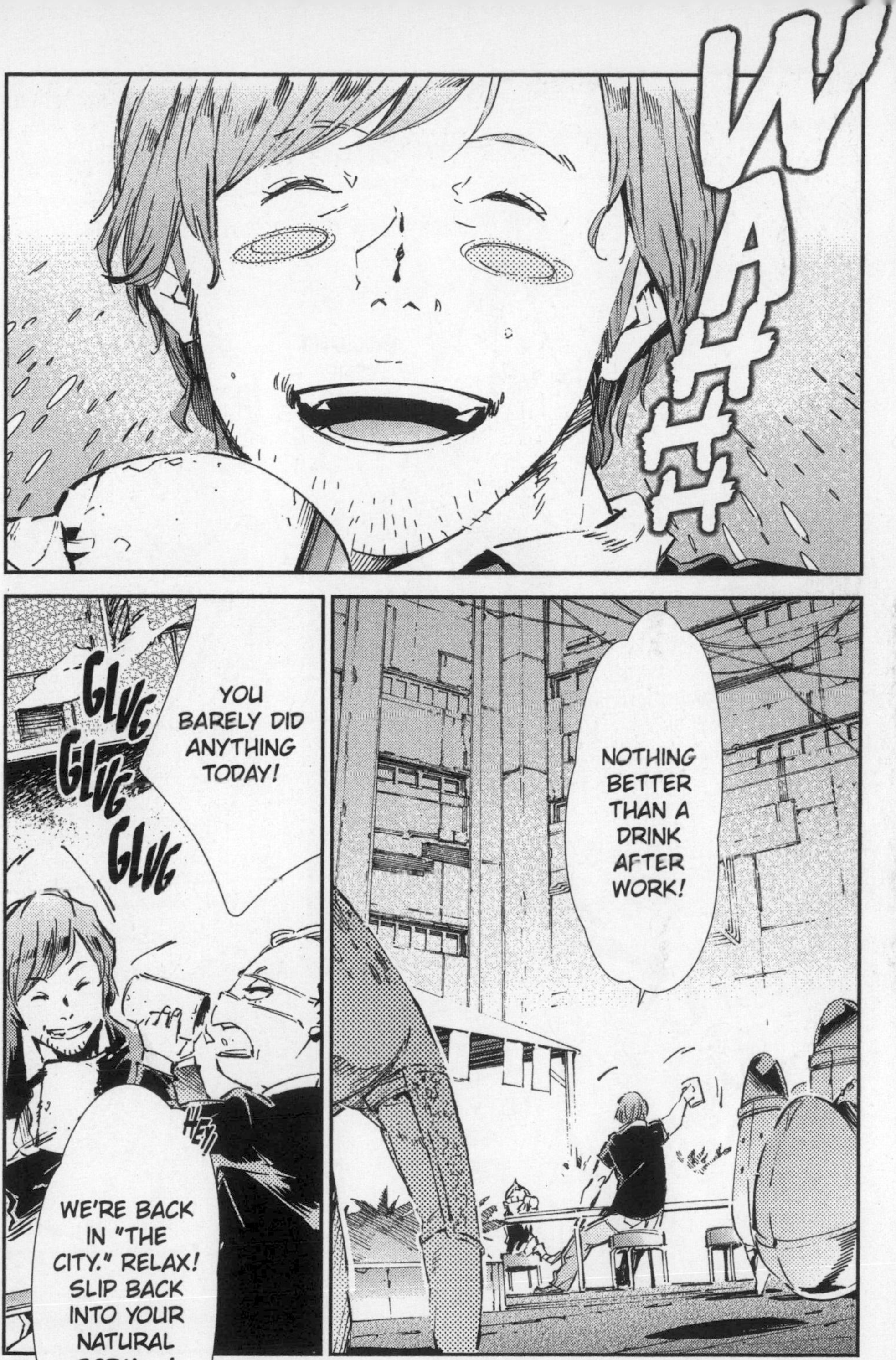
WAHHH
NOTHING BETTER THAN A DRINK AFTER WORK!
YOU BARELY DID ANYTHING TODAY!
GLUG GLUG GLUG
HEH
WE'RE BACK IN "THE CITY." RELAX! SLIP BACK INTO YOUR NATURAL FORM...!

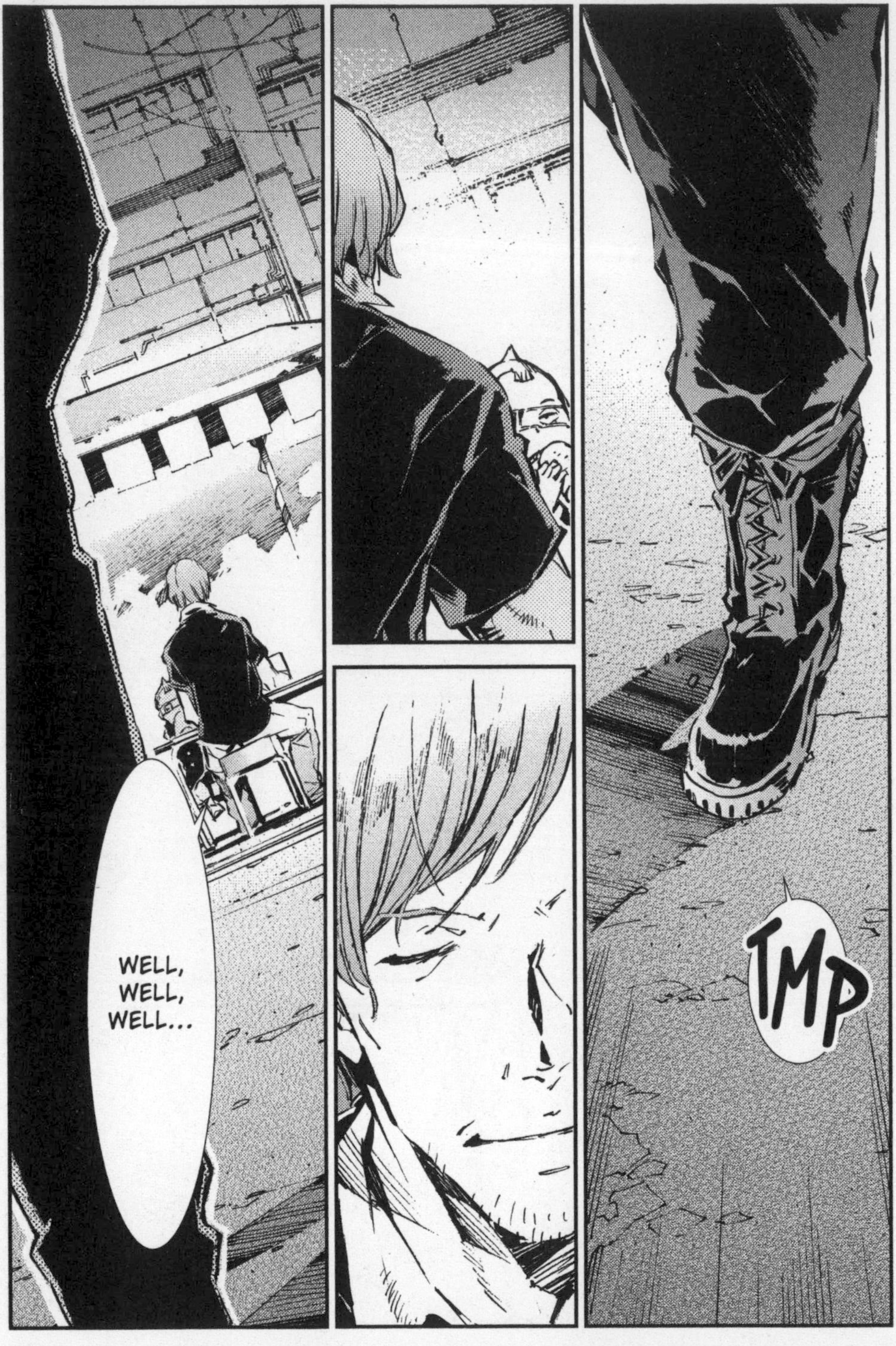
TMP
WELL, WELL, WELL...

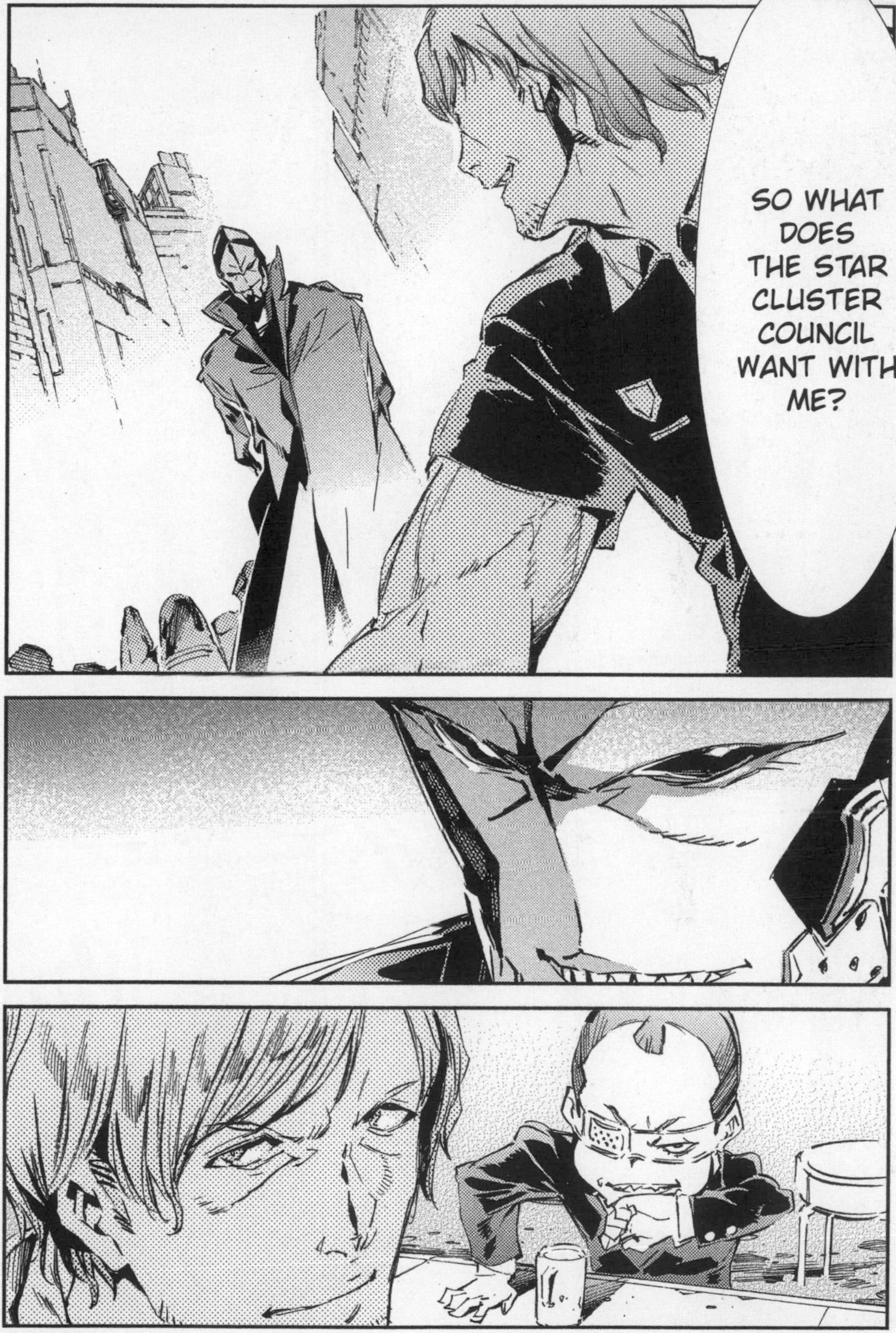
SO WHAT DOES THE STAR CLUSTER COUNCIL WANT WITH ME?

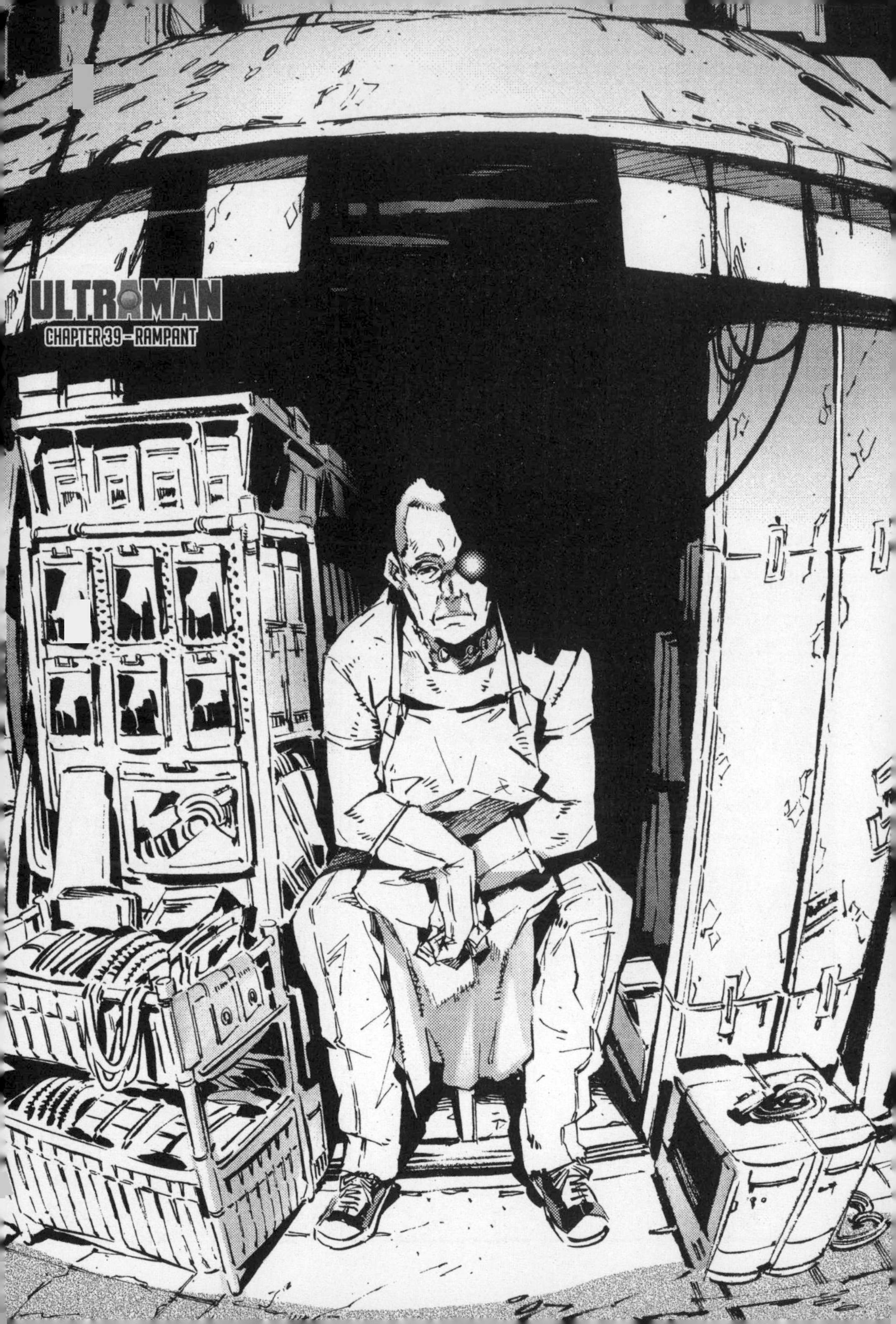
ULTRAMAN
CHAPTER 39 – RAMPANT

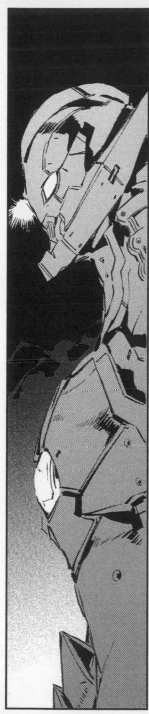
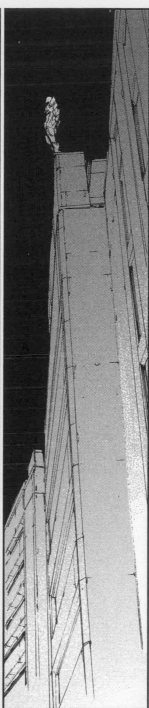
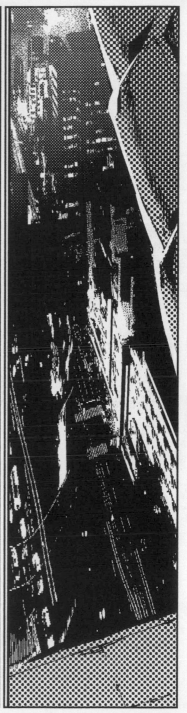

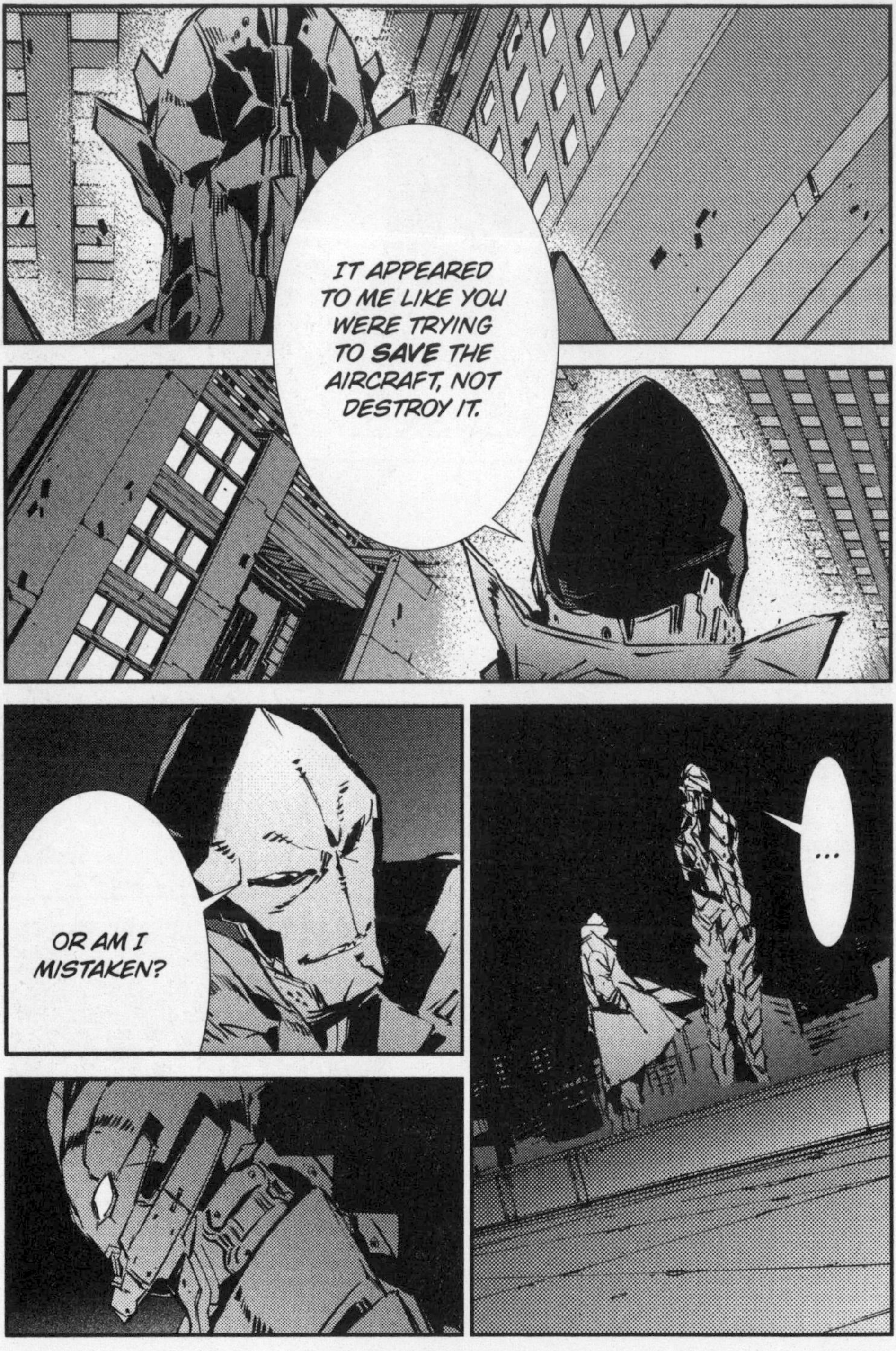
IT APPEARED TO ME LIKE YOU WERE TRYING TO **SAVE** THE AIRCRAFT, NOT DESTROY IT.
...
OR AM I MISTAKEN?

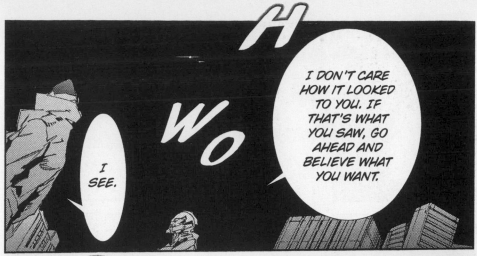

I DON'T CARE HOW IT LOOKED TO YOU. IF THAT'S WHAT YOU SAW, GO AHEAD AND BELIEVE WHAT YOU WANT.

I SEE.

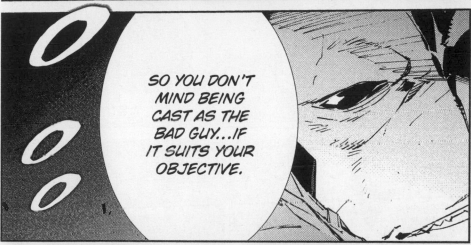

SO YOU DON'T MIND BEING CAST AS THE BAD GUY...IF IT SUITS YOUR OBJECTIVE.

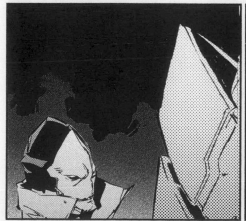

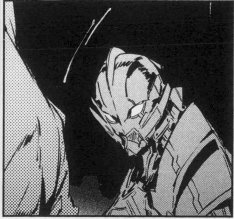

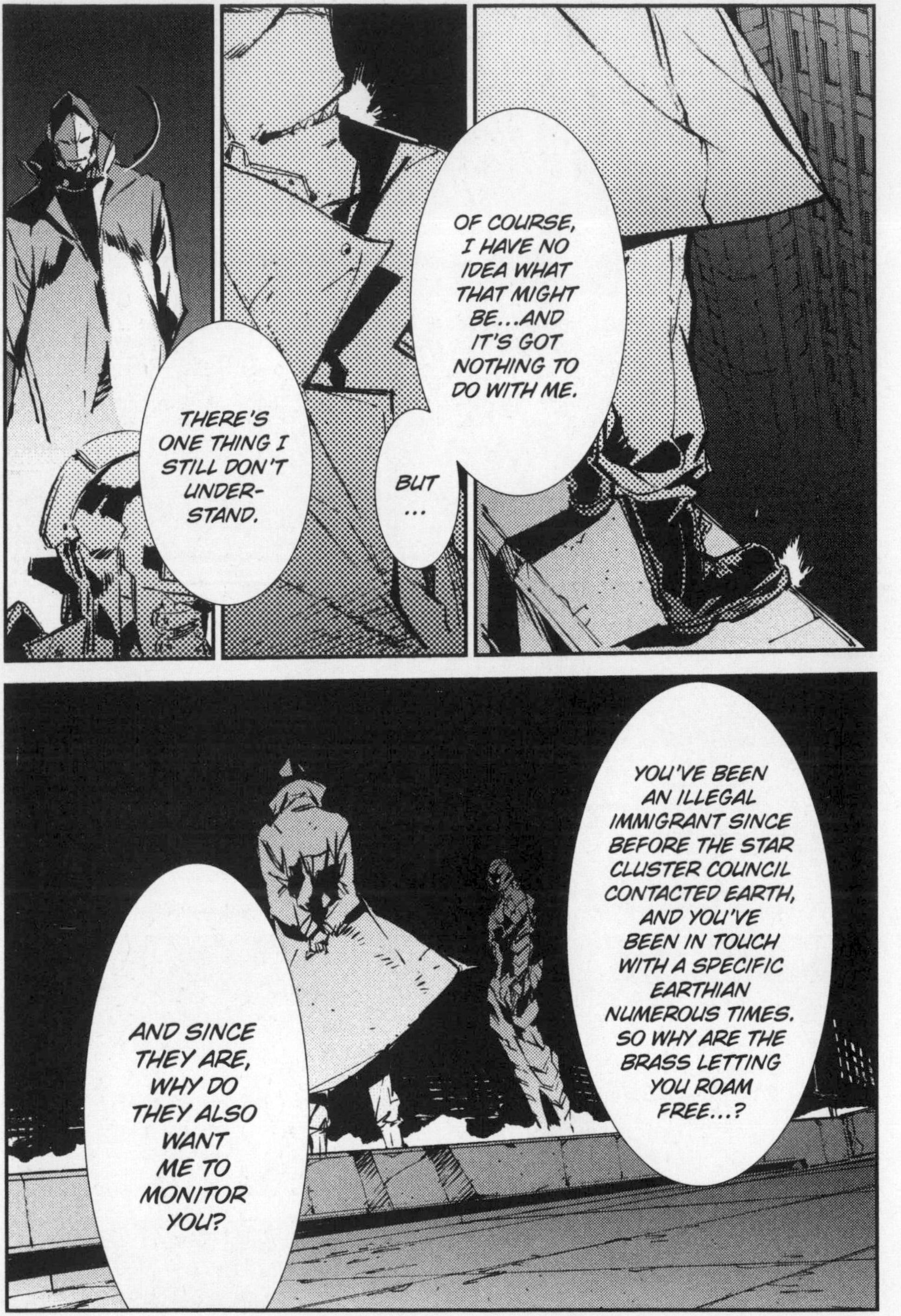
OF COURSE, I HAVE NO IDEA WHAT THAT MIGHT BE...AND IT'S GOT NOTHING TO DO WITH ME.
BUT ...
THERE'S ONE THING I STILL DON'T UNDER-STAND.
YOU'VE BEEN AN ILLEGAL IMMIGRANT SINCE BEFORE THE STAR CLUSTER COUNCIL CONTACTED EARTH, AND YOU'VE BEEN IN TOUCH WITH A SPECIFIC EARTHIAN NUMEROUS TIMES. SO WHY ARE THE BRASS LETTING YOU ROAM FREE...?
AND SINCE THEY ARE, WHY DO THEY ALSO WANT ME TO MONITOR YOU?

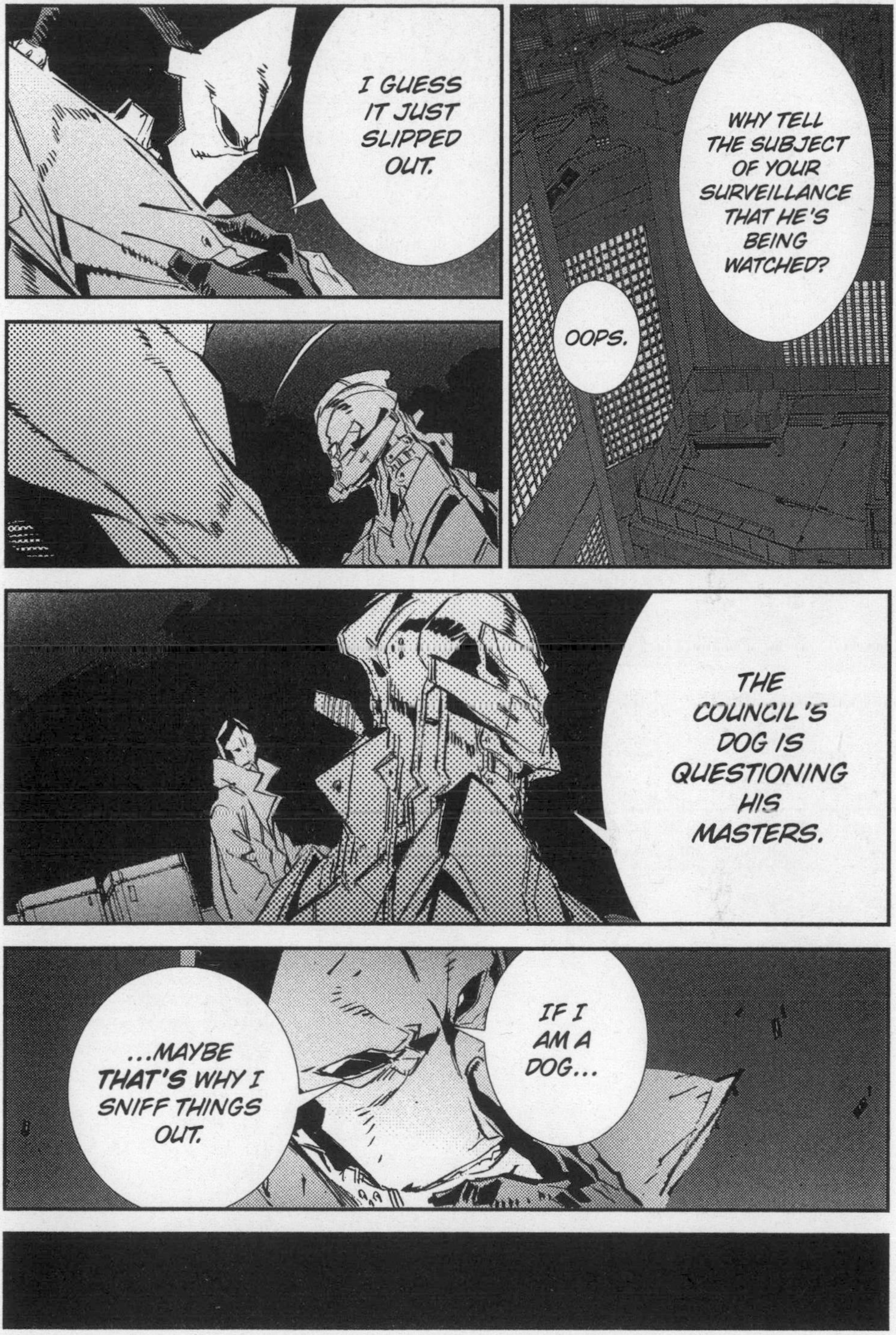
WHY TELL THE SUBJECT OF YOUR SURVEILLANCE THAT HE'S BEING WATCHED?
OOPS.
I GUESS IT JUST SLIPPED OUT.
THE COUNCIL'S DOG IS QUESTIONING HIS MASTERS.
IF I AM A DOG...
...MAYBE THAT'S WHY I SNIFF THINGS OUT.

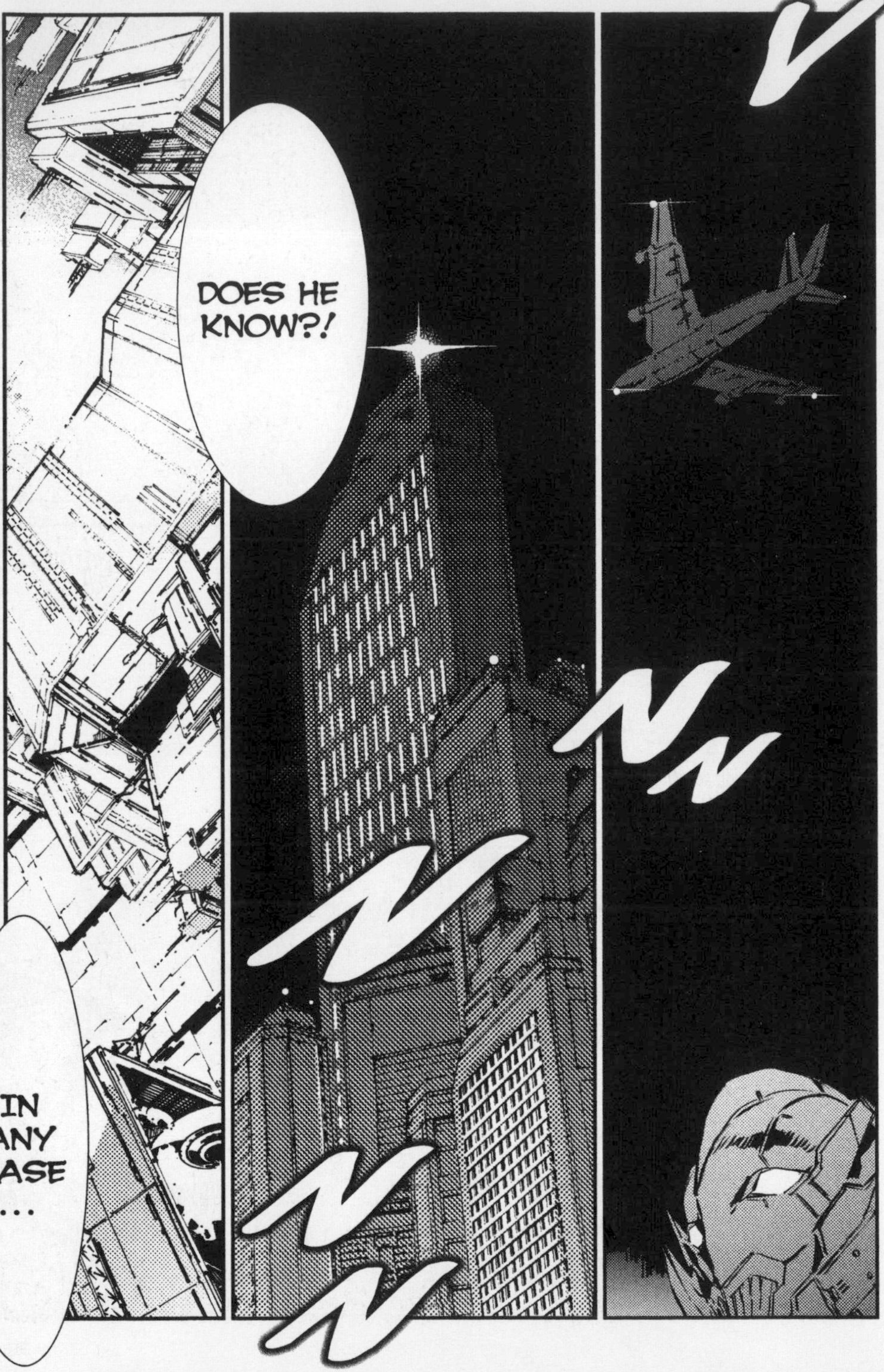
DOES HE KNOW?!
IN ANY CASE ...

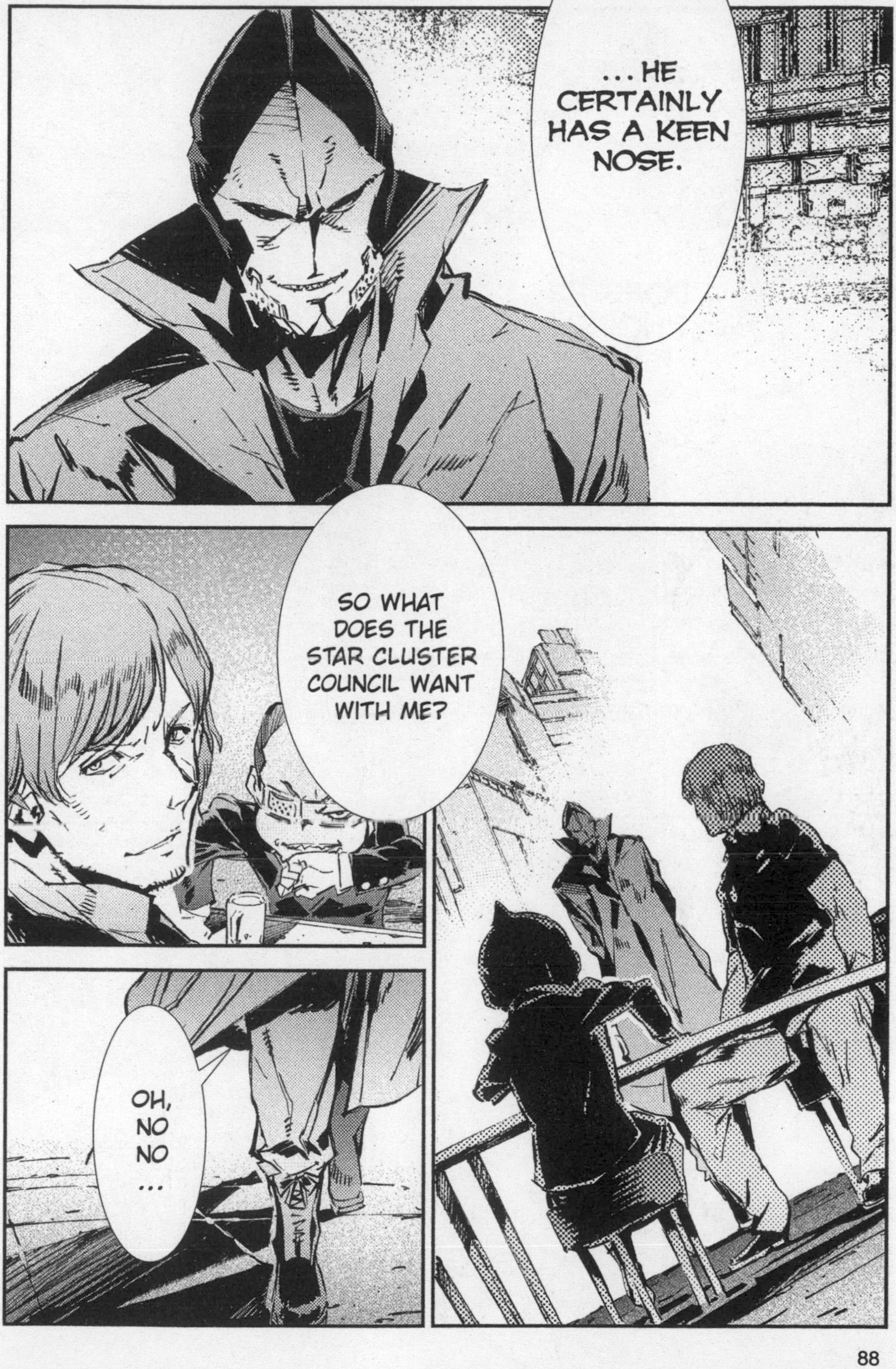
...HE CERTAINLY HAS A KEEN NOSE.
SO WHAT DOES THE STAR CLUSTER COUNCIL WANT WITH ME?
OH, NO NO ...

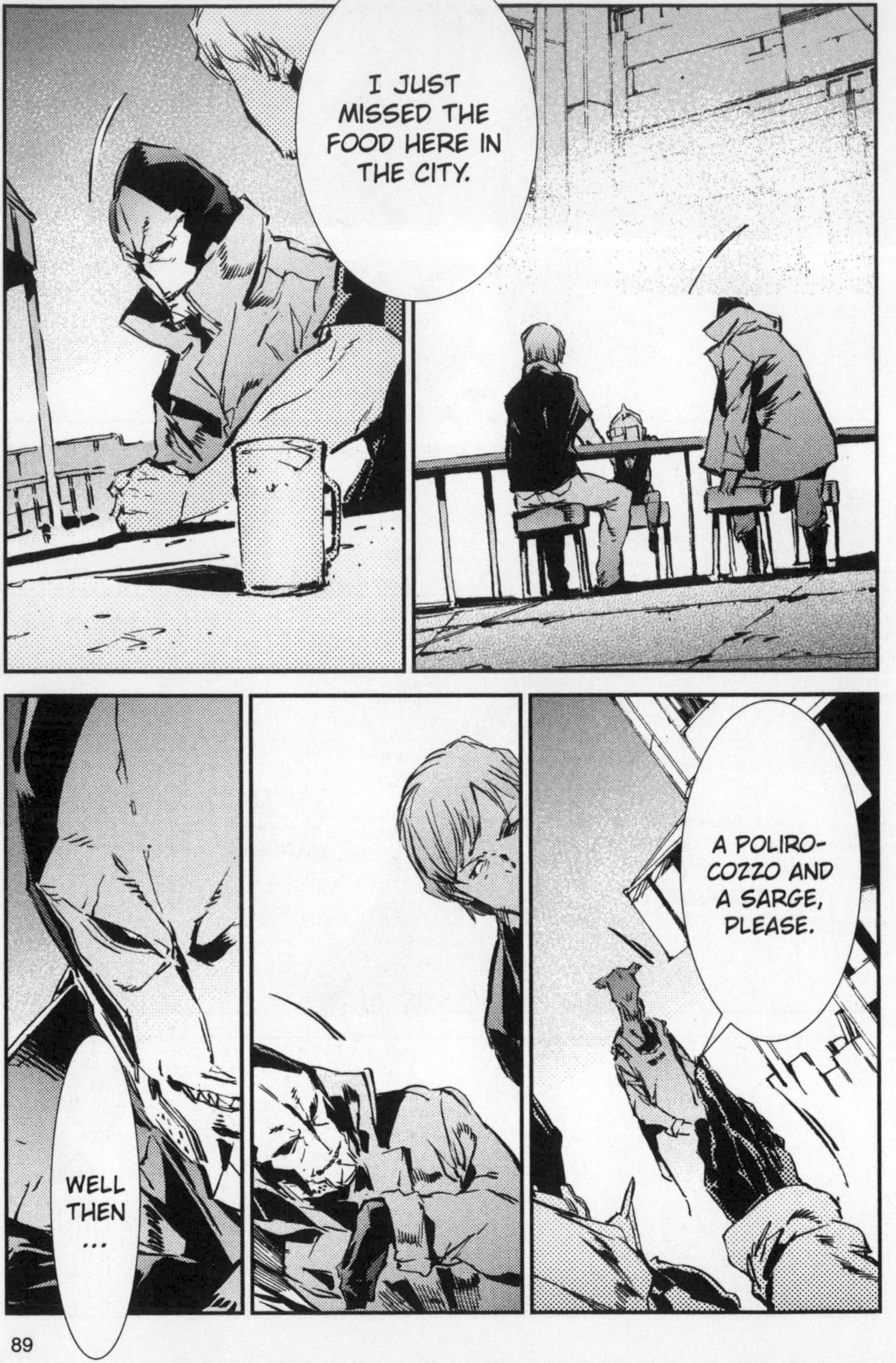
I JUST MISSED THE FOOD HERE IN THE CITY.
A POLIRO-COZZO AND A SARGE, PLEASE.
WELL THEN ...

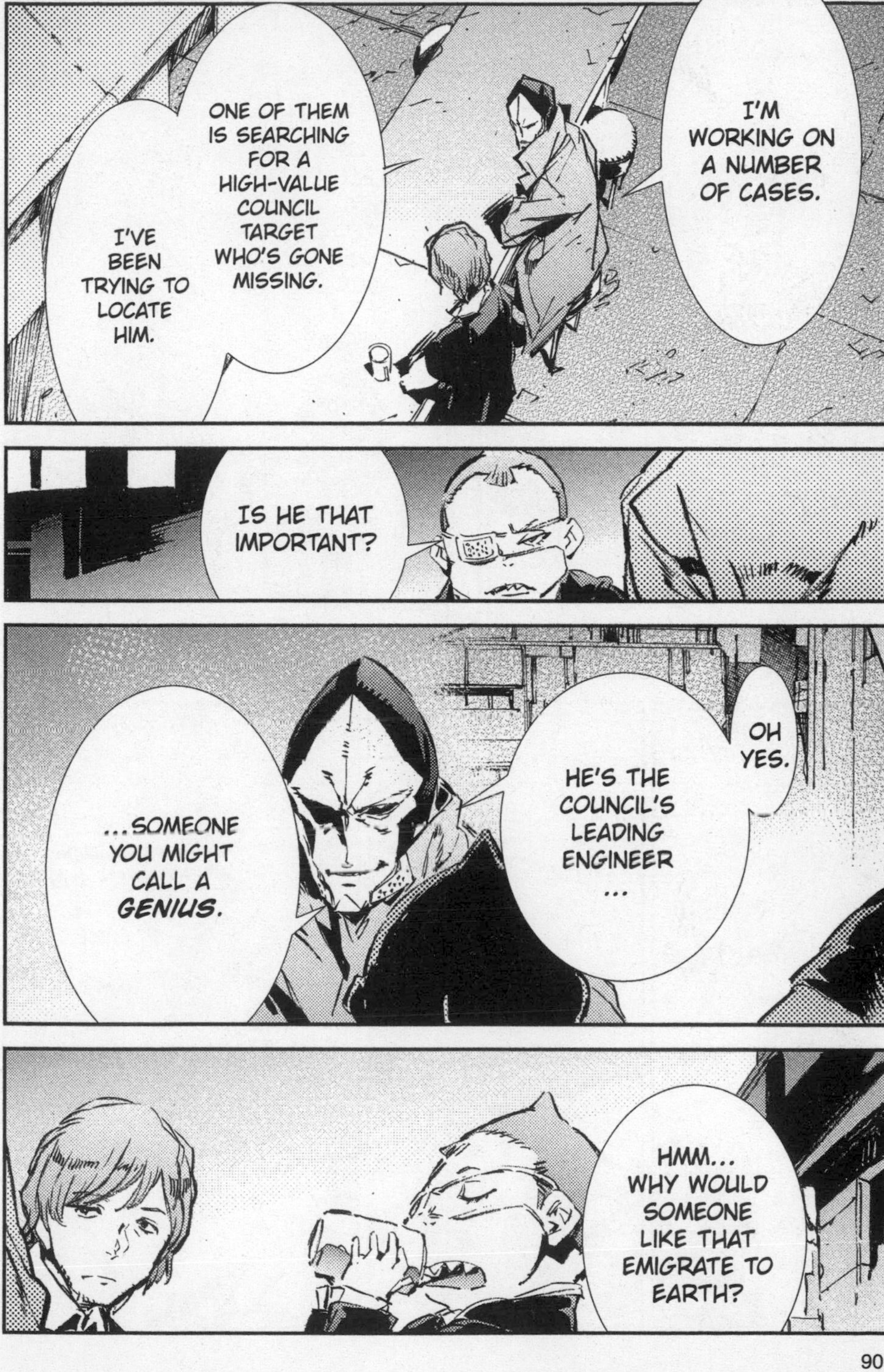
I'M WORKING ON A NUMBER OF CASES.
ONE OF THEM IS SEARCHING FOR A HIGH-VALUE COUNCIL TARGET WHO'S GONE MISSING.
I'VE BEEN TRYING TO LOCATE HIM.
IS HE THAT IMPORTANT?
OH YES.
HE'S THE COUNCIL'S LEADING ENGINEER ...
...SOMEONE YOU MIGHT CALL A *GENIUS*.
HMM... WHY WOULD SOMEONE LIKE THAT EMIGRATE TO EARTH?

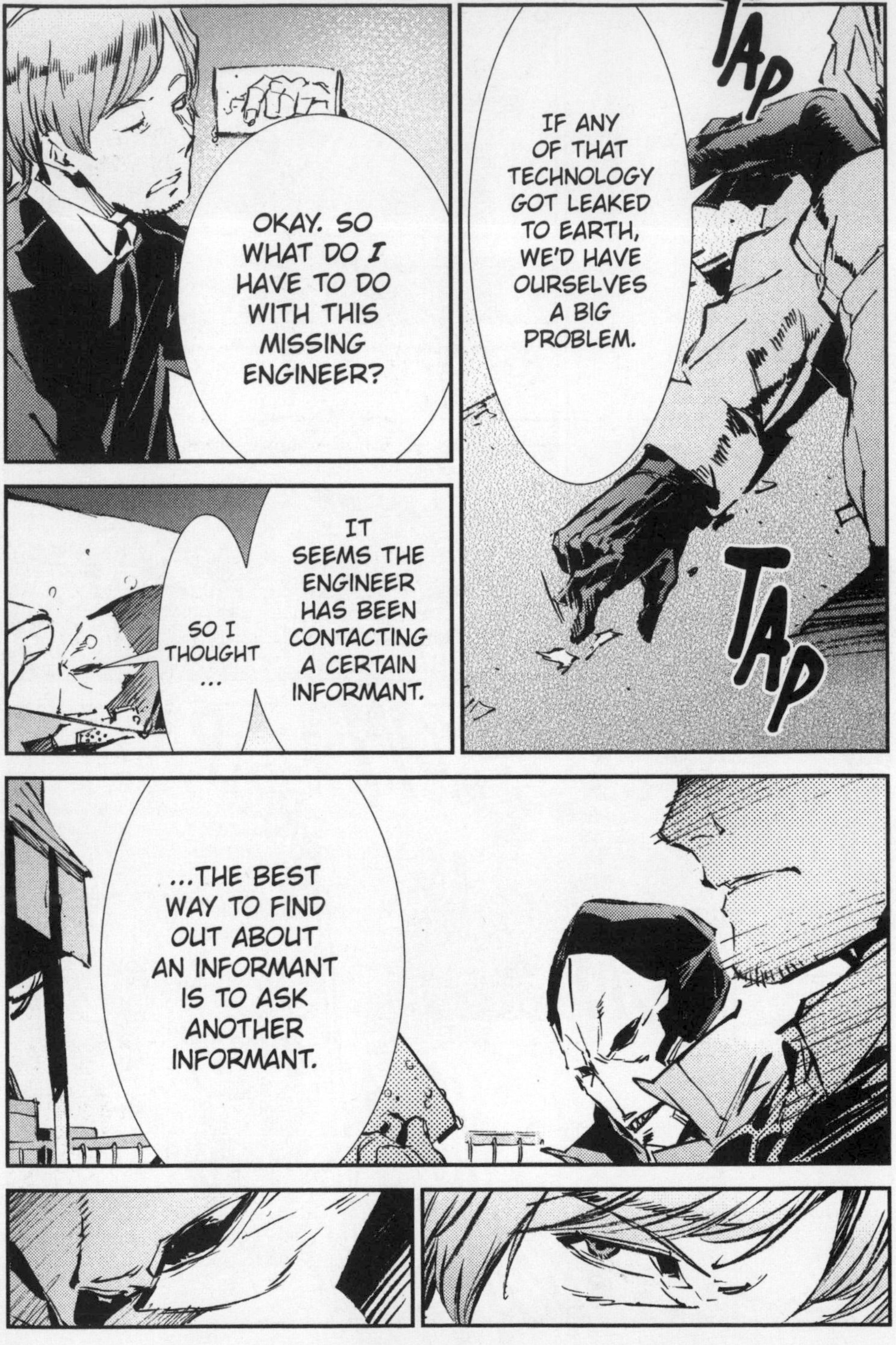
TAP
IF ANY OF THAT TECHNOLOGY GOT LEAKED TO EARTH, WE'D HAVE OURSELVES A BIG PROBLEM.
TAP
OKAY. SO WHAT DO *I* HAVE TO DO WITH THIS MISSING ENGINEER?
IT SEEMS THE ENGINEER HAS BEEN CONTACTING A CERTAIN INFORMANT.
SO I THOUGHT ...
...THE BEST WAY TO FIND OUT ABOUT AN INFORMANT IS TO ASK ANOTHER INFORMANT.

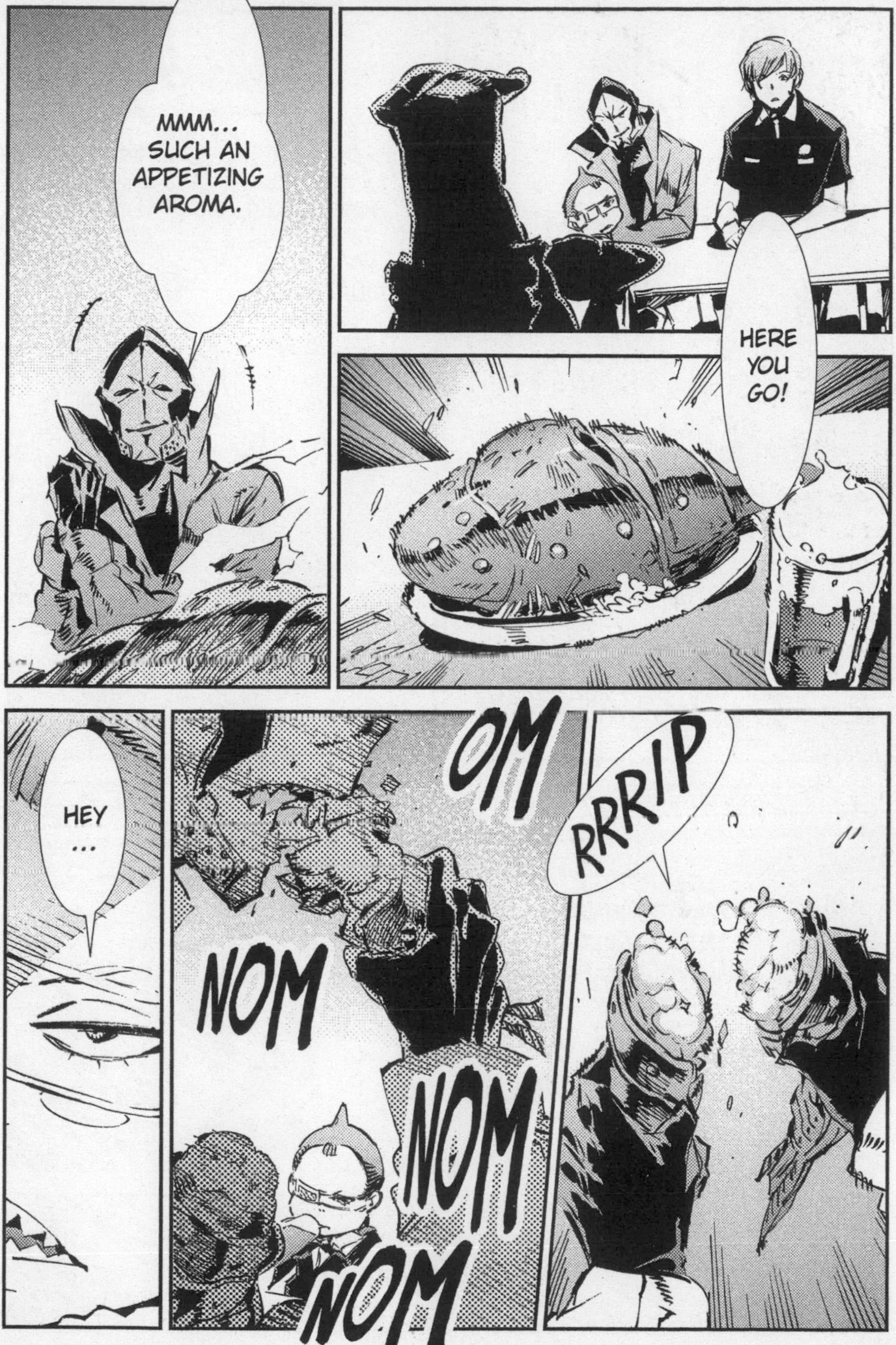
HERE YOU GO!
MMM... SUCH AN APPETIZING AROMA.
RRRIP
OM
NOM
NOM
NOM
HEY ...

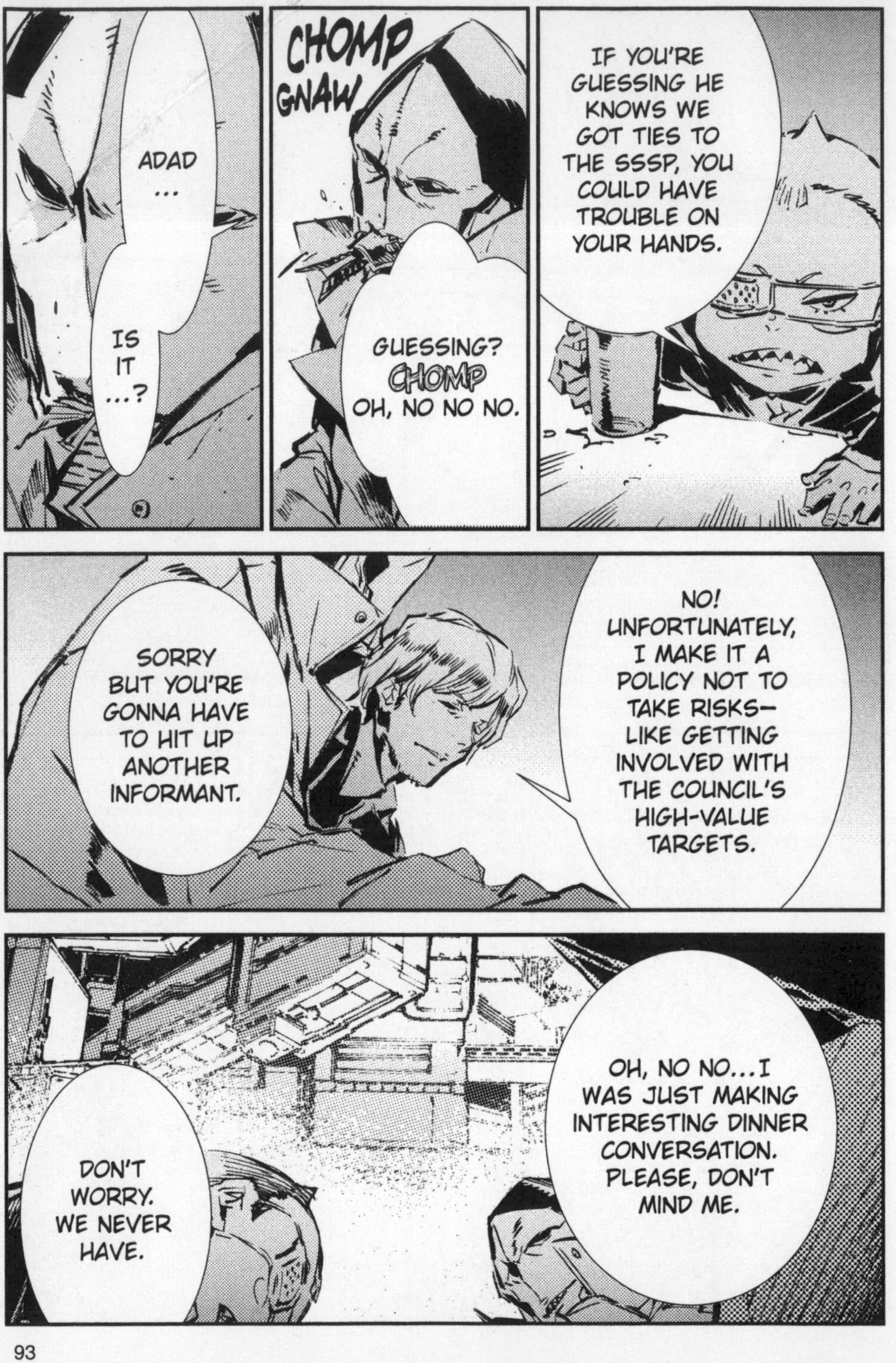
IF YOU'RE GUESSING HE KNOWS WE GOT TIES TO THE SSSP, YOU COULD HAVE TROUBLE ON YOUR HANDS.
CHOMP
GNAW
GUESSING? CHOMP OH, NO NO NO.
ADAD ...
IS IT ...?
NO! UNFORTUNATELY, I MAKE IT A POLICY NOT TO TAKE RISKS— LIKE GETTING INVOLVED WITH THE COUNCIL'S HIGH-VALUE TARGETS.
SORRY BUT YOU'RE GONNA HAVE TO HIT UP ANOTHER INFORMANT.
OH, NO NO...I WAS JUST MAKING INTERESTING DINNER CONVERSATION. PLEASE, DON'T MIND ME.
DON'T WORRY. WE NEVER HAVE.

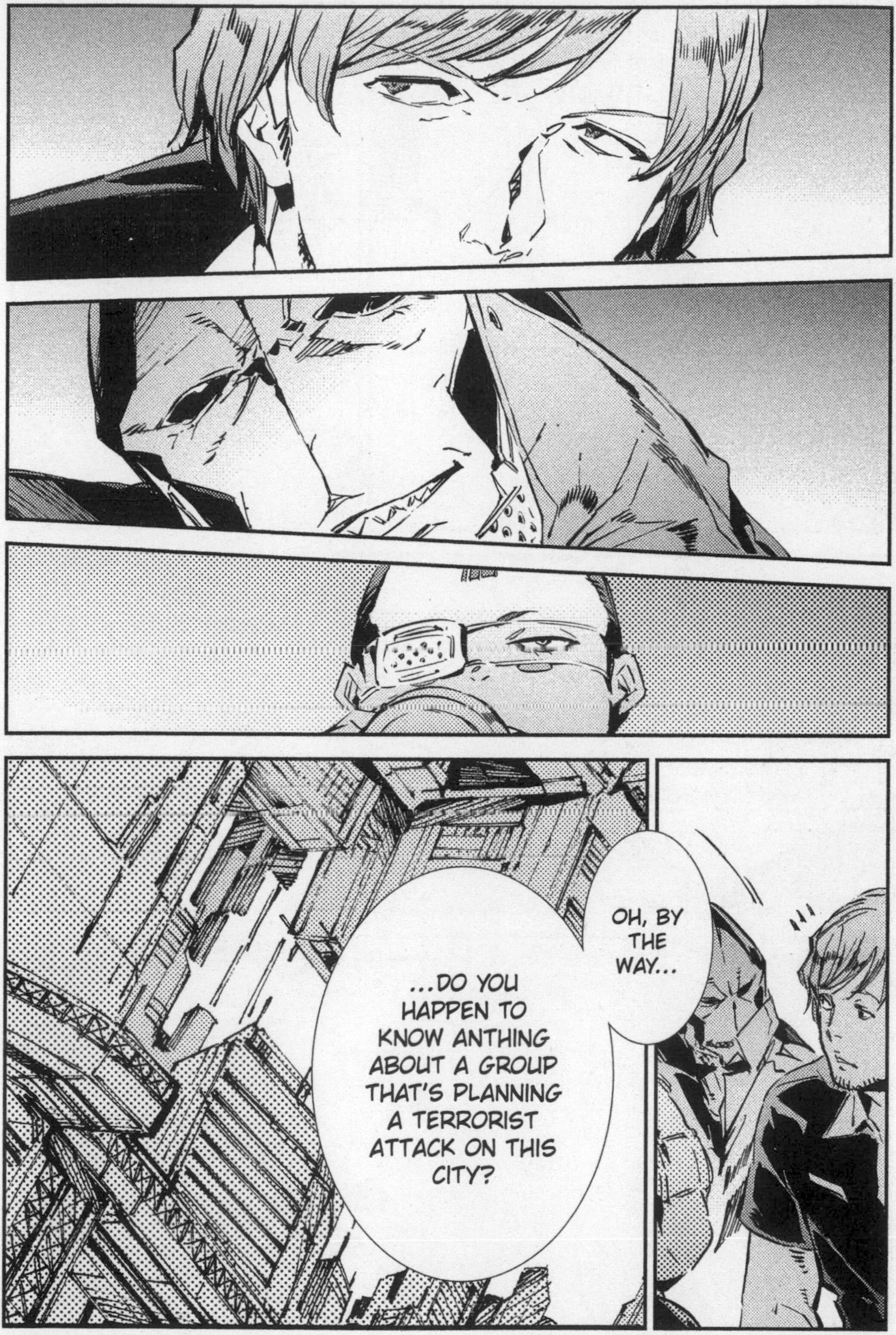
OH, BY THE WAY...
...DO YOU HAPPEN TO KNOW ANTHING ABOUT A GROUP THAT'S PLANNING A TERRORIST ATTACK ON THIS CITY?

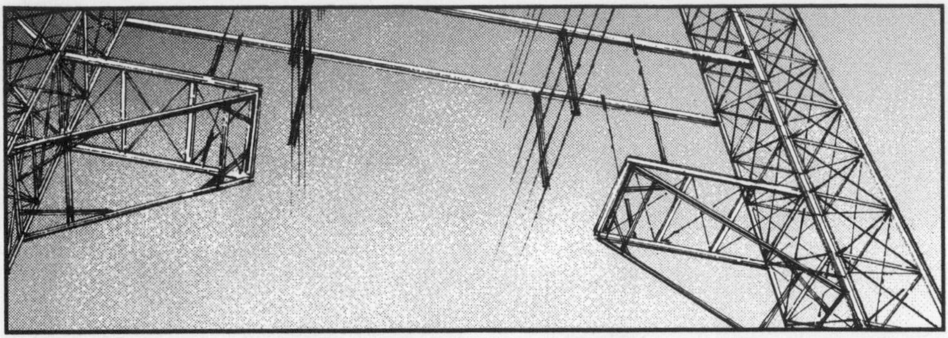
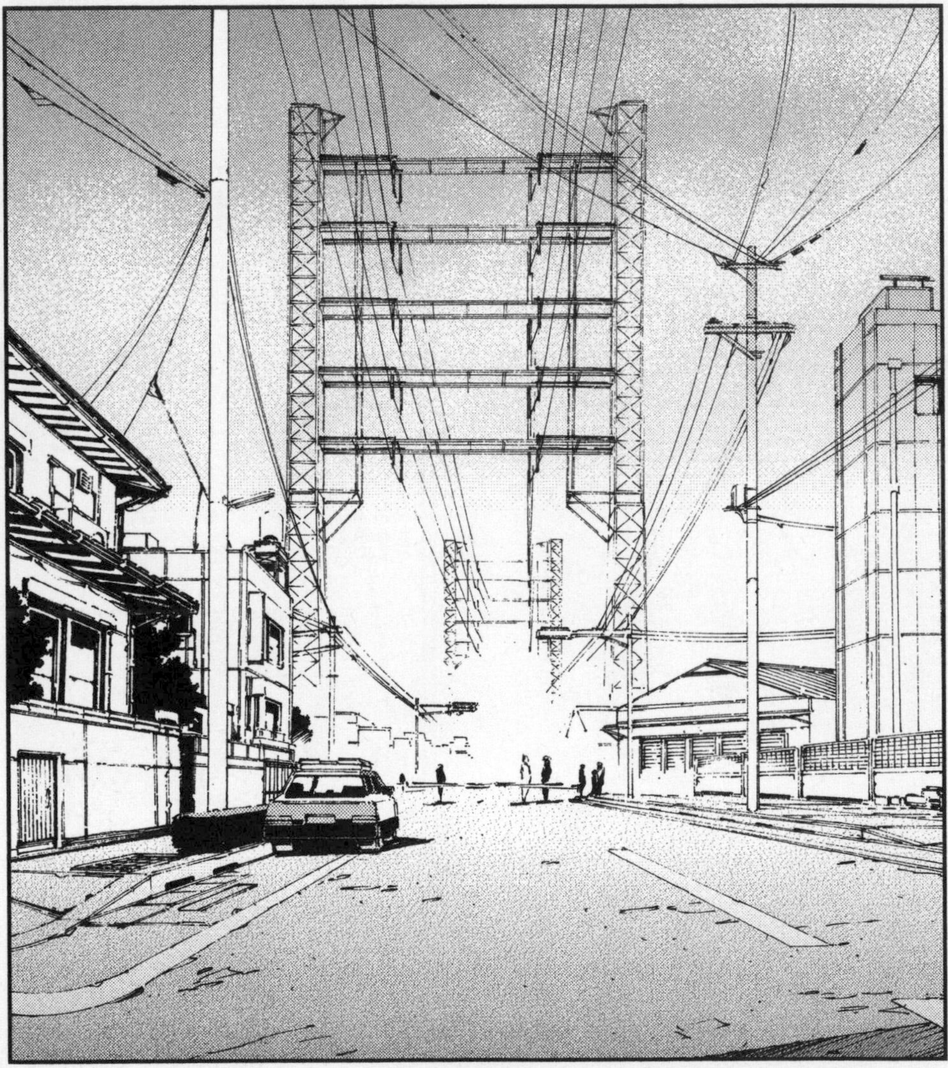

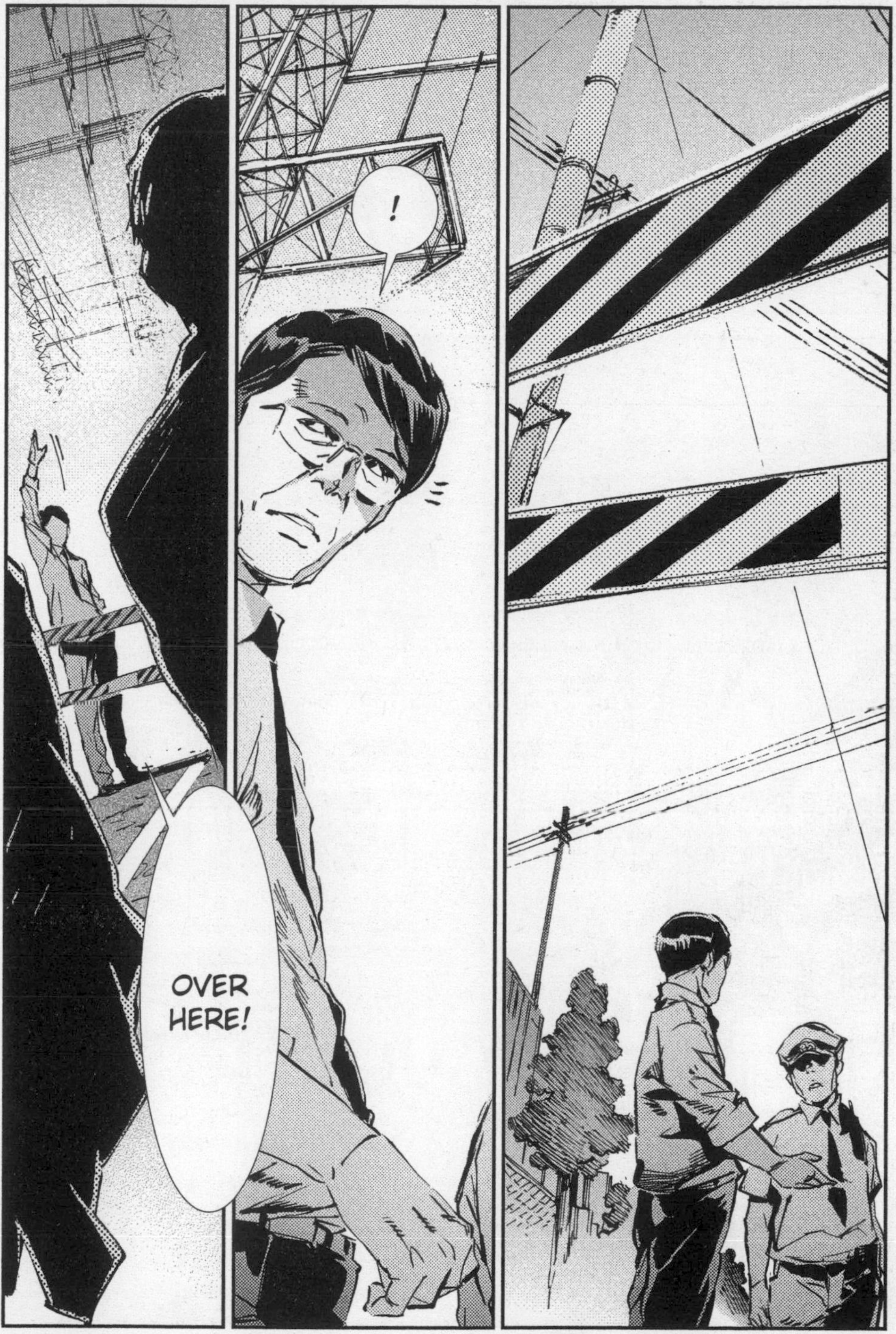
!
OVER HERE!

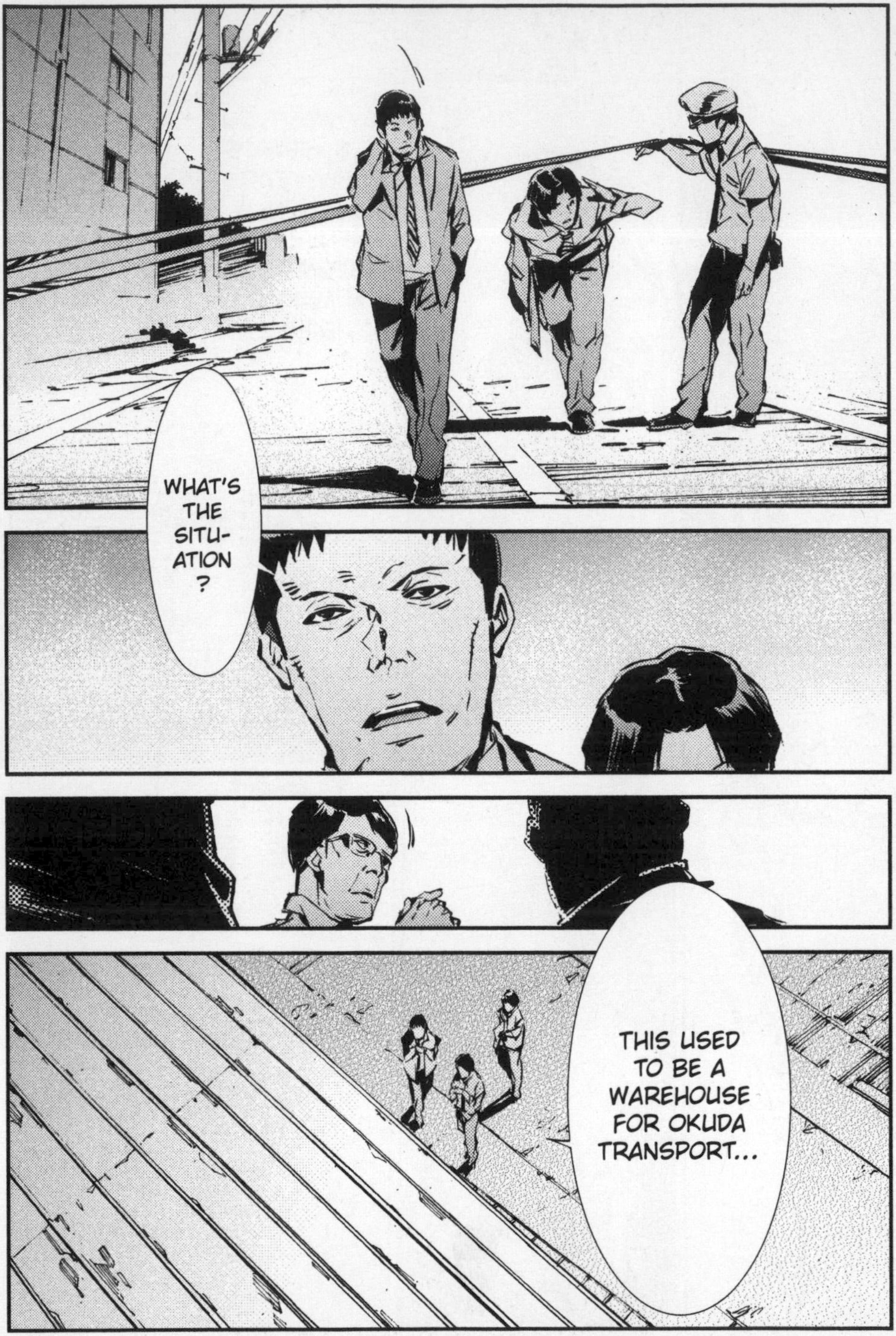
WHAT'S THE SITU-ATION?
THIS USED TO BE A WAREHOUSE FOR OKUDA TRANSPORT...

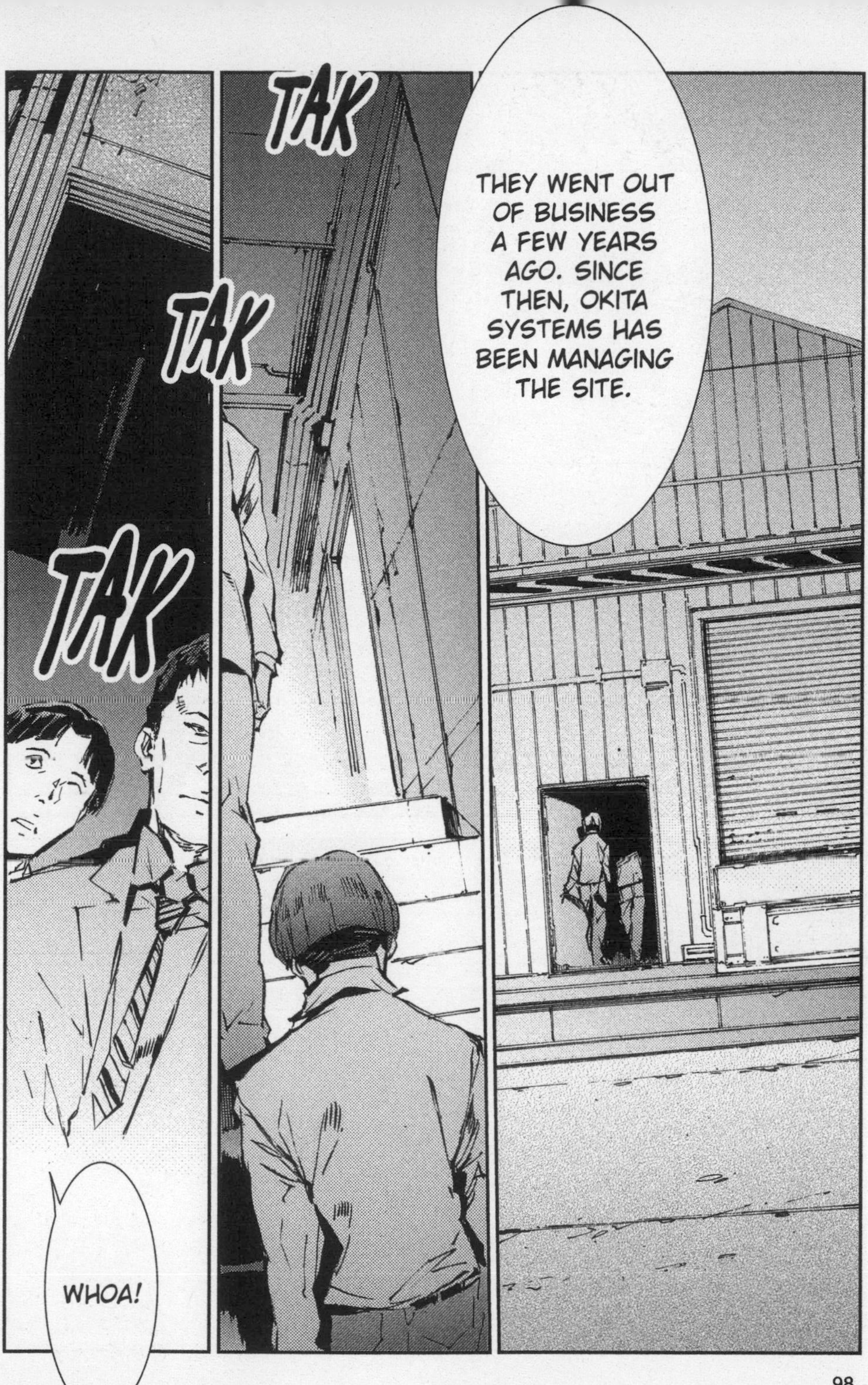
THEY WENT OUT OF BUSINESS A FEW YEARS AGO. SINCE THEN, OKITA SYSTEMS HAS BEEN MANAGING THE SITE.
TAK
TAK
TAK
WHOA!

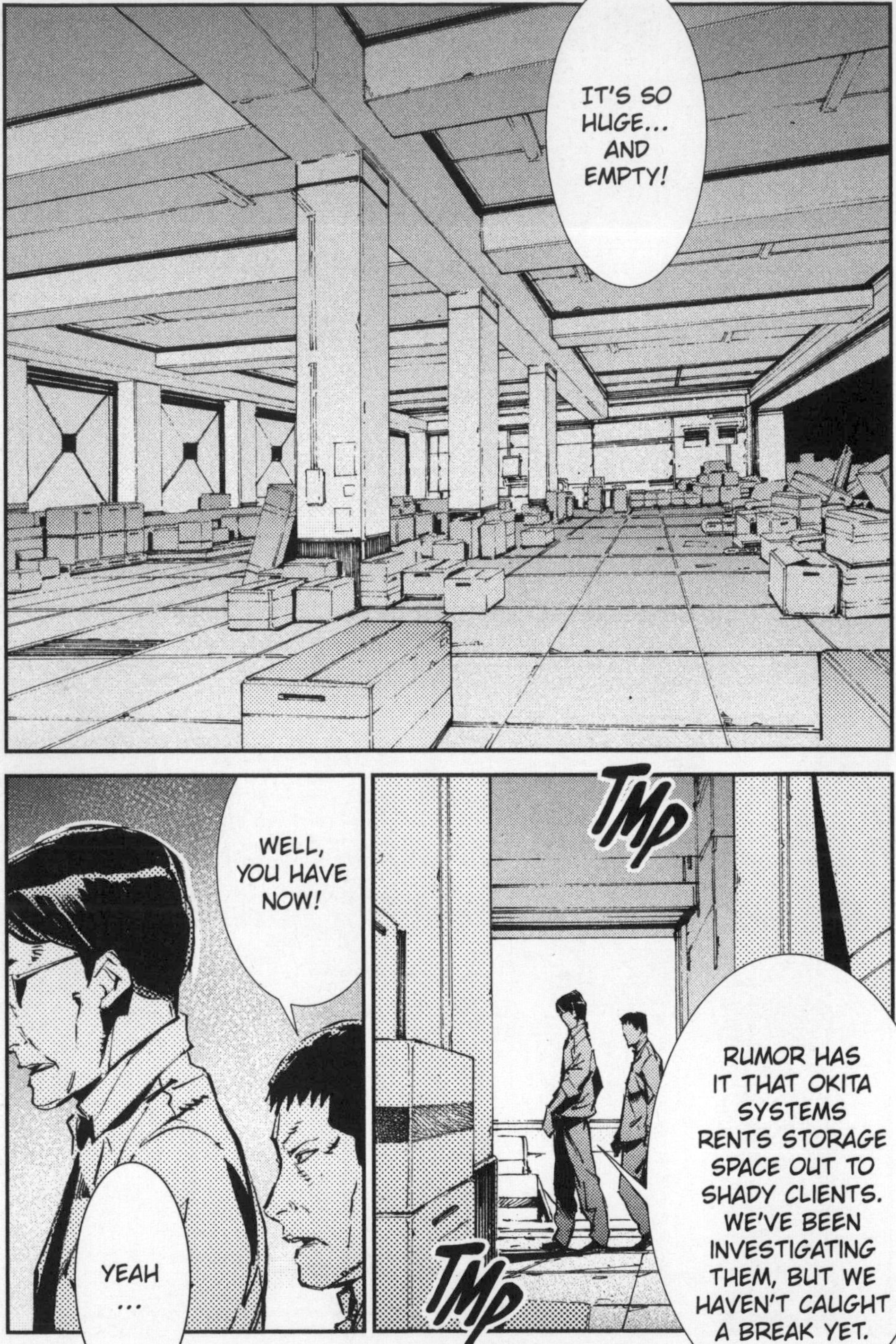
IT'S SO HUGE... AND EMPTY!
TMP
TMP
RUMOR HAS IT THAT OKITA SYSTEMS RENTS STORAGE SPACE OUT TO SHADY CLIENTS. WE'VE BEEN INVESTIGATING THEM, BUT WE HAVEN'T CAUGHT A BREAK YET.
WELL, YOU HAVE NOW!
YEAH ...

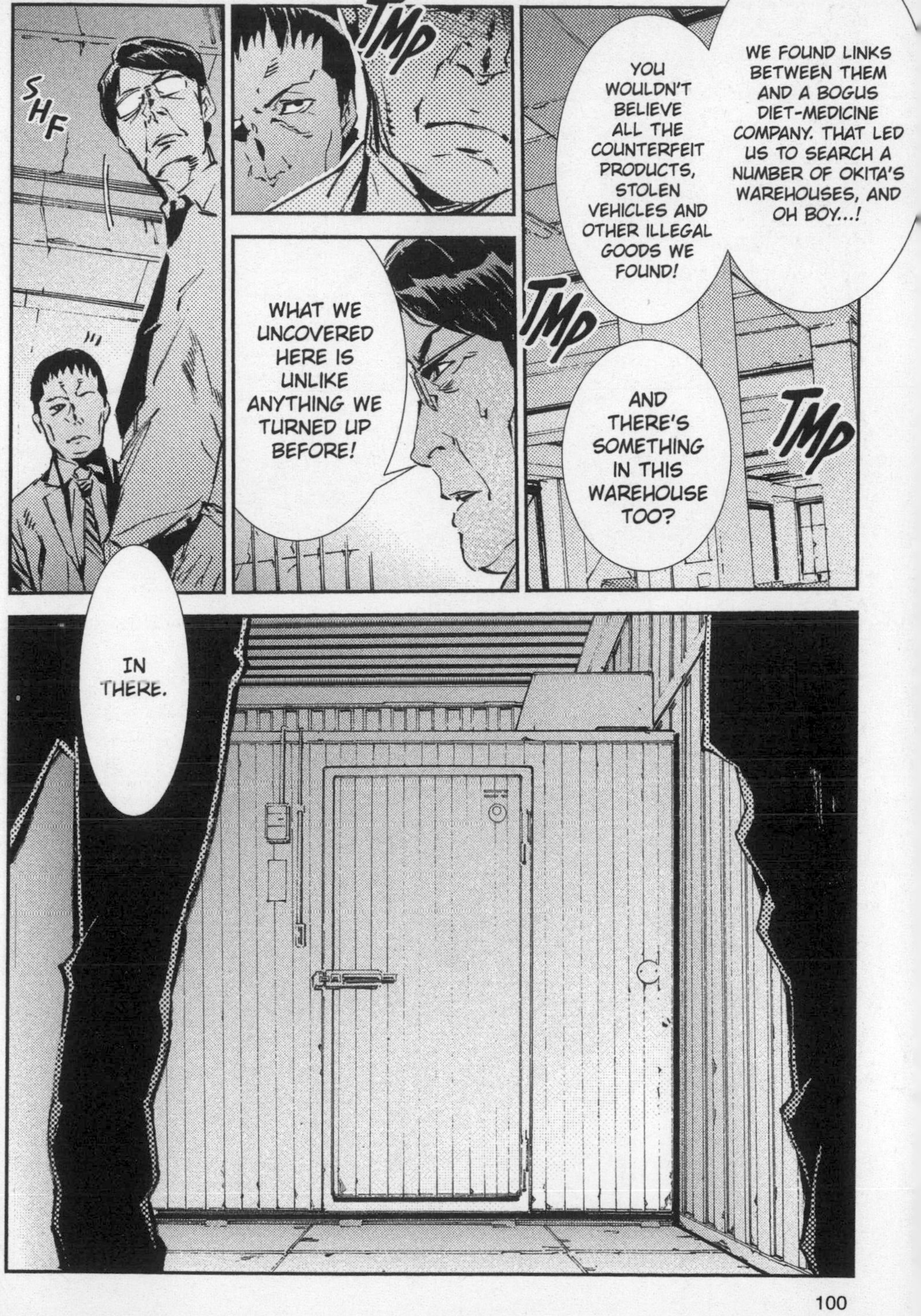
WE FOUND LINKS BETWEEN THEM AND A BOGUS DIET-MEDICINE COMPANY. THAT LED US TO SEARCH A NUMBER OF OKITA'S WAREHOUSES, AND OH BOY...!
YOU WOULDN'T BELIEVE ALL THE COUNTERFEIT PRODUCTS, STOLEN VEHICLES AND OTHER ILLEGAL GOODS WE FOUND!
TMP
AND THERE'S SOMETHING IN THIS WAREHOUSE TOO?
TMP
TMP
WHAT WE UNCOVERED HERE IS UNLIKE ANYTHING WE TURNED UP BEFORE!
SHF
IN THERE.

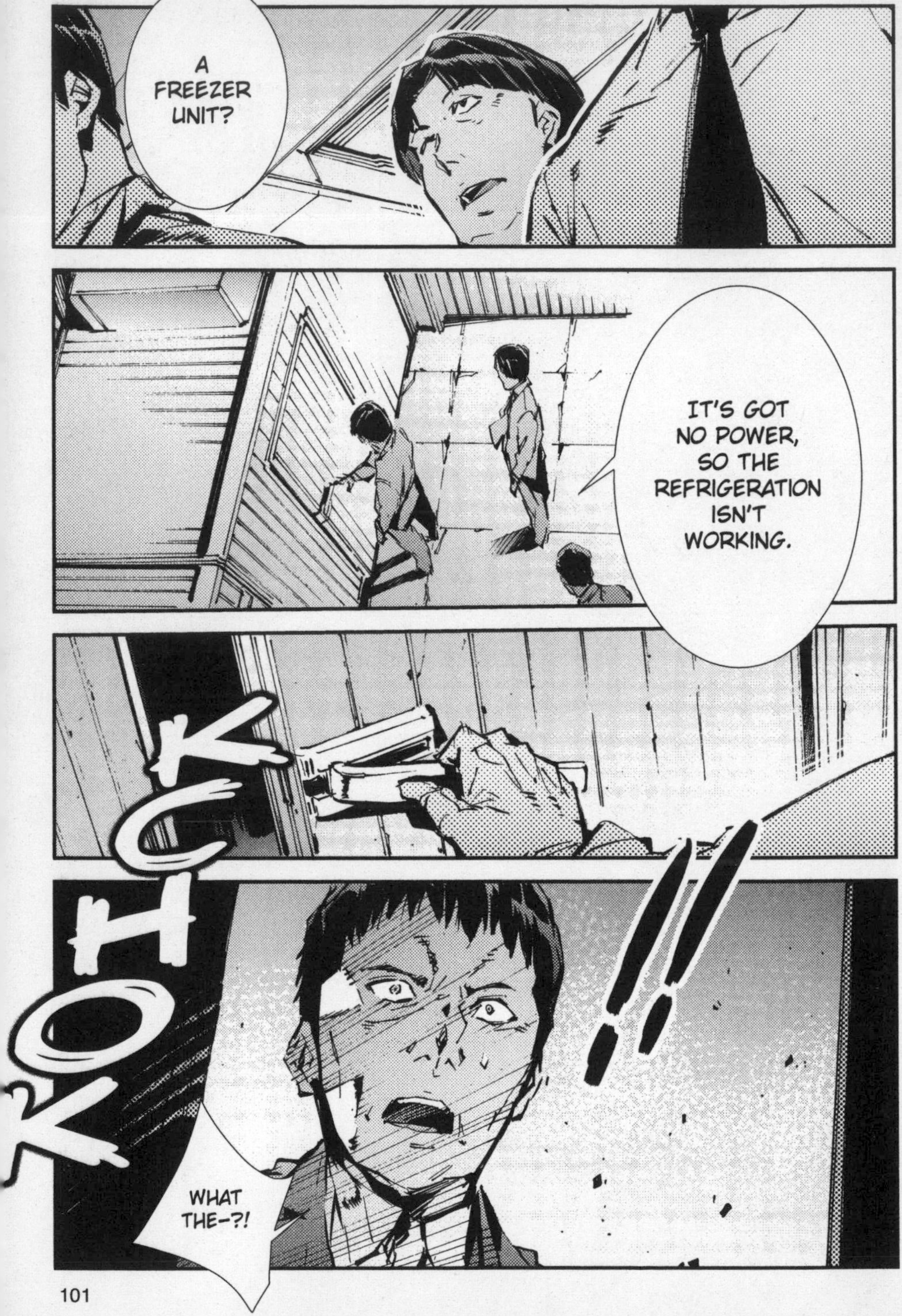
A FREEZER UNIT?
IT'S GOT NO POWER, SO THE REFRIGERATION ISN'T WORKING.
KCHOK
!!
WHAT THE-?!

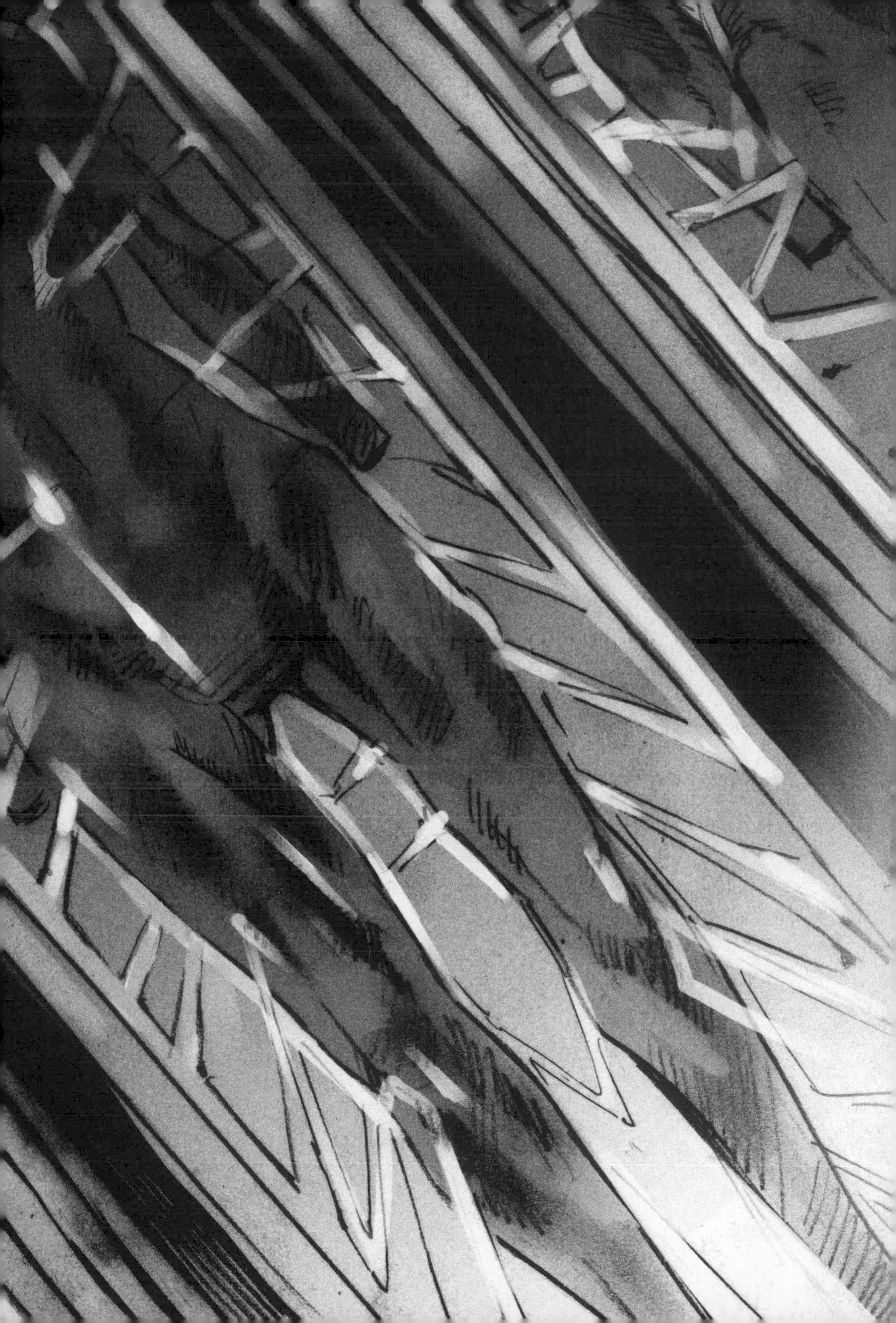

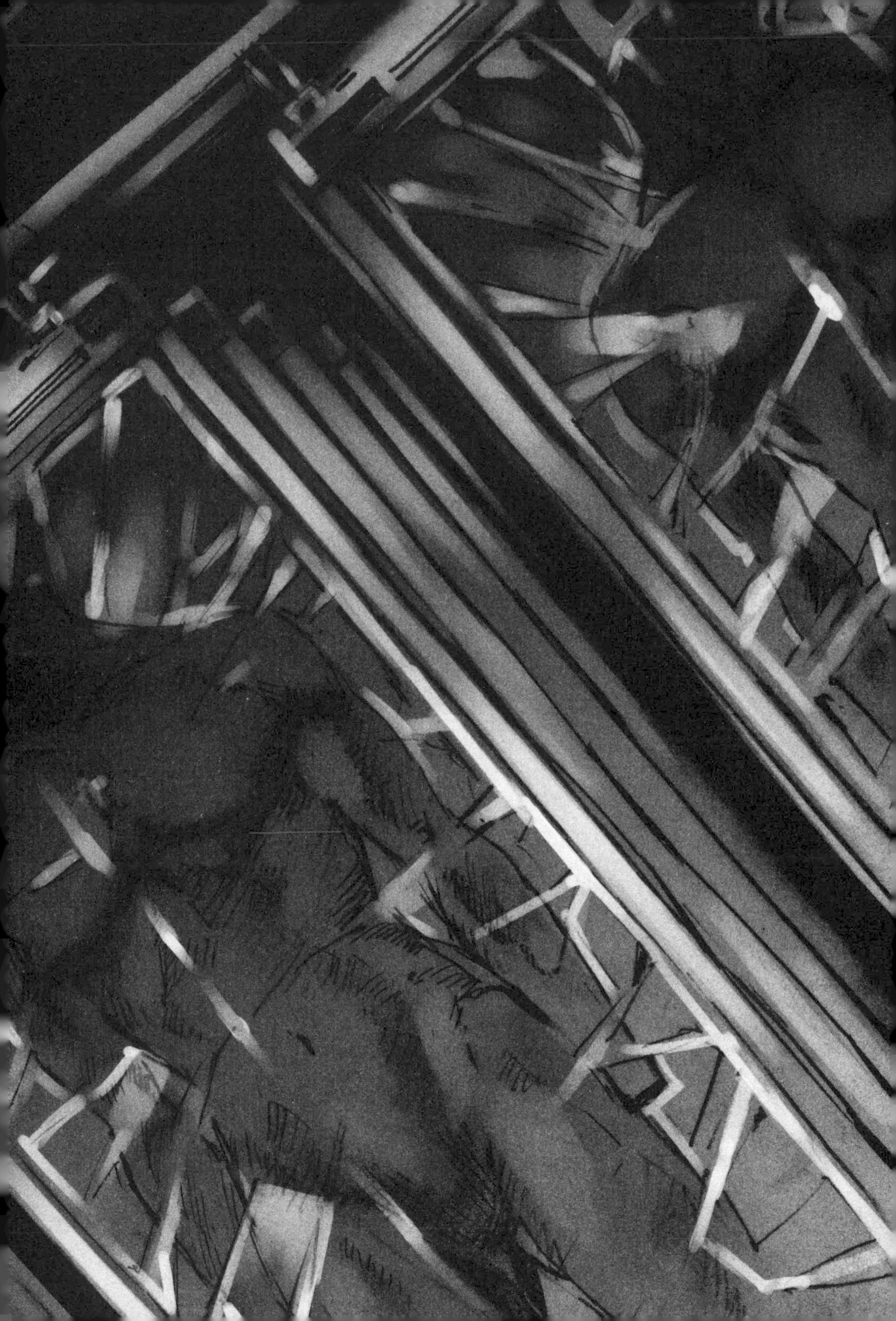

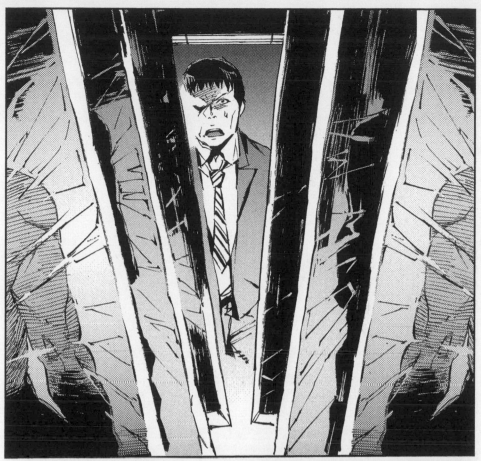

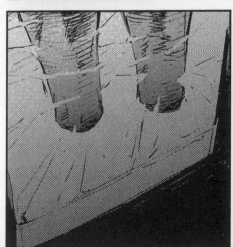

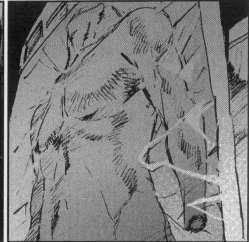

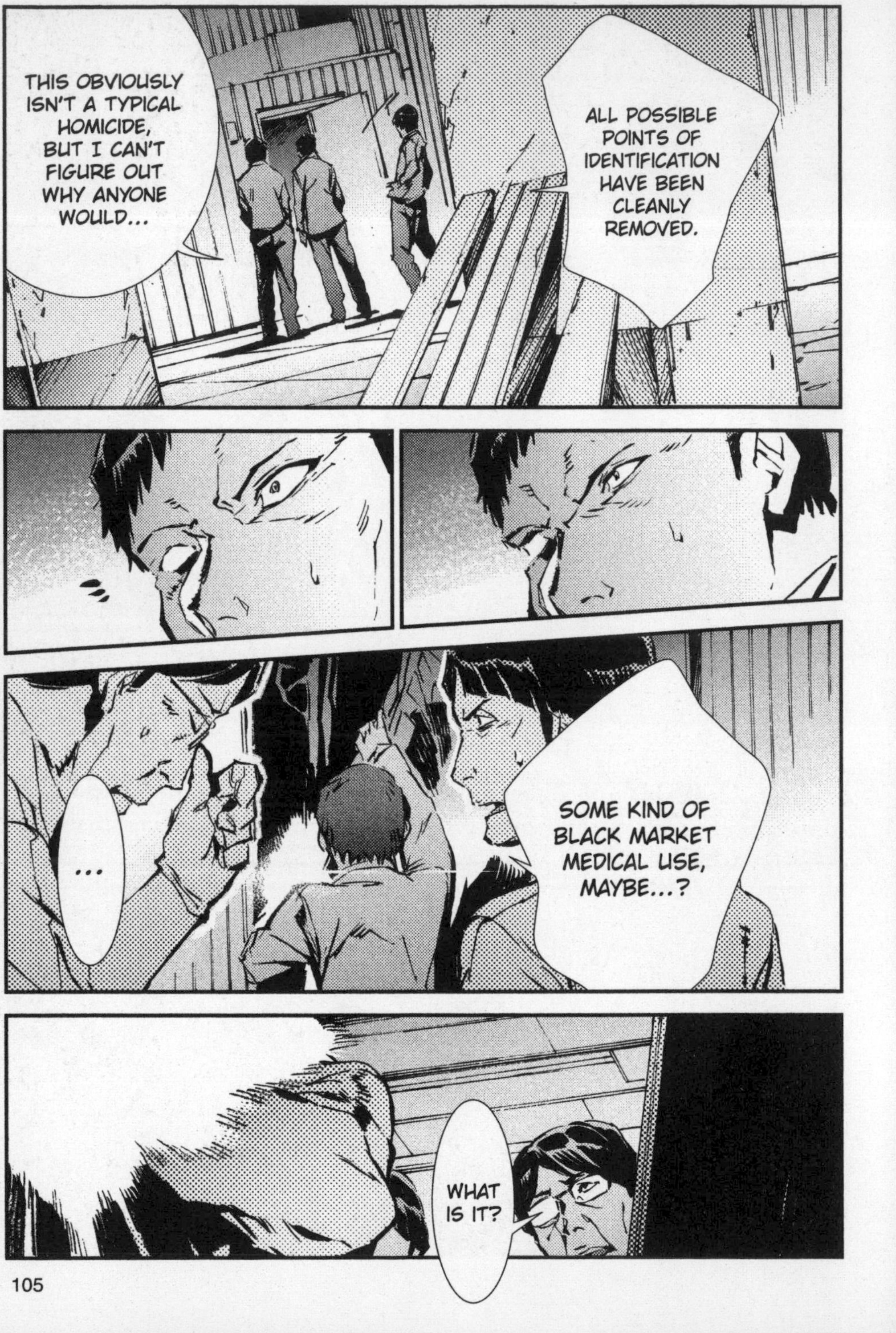
ALL POSSIBLE POINTS OF IDENTIFICATION HAVE BEEN CLEANLY REMOVED.
THIS OBVIOUSLY ISN'T A TYPICAL HOMICIDE, BUT I CAN'T FIGURE OUT WHY ANYONE WOULD...
SOME KIND OF BLACK MARKET MEDICAL USE, MAYBE...?
...
WHAT IS IT?

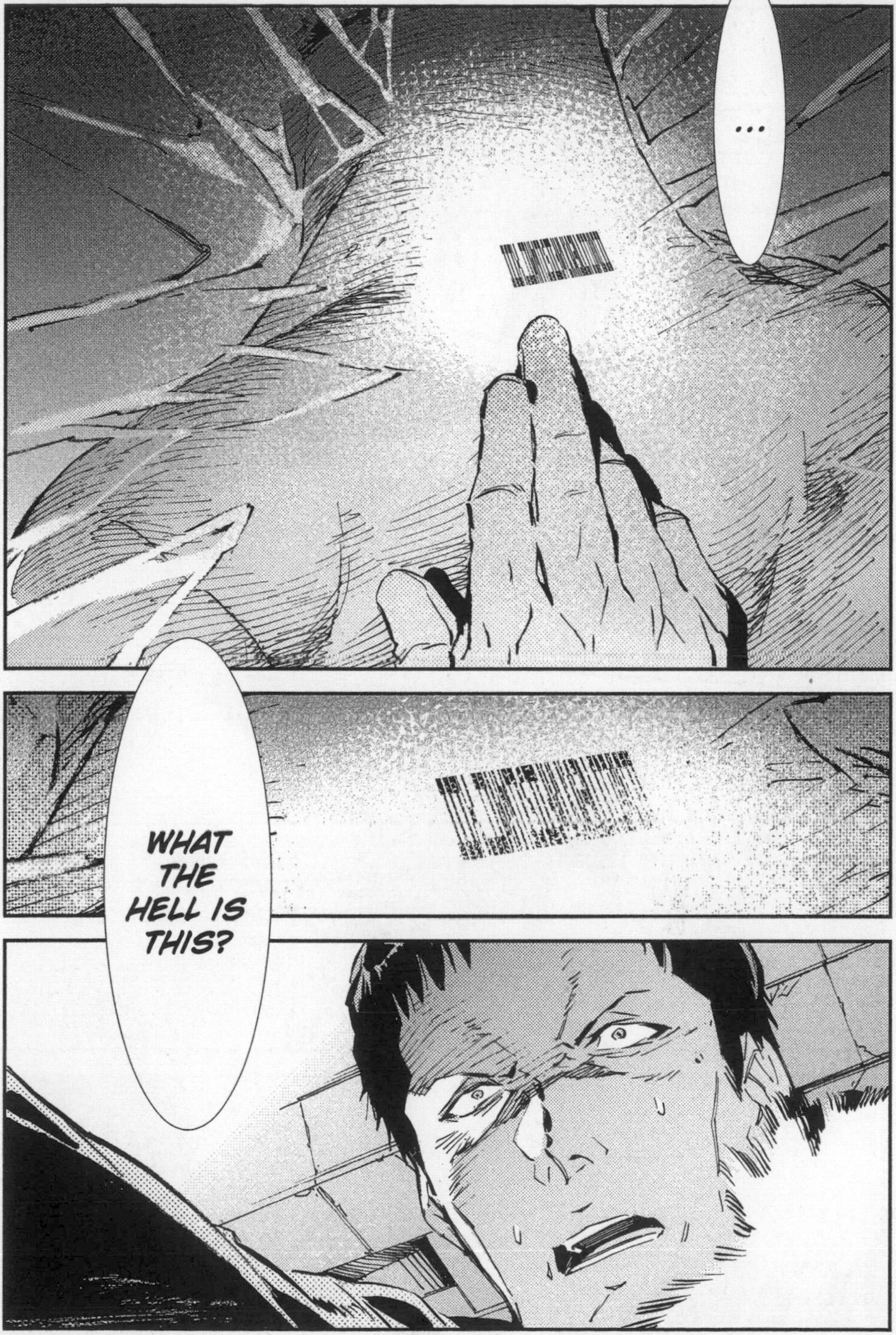
...
WHAT THE HELL IS THIS?

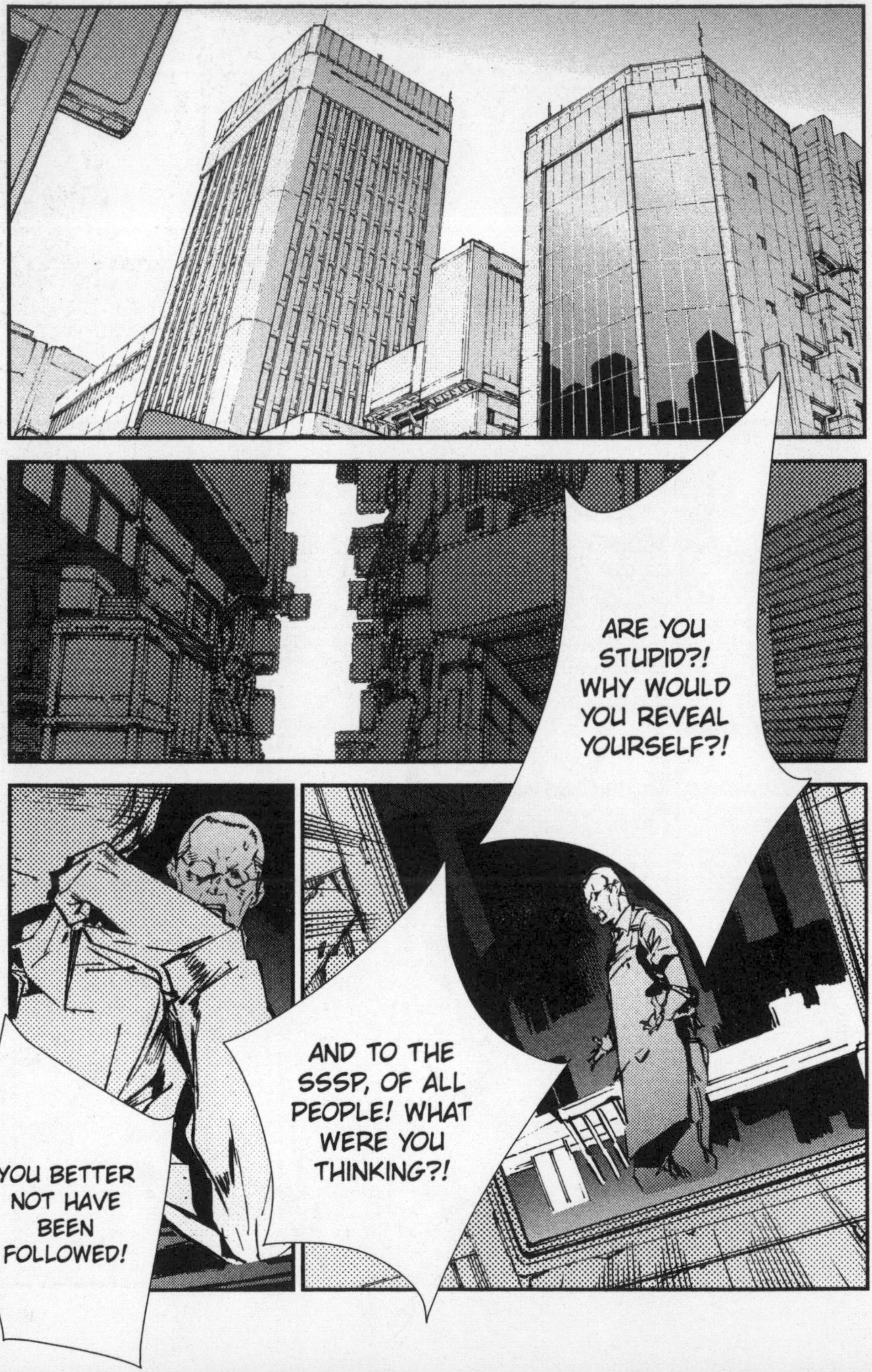
ARE YOU STUPID?! WHY WOULD YOU REVEAL YOURSELF?!
AND TO THE SSSP, OF ALL PEOPLE! WHAT WERE YOU THINKING?!
YOU BETTER NOT HAVE BEEN FOLLOWED!

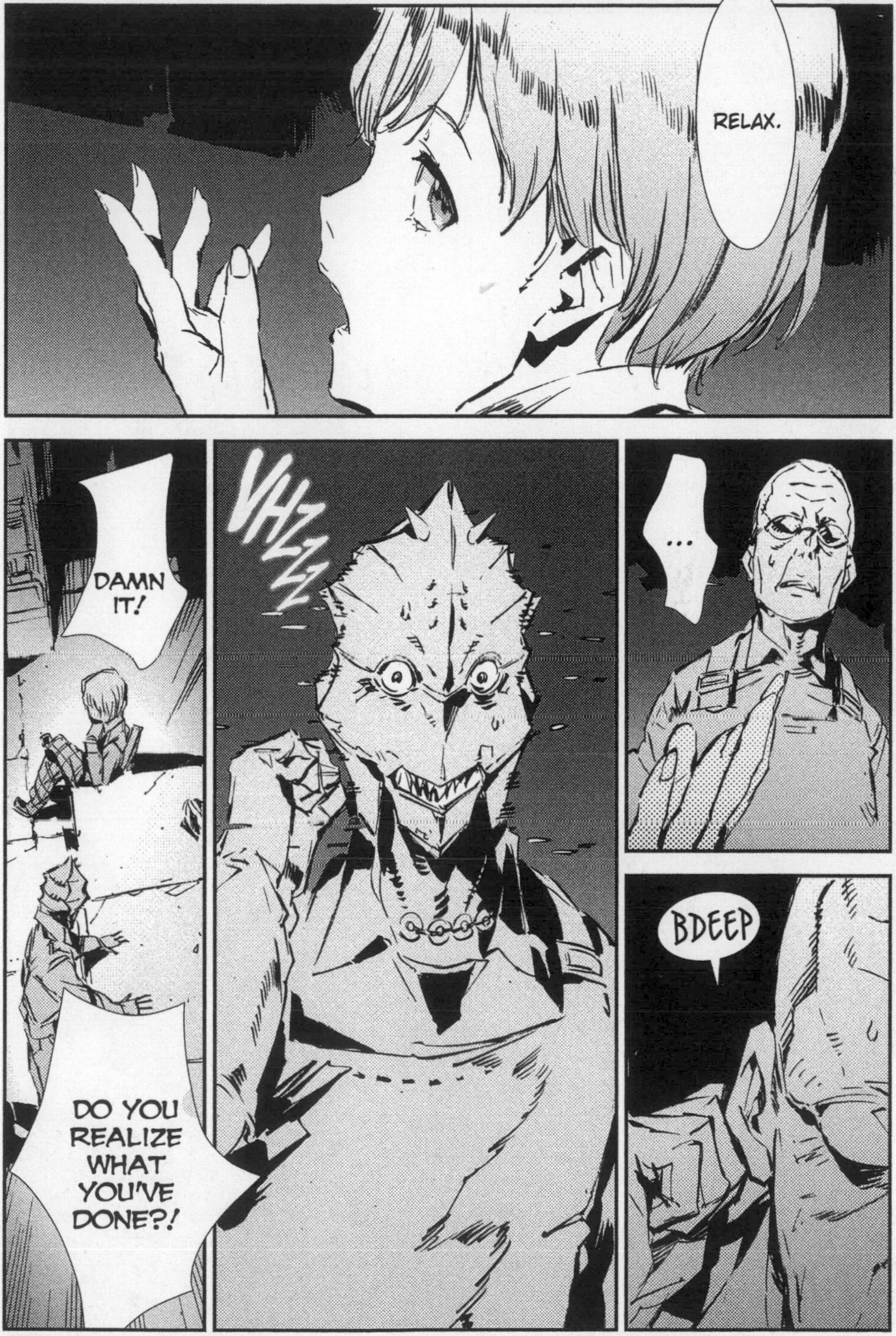
RELAX.
...
BDEEP
VHZZZ
DAMN IT!
DO YOU REALIZE WHAT YOU'VE DONE?!

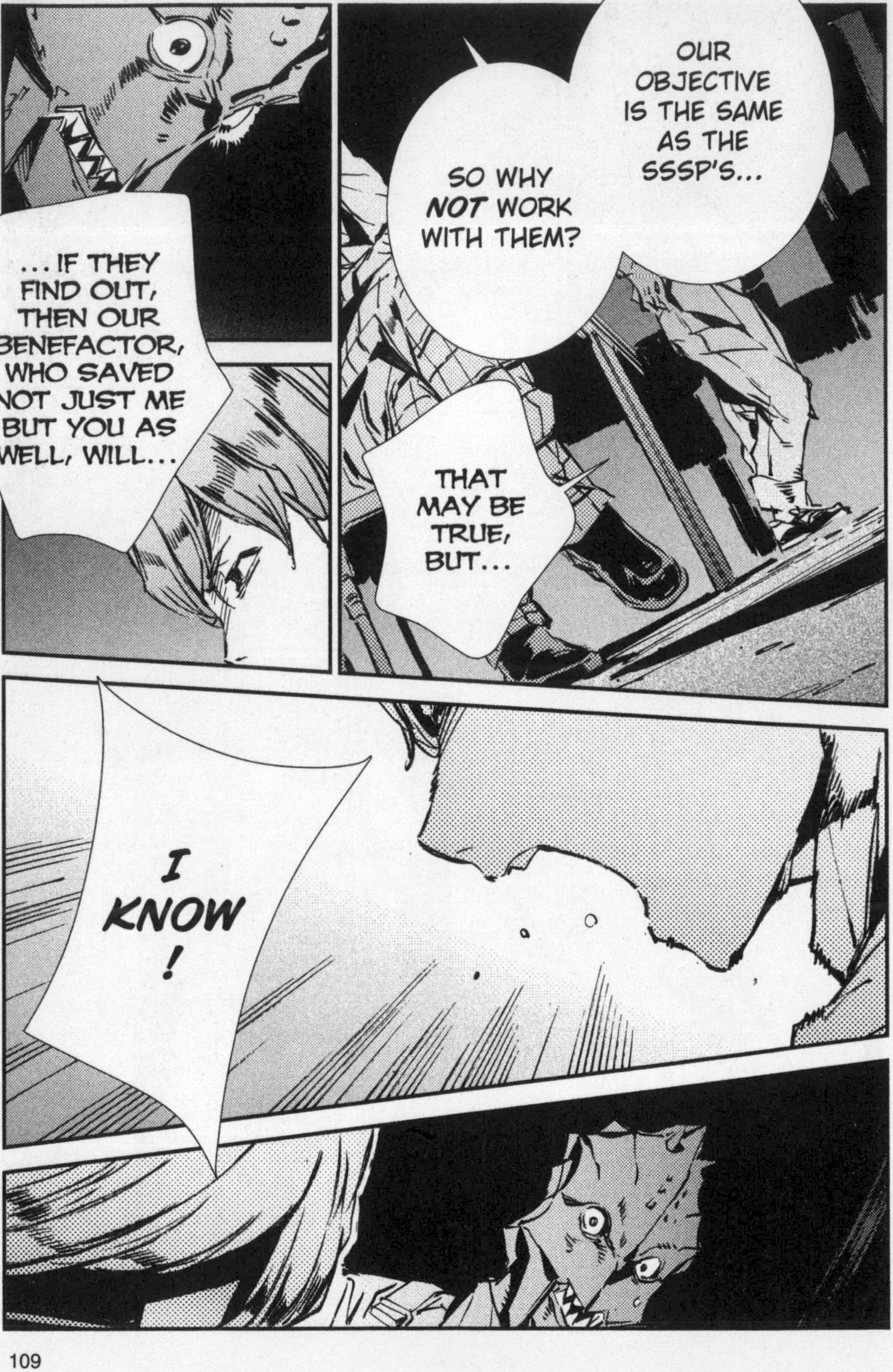
OUR OBJECTIVE IS THE SAME AS THE SSSP'S...
SO WHY *NOT* WORK WITH THEM?
THAT MAY BE TRUE, BUT...
...IF THEY FIND OUT, THEN OUR BENEFACTOR, WHO SAVED NOT JUST ME BUT YOU AS WELL, WILL...
I KNOW!

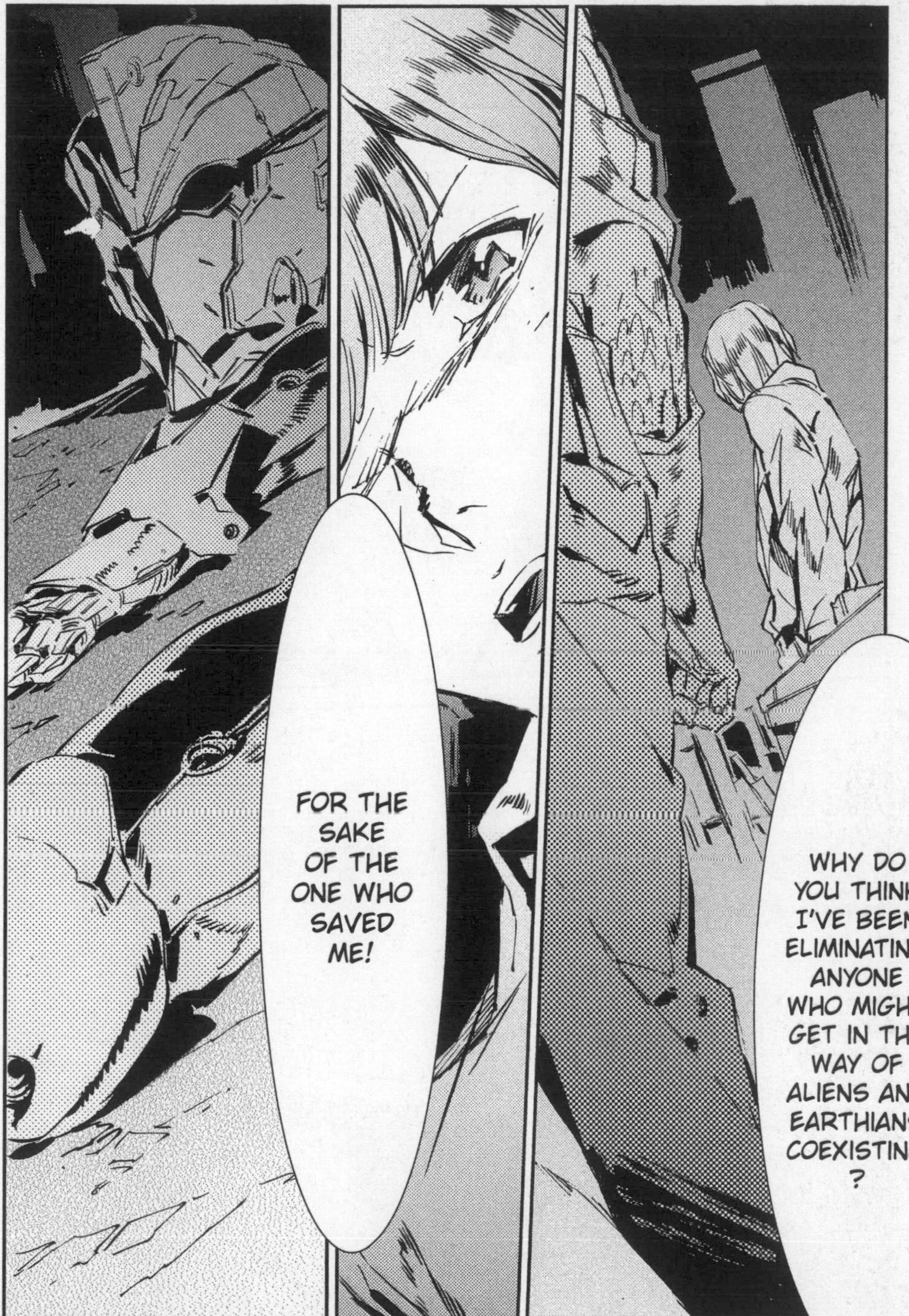
WHY DO YOU THINK I'VE BEEN ELIMINATING ANYONE WHO MIGHT GET IN THE WAY OF ALIENS AND EARTHIANS COEXISTING?
FOR THE SAKE OF THE ONE WHO SAVED ME!

ULTRAMAN

CHAPTER 40 — IN AND OUT OF SIGHT

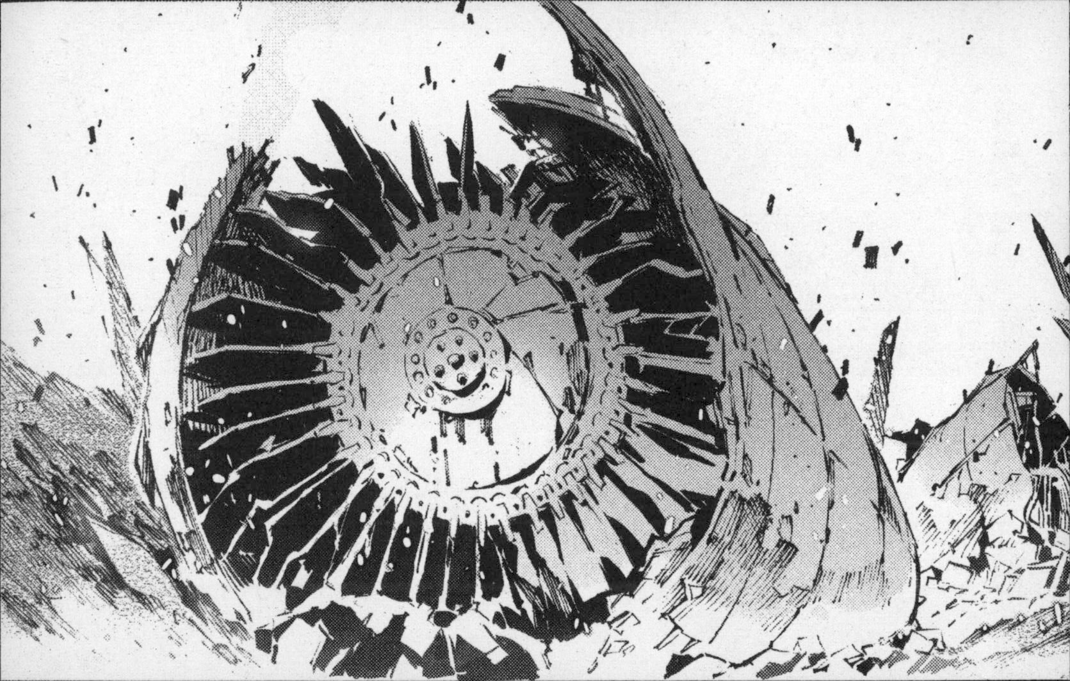

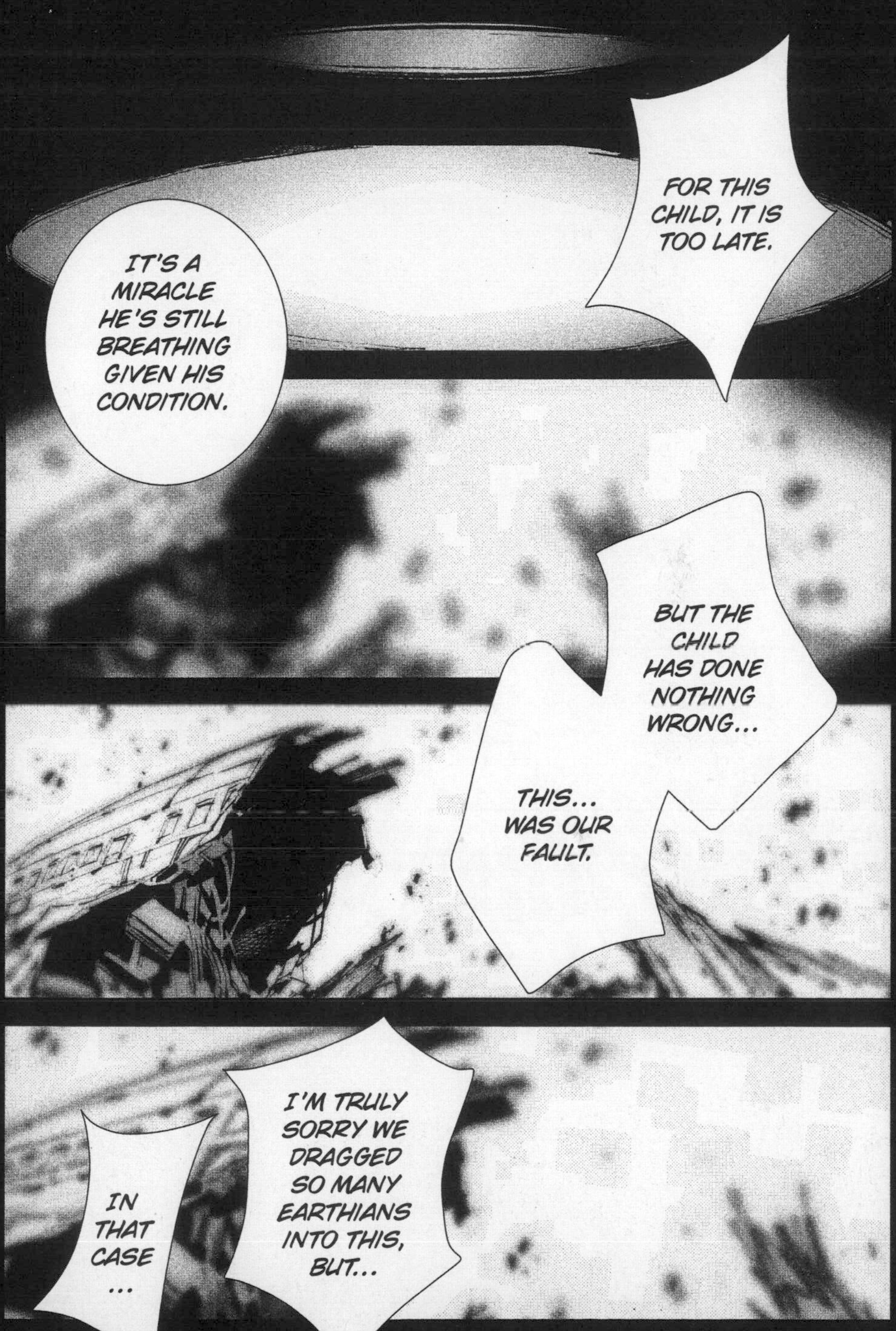
FOR THIS CHILD, IT IS TOO LATE.
IT'S A MIRACLE HE'S STILL BREATHING GIVEN HIS CONDITION.
BUT THE CHILD HAS DONE NOTHING WRONG...
THIS... WAS OUR FAULT.
I'M TRULY SORRY WE DRAGGED SO MANY EARTHIANS INTO THIS, BUT...
IN THAT CASE ...

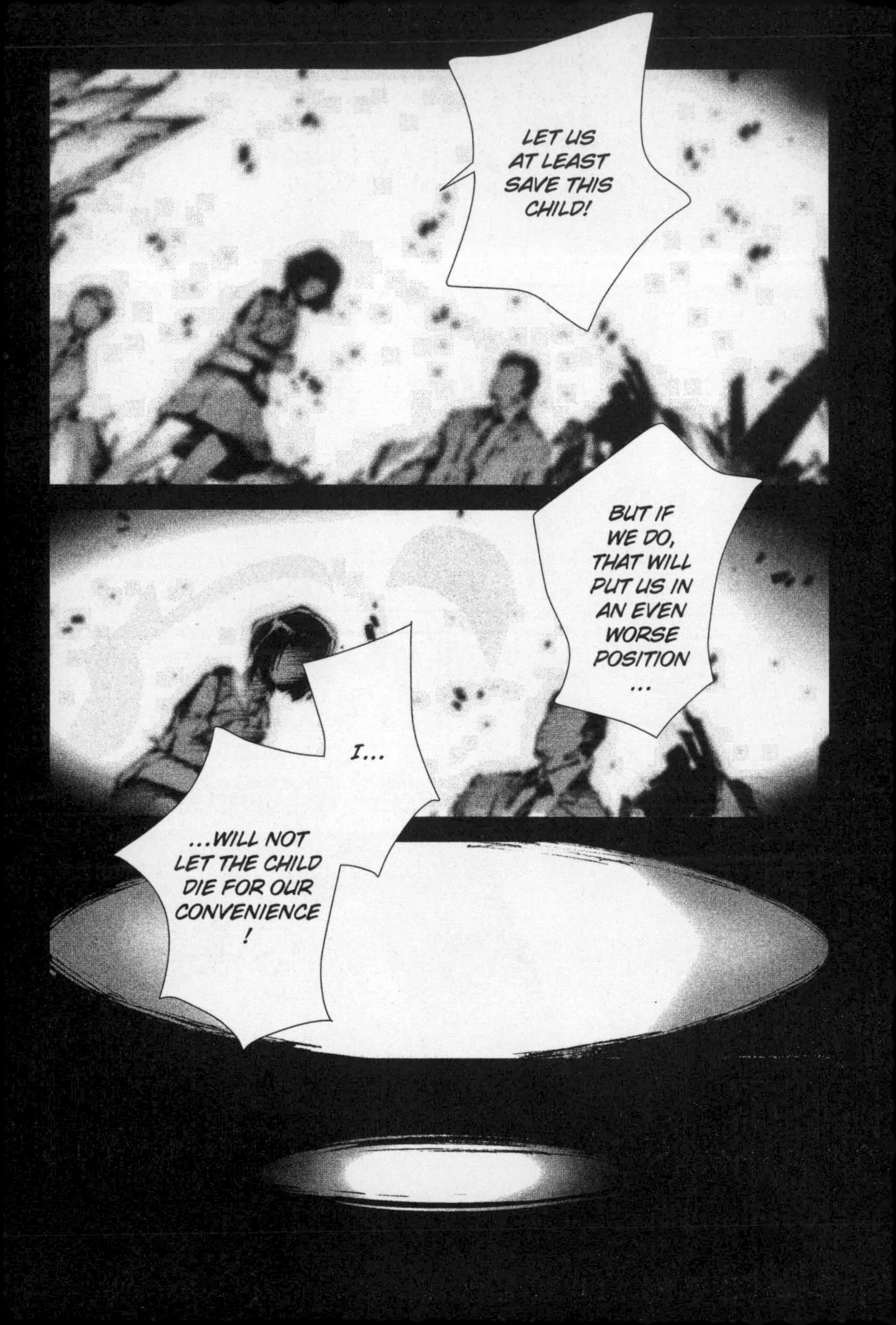
LET US AT LEAST SAVE THIS CHILD!
BUT IF WE DO, THAT WILL PUT US IN AN EVEN WORSE POSITION...
I...
...WILL NOT LET THE CHILD DIE FOR OUR CONVENIENCE!

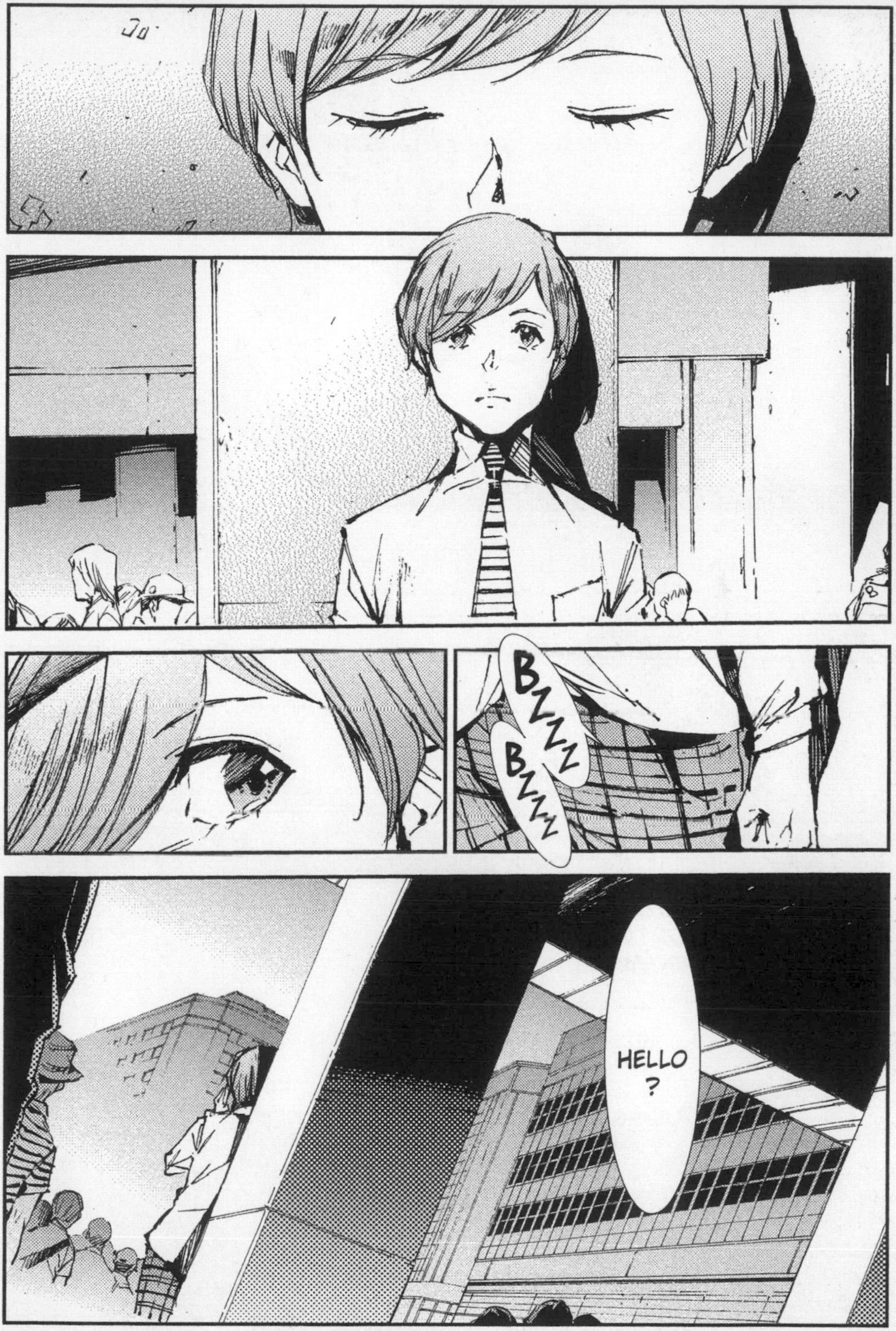
BZZZ
BZZZ
HELLO ?

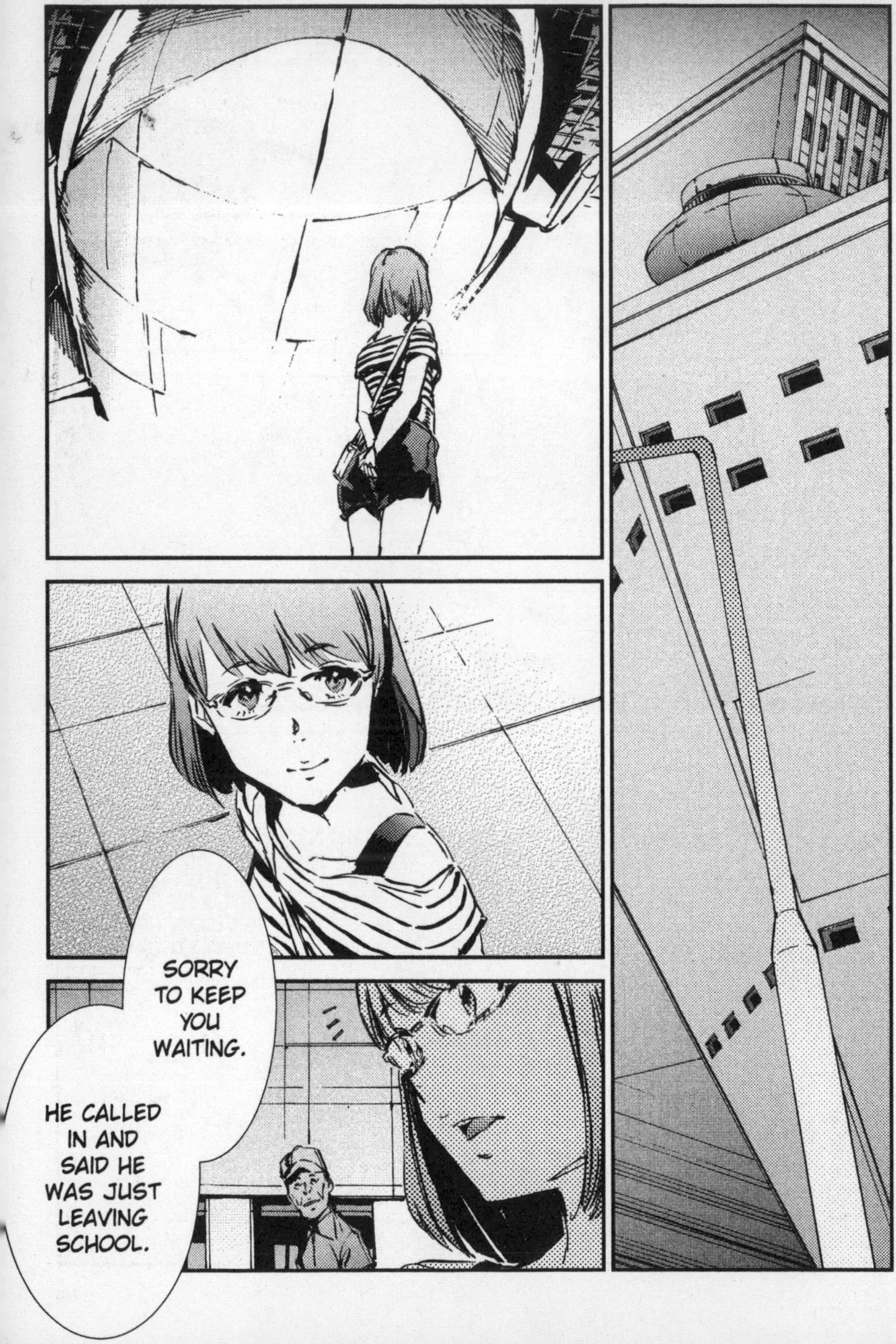
SORRY TO KEEP YOU WAITING.
HE CALLED IN AND SAID HE WAS JUST LEAVING SCHOOL.

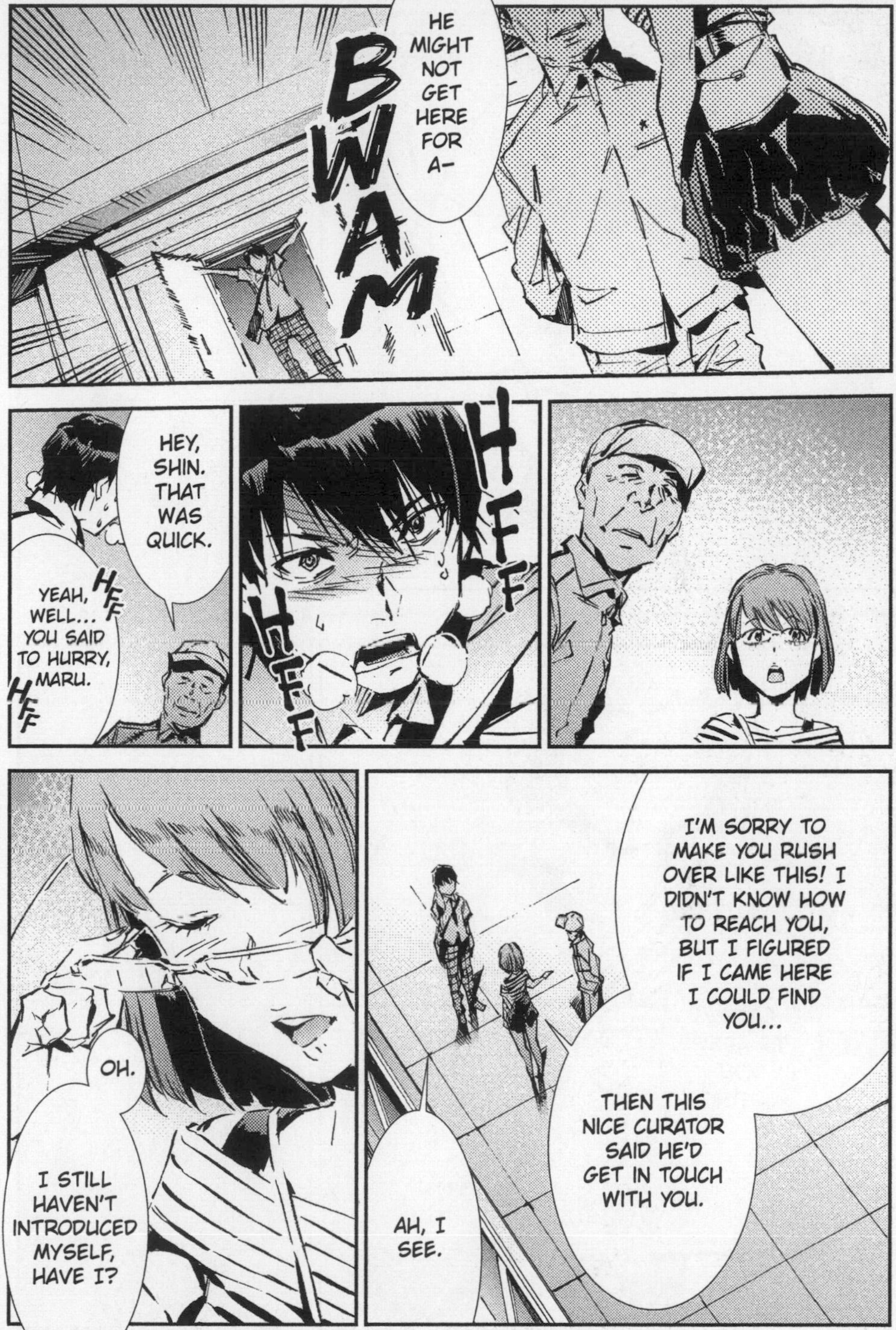
HE MIGHT NOT GET HERE FOR A-
BWAM
HFF
HFF
HEY, SHIN. THAT WAS QUICK.
YEAH, WELL... YOU SAID TO HURRY, MARU.
HFF
HFF
I'M SORRY TO MAKE YOU RUSH OVER LIKE THIS! I DIDN'T KNOW HOW TO REACH YOU, BUT I FIGURED IF I CAME HERE I COULD FIND YOU...
THEN THIS NICE CURATOR SAID HE'D GET IN TOUCH WITH YOU.
AH, I SEE.
OH.
I STILL HAVEN'T INTRODUCED MYSELF, HAVE I?

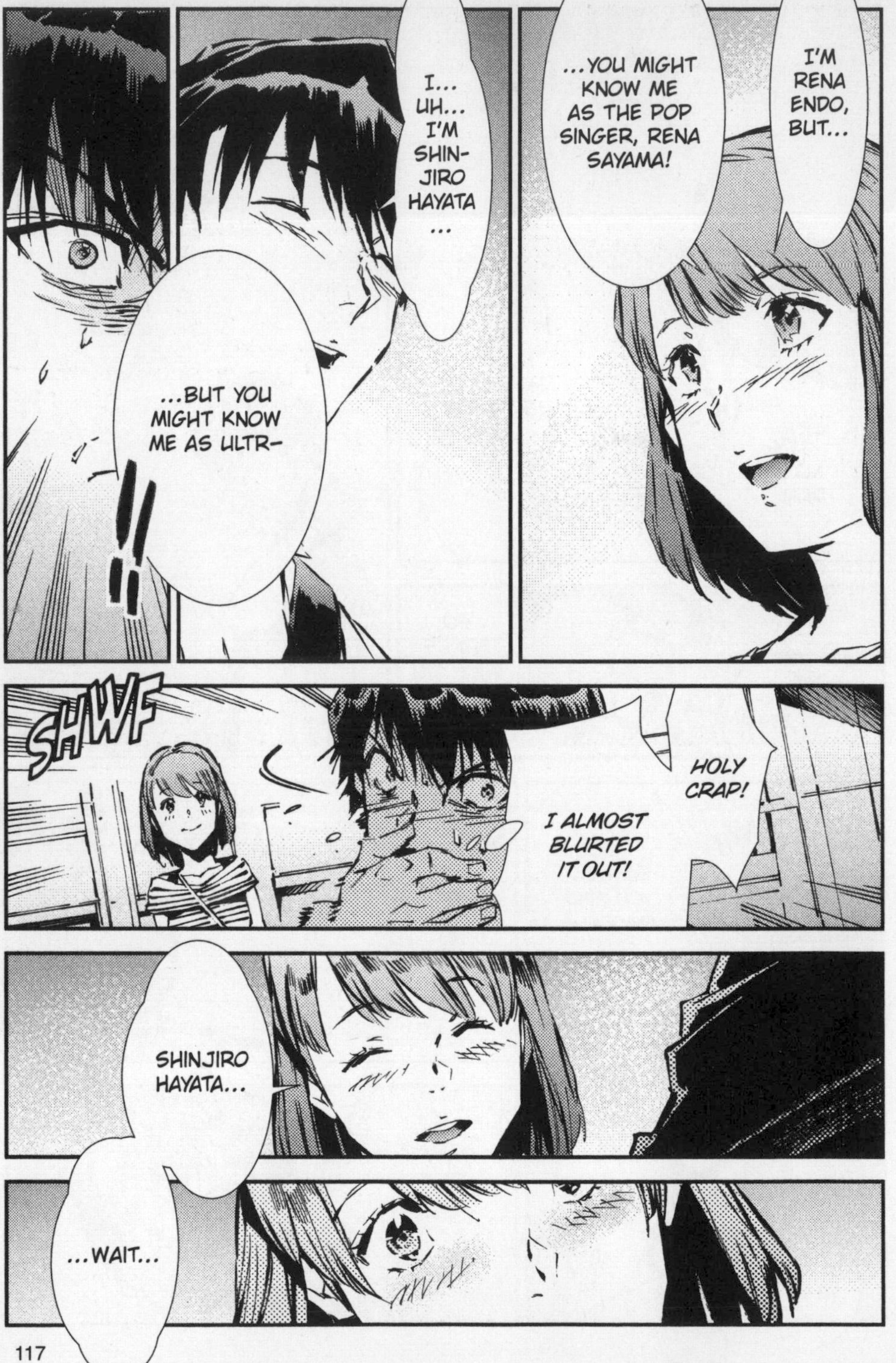
I'M RENA ENDO, BUT...
...YOU MIGHT KNOW ME AS THE POP SINGER, RENA SAYAMA!
I... UH... I'M SHINJIRO HAYATA...
...BUT YOU MIGHT KNOW ME AS ULTR-
!!
HOLY CRAP!
I ALMOST BLURTED IT OUT!
SHWF
SHINJIRO HAYATA...
...WAIT...

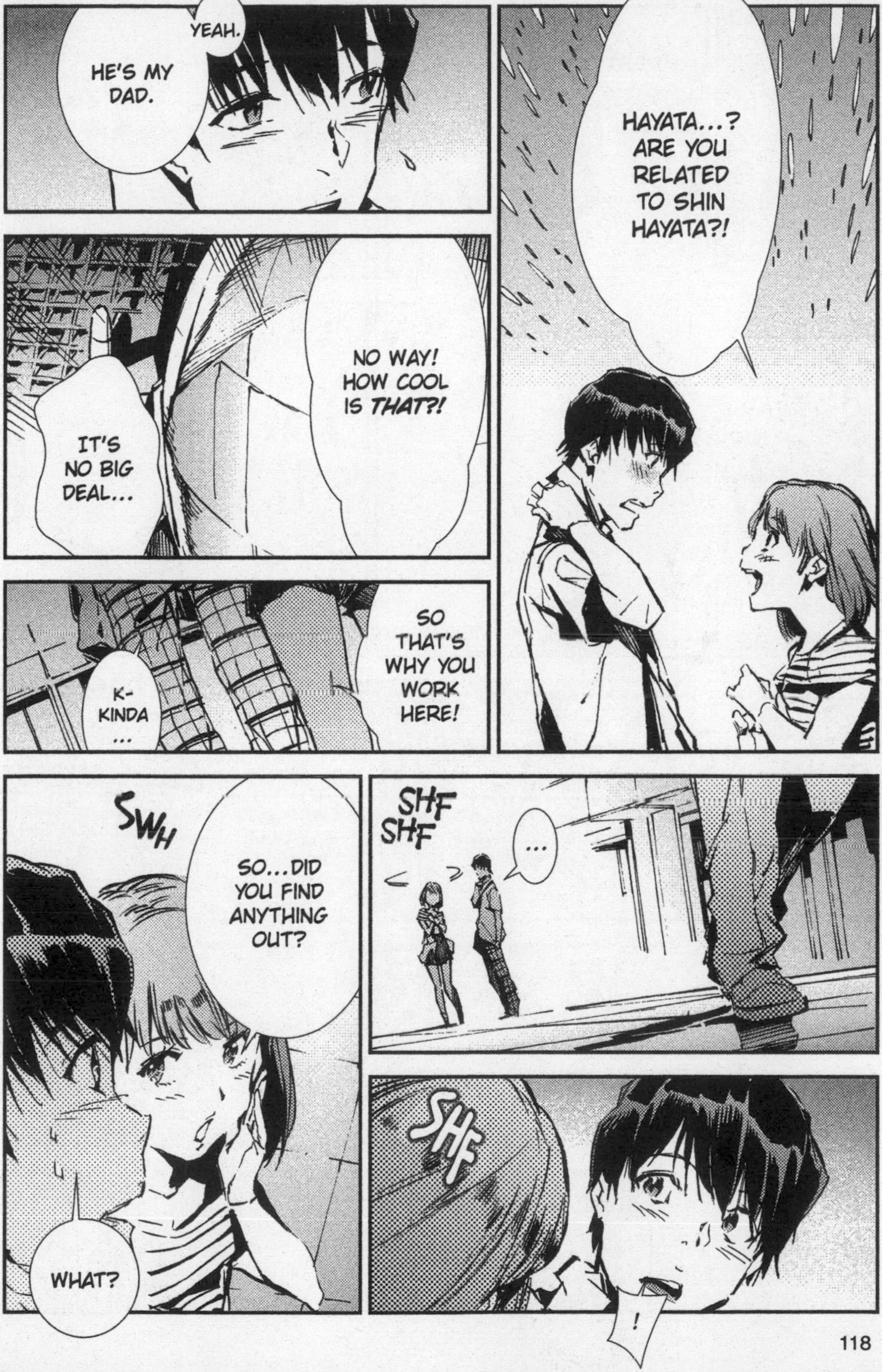
HAYATA...? ARE YOU RELATED TO SHIN HAYATA?!
YEAH.
HE'S MY DAD.
NO WAY! HOW COOL IS *THAT*?!
IT'S NO BIG DEAL...
SO THAT'S WHY YOU WORK HERE!
K-KINDA ...
SHF SHF
...
SHF
!
SWH
SO...DID YOU FIND ANYTHING OUT?
WHAT?

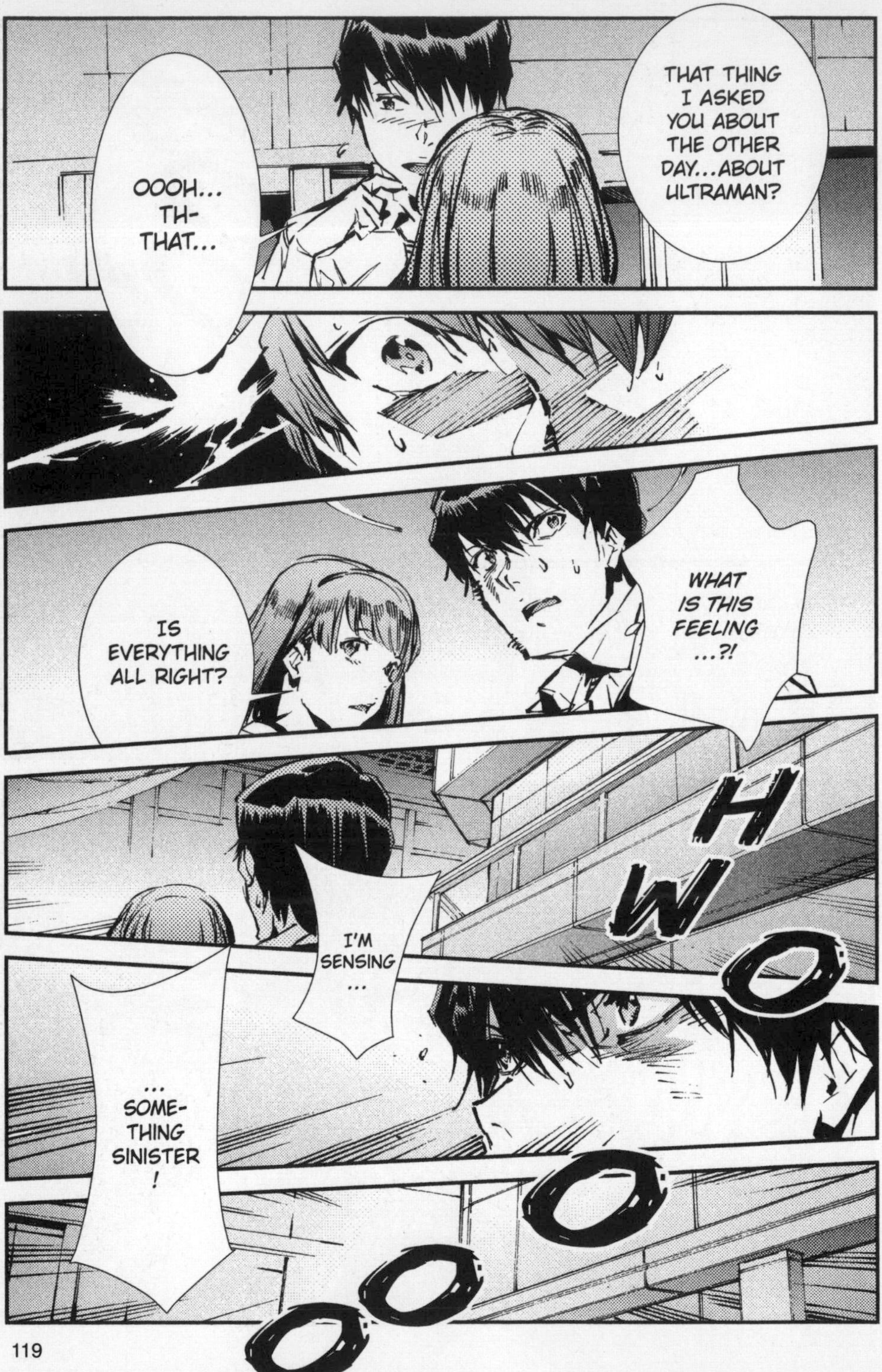
THAT THING I ASKED YOU ABOUT THE OTHER DAY...ABOUT ULTRAMAN?
OOOH... TH- THAT...
WHAT IS THIS FEELING ...?!
IS EVERYTHING ALL RIGHT?
I'M SENSING ...
HWOOOOO
... SOME- THING SINISTER !

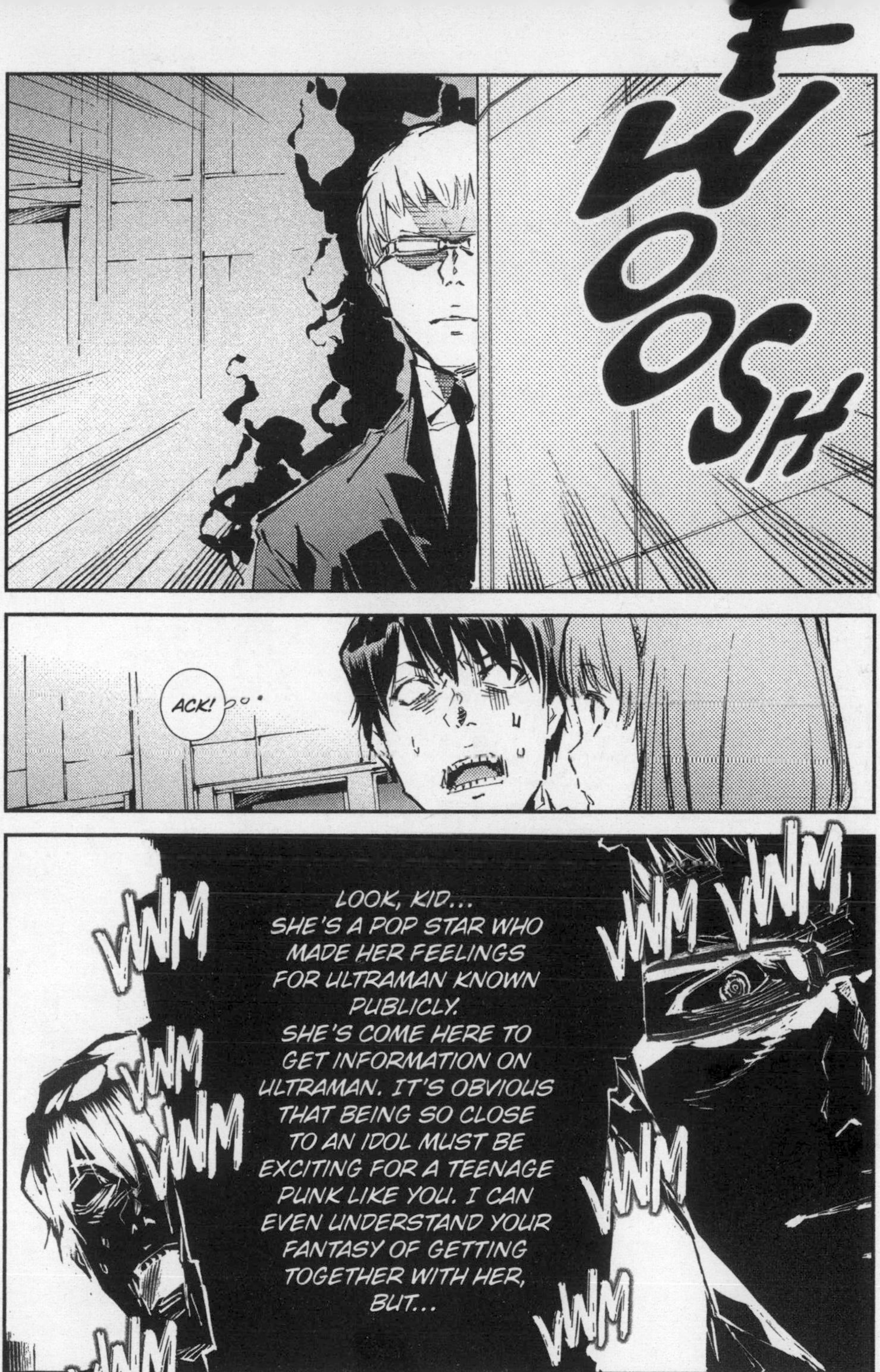
WHOOSH
ACK!
VWM VWM
VWM
LOOK, KID...
SHE'S A POP STAR WHO
MADE HER FEELINGS
FOR ULTRAMAN KNOWN
PUBLICLY.
SHE'S COME HERE TO
GET INFORMATION ON
ULTRAMAN. IT'S OBVIOUS
THAT BEING SO CLOSE
TO AN IDOL MUST BE
EXCITING FOR A TEENAGE
PUNK LIKE YOU. I CAN
EVEN UNDERSTAND YOUR
FANTASY OF GETTING
TOGETHER WITH HER,
BUT...
VWM
VWM
VWM
VWM
VWM
VWM

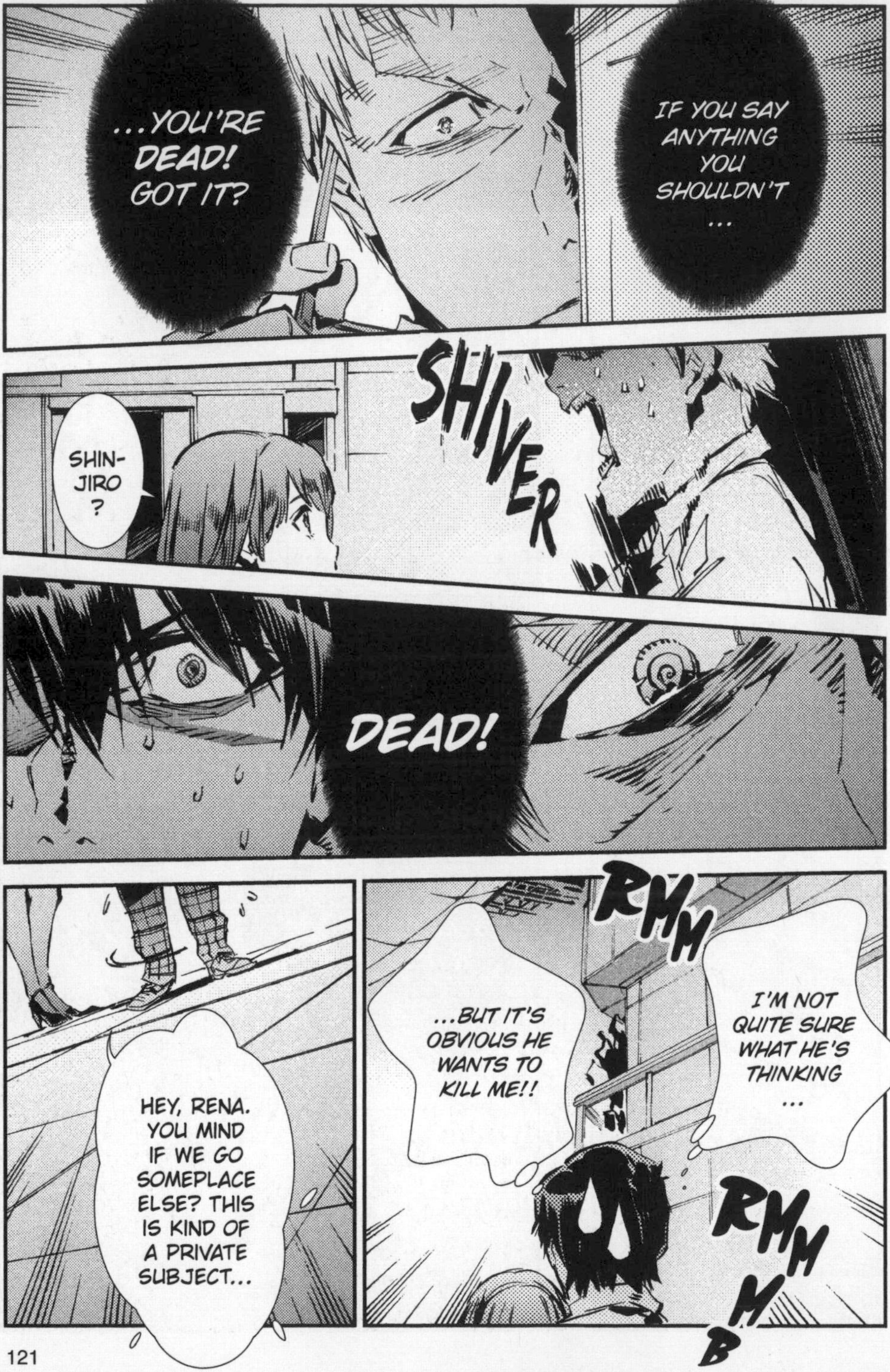
IF YOU SAY ANYTHING YOU SHOULDN'T ...
...YOU'RE DEAD! GOT IT?
SHIVER
SHIN-JIRO?
DEAD!
RMM
I'M NOT QUITE SURE WHAT HE'S THINKING ...
...BUT IT'S OBVIOUS HE WANTS TO KILL ME!!
RMMMB
HEY, RENA. YOU MIND IF WE GO SOMEPLACE ELSE? THIS IS KIND OF A PRIVATE SUBJECT...

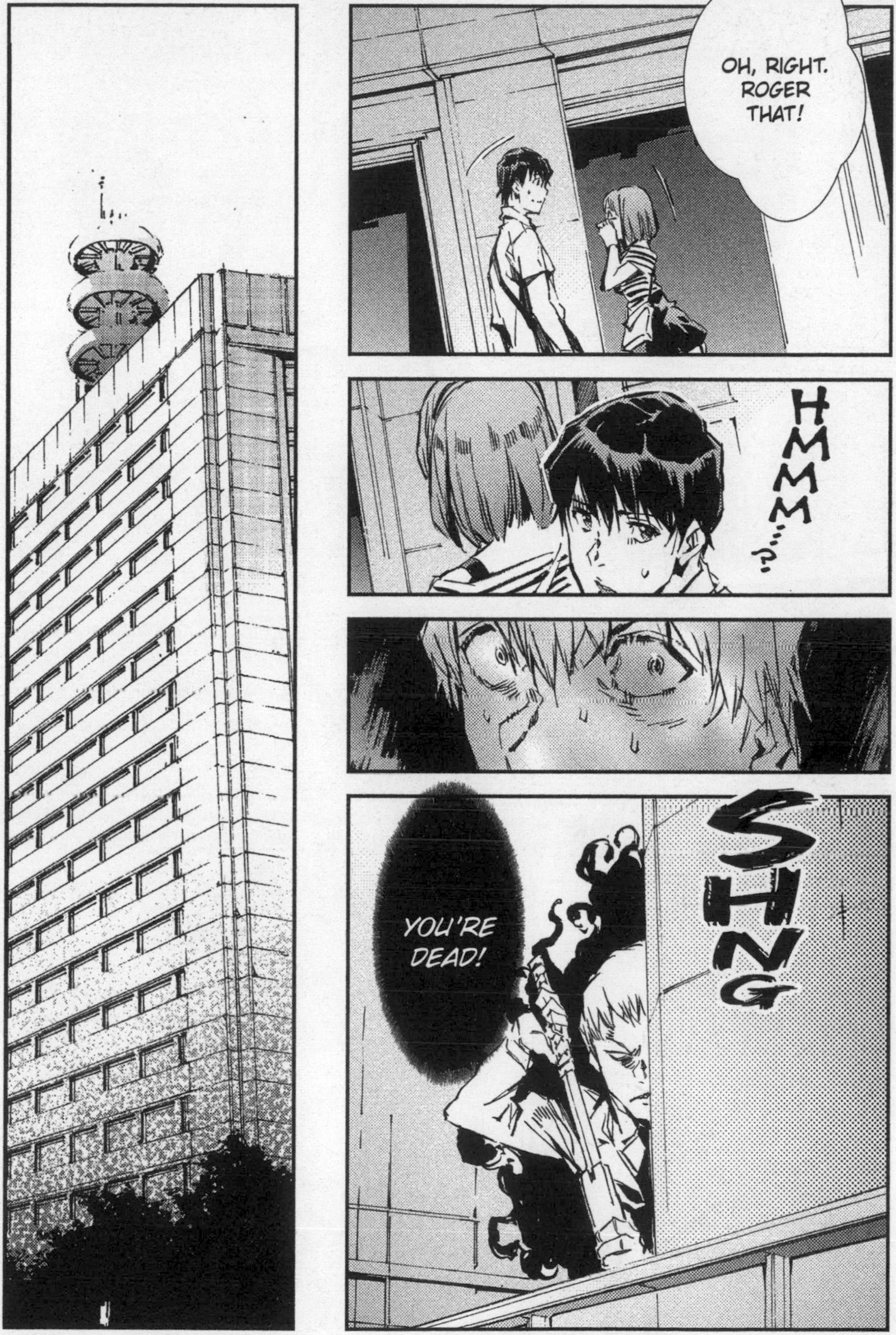
OH, RIGHT. ROGER THAT!
HMMM...?
SHNG
YOU'RE DEAD!

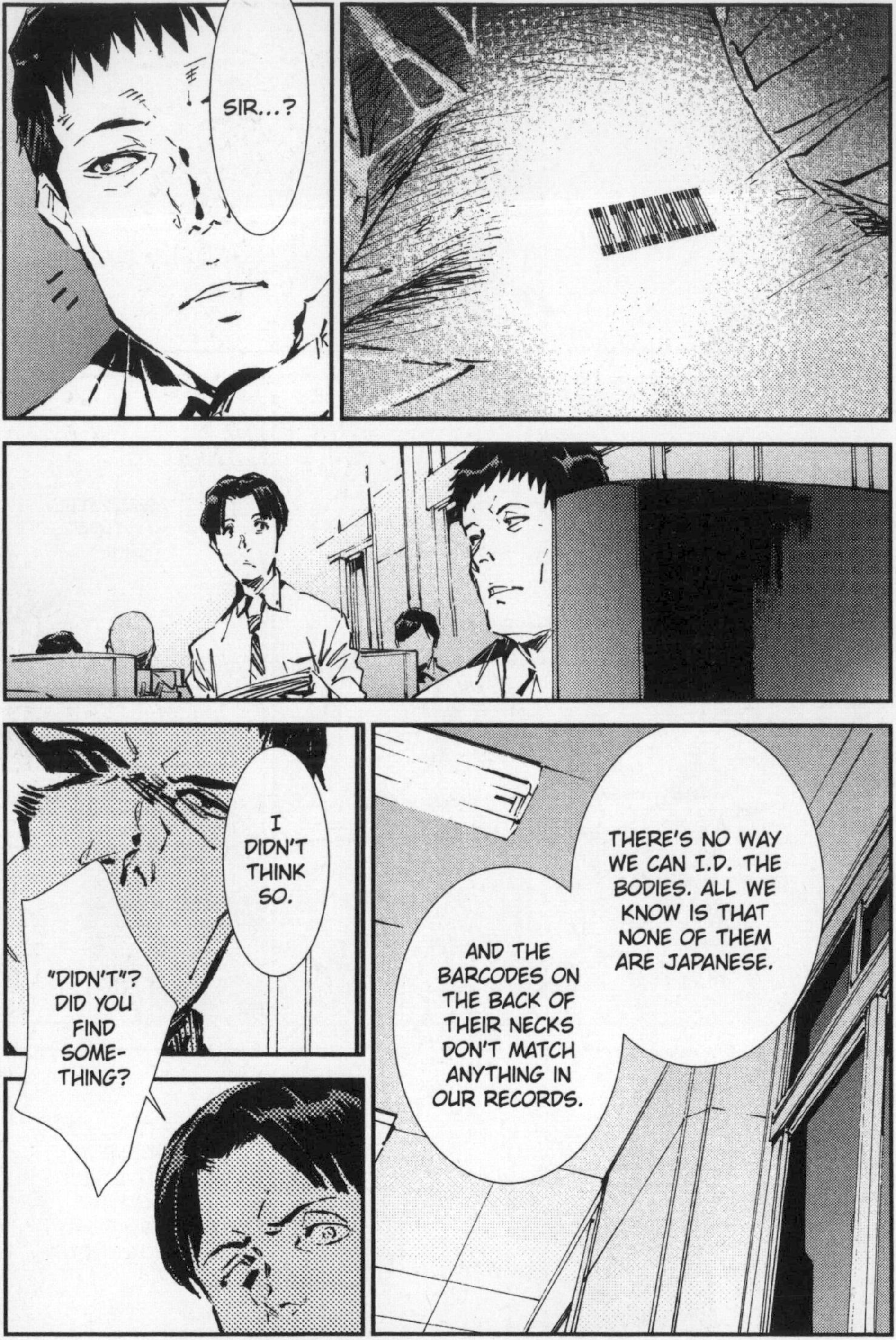
SIR...?
THERE'S NO WAY WE CAN I.D. THE BODIES. ALL WE KNOW IS THAT NONE OF THEM ARE JAPANESE.
AND THE BARCODES ON THE BACK OF THEIR NECKS DON'T MATCH ANYTHING IN OUR RECORDS.
I DIDN'T THINK SO.
"DIDN'T"? DID YOU FIND SOME-THING?

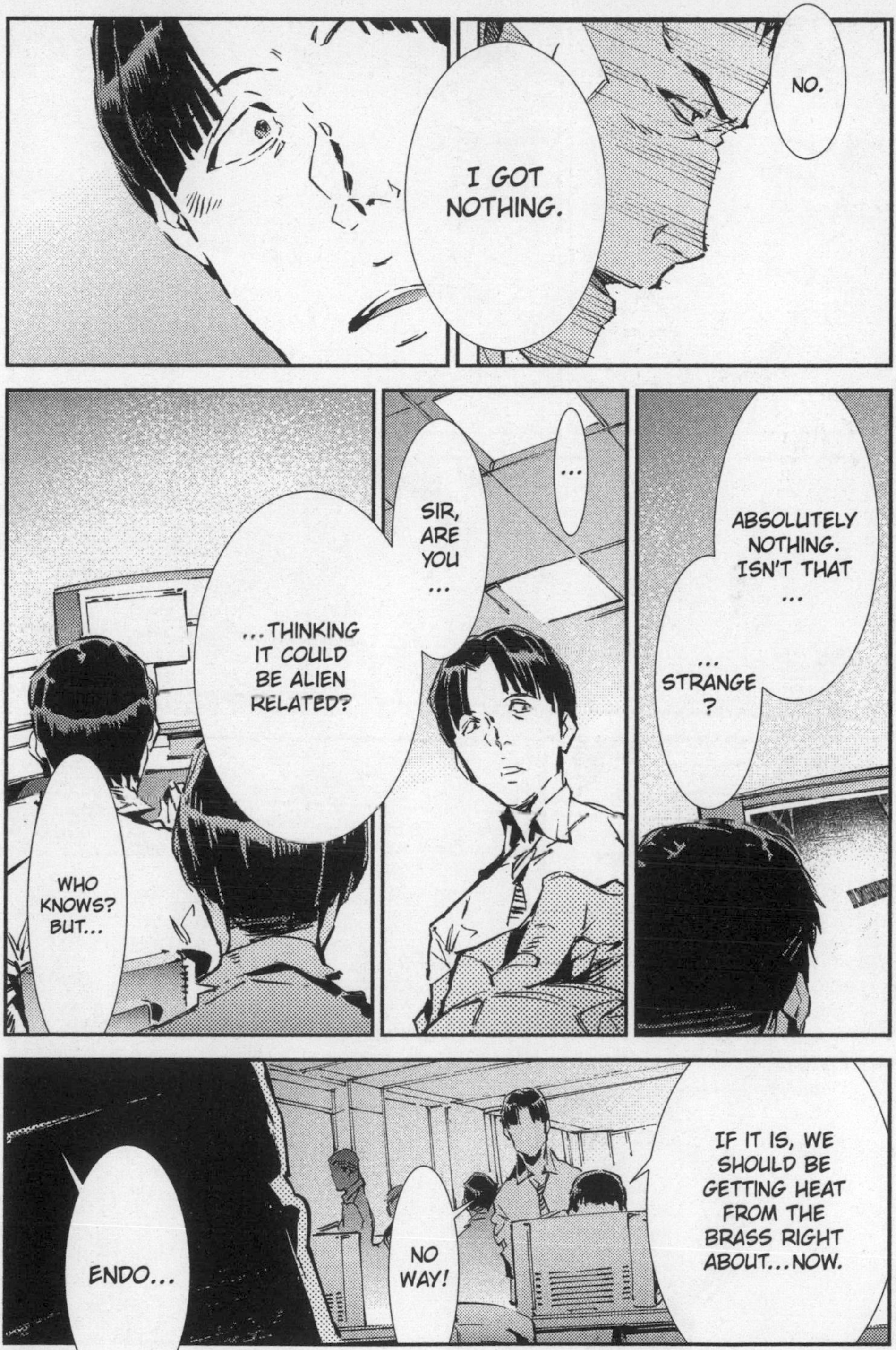
NO.
I GOT NOTHING.
ABSOLUTELY NOTHING. ISN'T THAT ...
... STRANGE ?
...
SIR, ARE YOU ...
...THINKING IT COULD BE ALIEN RELATED?
WHO KNOWS? BUT...
IF IT IS, WE SHOULD BE GETTING HEAT FROM THE BRASS RIGHT ABOUT...NOW.
NO WAY!
ENDO...

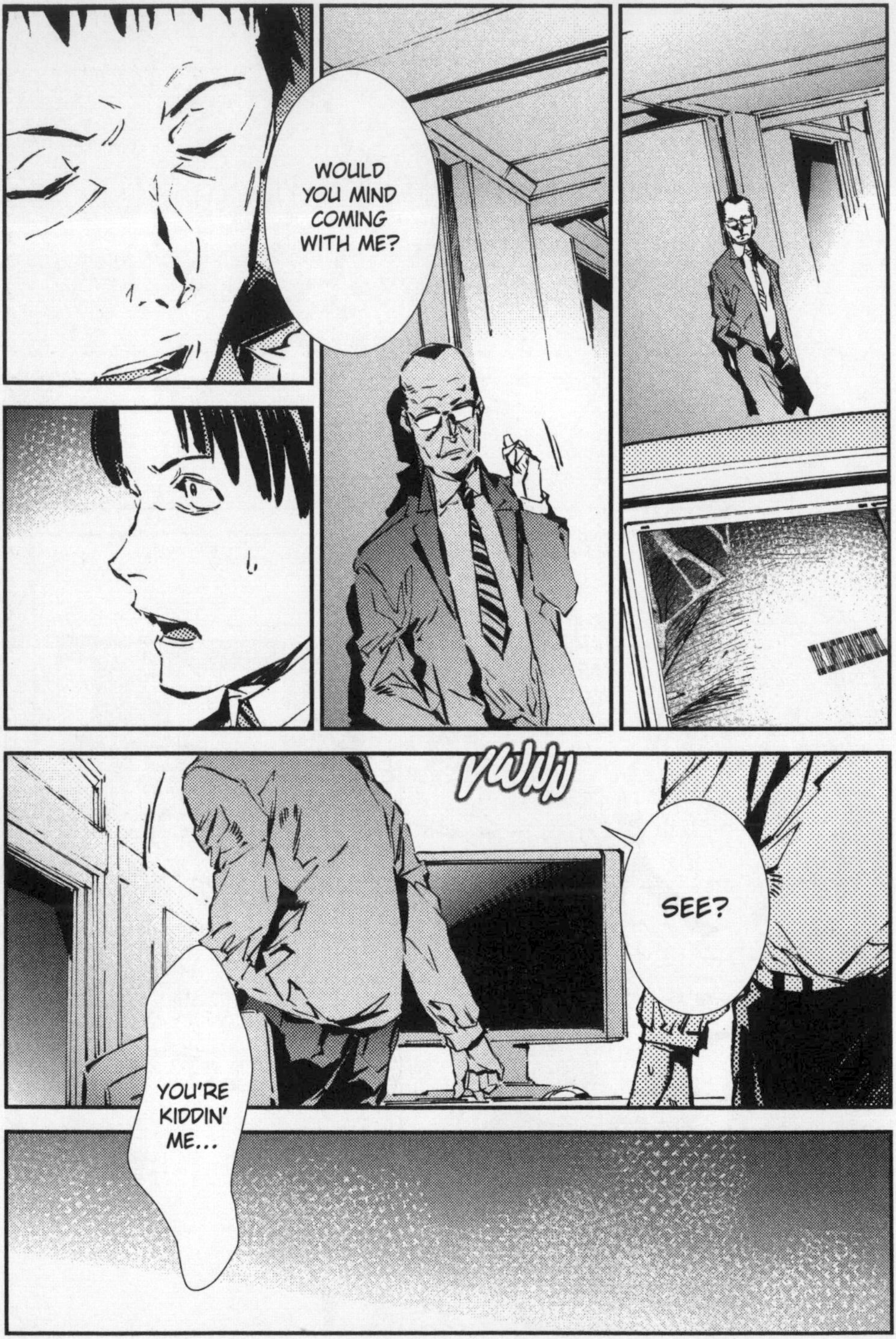
WOULD YOU MIND COMING WITH ME?
SEE?
YOU'RE KIDDIN' ME...

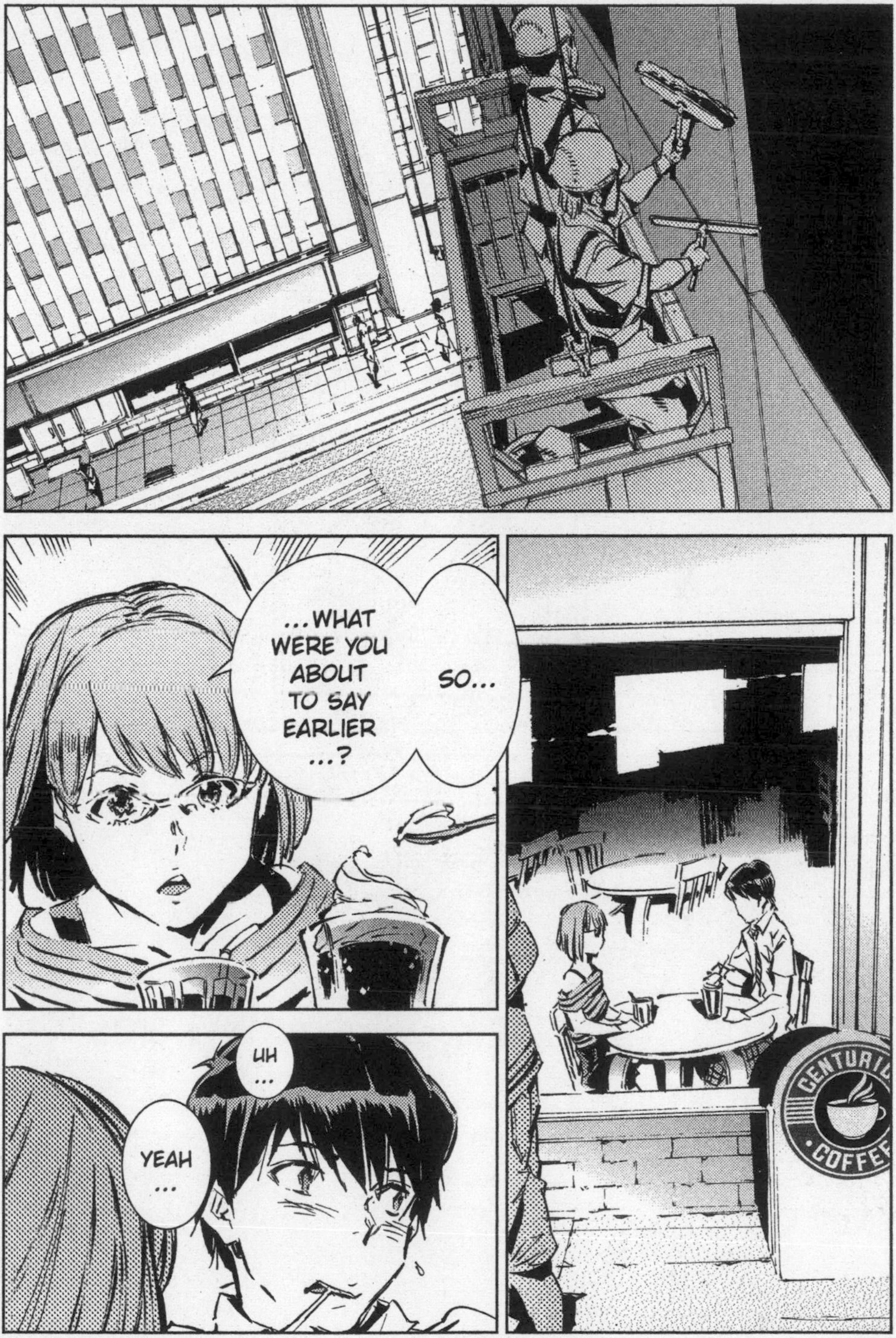
SO...
...WHAT WERE YOU ABOUT TO SAY EARLIER ...?
UH ...
YEAH ...

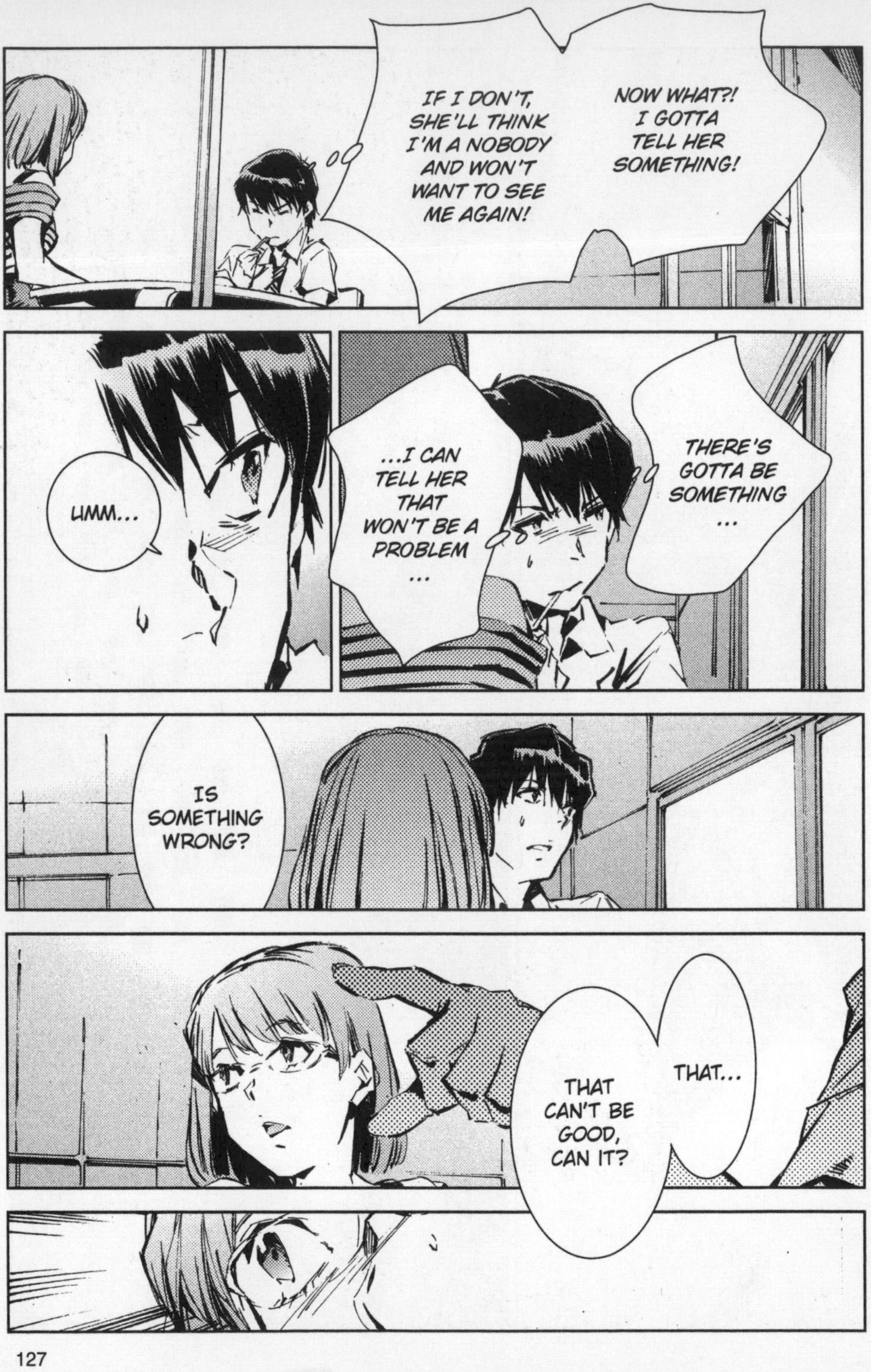
NOW WHAT?! I GOTTA TELL HER SOMETHING!
IF I DON'T, SHE'LL THINK I'M A NOBODY AND WON'T WANT TO SEE ME AGAIN!
THERE'S GOTTA BE SOMETHING ...
...I CAN TELL HER THAT WON'T BE A PROBLEM ...
UMM...
IS SOMETHING WRONG?
THAT...
THAT CAN'T BE GOOD, CAN IT?

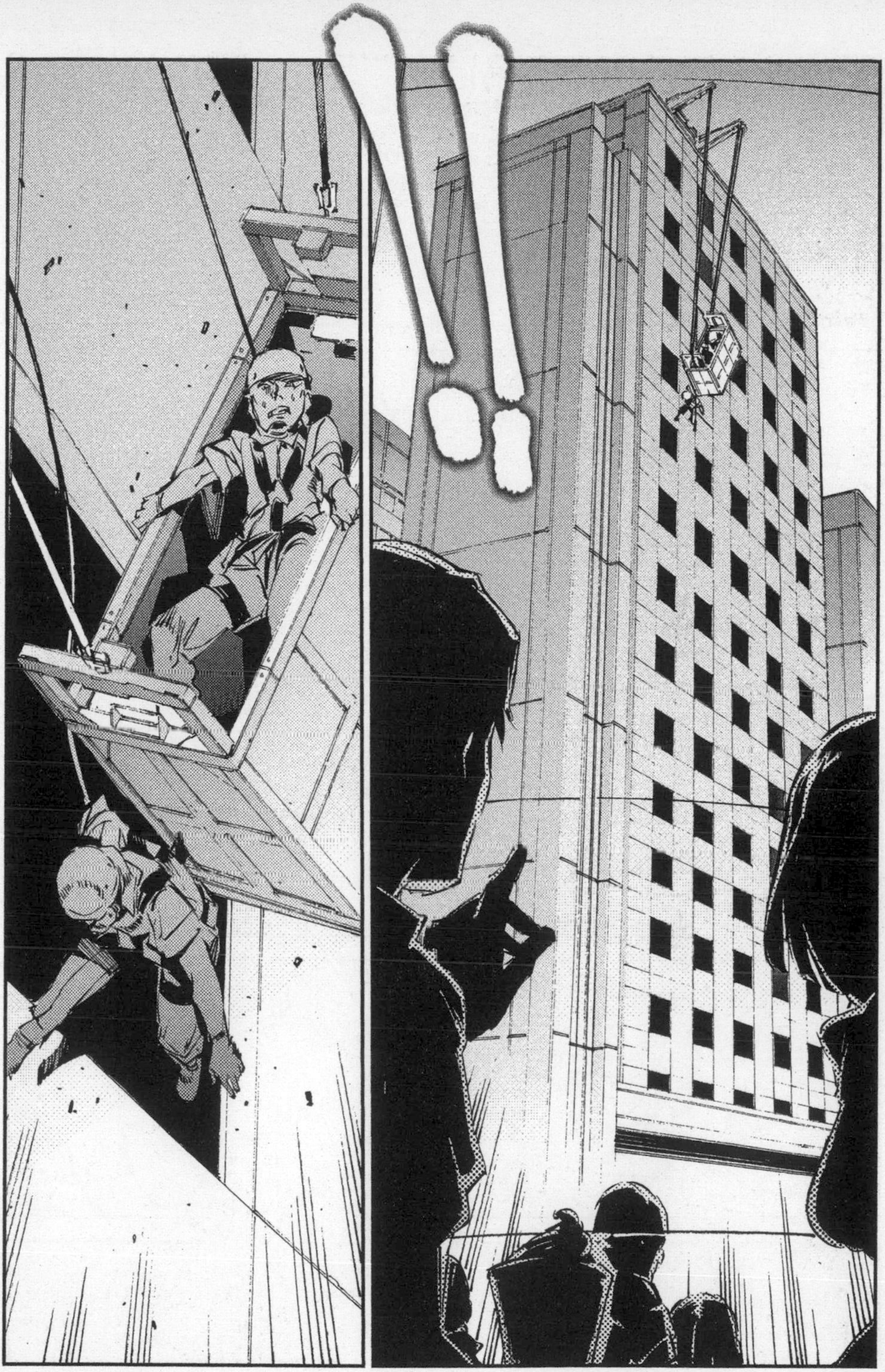
!!

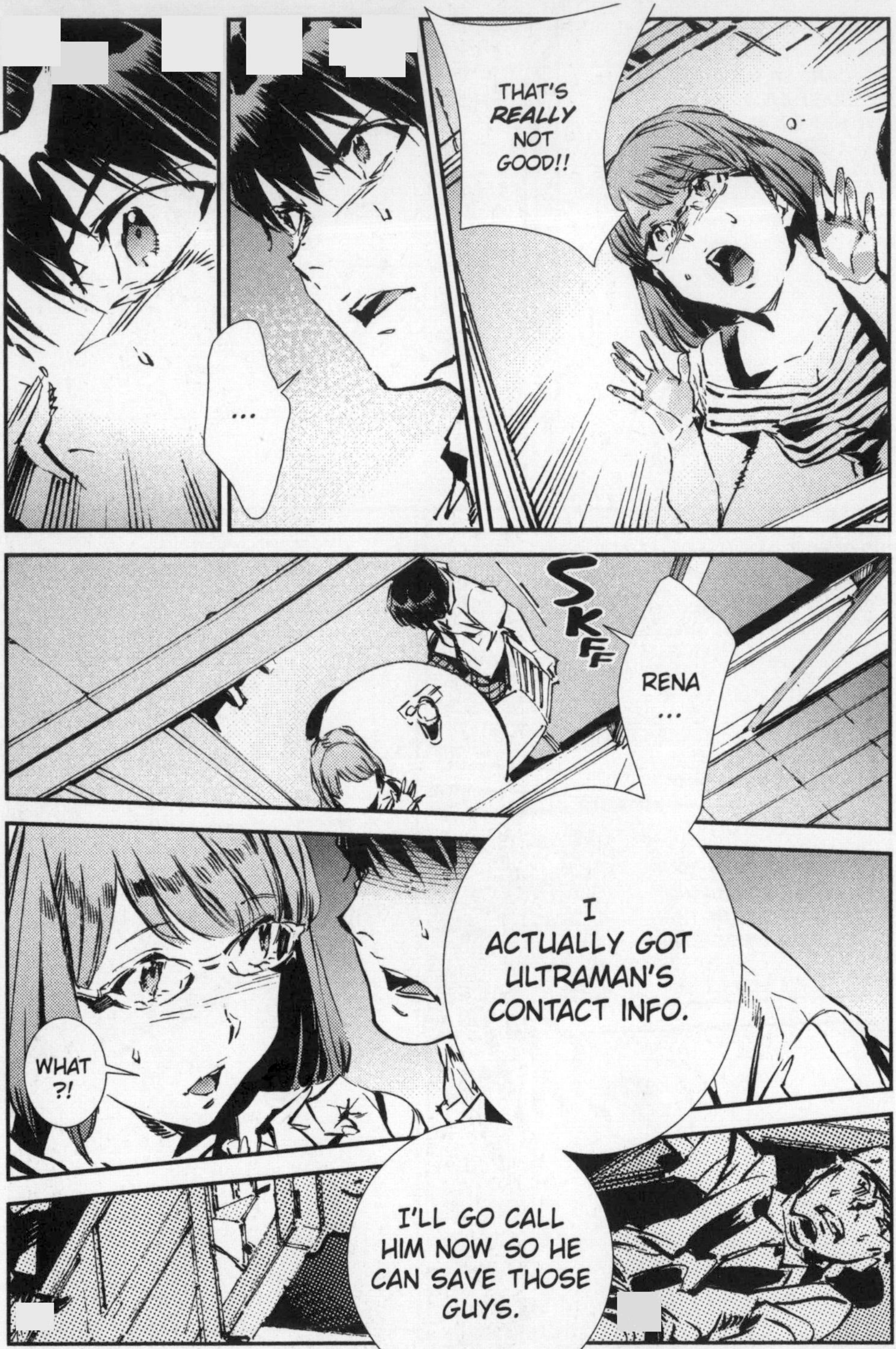
THAT'S *REALLY* NOT GOOD!!
...
SKFF
RENA ...
I ACTUALLY GOT ULTRAMAN'S CONTACT INFO.
WHAT ?!
I'LL GO CALL HIM NOW SO HE CAN SAVE THOSE GUYS.

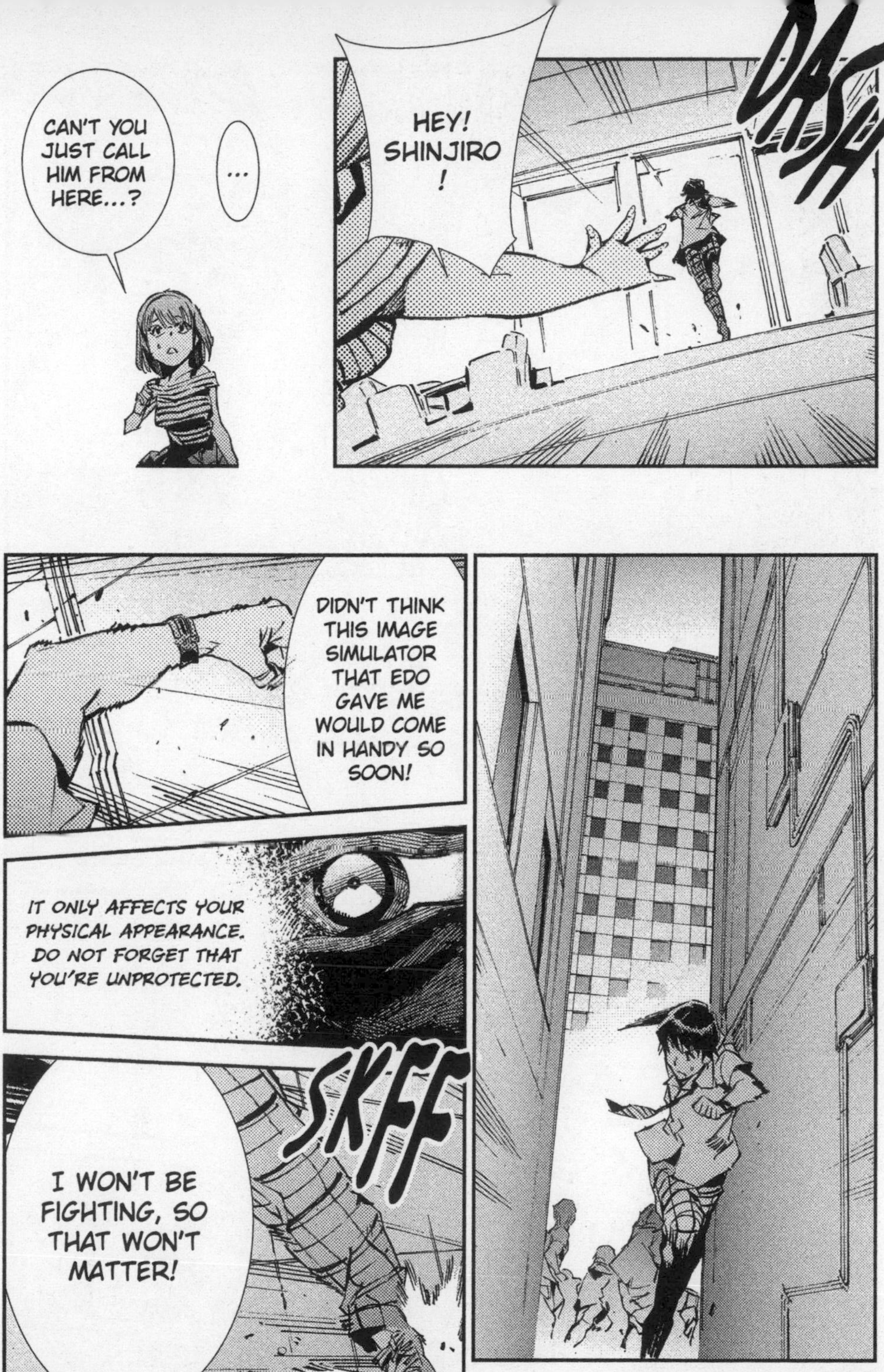
DASH
HEY! SHINJIRO!
...
CAN'T YOU JUST CALL HIM FROM HERE...?
DIDN'T THINK THIS IMAGE SIMULATOR THAT EDO GAVE ME WOULD COME IN HANDY SO SOON!
IT ONLY AFFECTS YOUR PHYSICAL APPEARANCE. DO NOT FORGET THAT YOU'RE UNPROTECTED.
SKFF
I WON'T BE FIGHTING, SO THAT WON'T MATTER!

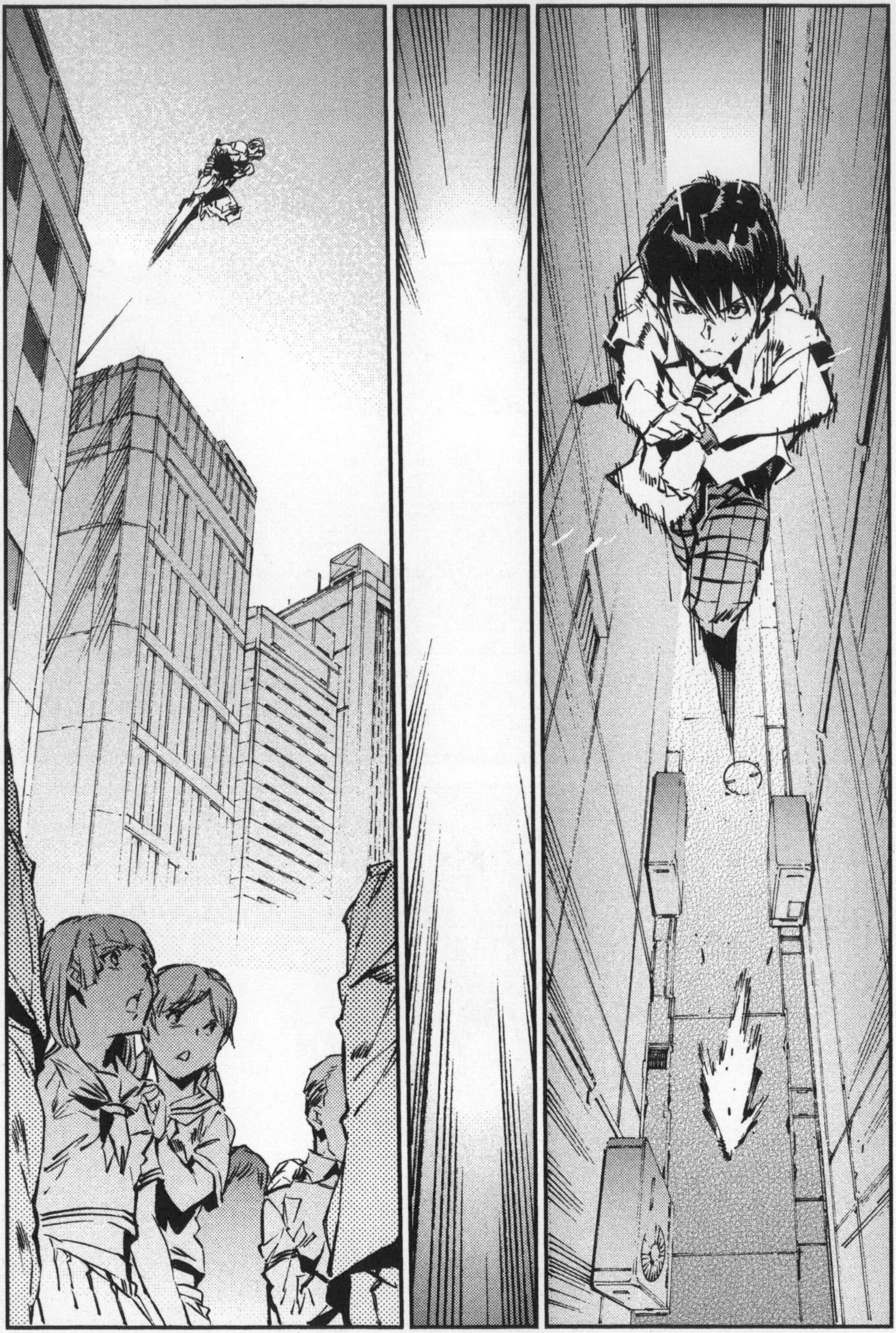

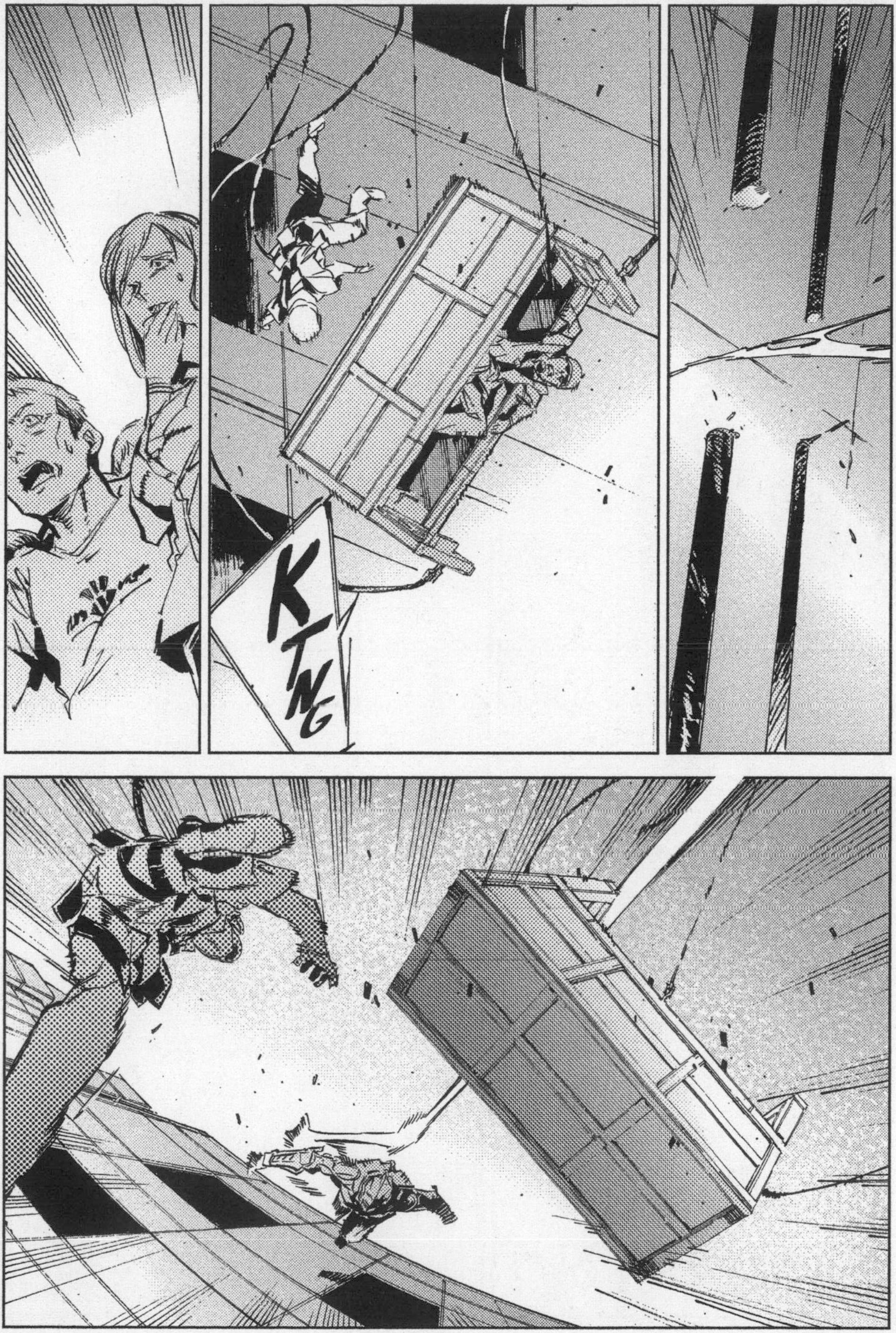
KTNG

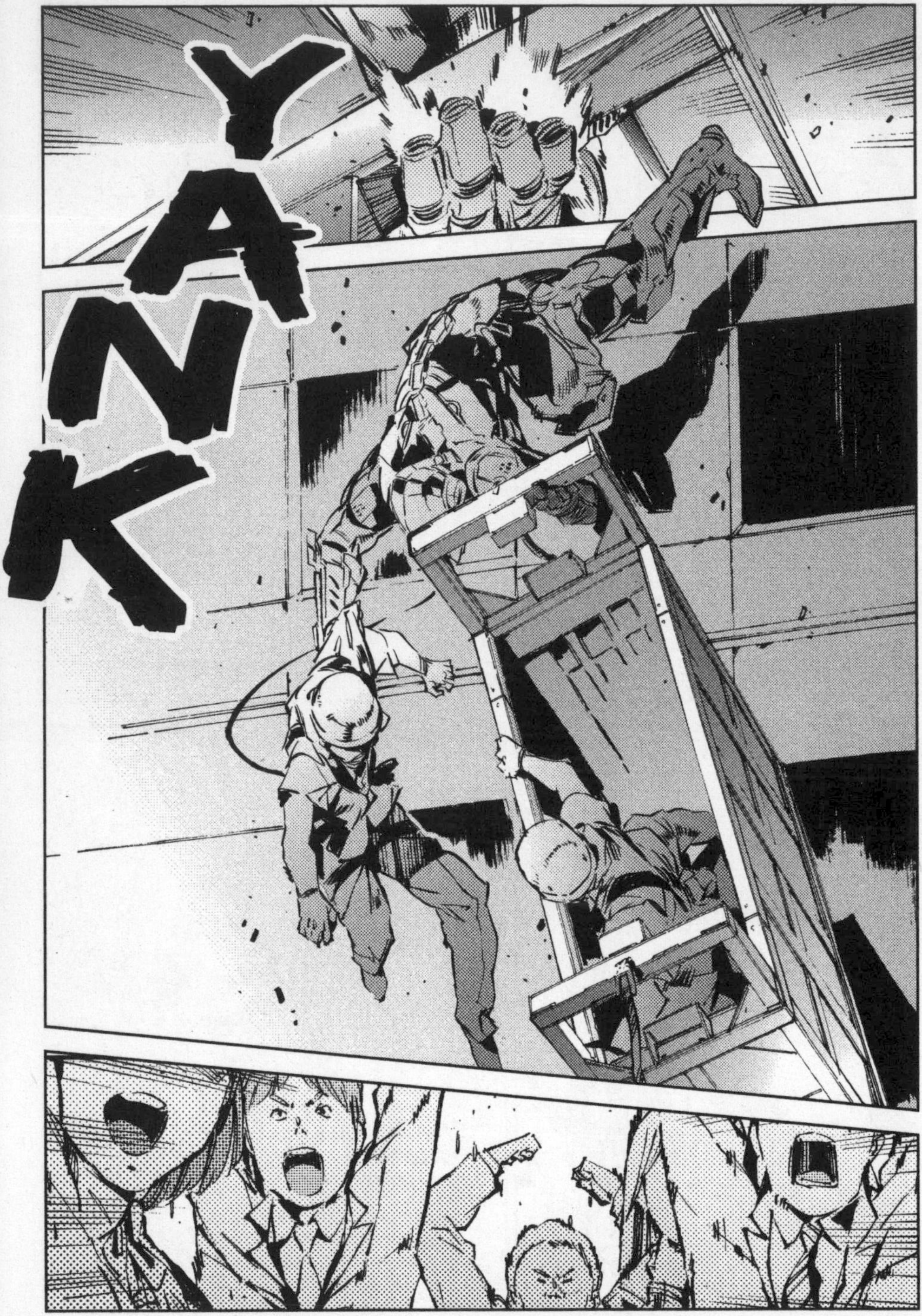
YANK

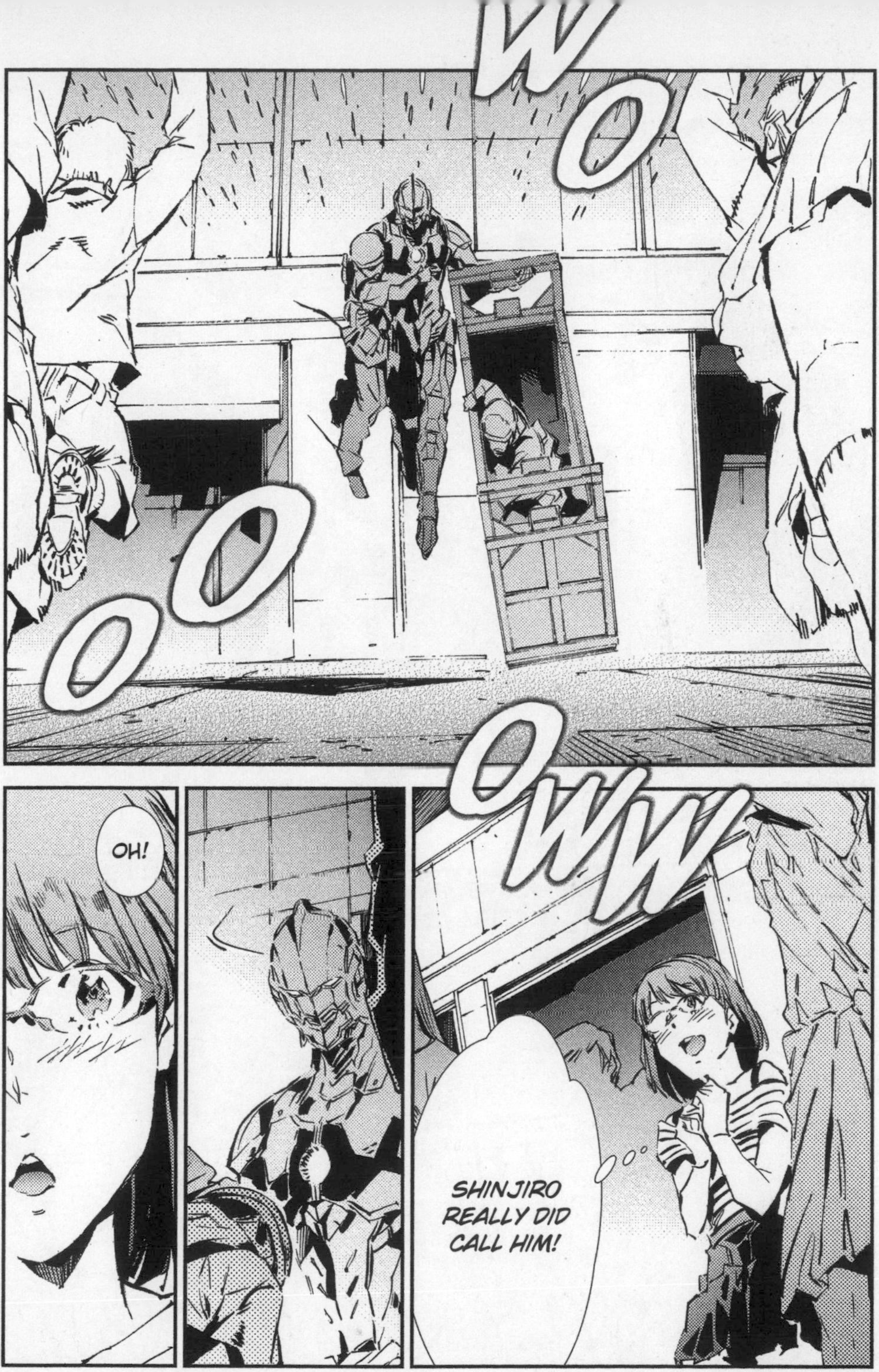
WOOOOWW
SHINJIRO REALLY DID CALL HIM!
OH!

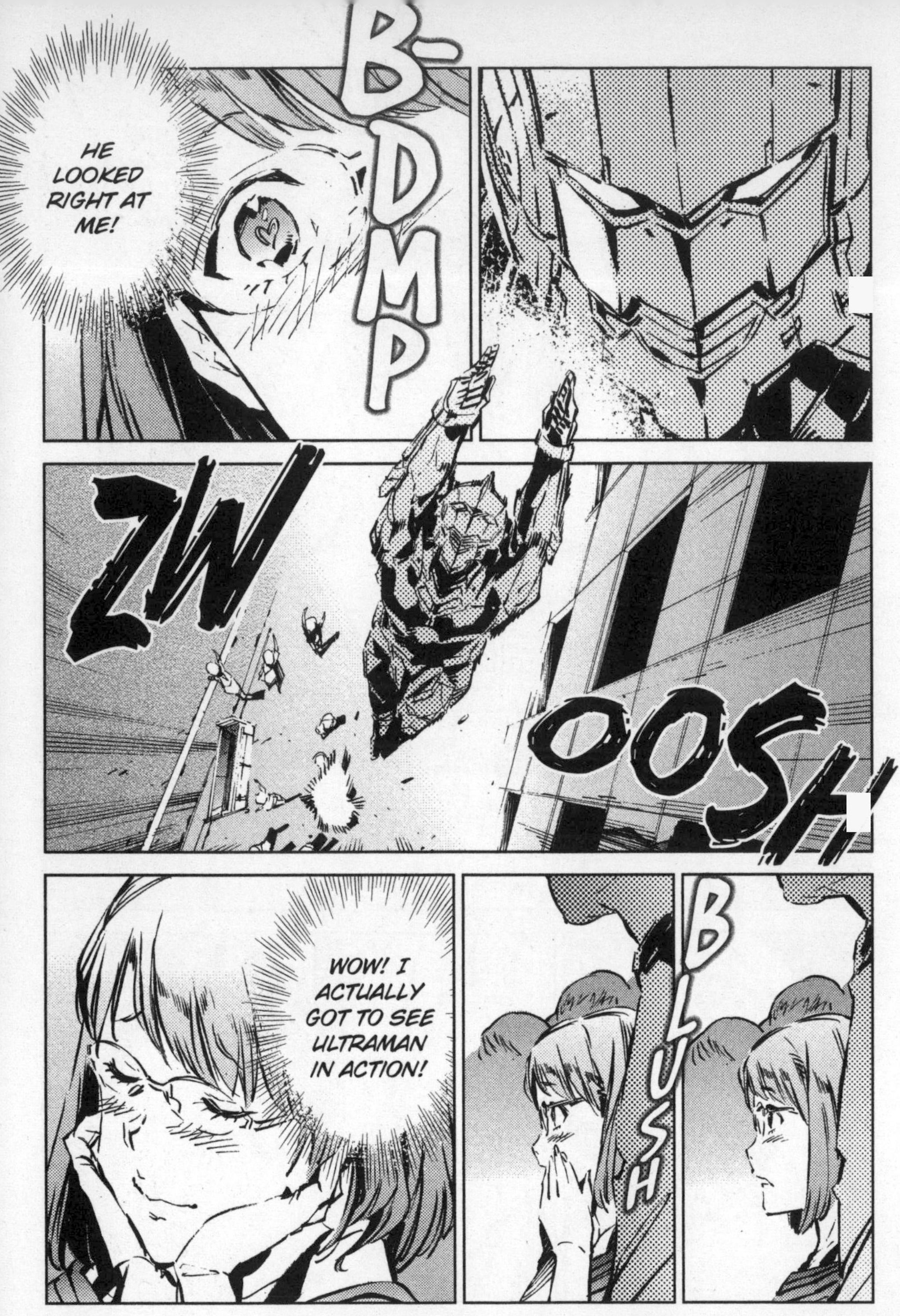
B-DMP
HE LOOKED RIGHT AT ME!
ZWOOSH
BLUSH
WOW! I ACTUALLY GOT TO SEE ULTRAMAN IN ACTION!

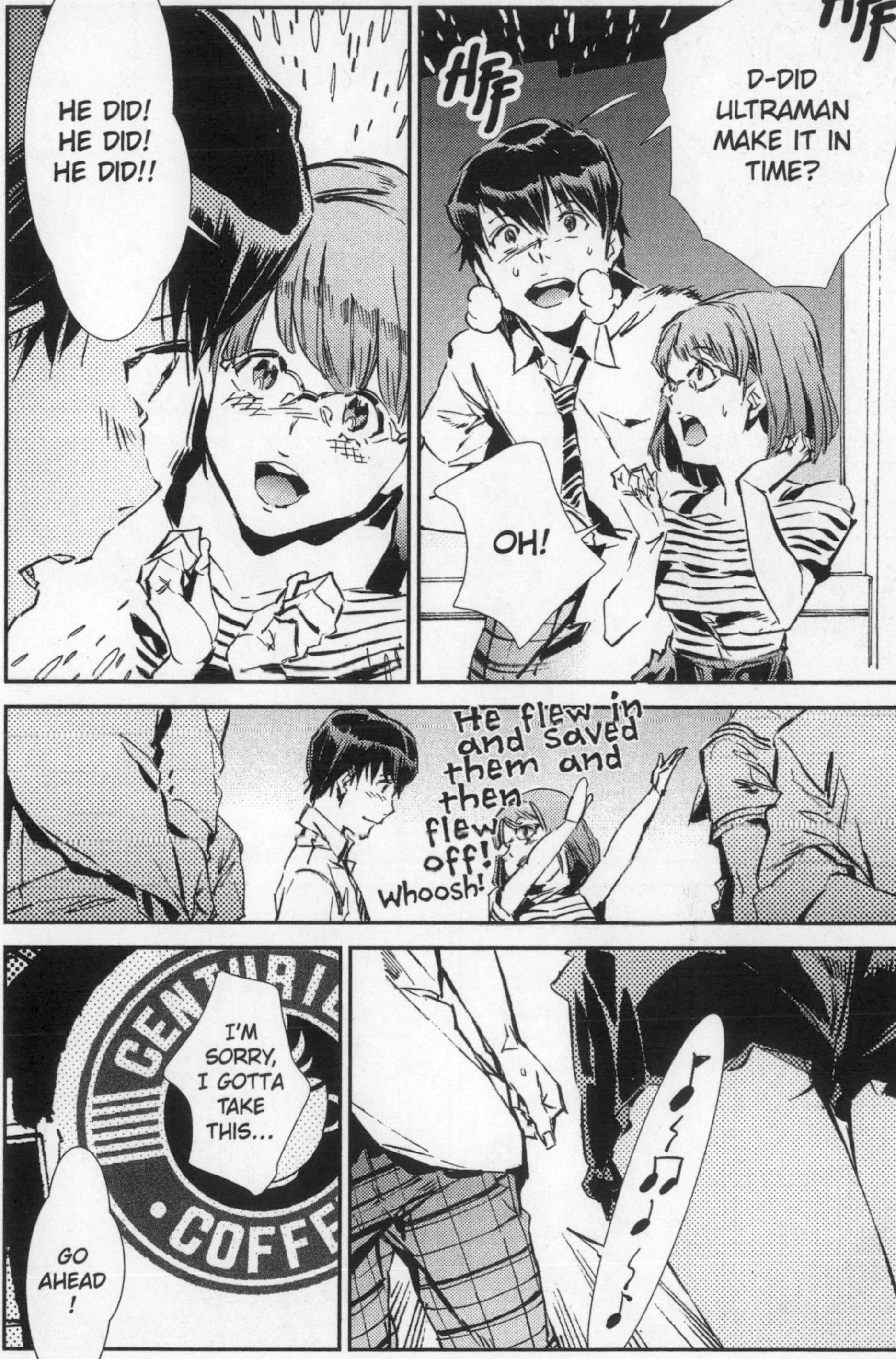
HFF
D-DID ULTRAMAN MAKE IT IN TIME?
HFF
OH!
HE DID! HE DID! HE DID!!
He flew in and saved them and then flew off!
Whoosh!
CENTURI
COFF
I'M SORRY, I GOTTA TAKE THIS...
GO AHEAD!

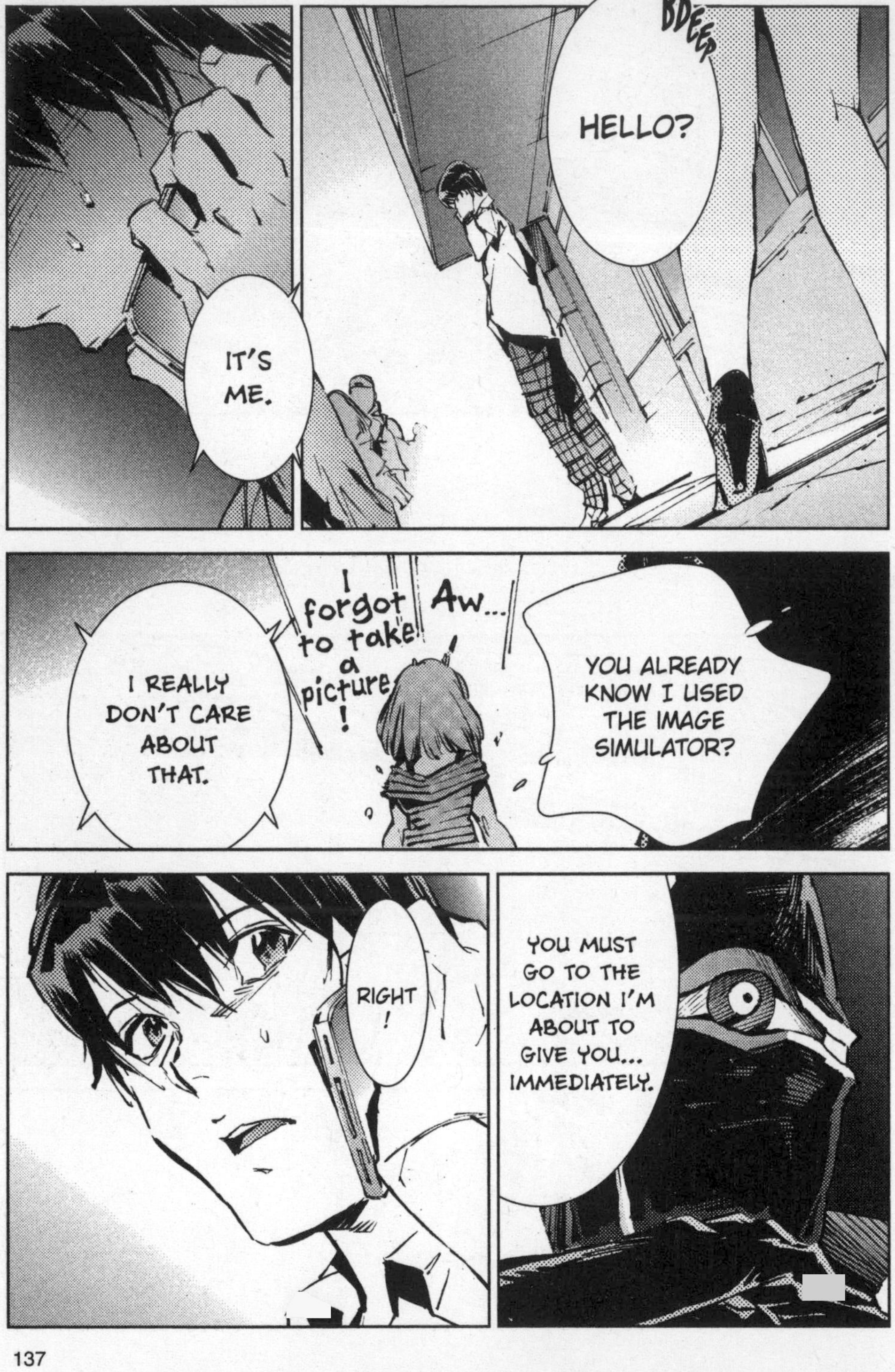
BDEEP
HELLO?
IT'S ME.
YOU ALREADY KNOW I USED THE IMAGE SIMULATOR?
Aw...
I forgot to take a picture!
I REALLY DON'T CARE ABOUT THAT.
YOU MUST GO TO THE LOCATION I'M ABOUT TO GIVE YOU... IMMEDIATELY.
RIGHT!

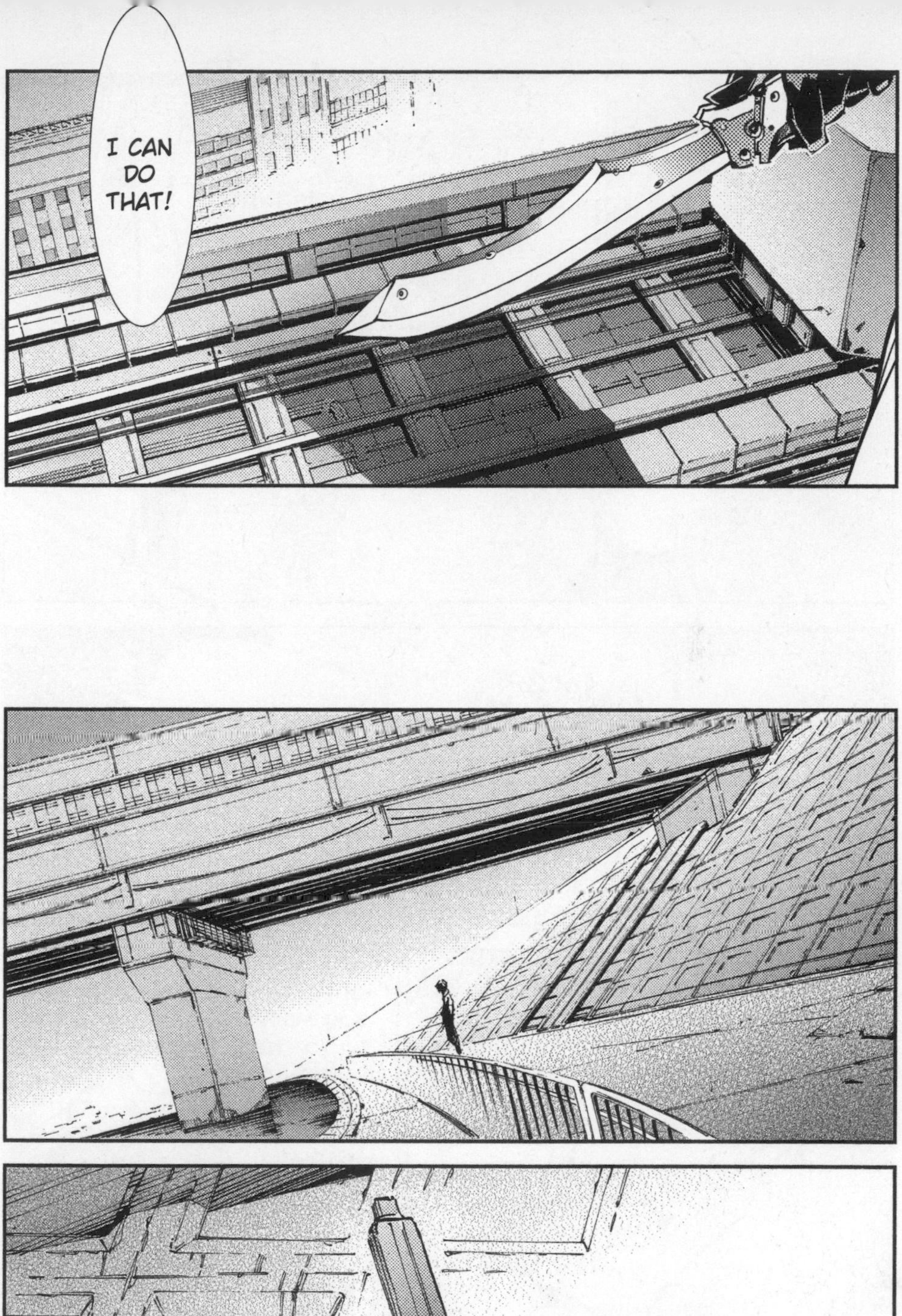
I CAN DO THAT!

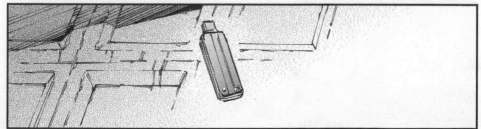

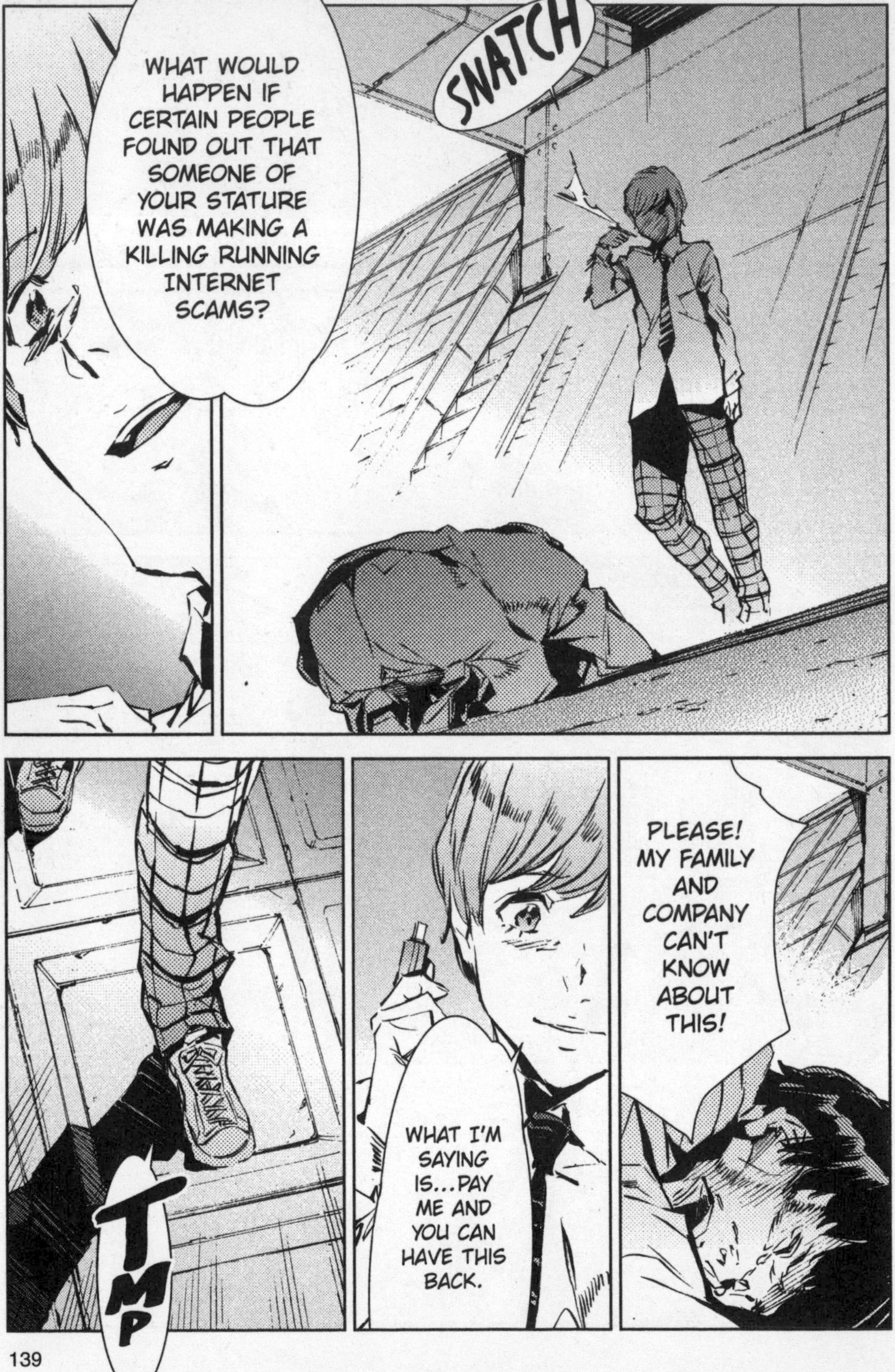
SNATCH
WHAT WOULD HAPPEN IF CERTAIN PEOPLE FOUND OUT THAT SOMEONE OF YOUR STATURE WAS MAKING A KILLING RUNNING INTERNET SCAMS?
PLEASE! MY FAMILY AND COMPANY CAN'T KNOW ABOUT THIS!
WHAT I'M SAYING IS...PAY ME AND YOU CAN HAVE THIS BACK.
TMP

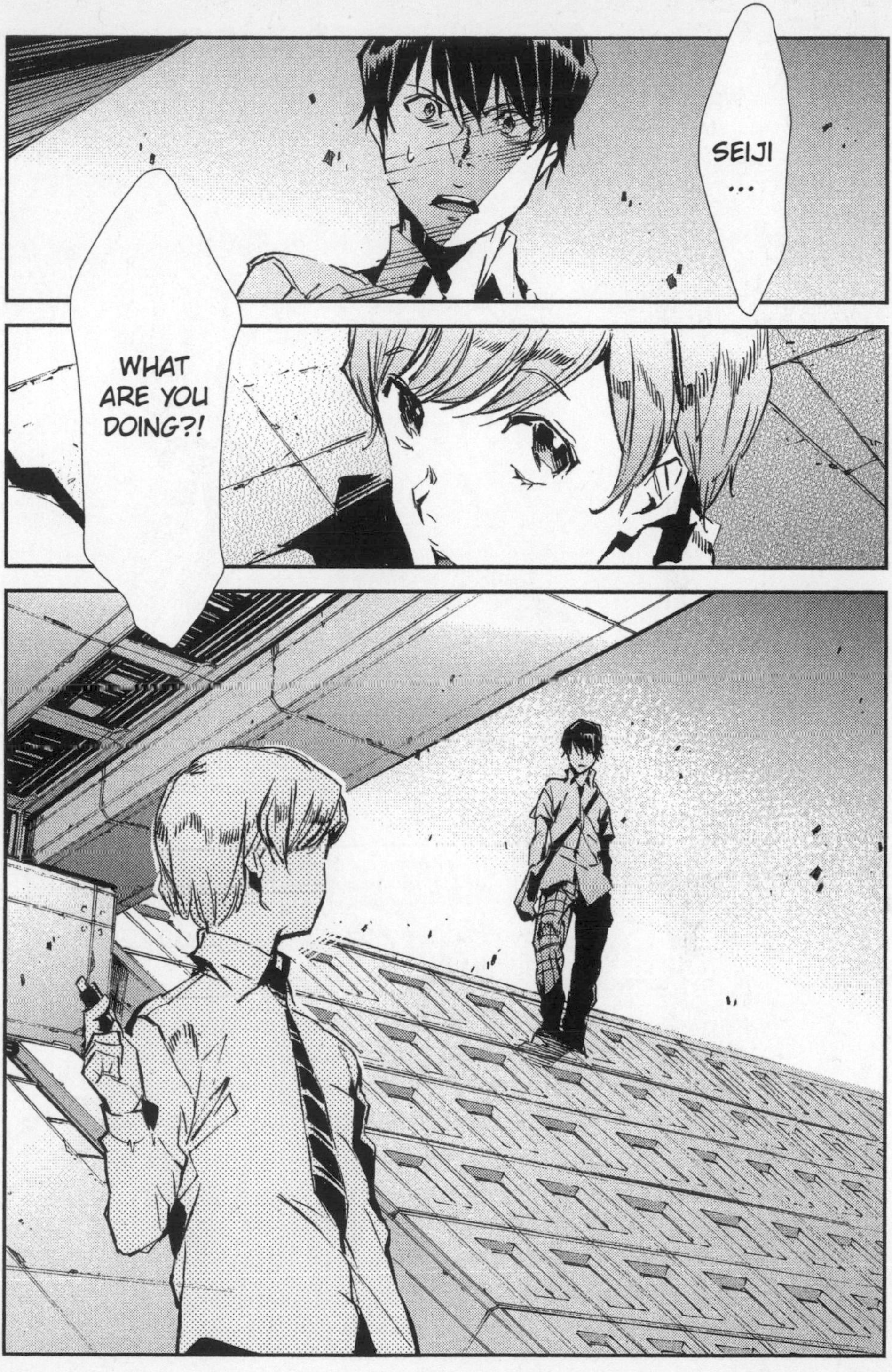
SEIJI ...
WHAT ARE YOU DOING?!

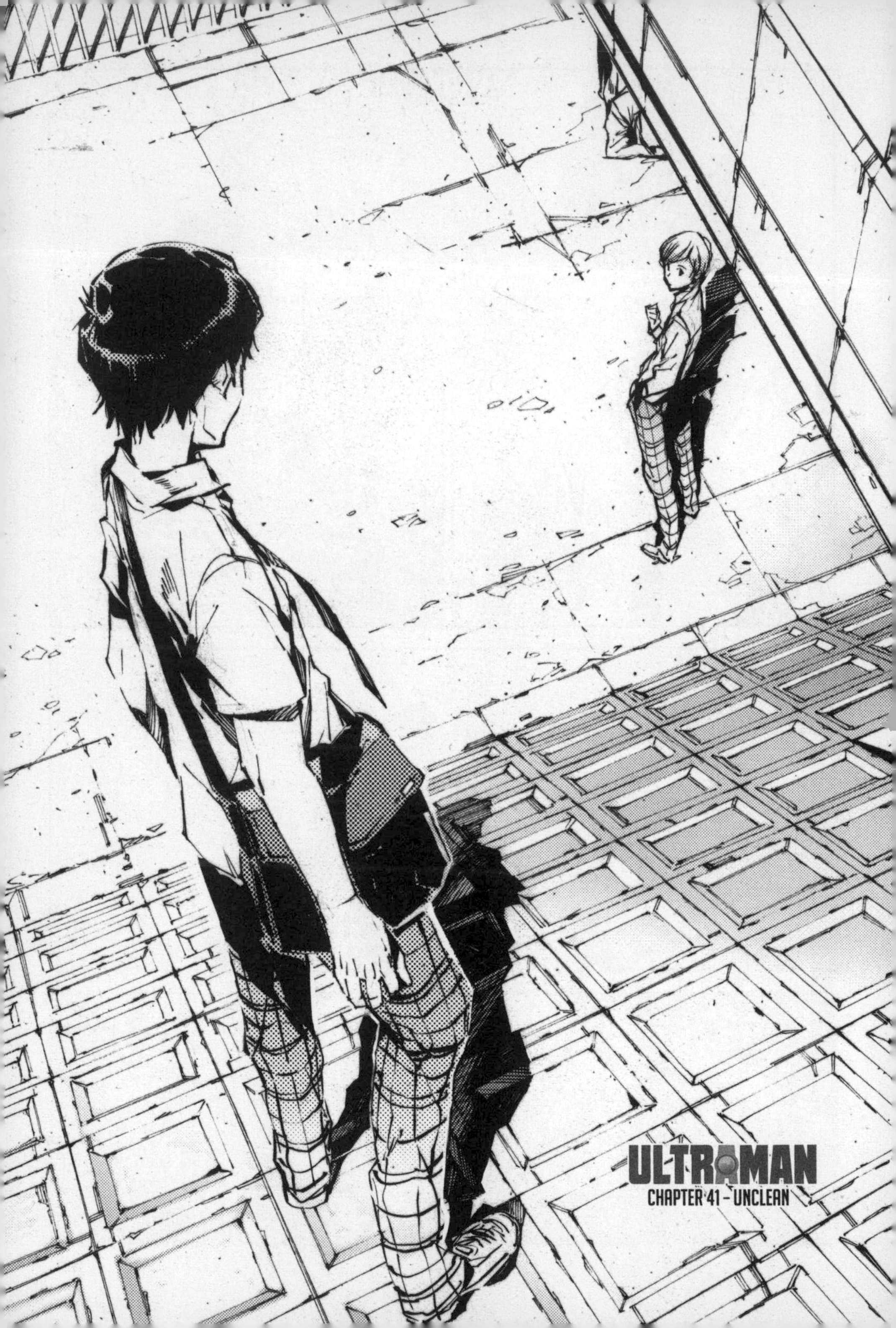
ULTRAMAN
CHAPTER 41 – UNCLEAN

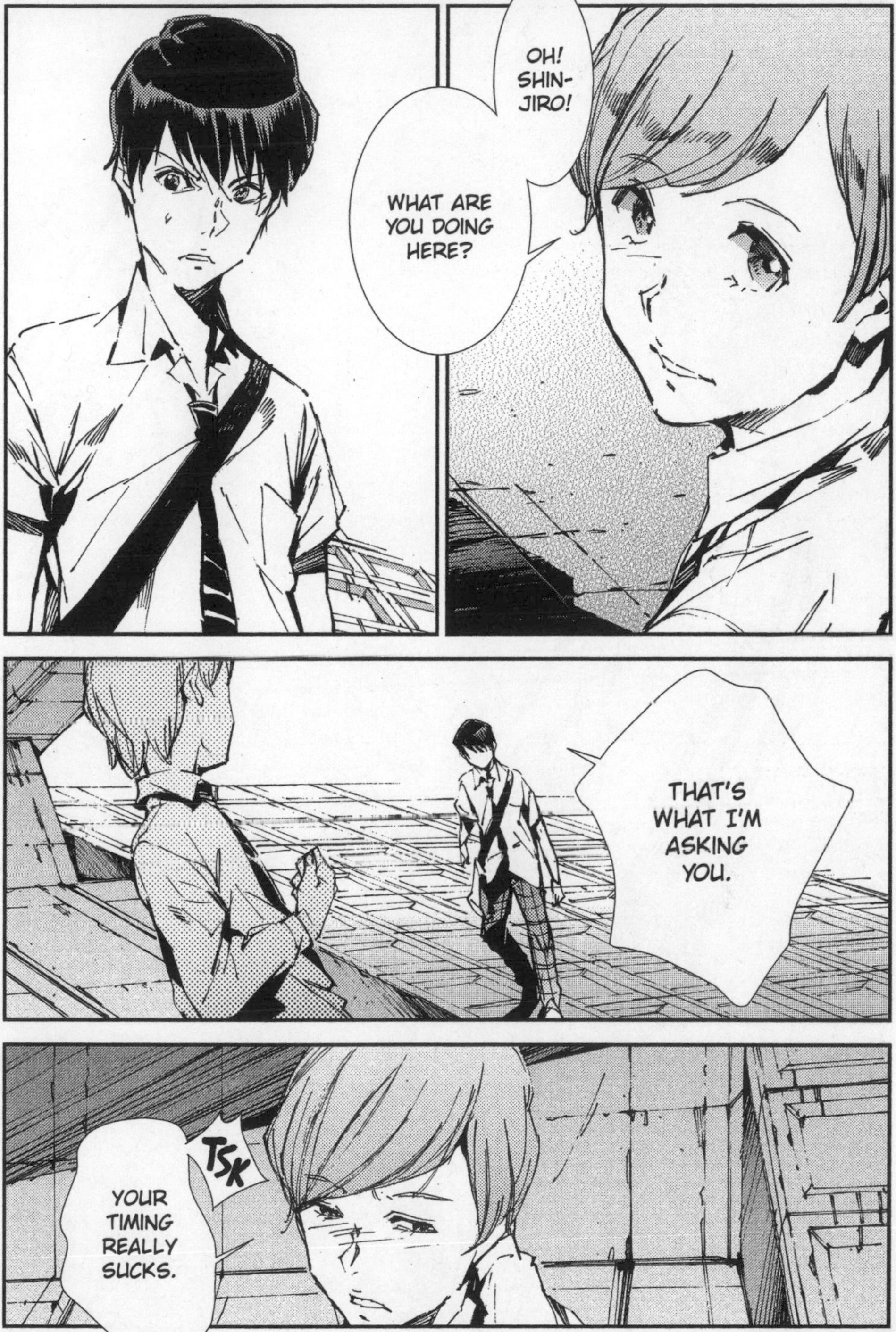
OH! SHIN-JIRO!
WHAT ARE YOU DOING HERE?
THAT'S WHAT I'M ASKING YOU.
TSK
YOUR TIMING REALLY SUCKS.

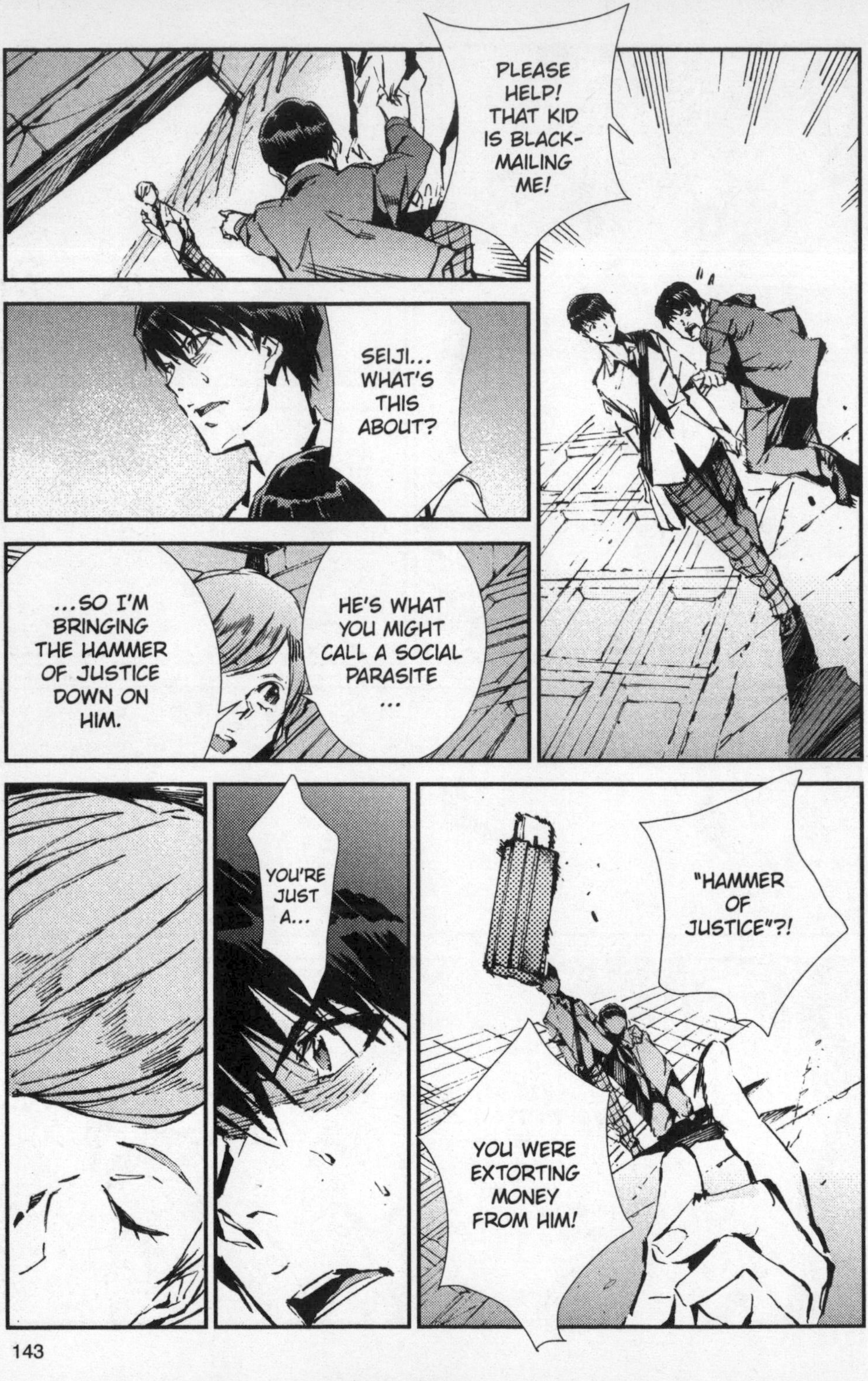
PLEASE HELP! THAT KID IS BLACK-MAILING ME!
SEIJI... WHAT'S THIS ABOUT?
HE'S WHAT YOU MIGHT CALL A SOCIAL PARASITE ...
...SO I'M BRINGING THE HAMMER OF JUSTICE DOWN ON HIM.
"HAMMER OF JUSTICE"?!
YOU WERE EXTORTING MONEY FROM HIM!
YOU'RE JUST A...

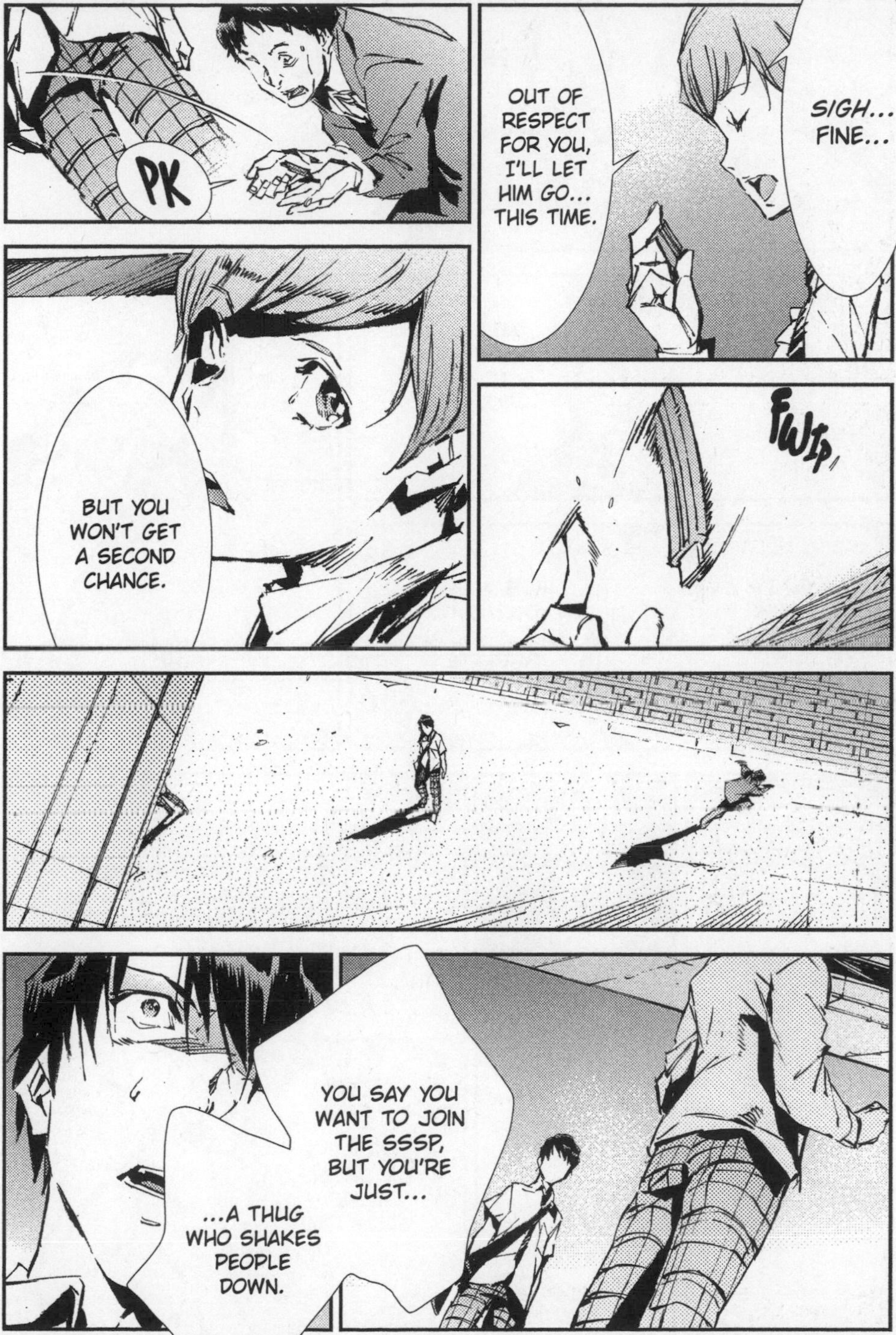
SIGH... FINE...
OUT OF RESPECT FOR YOU, I'LL LET HIM GO... THIS TIME.
PK
BUT YOU WON'T GET A SECOND CHANCE.
FWIP
YOU SAY YOU WANT TO JOIN THE SSSP, BUT YOU'RE JUST...
...A THUG WHO SHAKES PEOPLE DOWN.

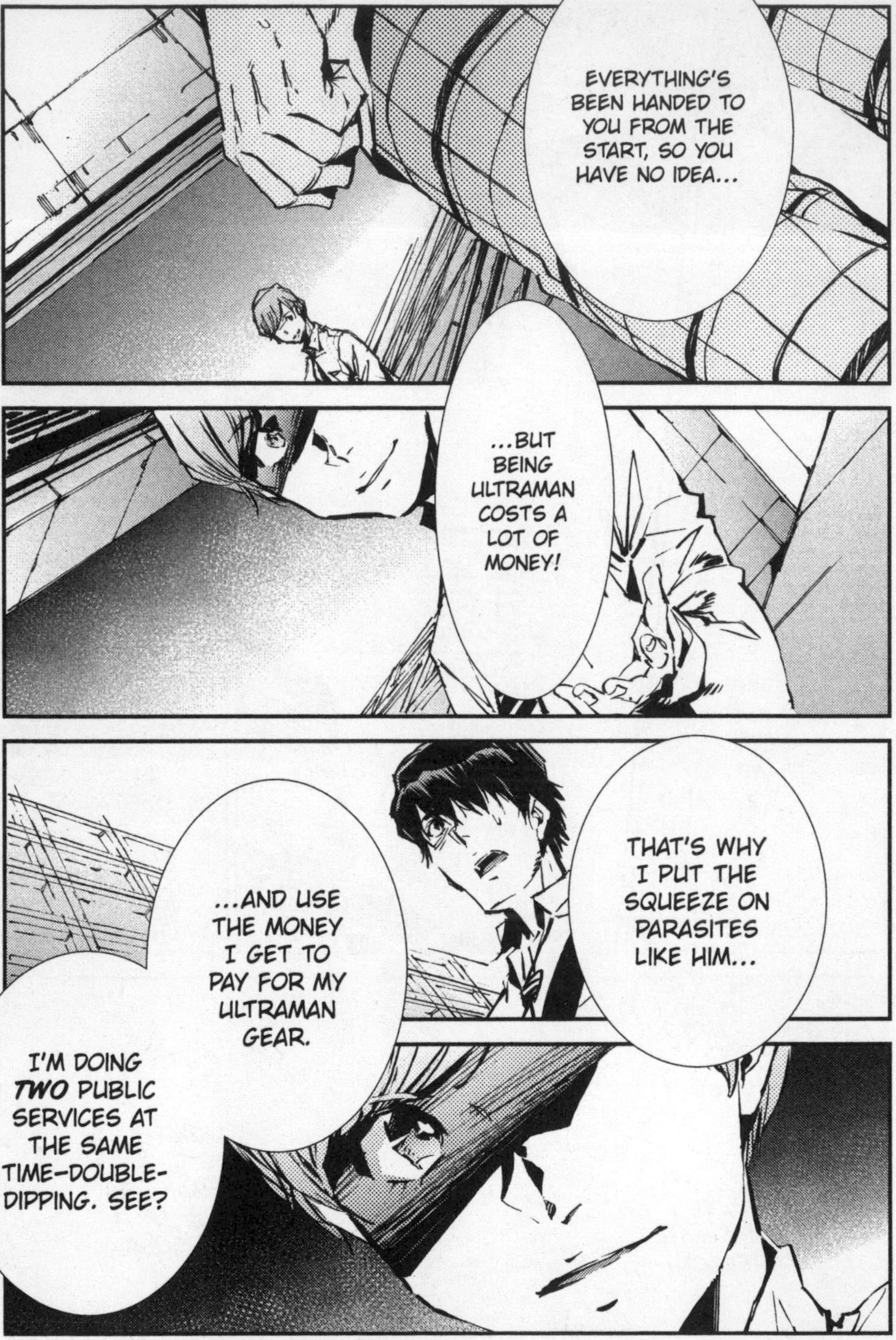
EVERYTHING'S BEEN HANDED TO YOU FROM THE START, SO YOU HAVE NO IDEA...
...BUT BEING ULTRAMAN COSTS A LOT OF MONEY!
THAT'S WHY I PUT THE SQUEEZE ON PARASITES LIKE HIM...
...AND USE THE MONEY I GET TO PAY FOR MY ULTRAMAN GEAR.
I'M DOING ***TWO*** PUBLIC SERVICES AT THE SAME TIME—DOUBLE-DIPPING. SEE?

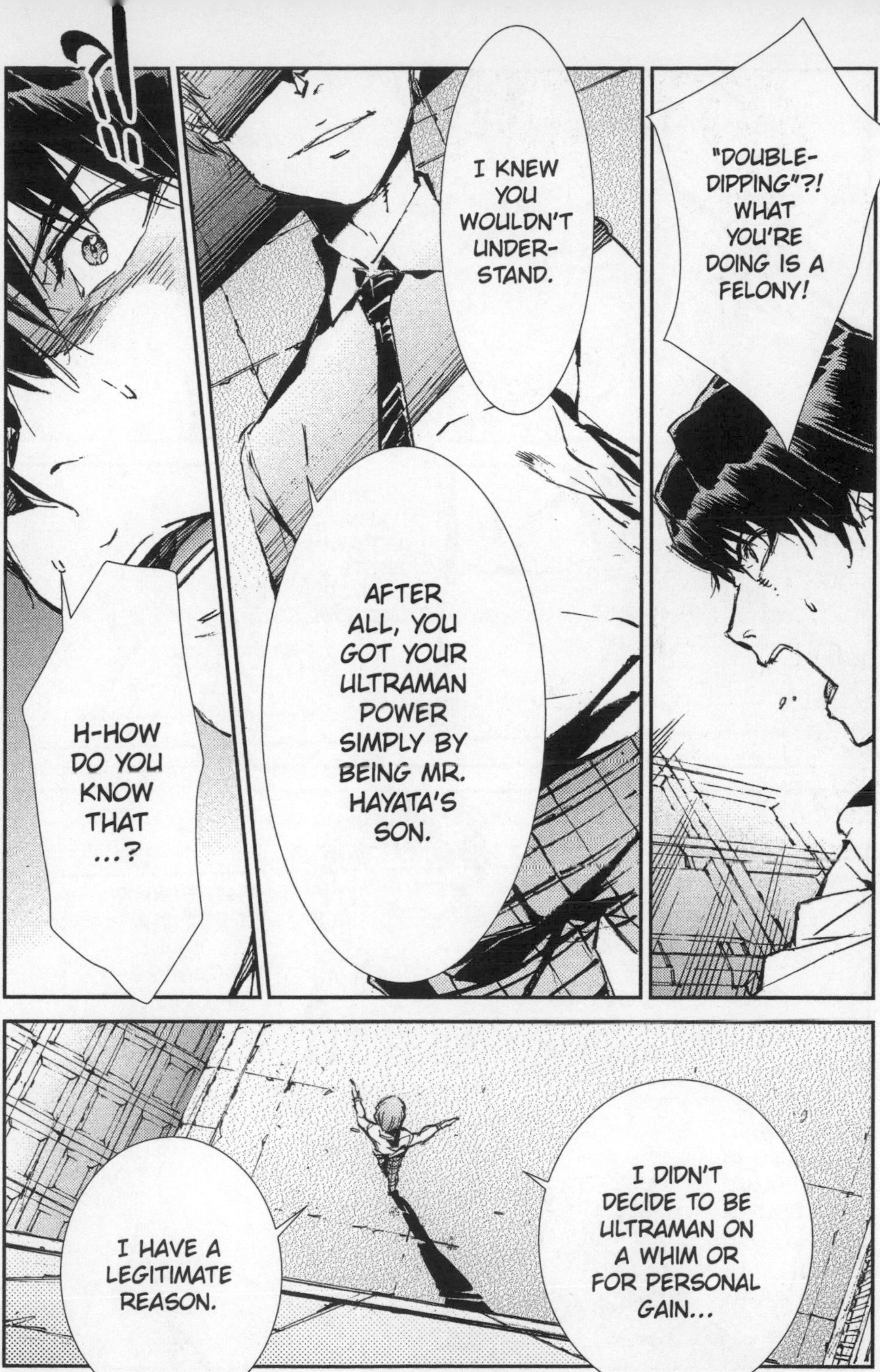
"DOUBLE-DIPPING"?! WHAT YOU'RE DOING IS A FELONY!
I KNEW YOU WOULDN'T UNDER-STAND.
AFTER ALL, YOU GOT YOUR ULTRAMAN POWER SIMPLY BY BEING MR. HAYATA'S SON.
H-HOW DO YOU KNOW THAT ...?
I DIDN'T DECIDE TO BE ULTRAMAN ON A WHIM OR FOR PERSONAL GAIN...
I HAVE A LEGITIMATE REASON.

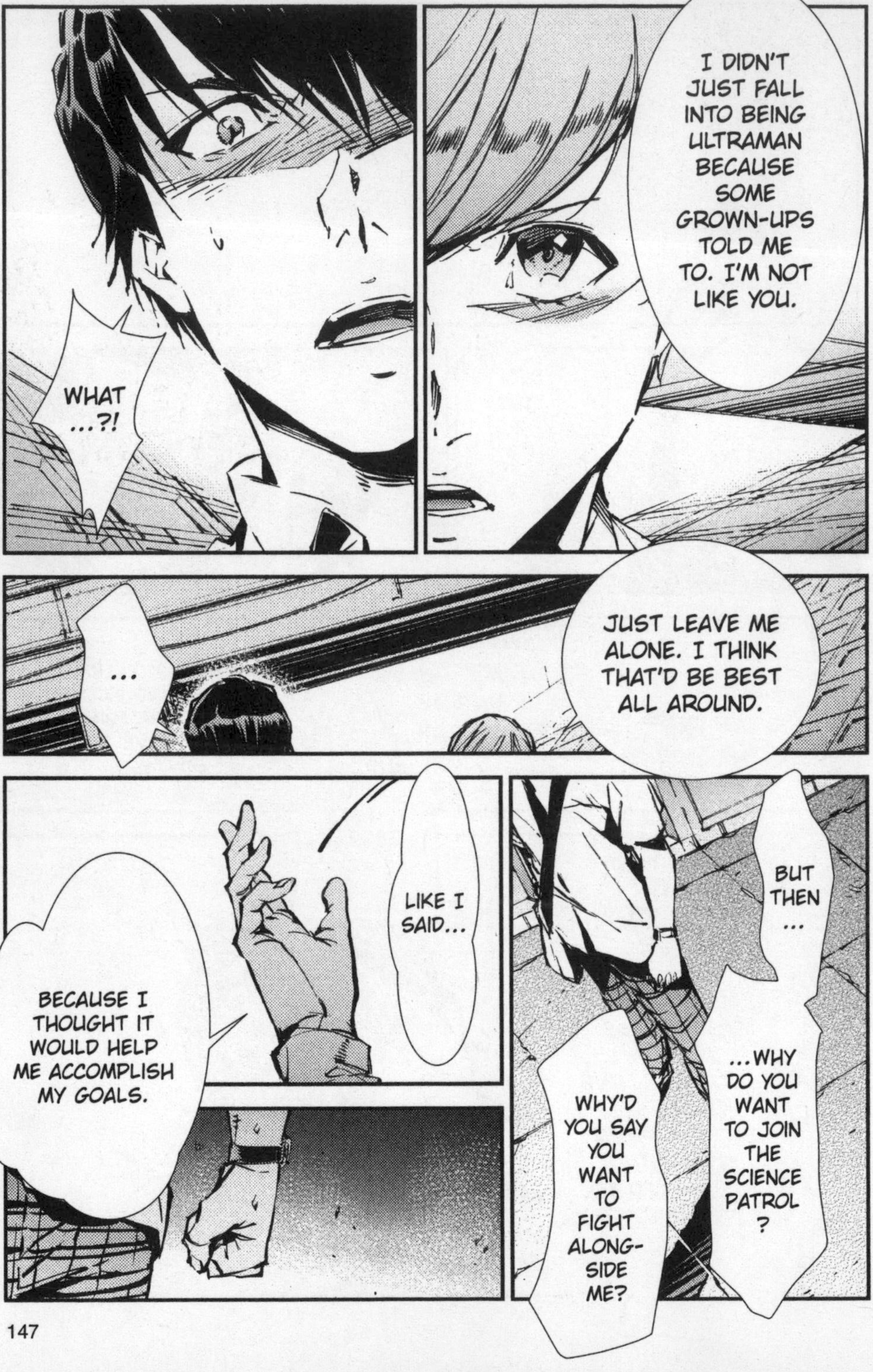
I DIDN'T JUST FALL INTO BEING ULTRAMAN BECAUSE SOME GROWN-UPS TOLD ME TO. I'M NOT LIKE YOU.
WHAT ...?!
JUST LEAVE ME ALONE. I THINK THAT'D BE BEST ALL AROUND.
...
BUT THEN ...
...WHY DO YOU WANT TO JOIN THE SCIENCE PATROL ?
WHY'D YOU SAY YOU WANT TO FIGHT ALONG-SIDE ME?
LIKE I SAID...
BECAUSE I THOUGHT IT WOULD HELP ME ACCOMPLISH MY GOALS.

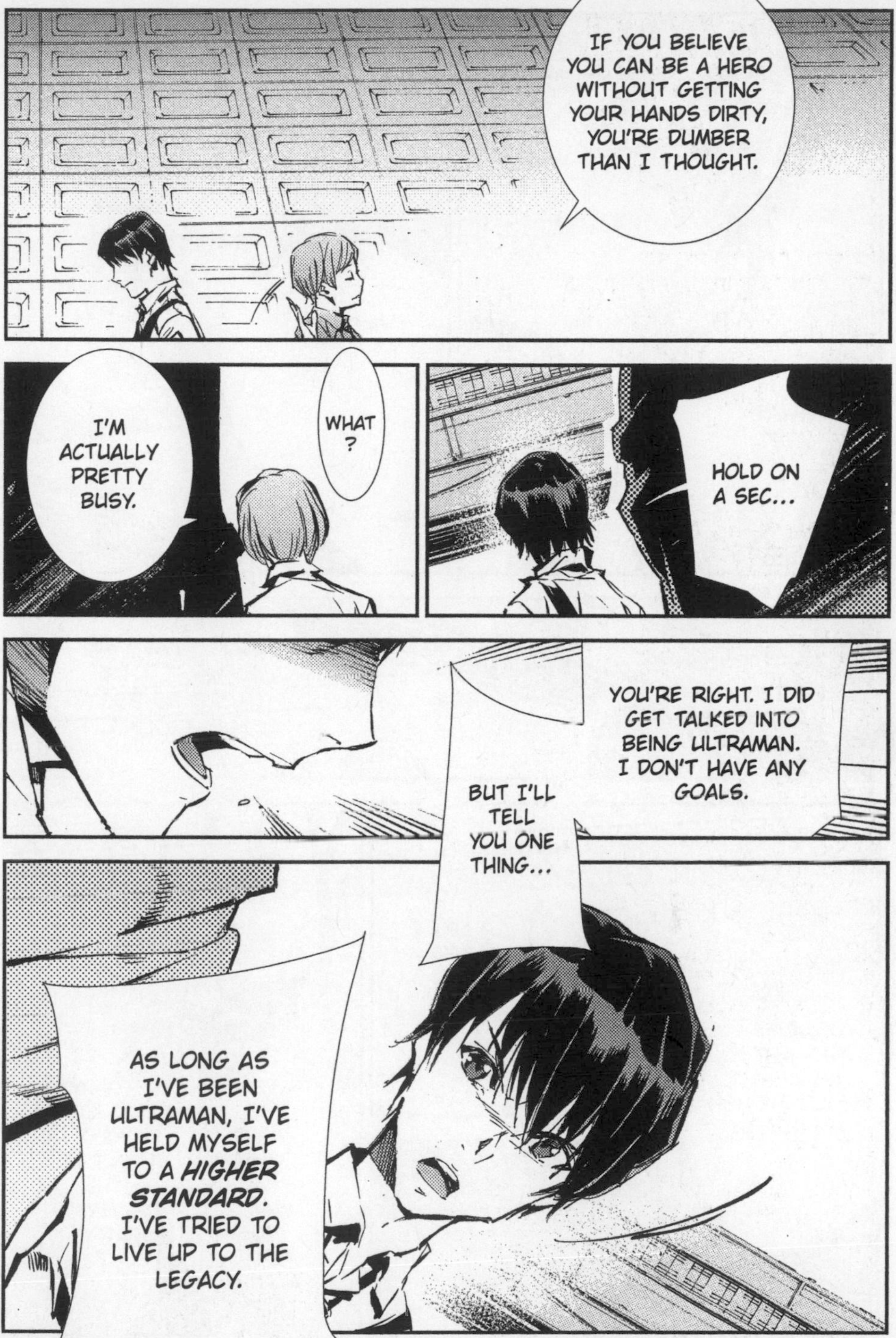
IF YOU BELIEVE YOU CAN BE A HERO WITHOUT GETTING YOUR HANDS DIRTY, YOU'RE DUMBER THAN I THOUGHT.
HOLD ON A SEC...
WHAT?
I'M ACTUALLY PRETTY BUSY.
YOU'RE RIGHT. I DID GET TALKED INTO BEING ULTRAMAN. I DON'T HAVE ANY GOALS.
BUT I'LL TELL YOU ONE THING...
AS LONG AS I'VE BEEN ULTRAMAN, I'VE HELD MYSELF TO A HIGHER STANDARD. I'VE TRIED TO LIVE UP TO THE LEGACY.

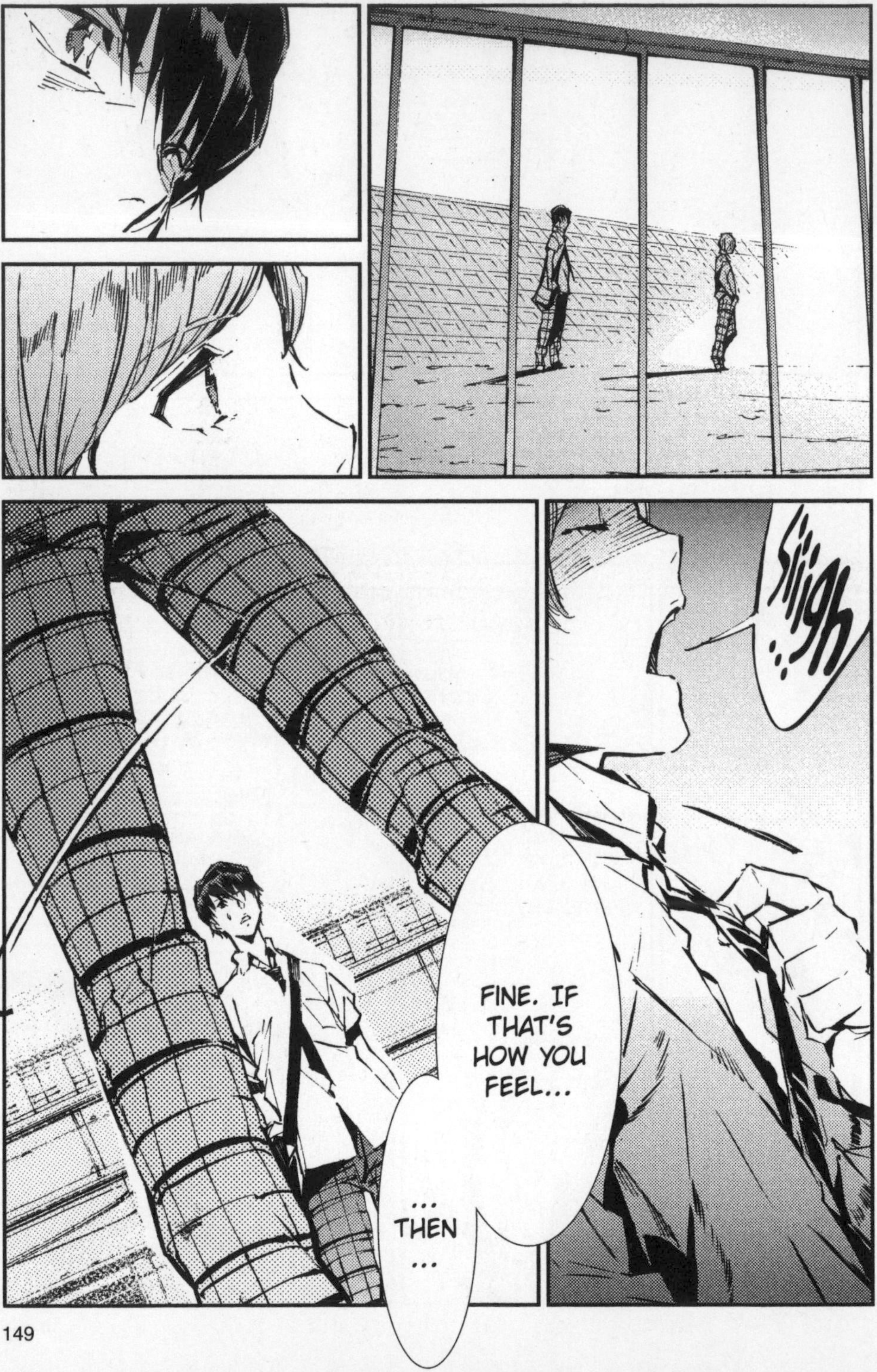
Siigh...
FINE. IF THAT'S HOW YOU FEEL...
...THEN...

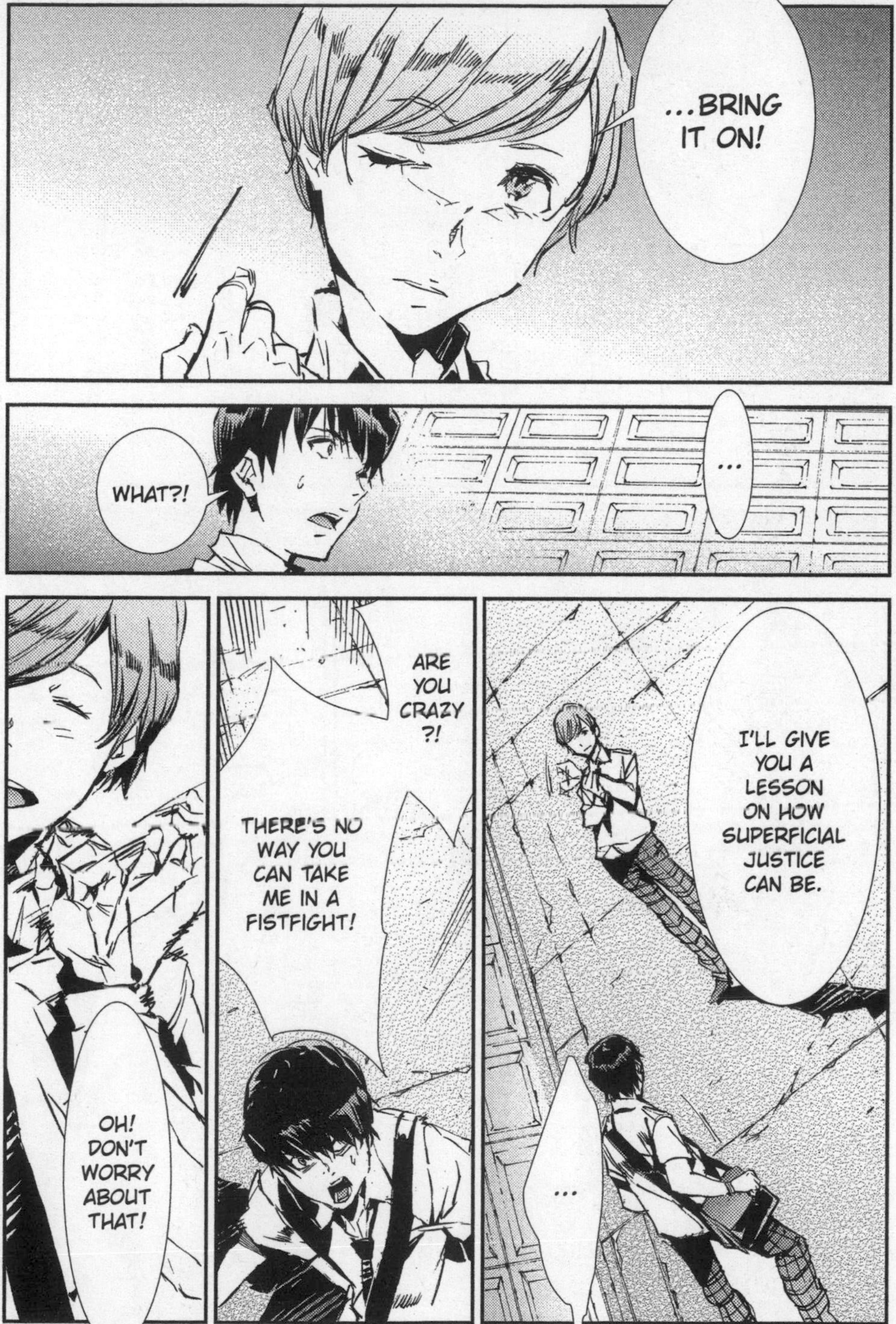
...BRING IT ON!
...
WHAT?!
I'LL GIVE YOU A LESSON ON HOW SUPERFICIAL JUSTICE CAN BE.
...
ARE YOU CRAZY?!
THERE'S NO WAY YOU CAN TAKE ME IN A FISTFIGHT!
OH! DON'T WORRY ABOUT THAT!

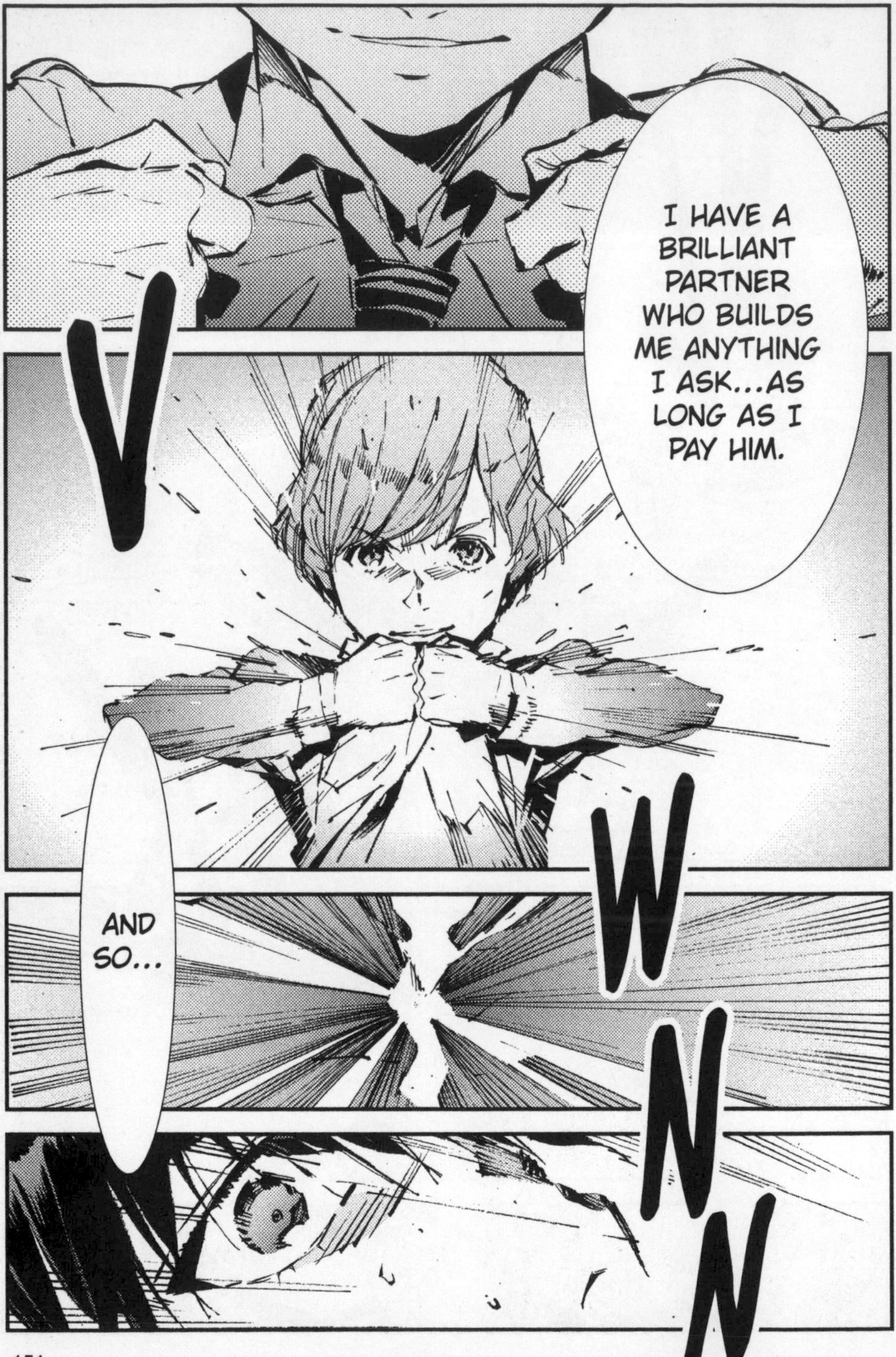
I HAVE A BRILLIANT PARTNER WHO BUILDS ME ANYTHING I ASK...AS LONG AS I PAY HIM.
V
AND SO...
WNNN

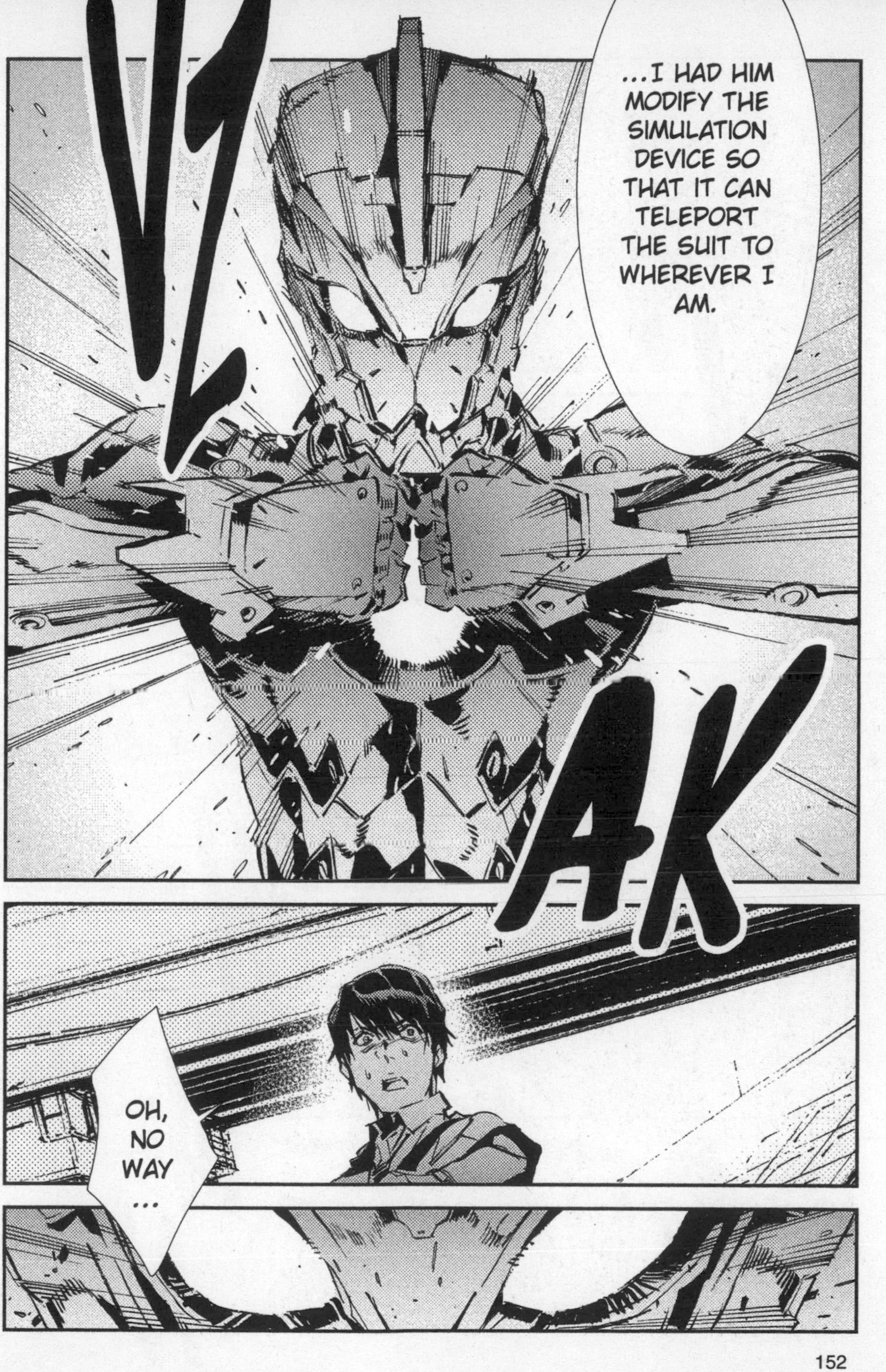
...I HAD HIM MODIFY THE SIMULATION DEVICE SO THAT IT CAN TELEPORT THE SUIT TO WHEREVER I AM.
AK
OH, NO WAY ...

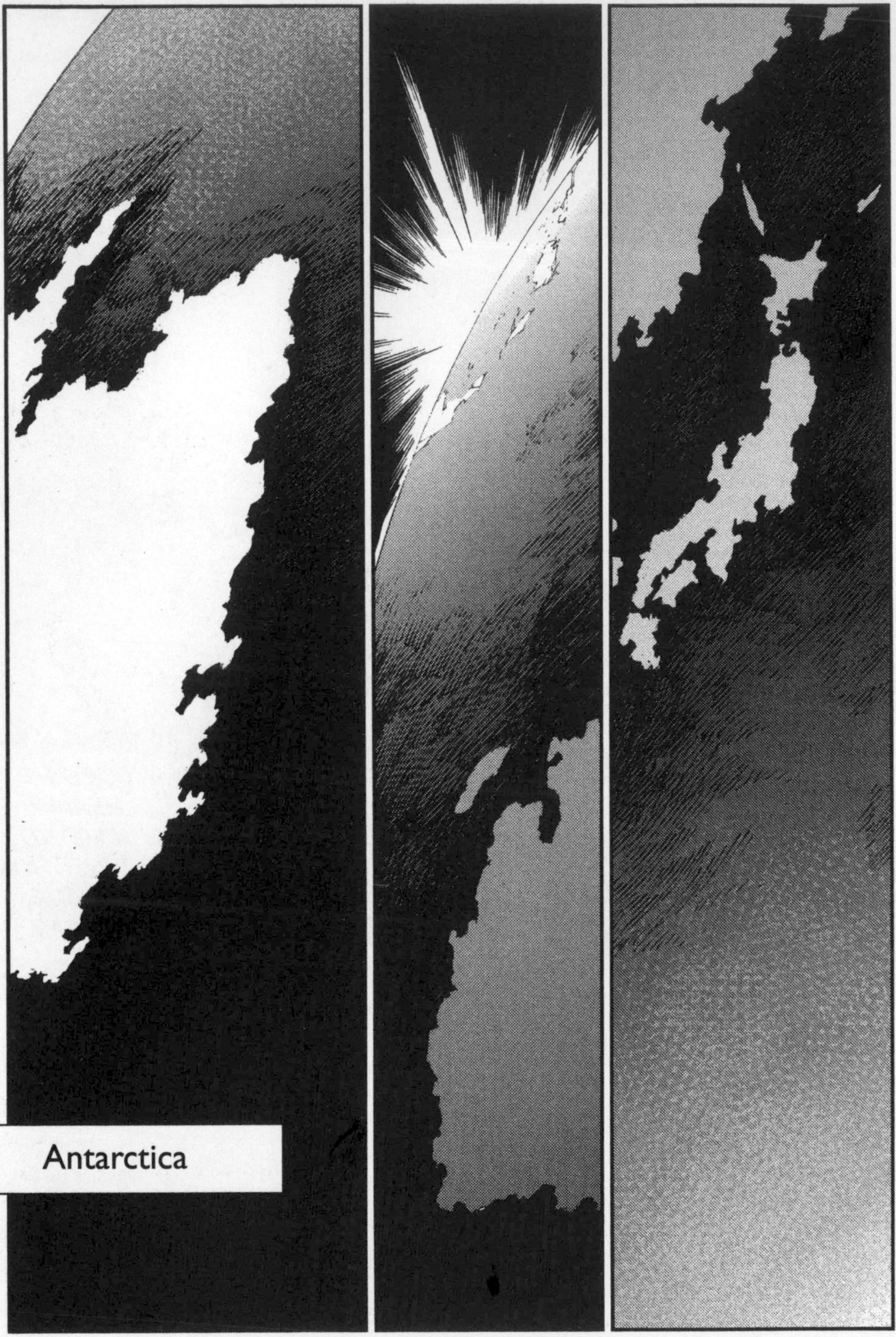
Antarctica

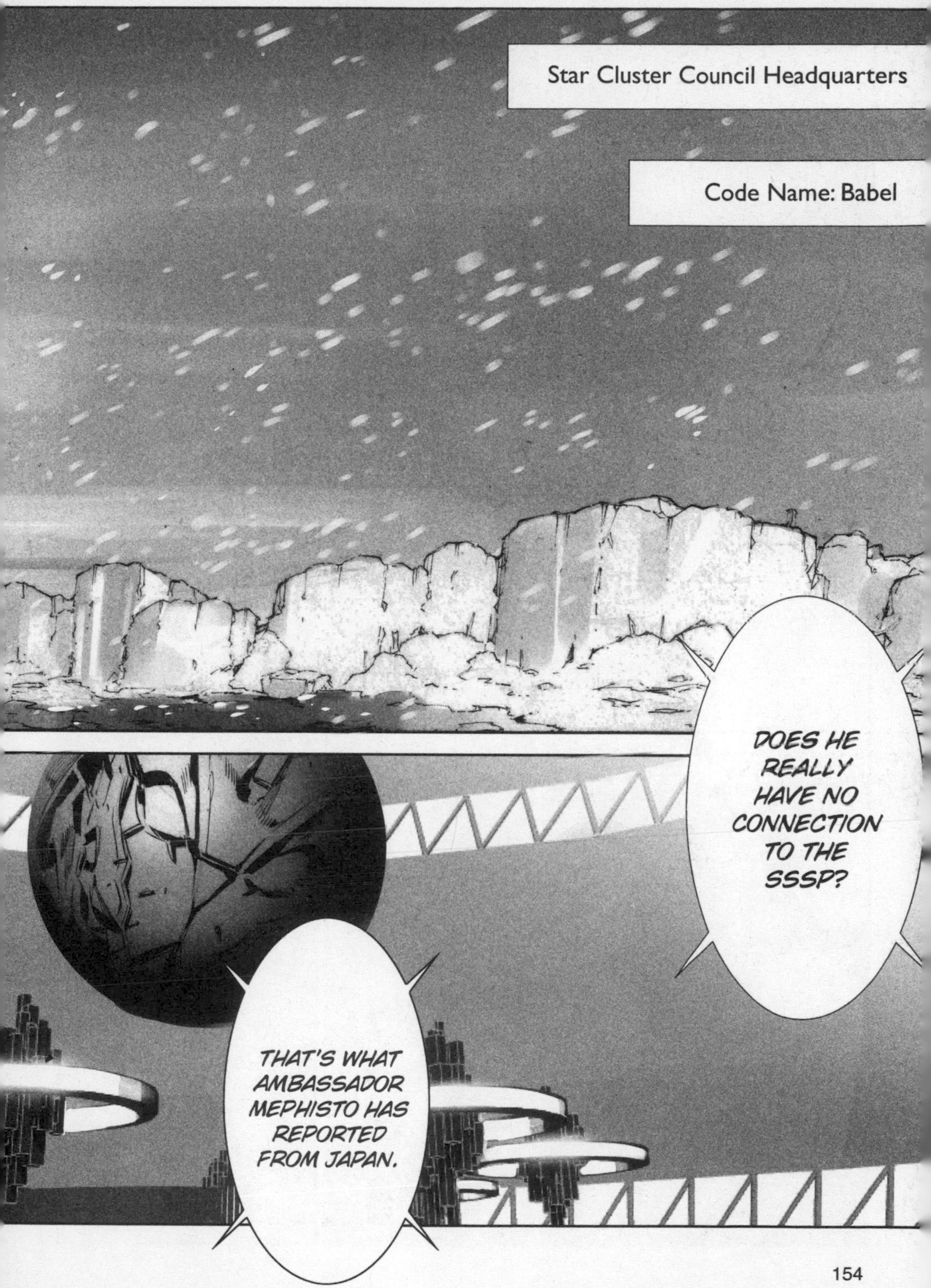
Star Cluster Council Headquarters
Code Name: Babel
DOES HE REALLY HAVE NO CONNECTION TO THE SSSP?
THAT'S WHAT AMBASSADOR MEPHISTO HAS REPORTED FROM JAPAN.

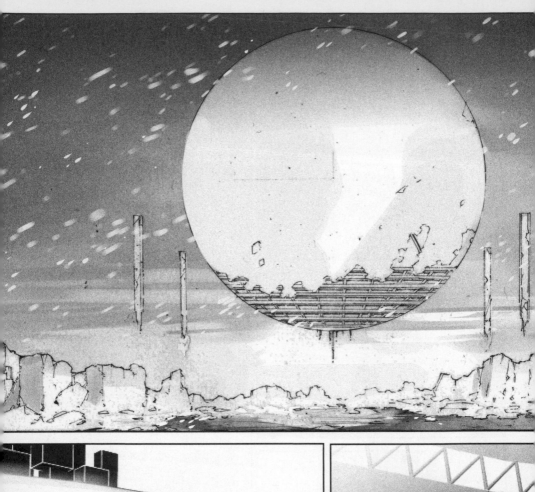

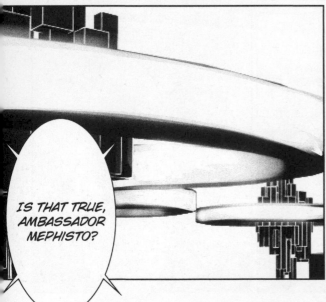

IS THAT TRUE,
AMBASSADOR
MEPHISTO?

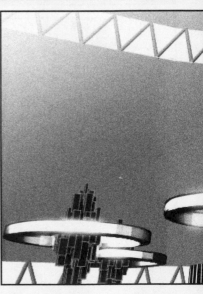

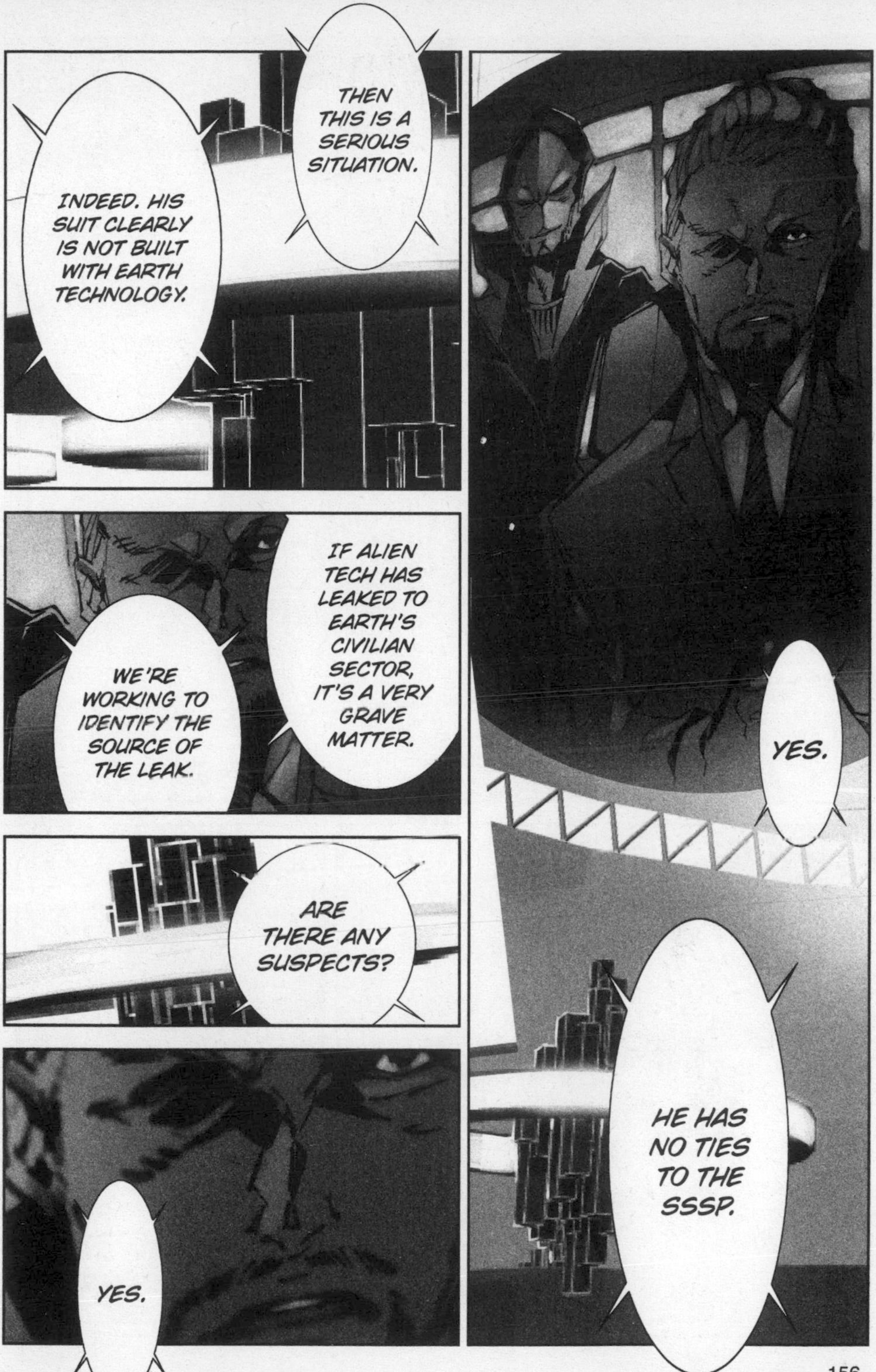
YES.
HE HAS NO TIES TO THE SSSP.
THEN THIS IS A SERIOUS SITUATION.
INDEED. HIS SUIT CLEARLY IS NOT BUILT WITH EARTH TECHNOLOGY.
IF ALIEN TECH HAS LEAKED TO EARTH'S CIVILIAN SECTOR, IT'S A VERY GRAVE MATTER.
WE'RE WORKING TO IDENTIFY THE SOURCE OF THE LEAK.
ARE THERE ANY SUSPECTS?
YES.

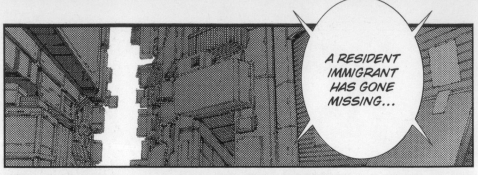

A RESIDENT IMMIGRANT HAS GONE MISSING...

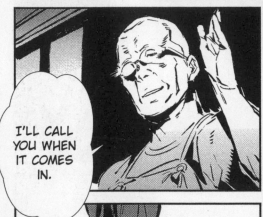

I'LL CALL YOU WHEN IT COMES IN.

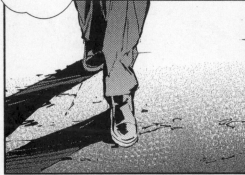

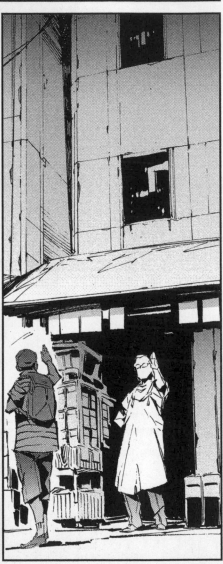

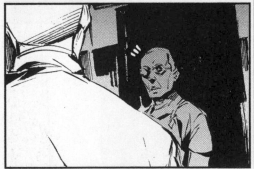

157

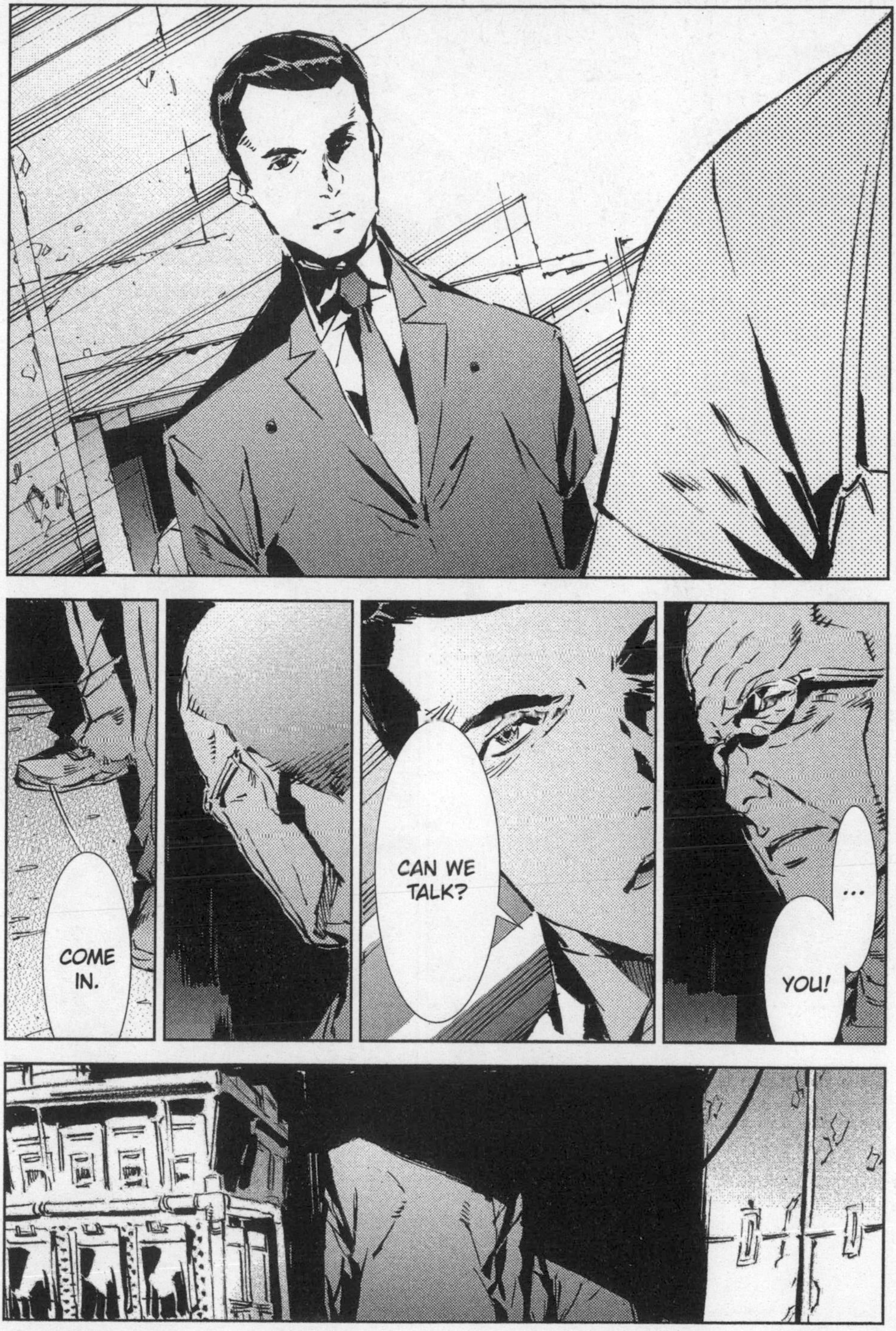
... YOU!
CAN WE TALK?
COME IN.

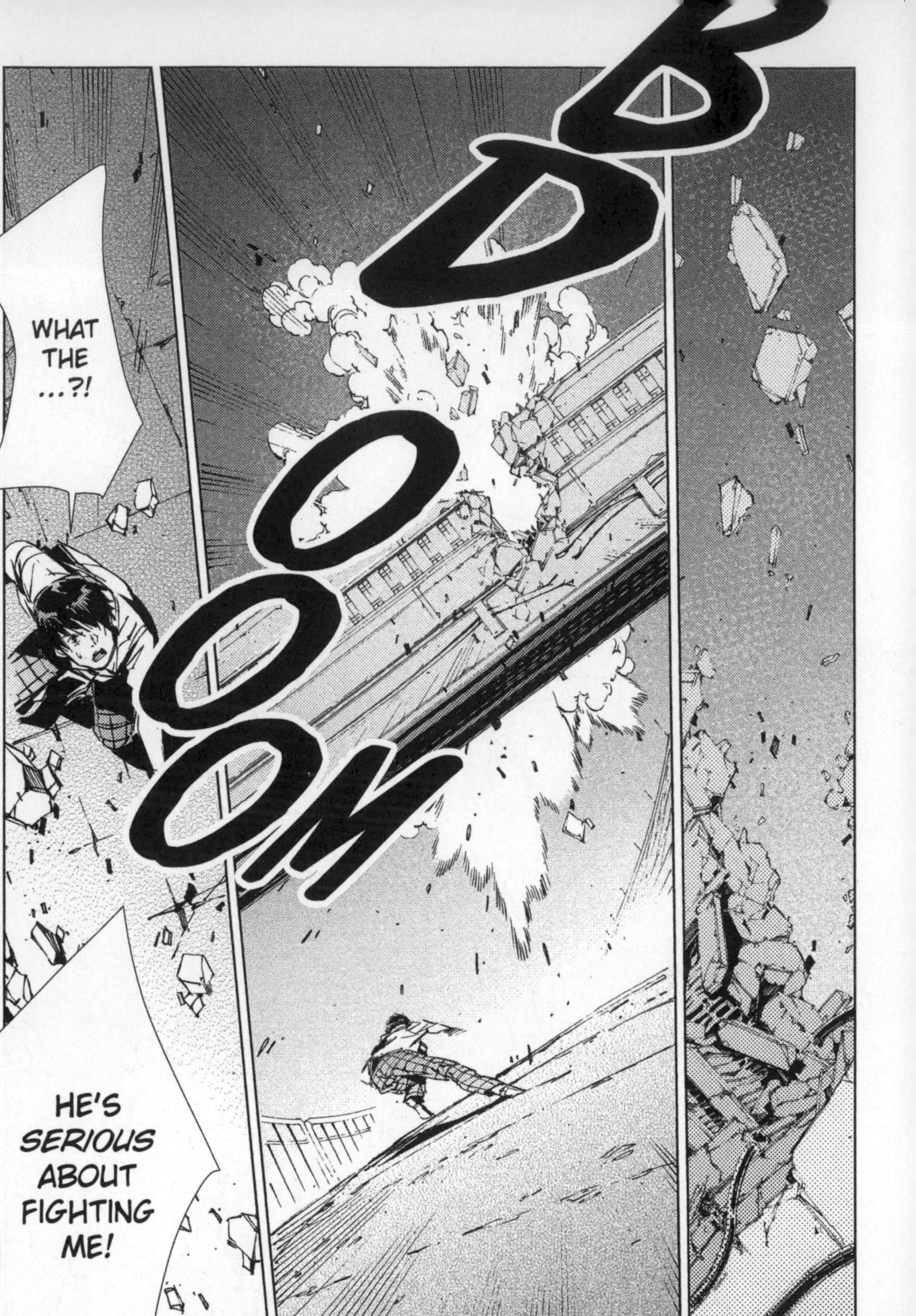
BDOOOM
WHAT THE ...?!
HE'S SERIOUS ABOUT FIGHTING ME!

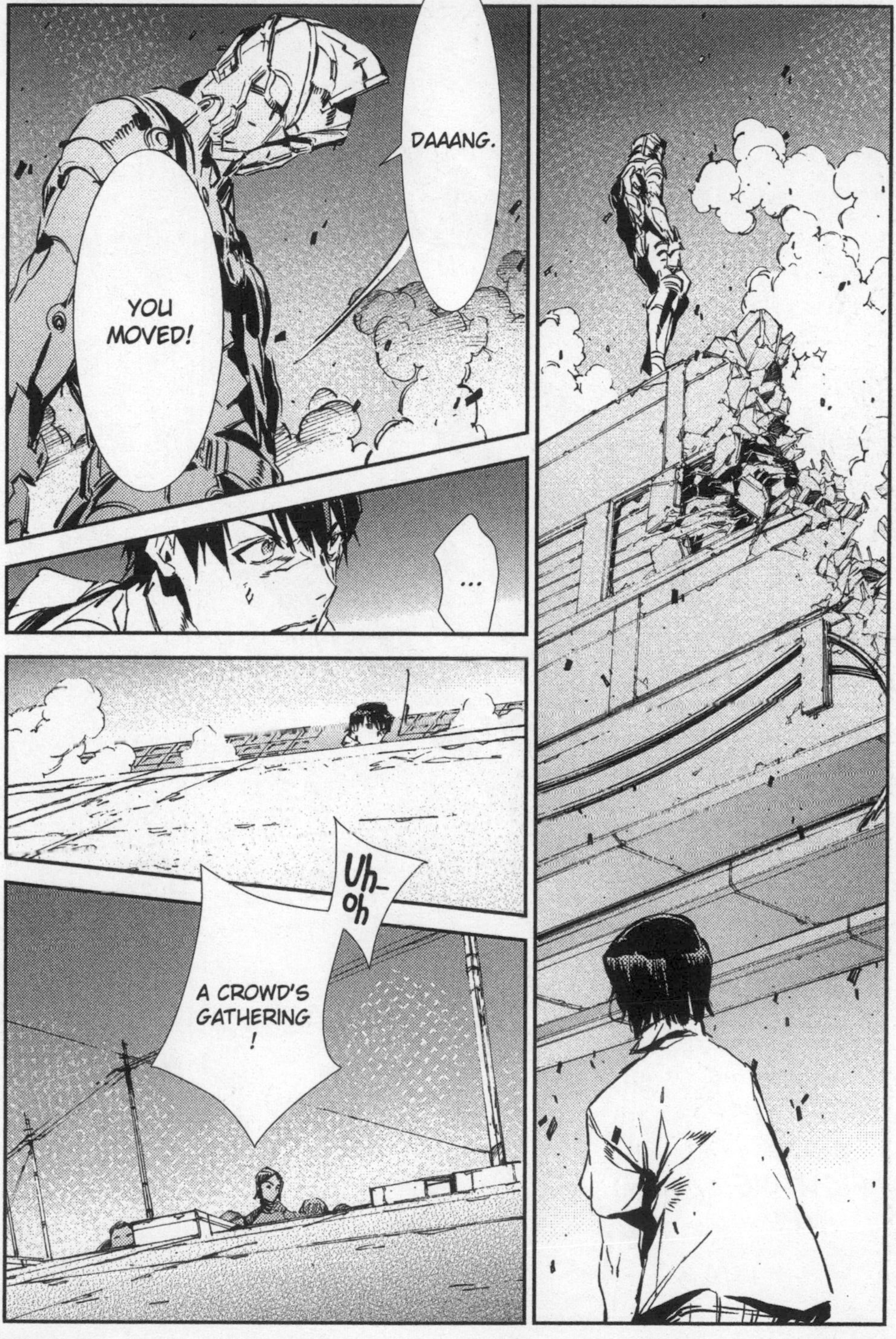
DAAANG.
YOU MOVED!
...
Uh-oh
A CROWD'S GATHERING!

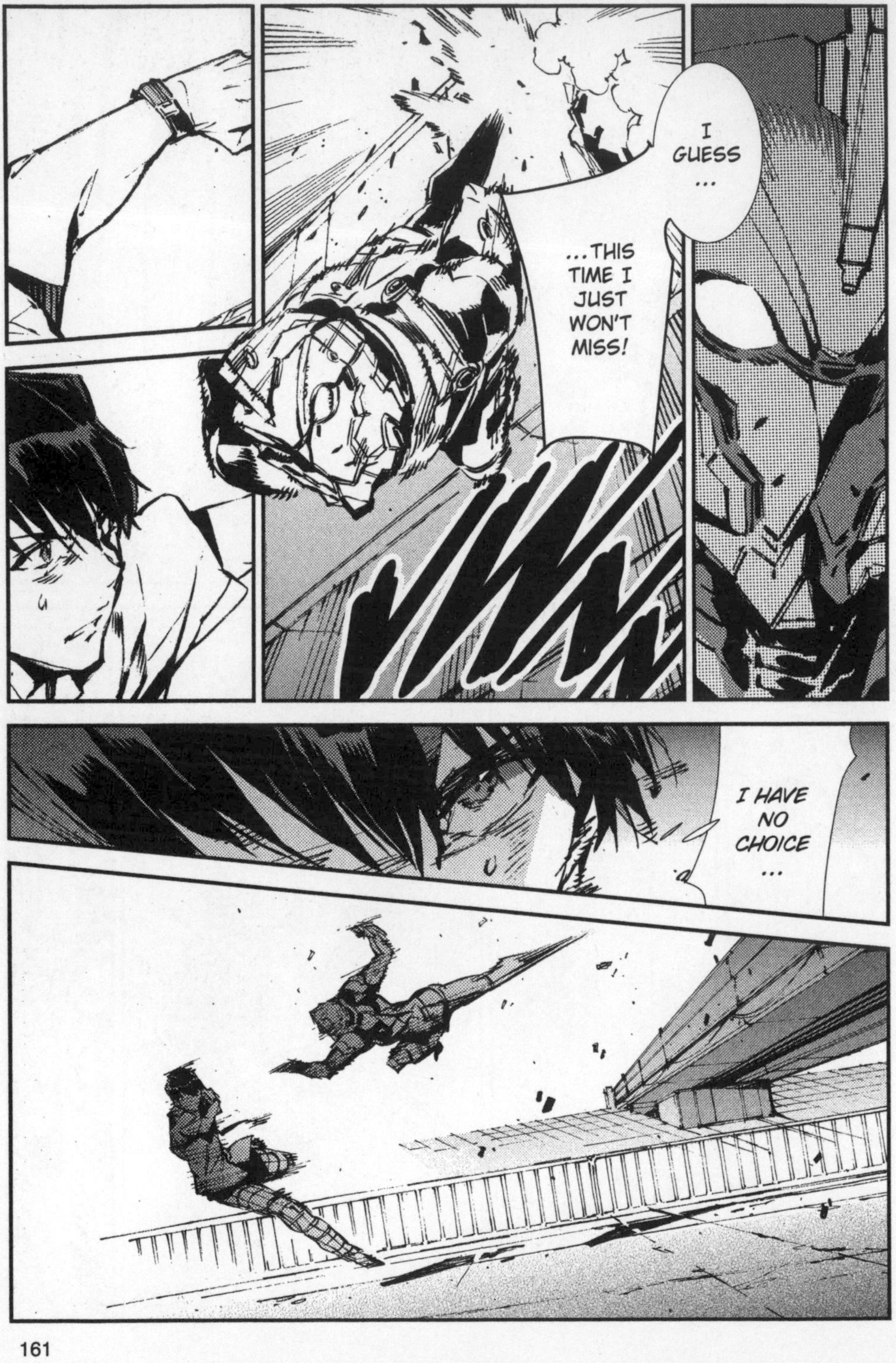
I GUESS ...
...THIS TIME I JUST WON'T MISS!
I HAVE NO CHOICE ...

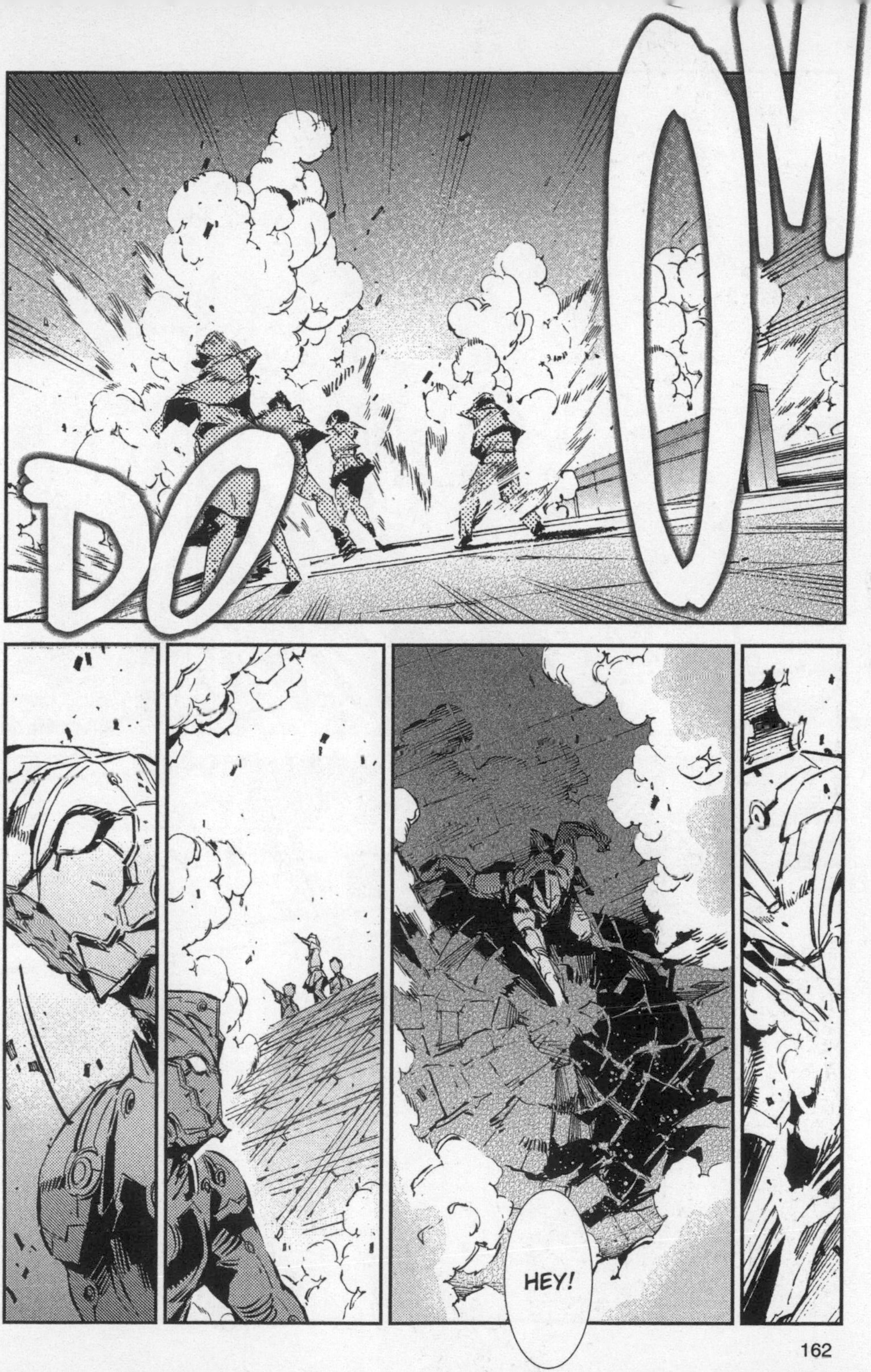
DOOOM
HEY!

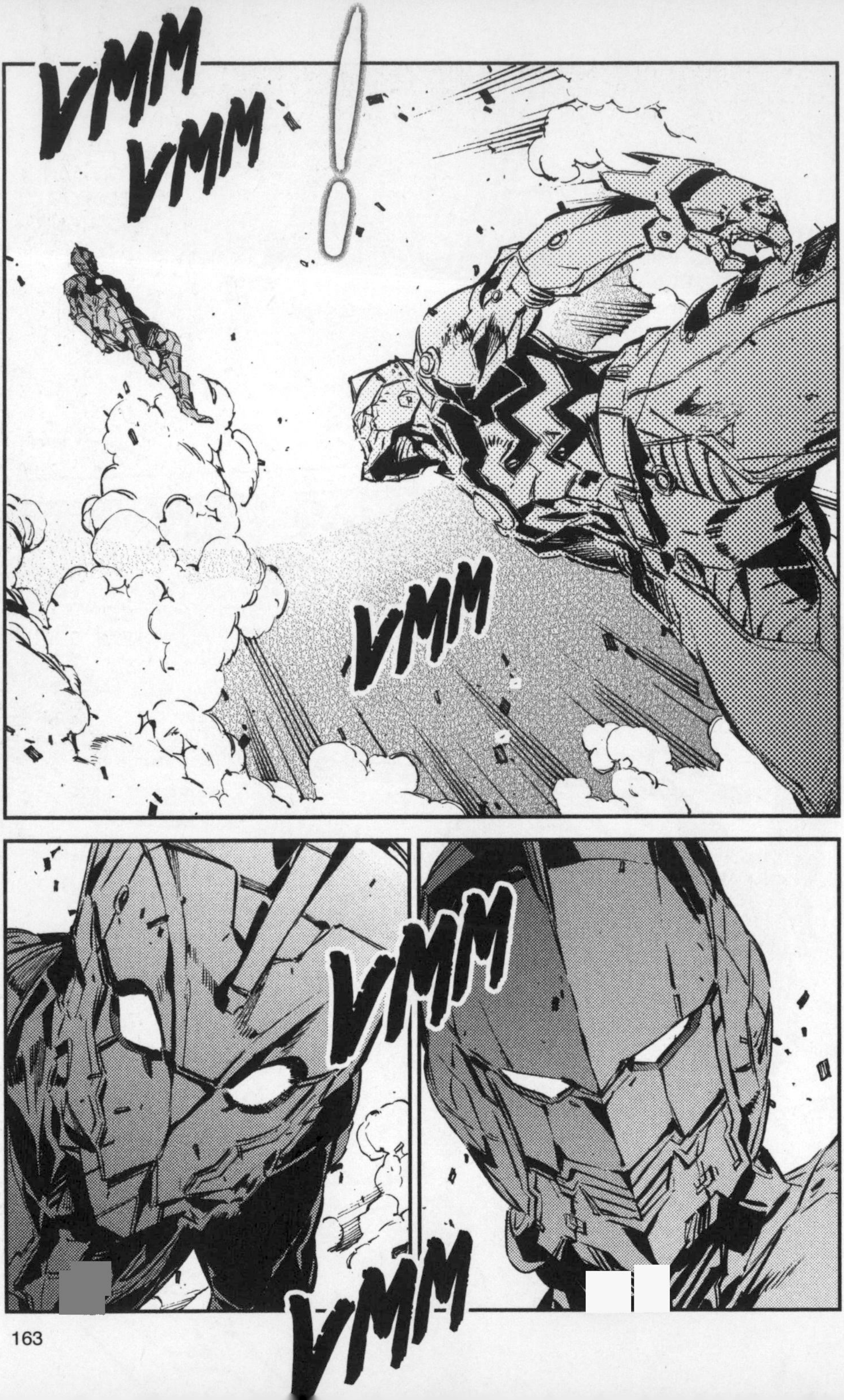
VMM
VMM
!
VMM
VMM
VMM

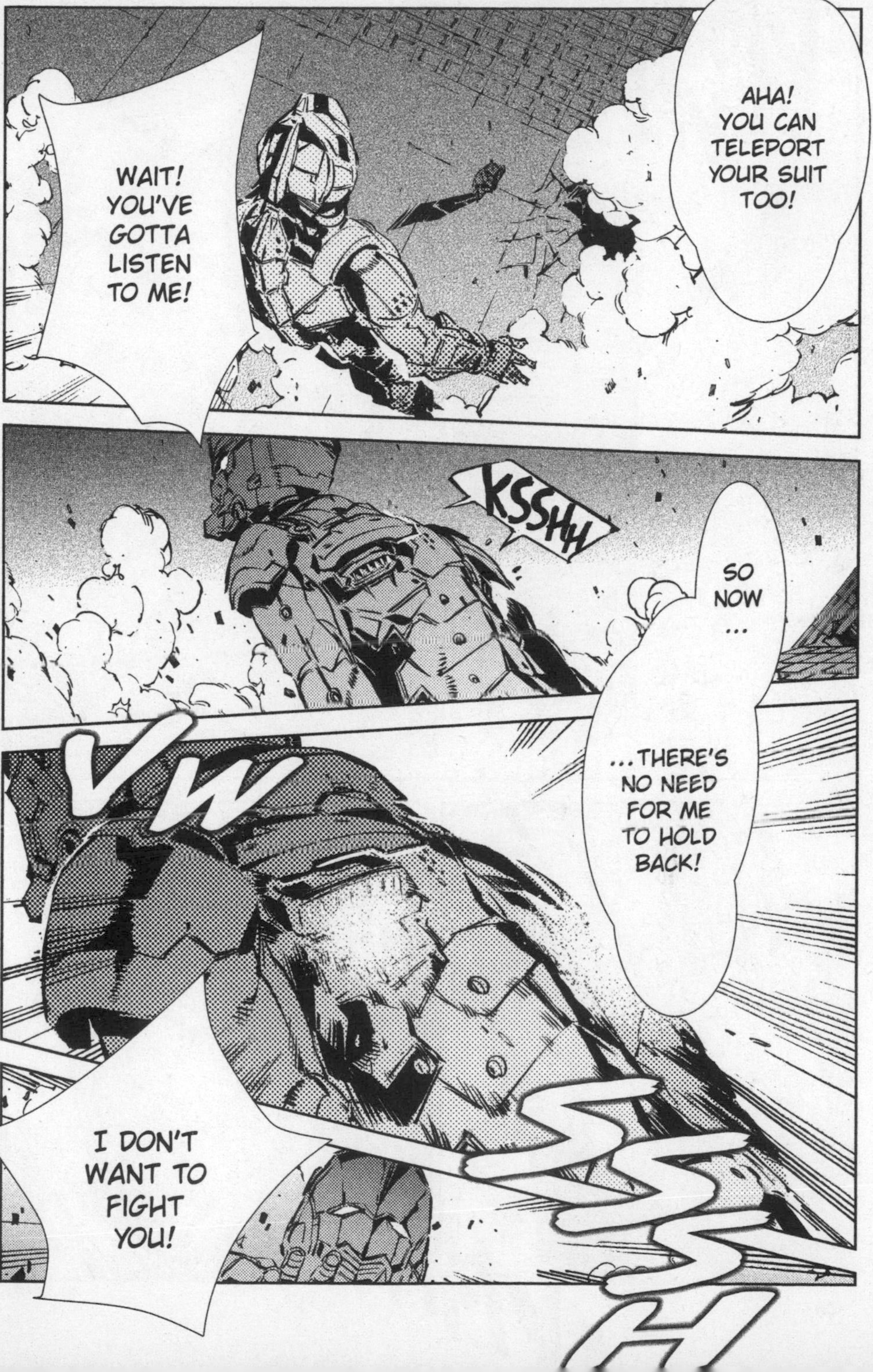
AHA! YOU CAN TELEPORT YOUR SUIT TOO!
WAIT! YOU'VE GOTTA LISTEN TO ME!
KSSHH
SO NOW ...
...THERE'S NO NEED FOR ME TO HOLD BACK!
VW
SSSH
I DON'T WANT TO FIGHT YOU!

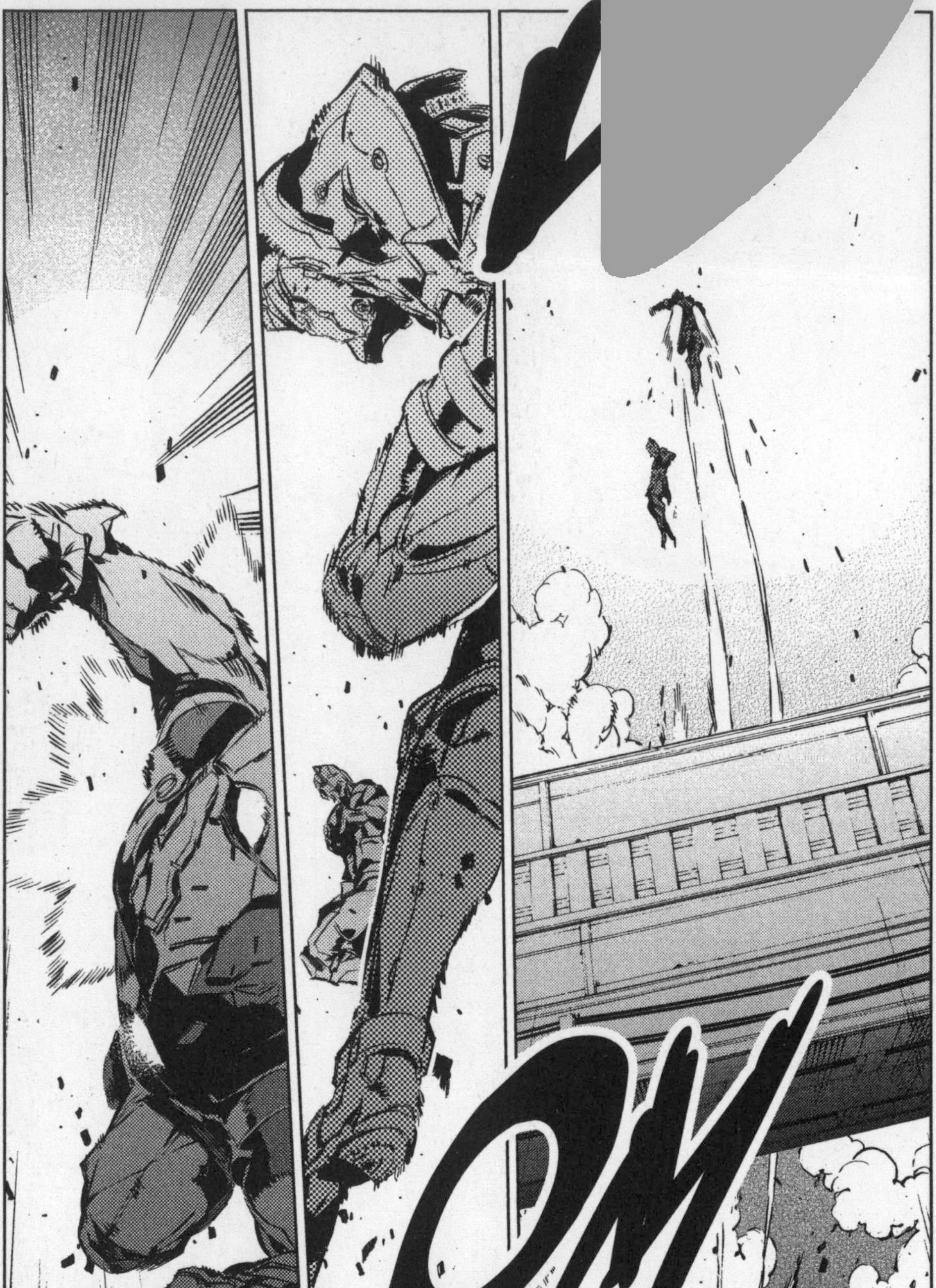

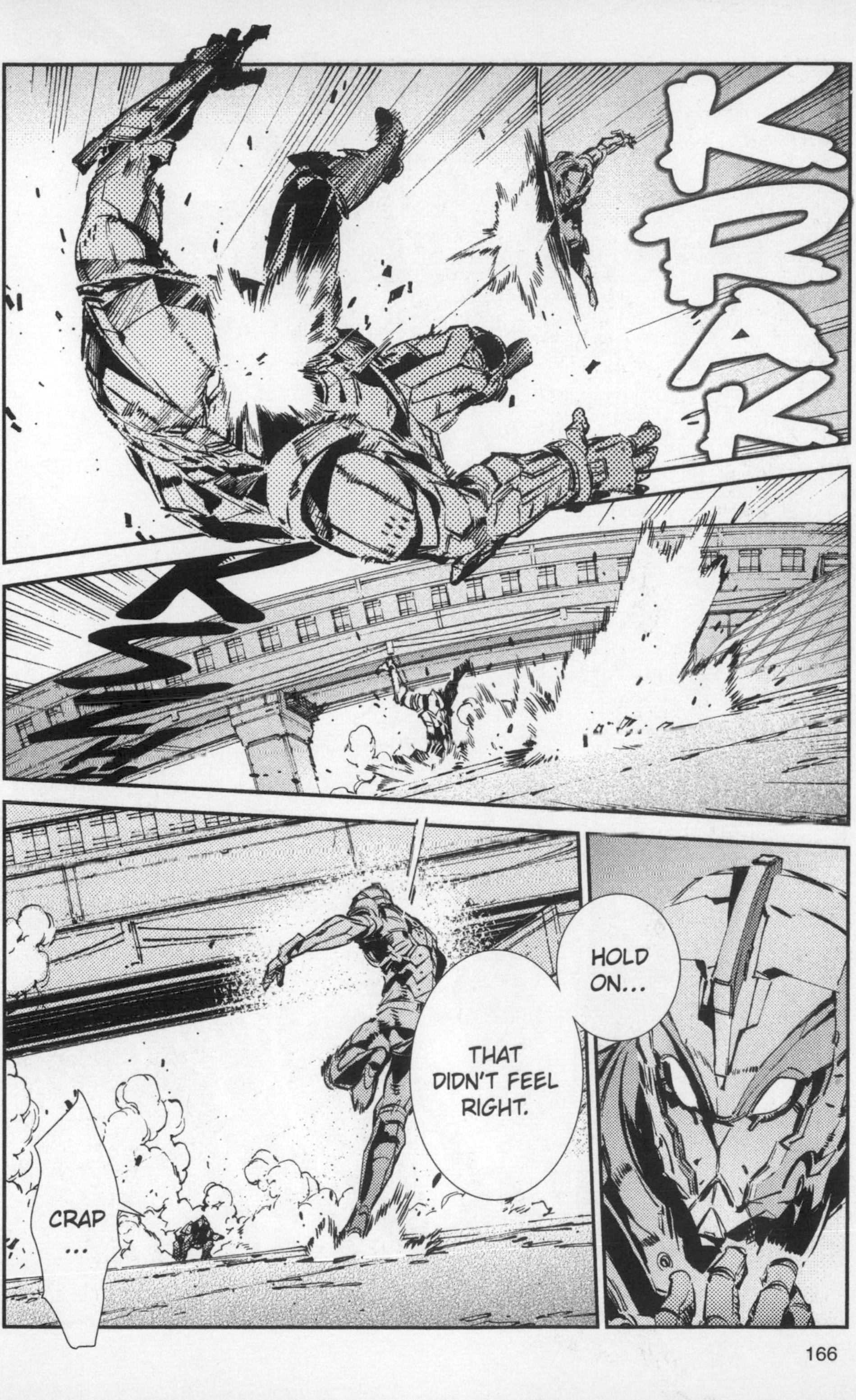
KRAK
HOLD ON...
THAT DIDN'T FEEL RIGHT.
CRAP ...

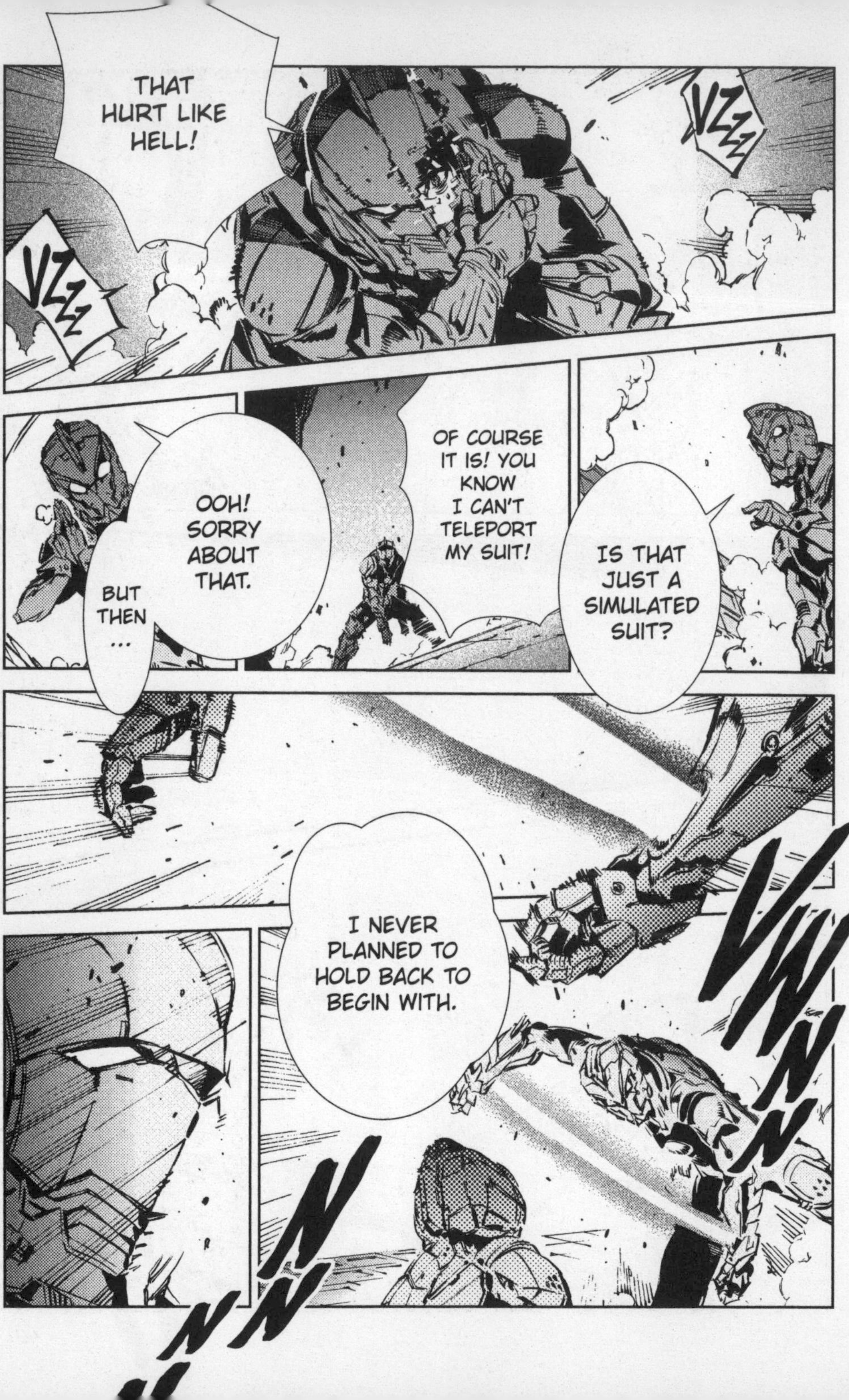
VZZZ
THAT HURT LIKE HELL!
VZZZ
IS THAT JUST A SIMULATED SUIT?
OF COURSE IT IS! YOU KNOW I CAN'T TELEPORT MY SUIT!
OOH! SORRY ABOUT THAT.
BUT THEN...
I NEVER PLANNED TO HOLD BACK TO BEGIN WITH.
VNNNN
NNN

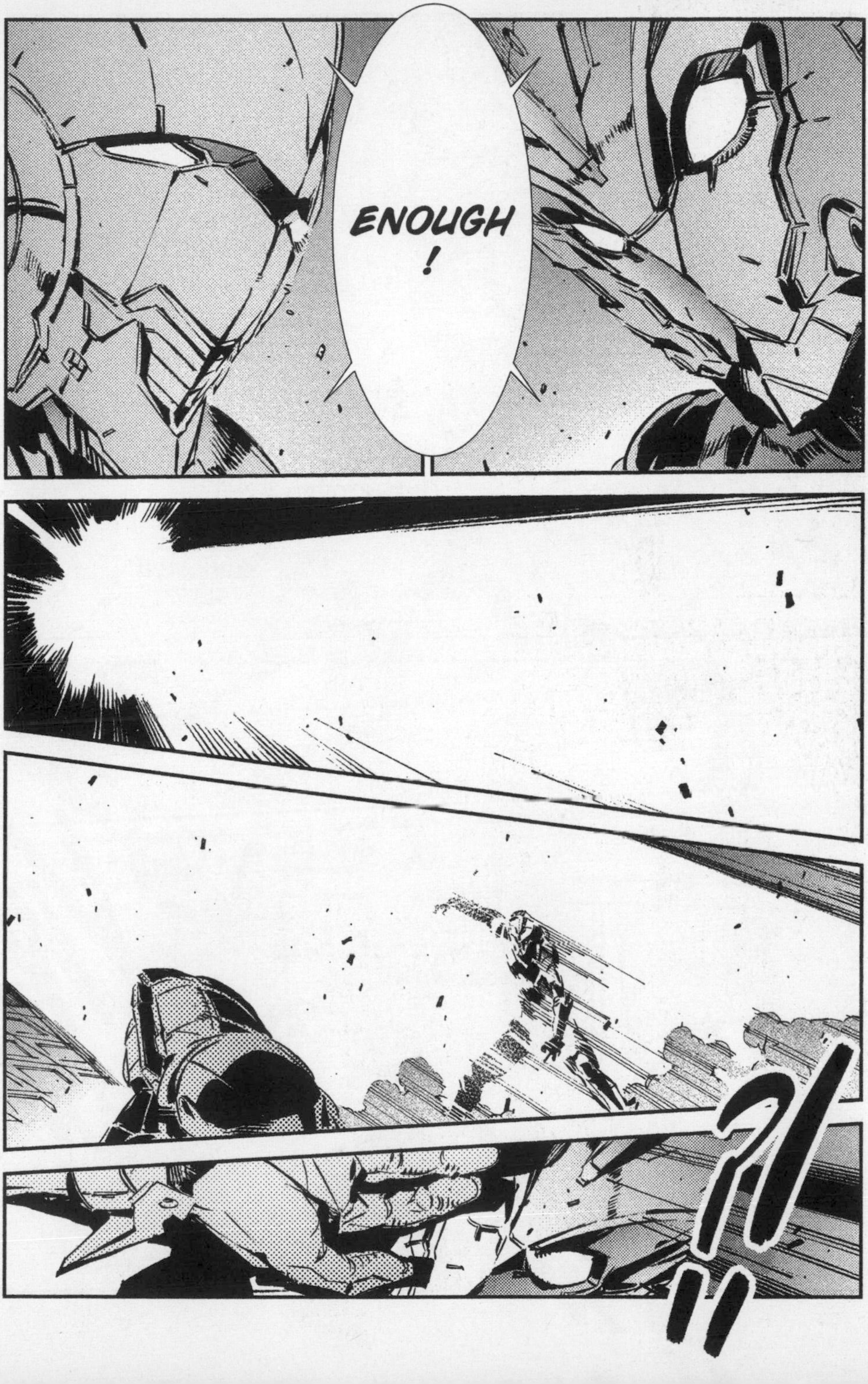
ENOUGH!
?!!

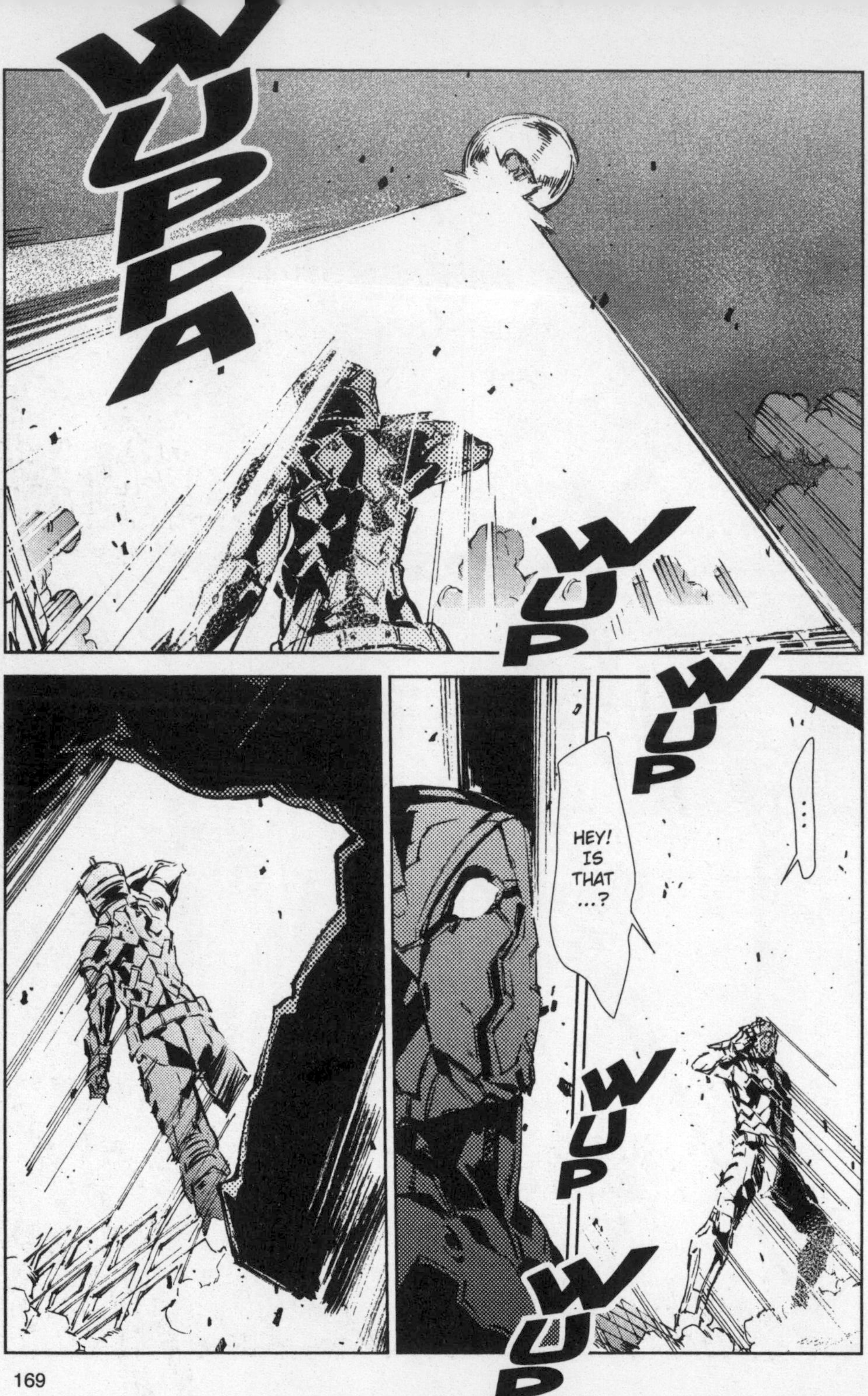
WUPPA
WUP
WUP
...
HEY! IS THAT ...?
WUP
WUP

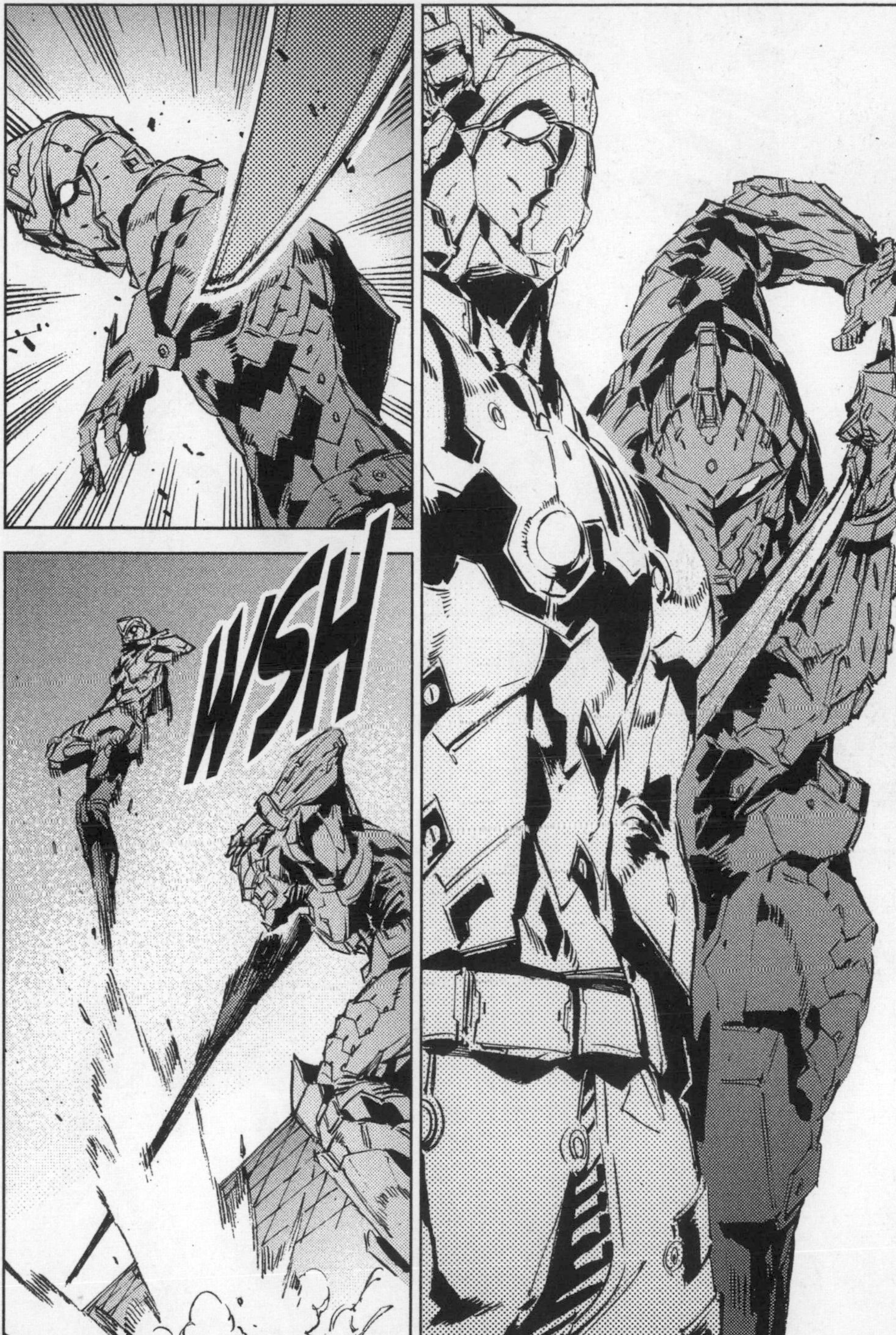
WSH

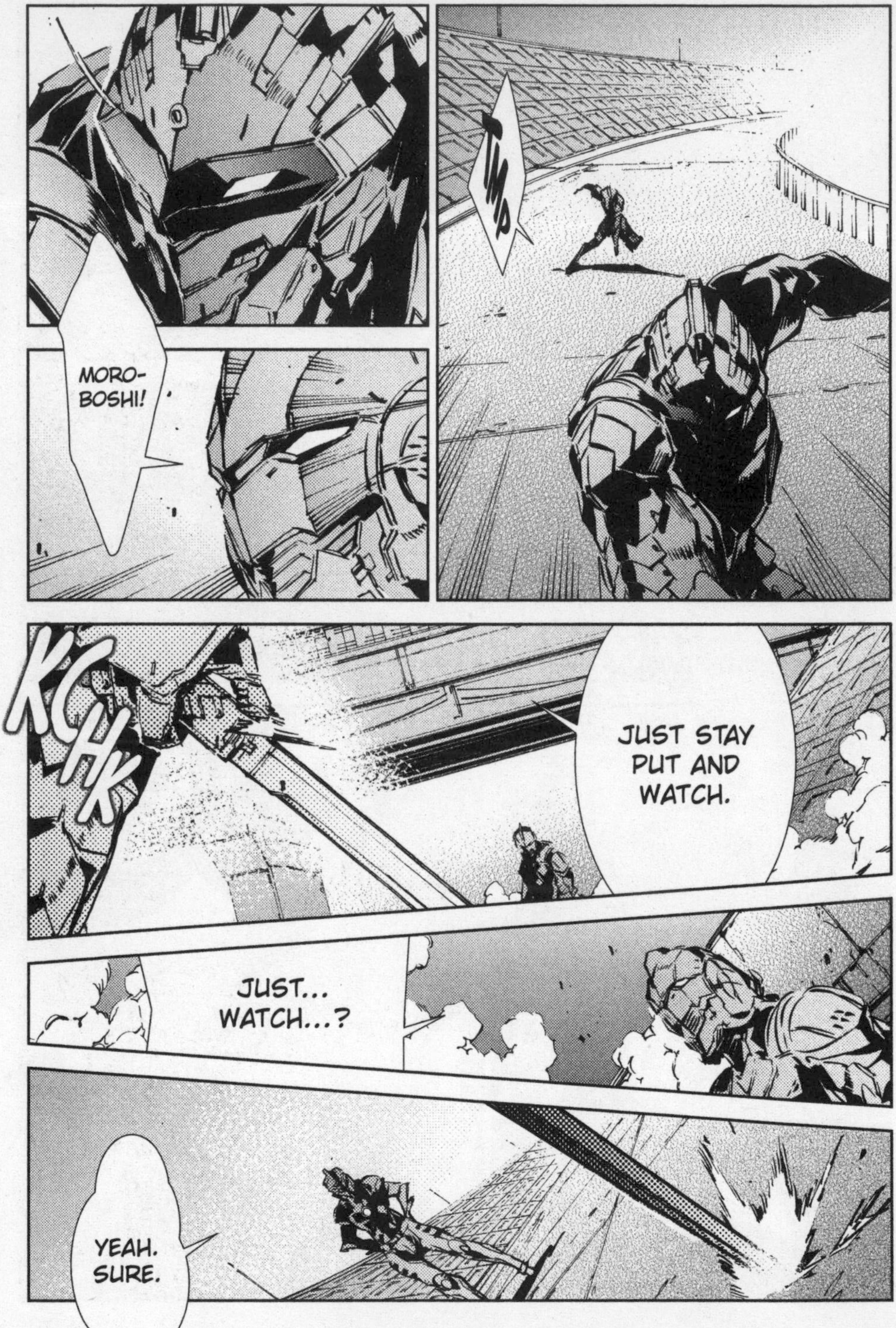
TMP
MORO-BOSHI!
JUST STAY PUT AND WATCH.
KCHK
JUST... WATCH...?
YEAH. SURE.

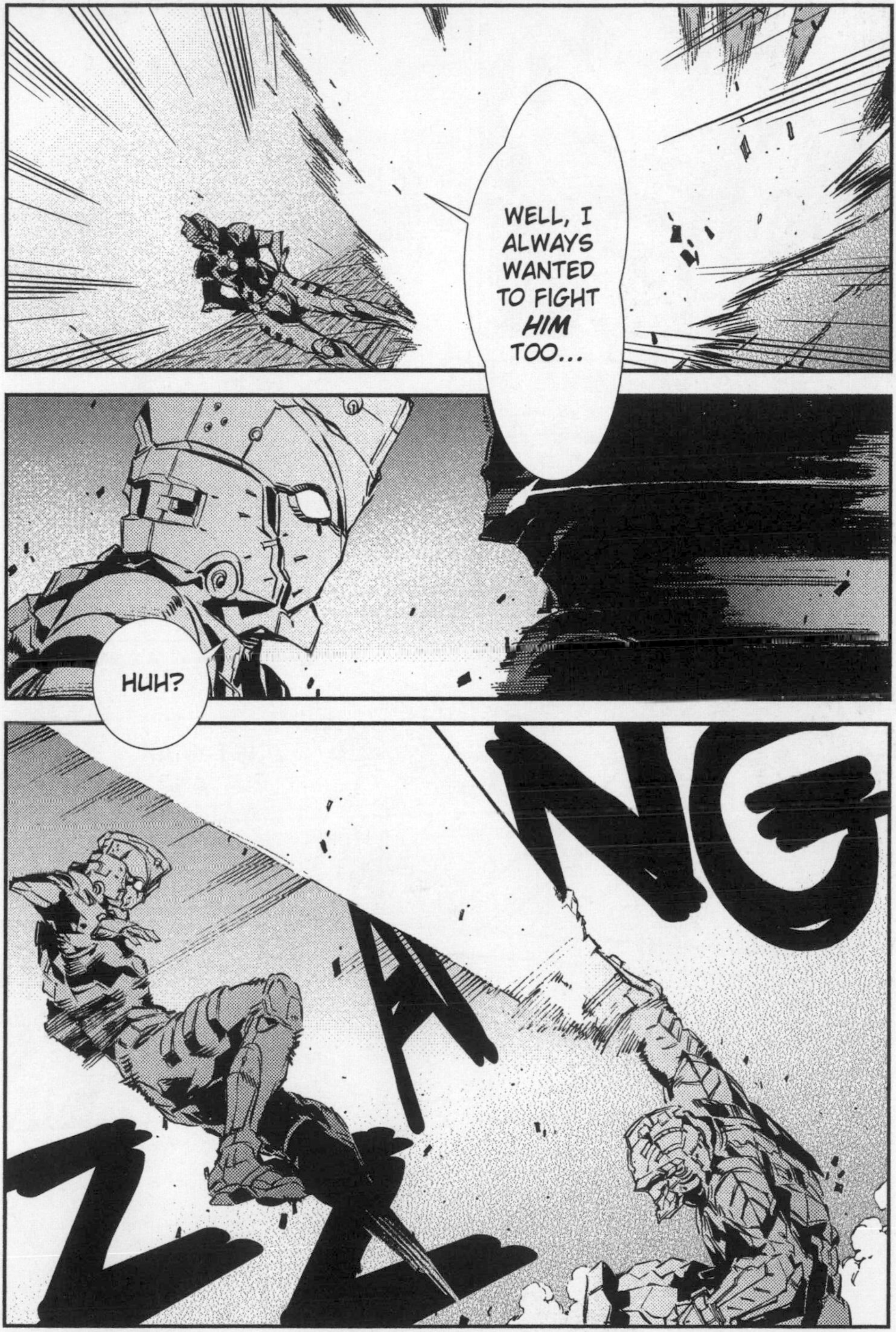
WELL, I ALWAYS WANTED TO FIGHT HIM TOO...
HUH?
ZZANG

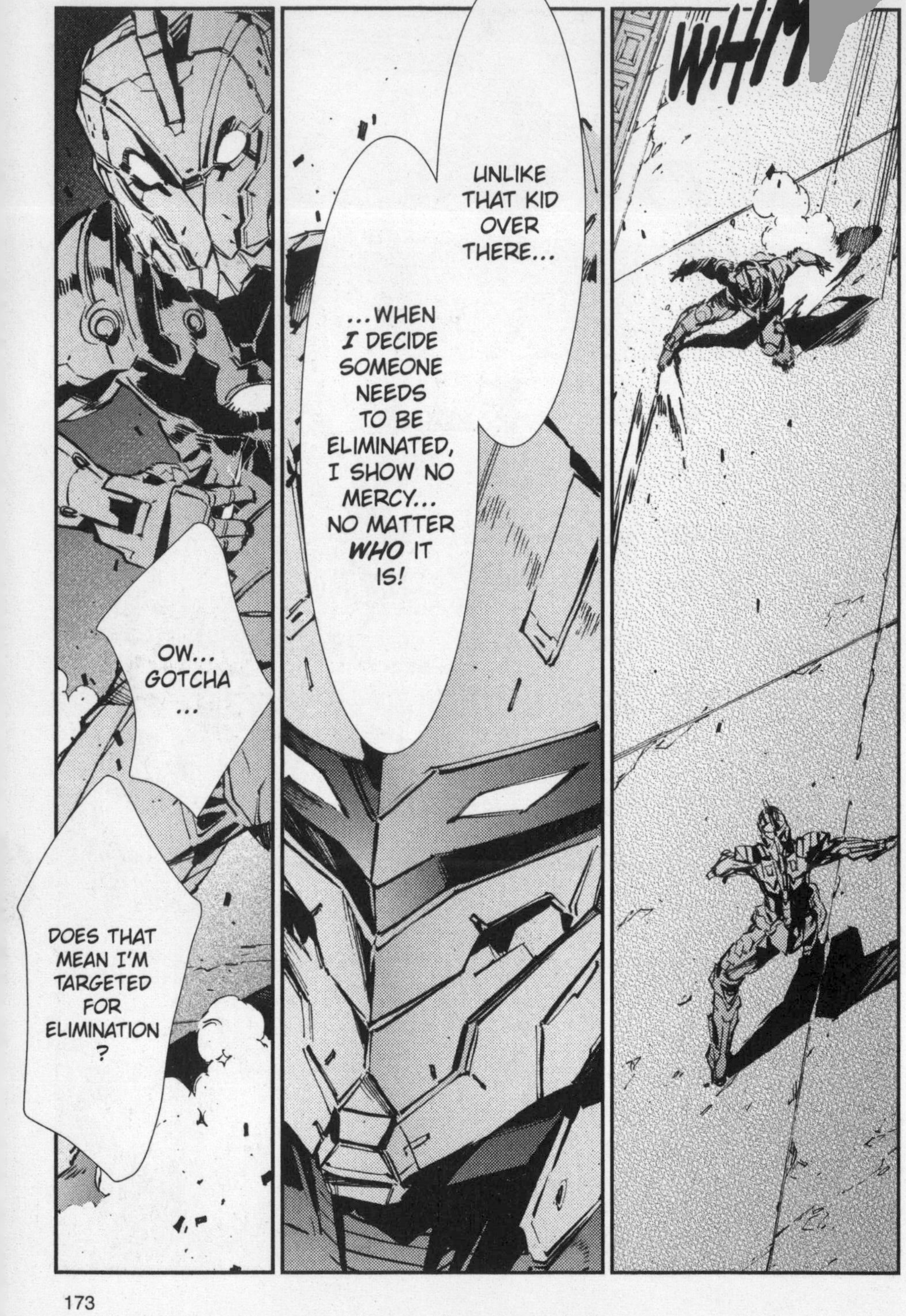
WHM
UNLIKE THAT KID OVER THERE...
...WHEN *I* DECIDE SOMEONE NEEDS TO BE ELIMINATED, I SHOW NO MERCY... NO MATTER *WHO* IT IS!
OW... GOTCHA ...
DOES THAT MEAN I'M TARGETED FOR ELIMINATION ?

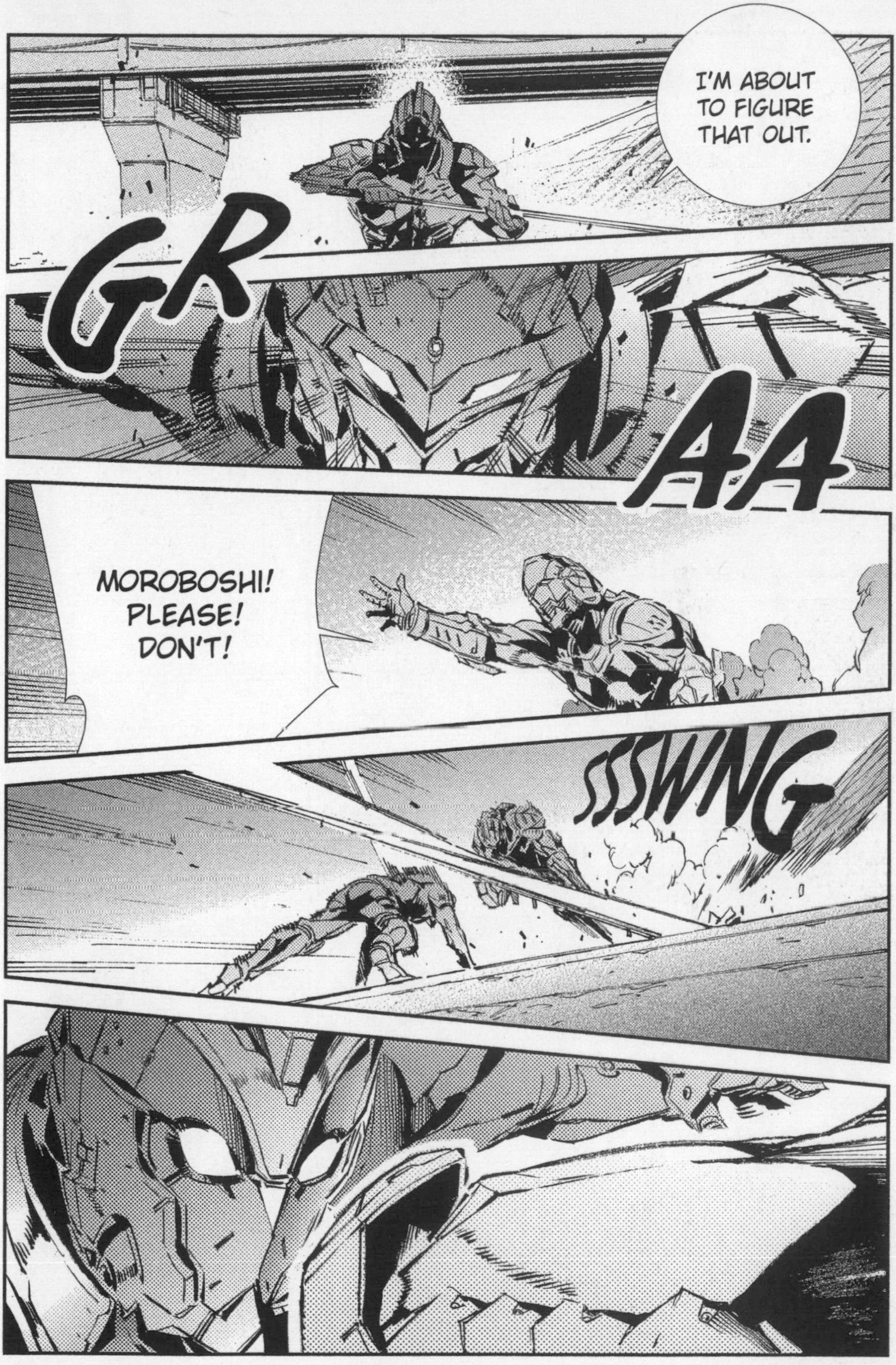
I'M ABOUT TO FIGURE THAT OUT.
GR
AA
MOROBOSHI! PLEASE! DON'T!
SSSWNG

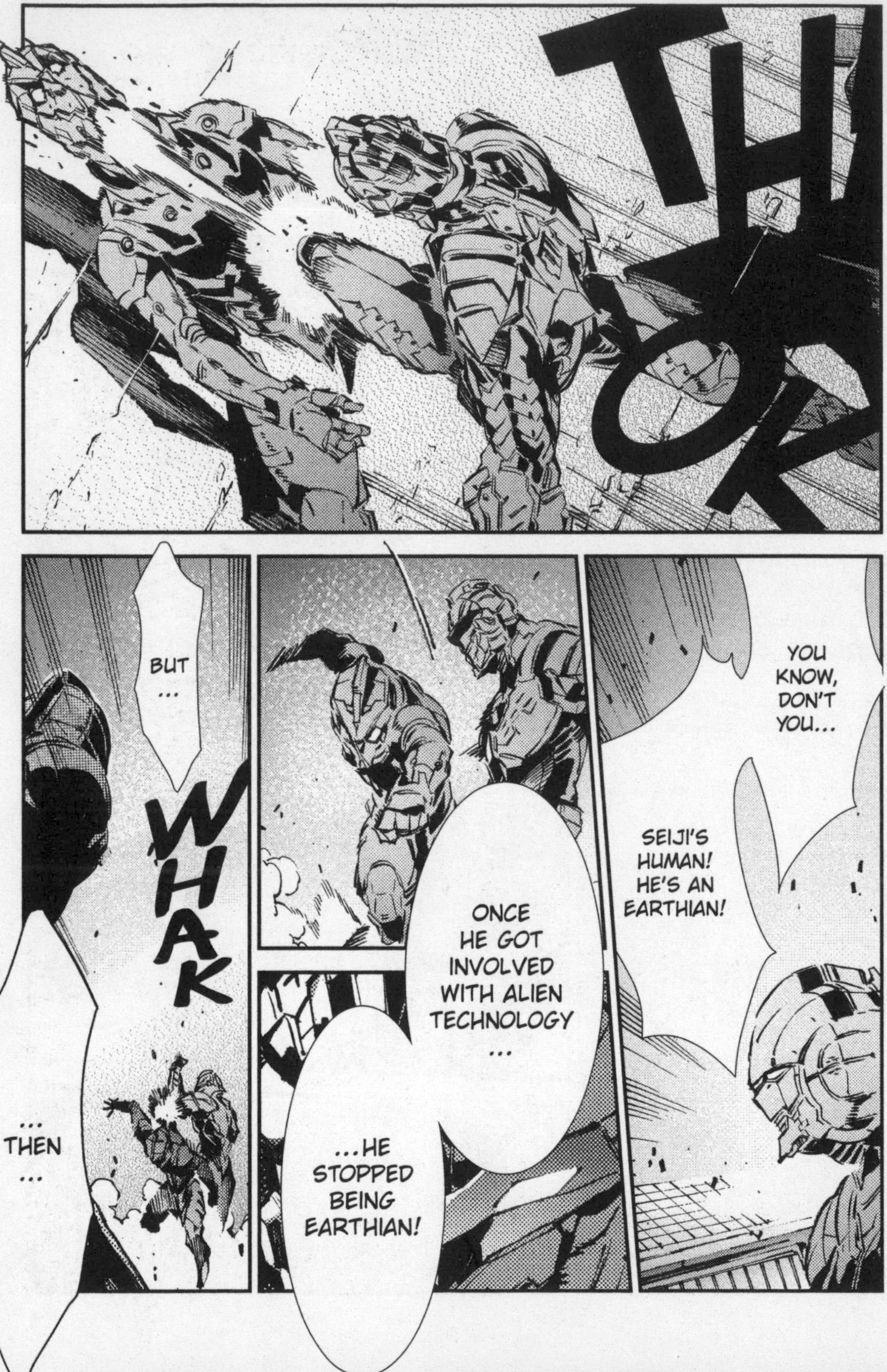
THOK
YOU KNOW, DON'T YOU...
SEIJI'S HUMAN! HE'S AN EARTHIAN!
ONCE HE GOT INVOLVED WITH ALIEN TECHNOLOGY ...
...HE STOPPED BEING EARTHIAN!
BUT ...
WHAK
... THEN ...

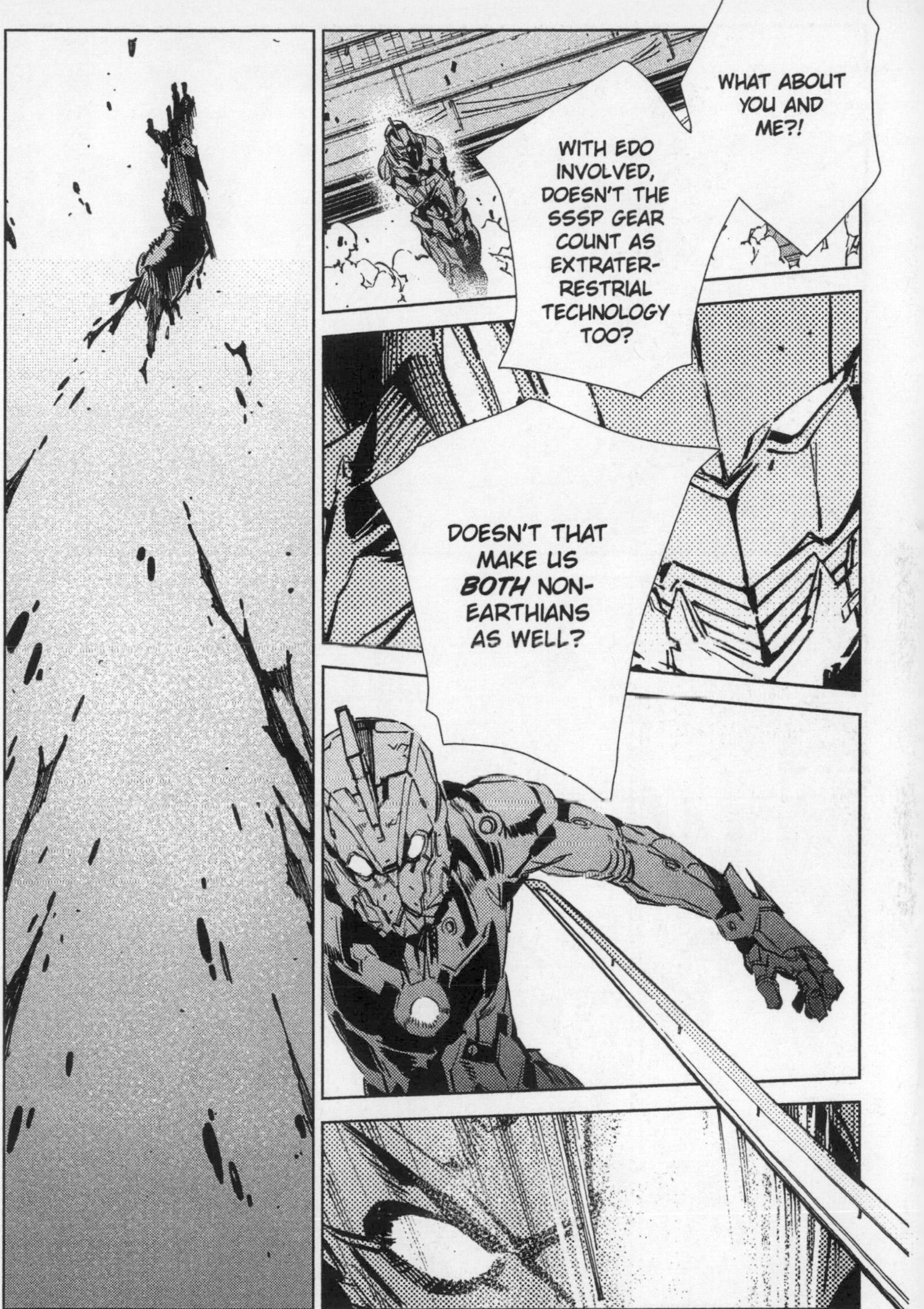
WHAT ABOUT YOU AND ME?!
WITH EDO INVOLVED, DOESN'T THE SSSP GEAR COUNT AS EXTRATER-RESTRIAL TECHNOLOGY TOO?
DOESN'T THAT MAKE US BOTH NON-EARTHIANS AS WELL?

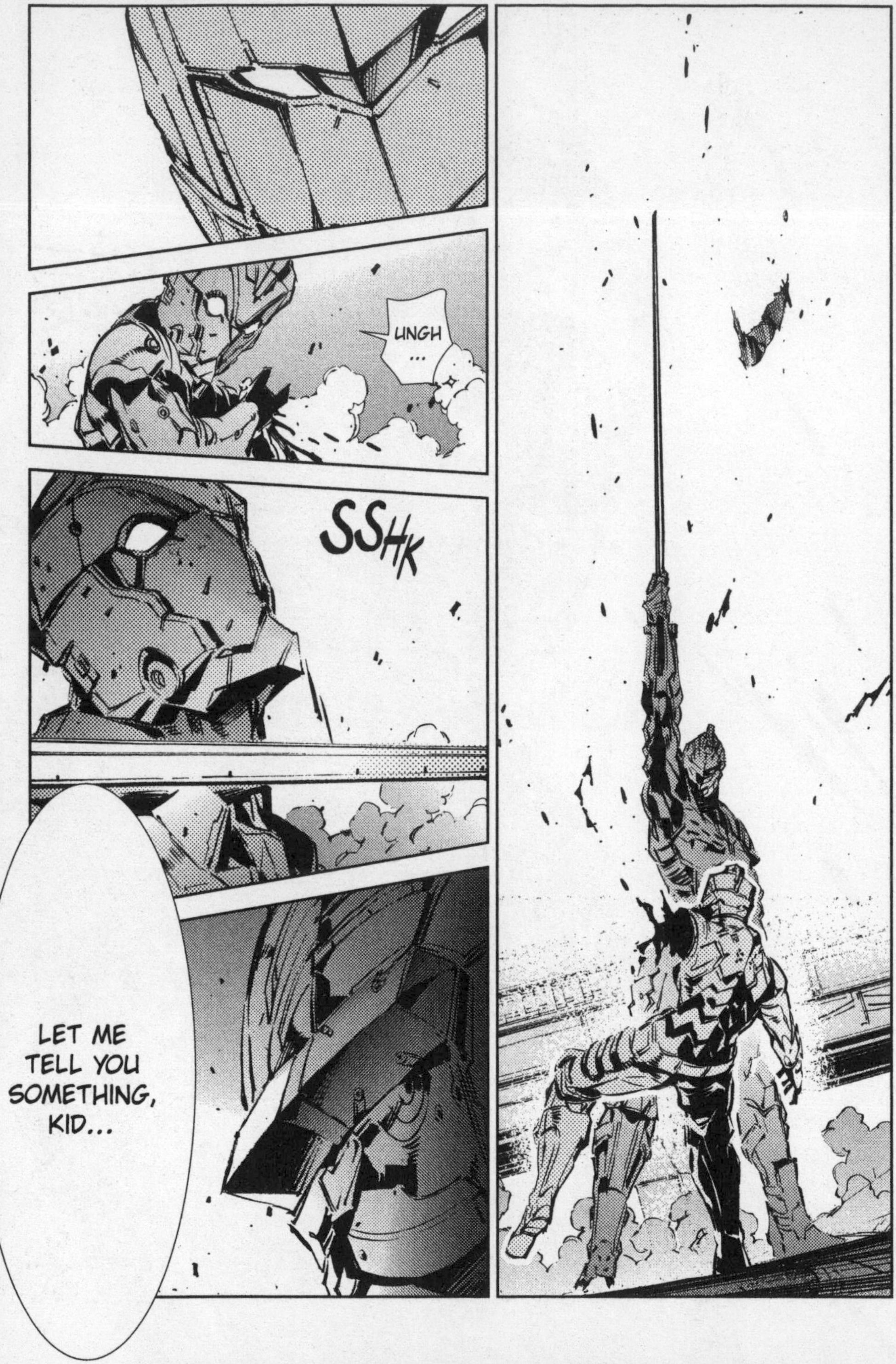
UNGH ...
SSHK
LET ME TELL YOU SOMETHING, KID...

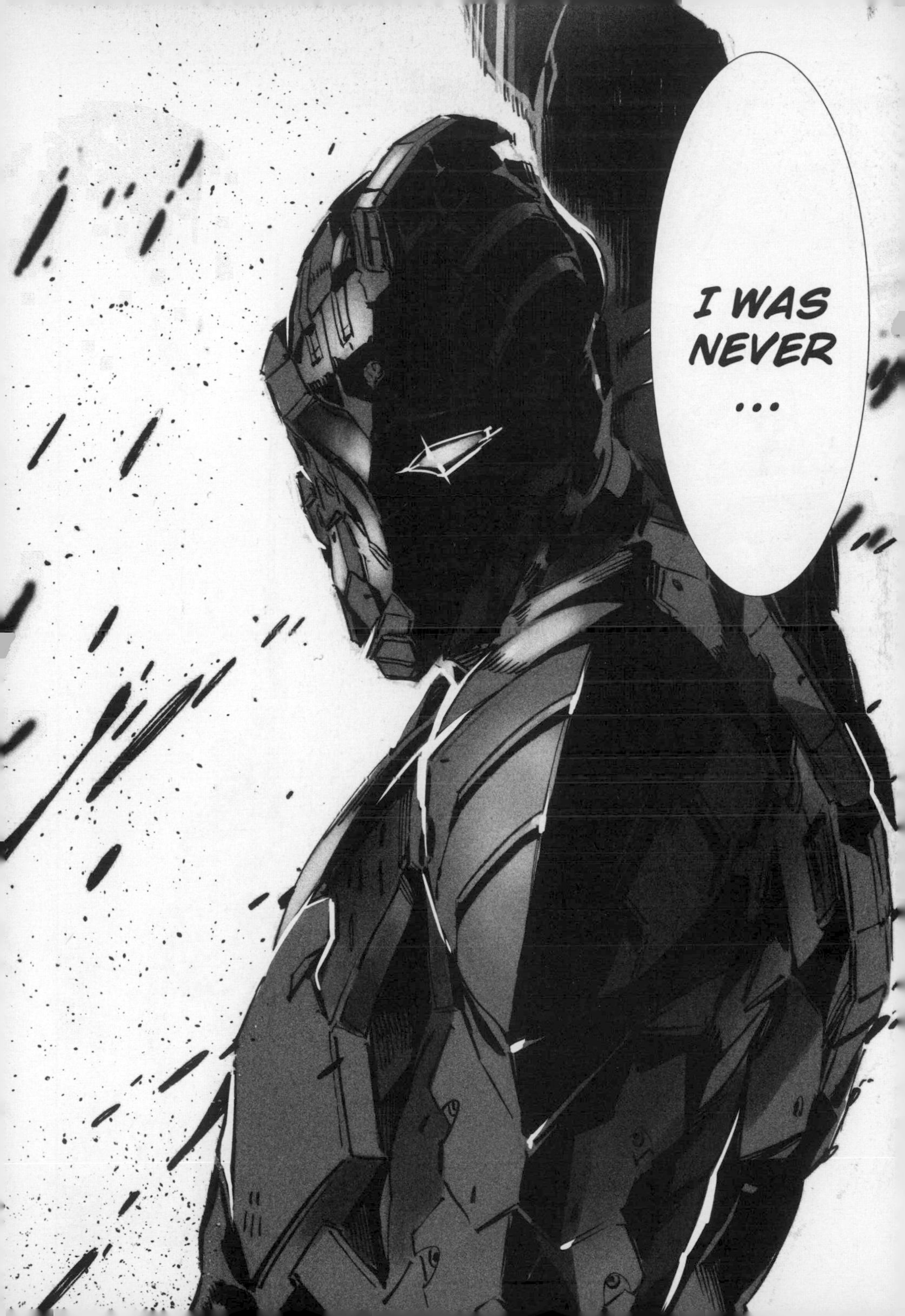
I WAS NEVER ...

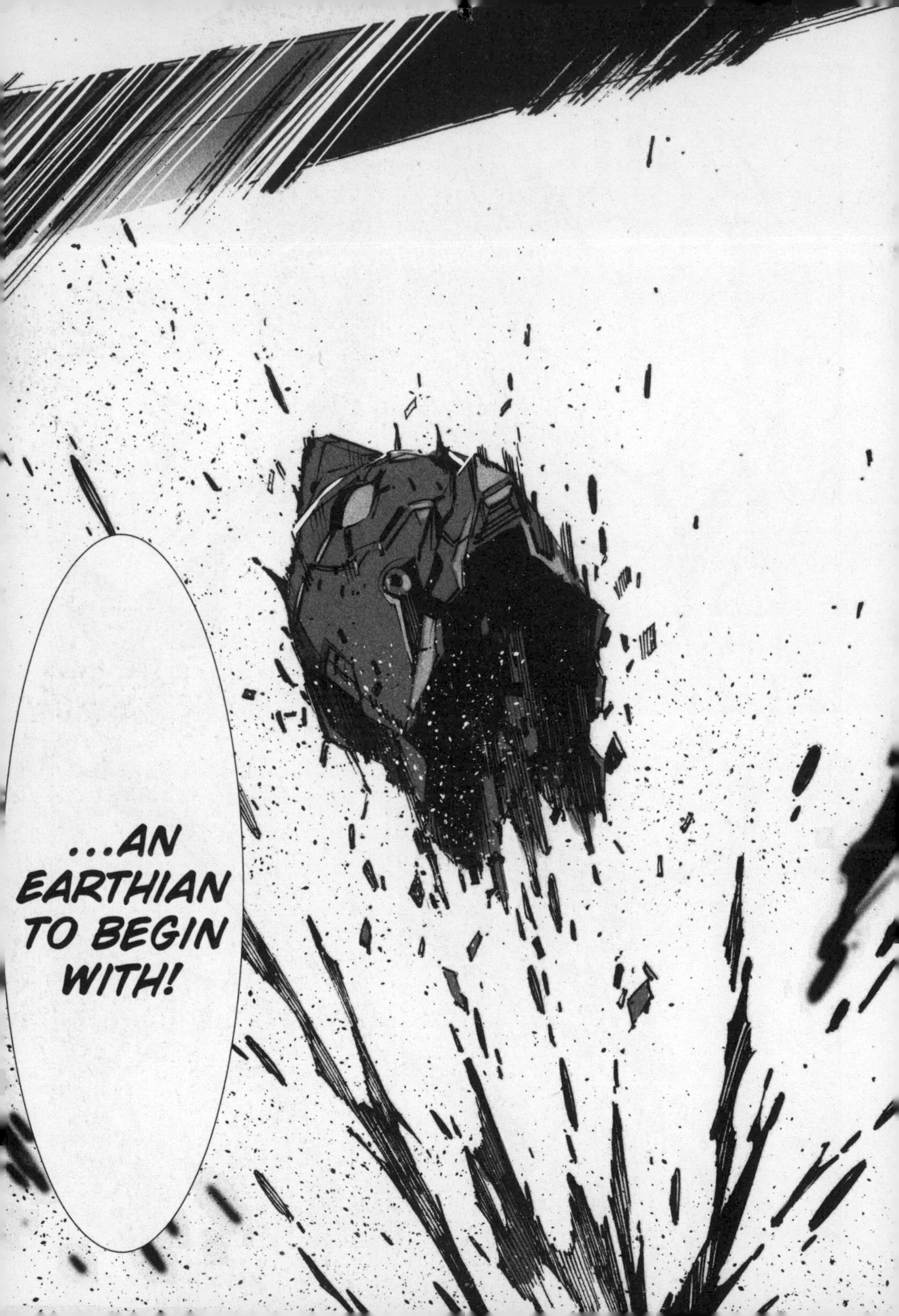
...AN EARTHIAN TO BEGIN WITH!

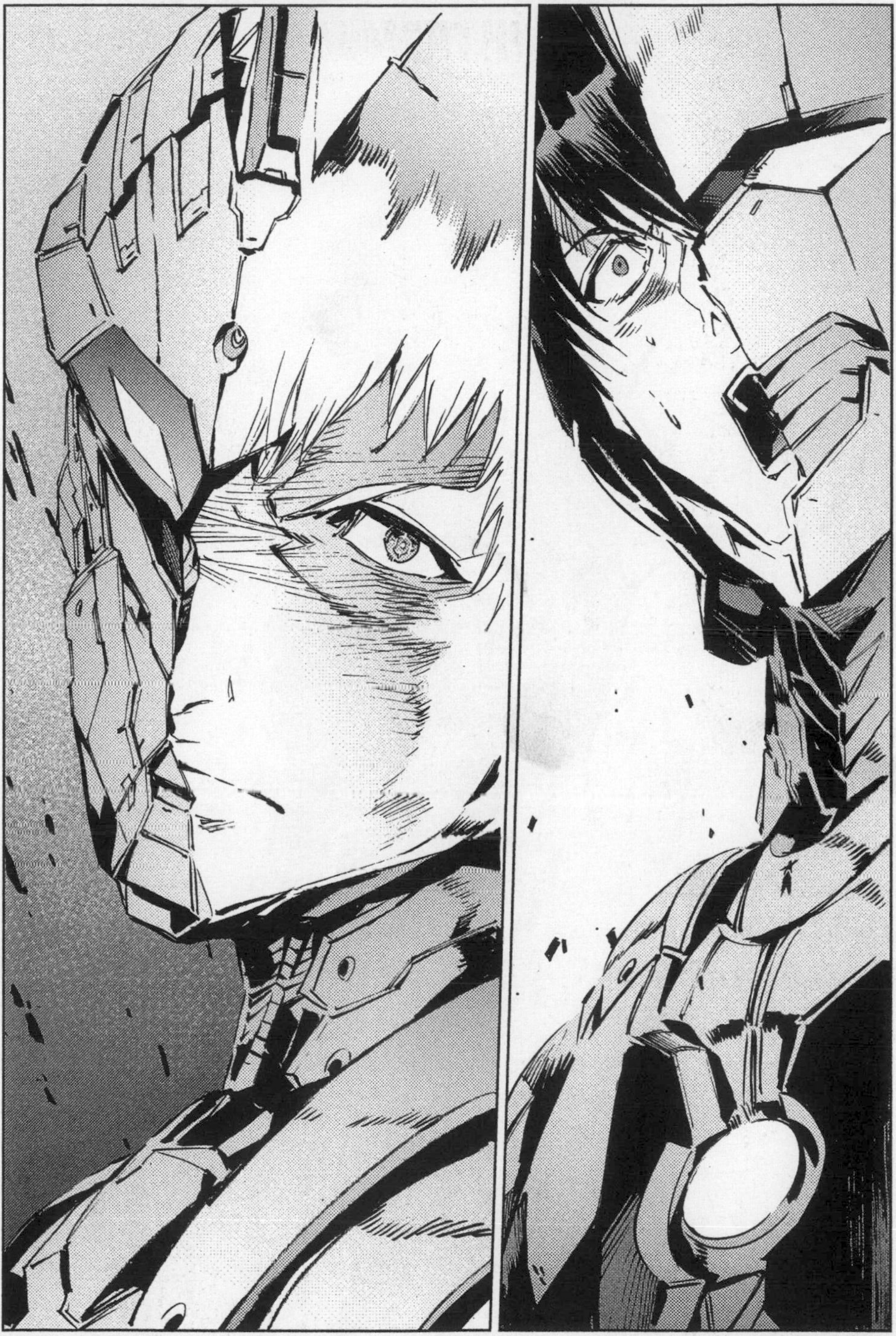

ULTRAMAN 6 – END

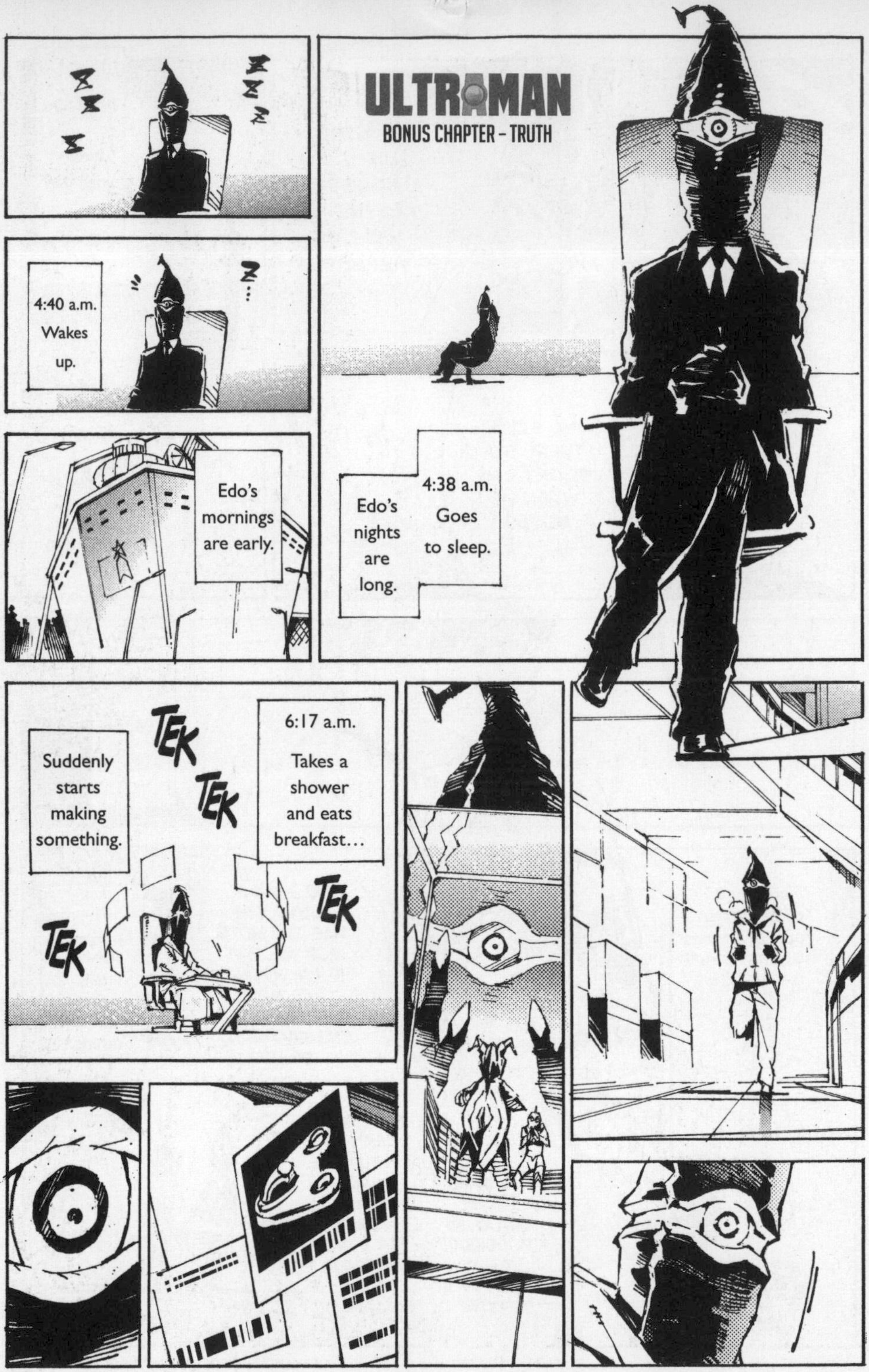
ULTRAMAN
BONUS CHAPTER – TRUTH
4:38 a.m. Goes to sleep.
Edo's nights are long.
4:40 a.m. Wakes up.
Edo's mornings are early.
6:17 a.m. Takes a shower and eats breakfast…
TEK
TEK
Suddenly starts making something.
TEK
TEK

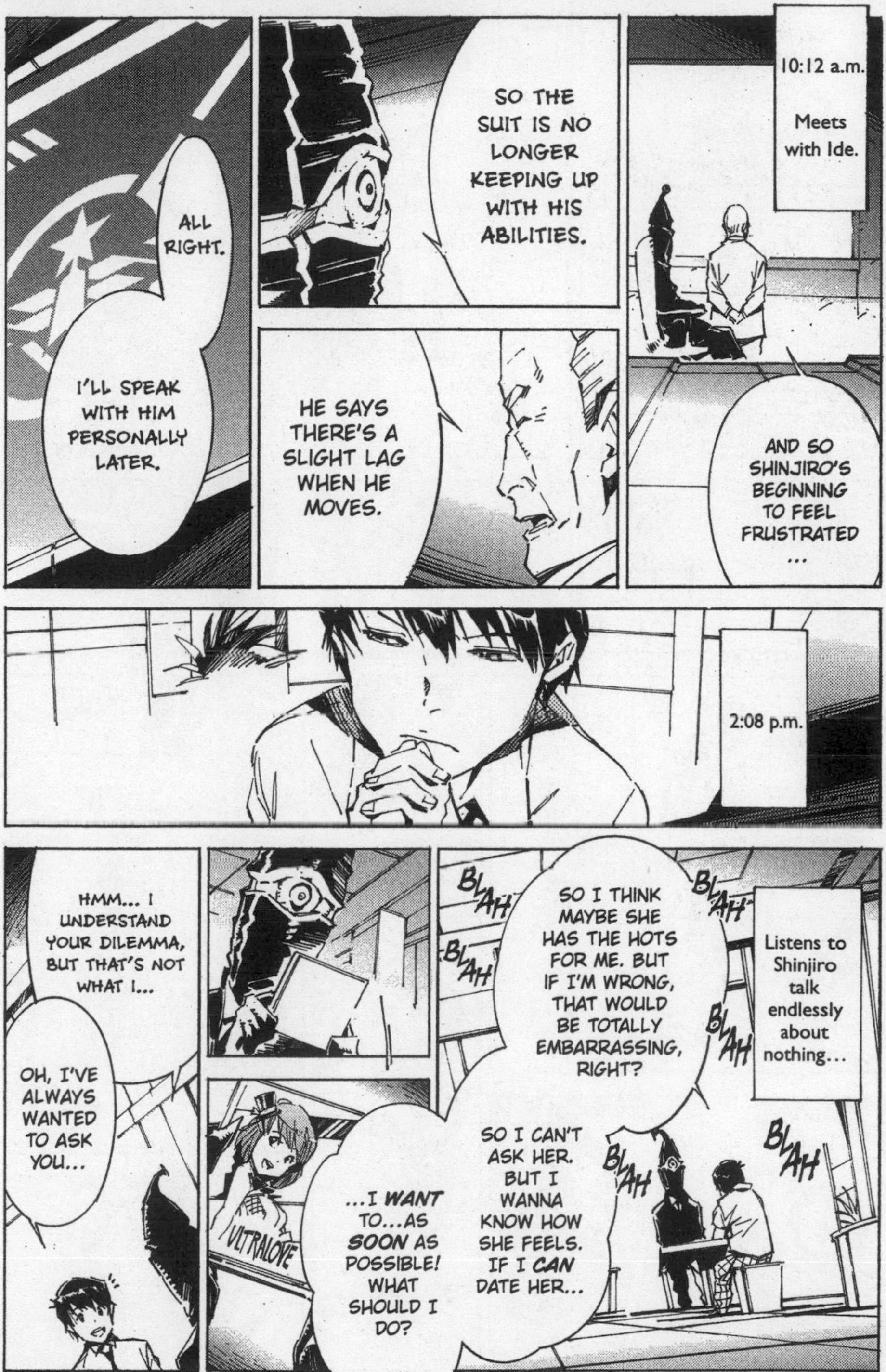
10:12 a.m.
Meets with Ide.
AND SO SHINJIRO'S BEGINNING TO FEEL FRUSTRATED...
SO THE SUIT IS NO LONGER KEEPING UP WITH HIS ABILITIES.
HE SAYS THERE'S A SLIGHT LAG WHEN HE MOVES.
ALL RIGHT.
I'LL SPEAK WITH HIM PERSONALLY LATER.
2:08 p.m.
Listens to Shinjiro talk endlessly about nothing...
BLAH
BLAH
BLAH
BLAH
BLAH
BLAH
BLAH
SO I THINK MAYBE SHE HAS THE HOTS FOR ME. BUT IF I'M WRONG, THAT WOULD BE TOTALLY EMBARRASSING, RIGHT?
SO I CAN'T ASK HER. BUT I WANNA KNOW HOW SHE FEELS. IF I CAN DATE HER...
...I WANT TO...AS SOON AS POSSIBLE! WHAT SHOULD I DO?
ULTRALOVE
HMM... I UNDERSTAND YOUR DILEMMA, BUT THAT'S NOT WHAT I...
OH, I'VE ALWAYS WANTED TO ASK YOU...

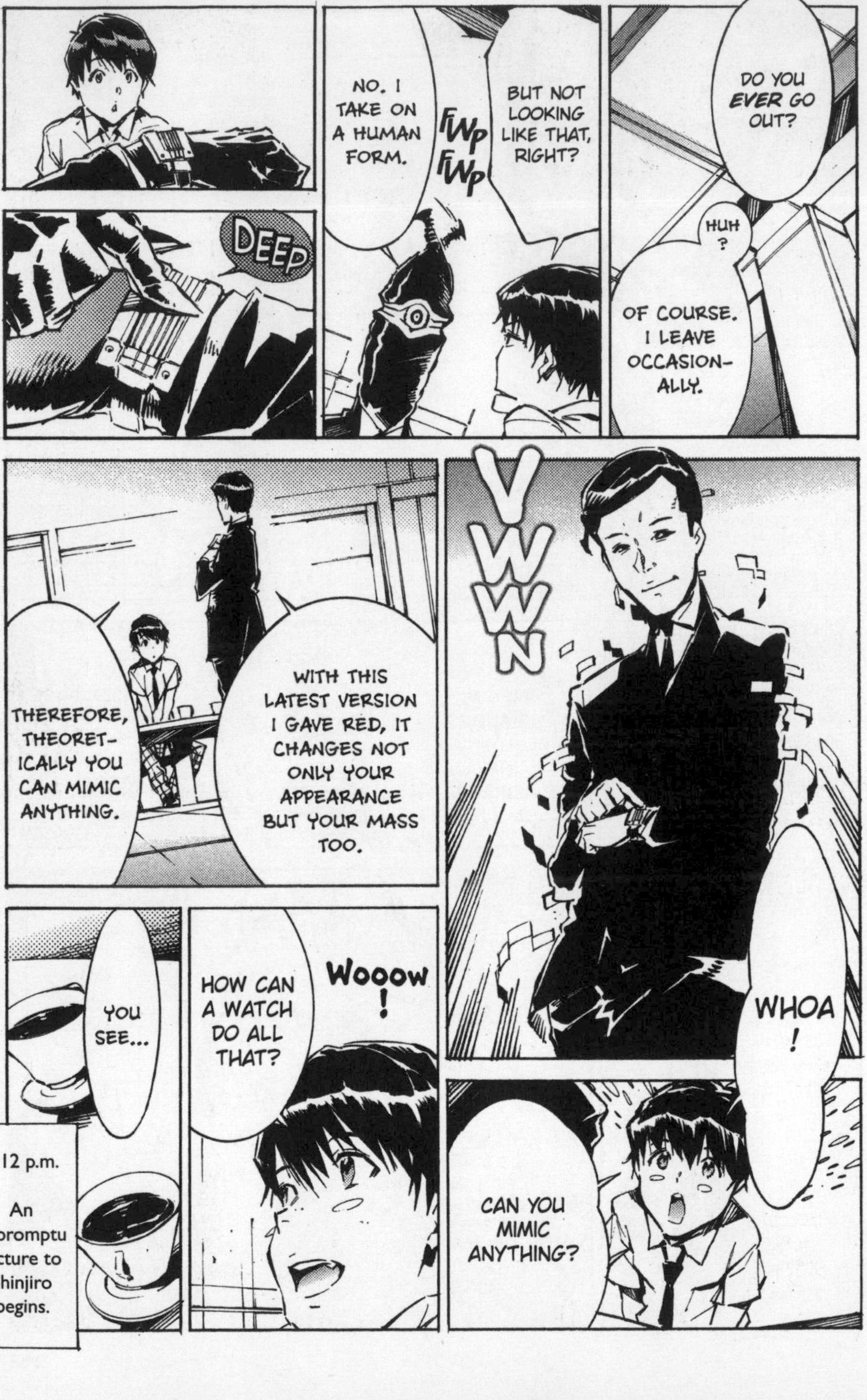
DO YOU EVER GO OUT?
HUH?
OF COURSE. I LEAVE OCCASION-ALLY.
BUT NOT LOOKING LIKE THAT, RIGHT?
FWP FWP
NO. I TAKE ON A HUMAN FORM.
DEEP
VWWN
WHOA!
CAN YOU MIMIC ANYTHING?
WITH THIS LATEST VERSION I GAVE RED, IT CHANGES NOT ONLY YOUR APPEARANCE BUT YOUR MASS TOO.
THEREFORE, THEORET-ICALLY YOU CAN MIMIC ANYTHING.
WOOOW!
HOW CAN A WATCH DO ALL THAT?
YOU SEE...
2:12 p.m.
An impromptu lecture to Shinjiro begins.

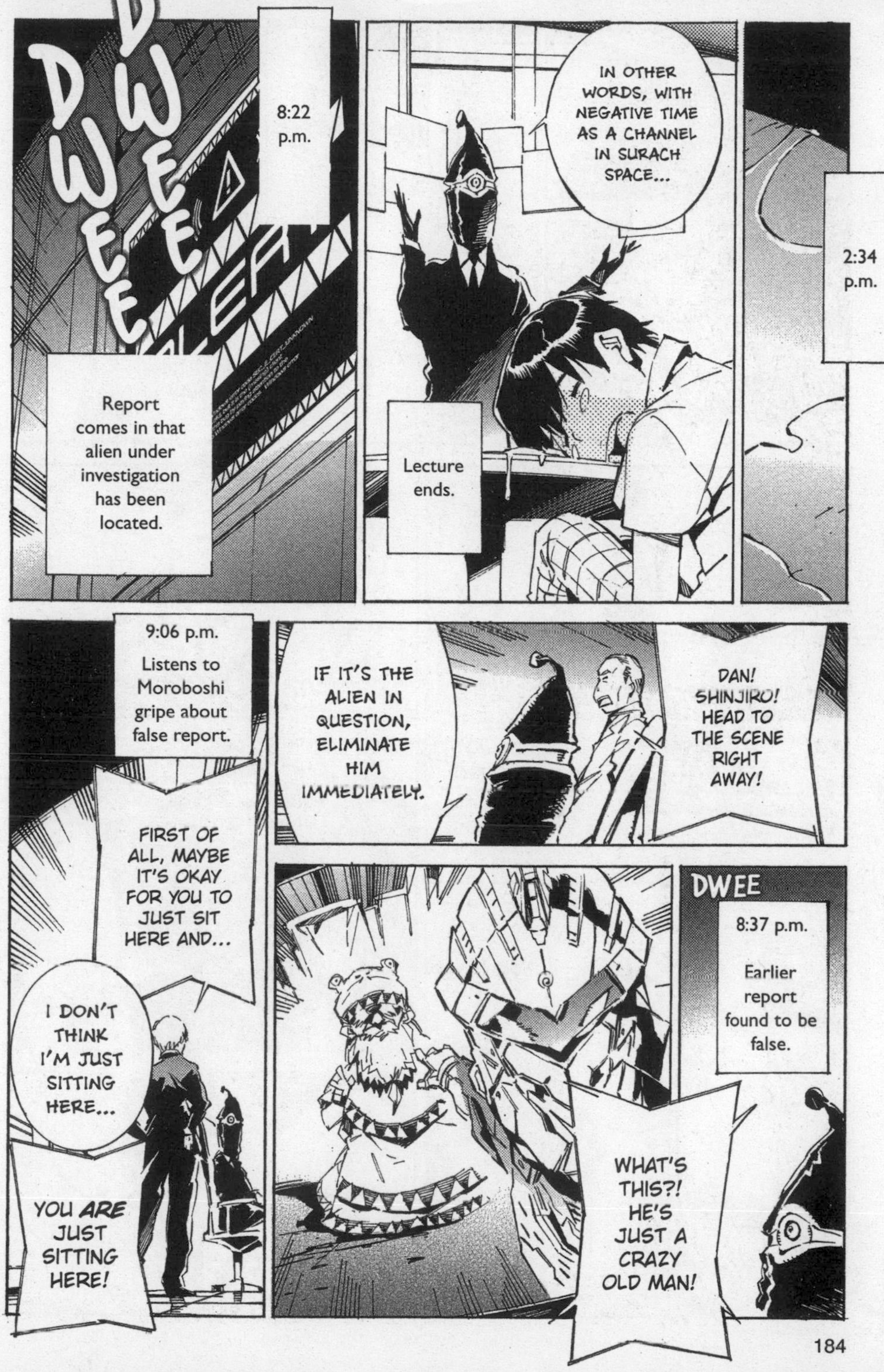
2:34 p.m.
IN OTHER WORDS, WITH NEGATIVE TIME AS A CHANNEL IN SURACH SPACE...
Lecture ends.
8:22 p.m.
DWEE
DWEE
Report comes in that alien under investigation has been located.
DAN! SHINJIRO! HEAD TO THE SCENE RIGHT AWAY!
IF IT'S THE ALIEN IN QUESTION, ELIMINATE HIM IMMEDIATELY.
DWEE
8:37 p.m.
Earlier report found to be false.
WHAT'S THIS?! HE'S JUST A CRAZY OLD MAN!
9:06 p.m.
Listens to Moroboshi gripe about false report.
FIRST OF ALL, MAYBE IT'S OKAY FOR YOU TO JUST SIT HERE AND...
I DON'T THINK I'M JUST SITTING HERE...
YOU *ARE* JUST SITTING HERE!

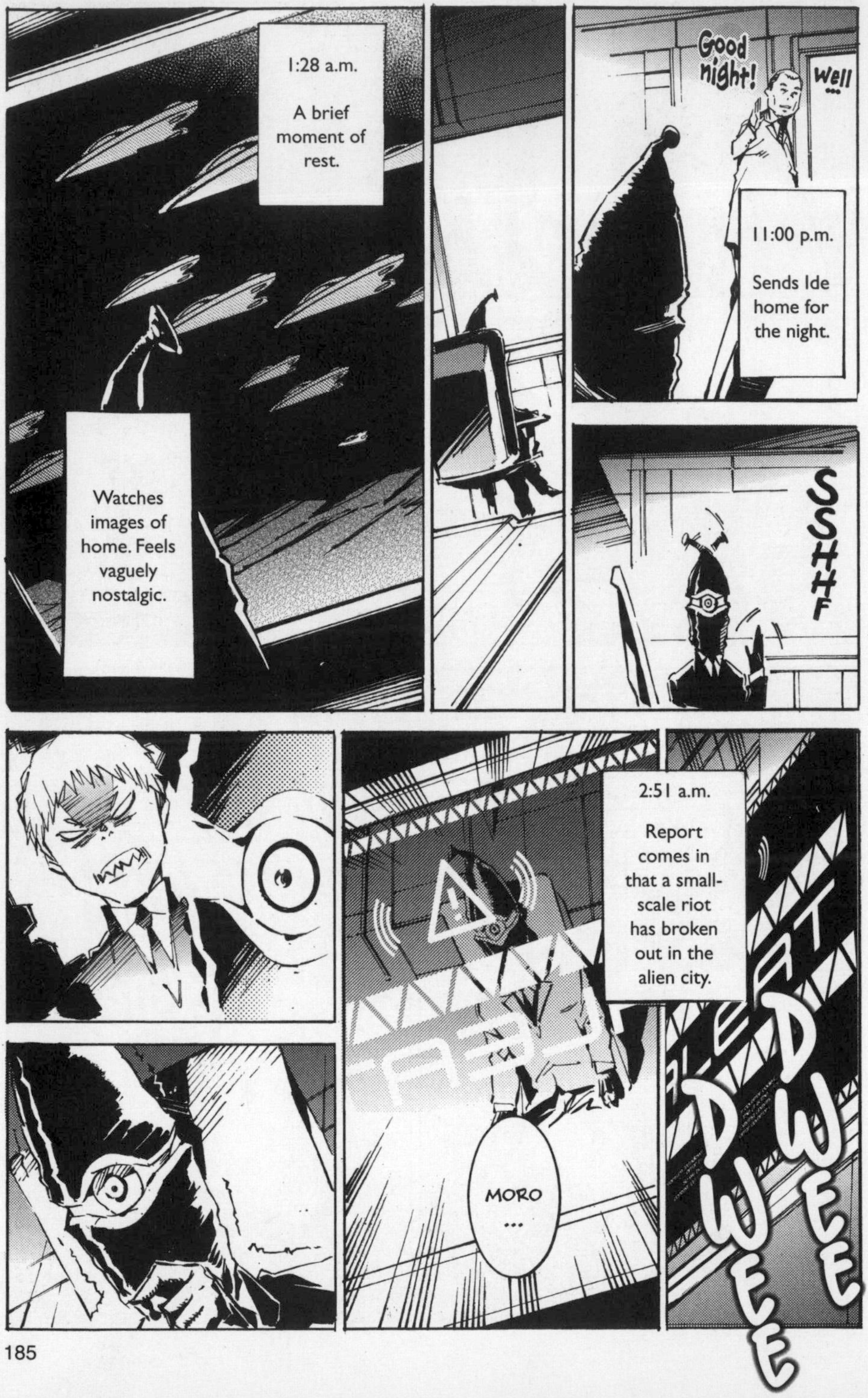
Well ...
Good night!
11:00 p.m.
Sends Ide home for the night.
SSHHF
1:28 a.m.
A brief moment of rest.
Watches images of home. Feels vaguely nostalgic.
2:51 a.m.
Report comes in that a small-scale riot has broken out in the alien city.
DWEE DWEE
MORO ...

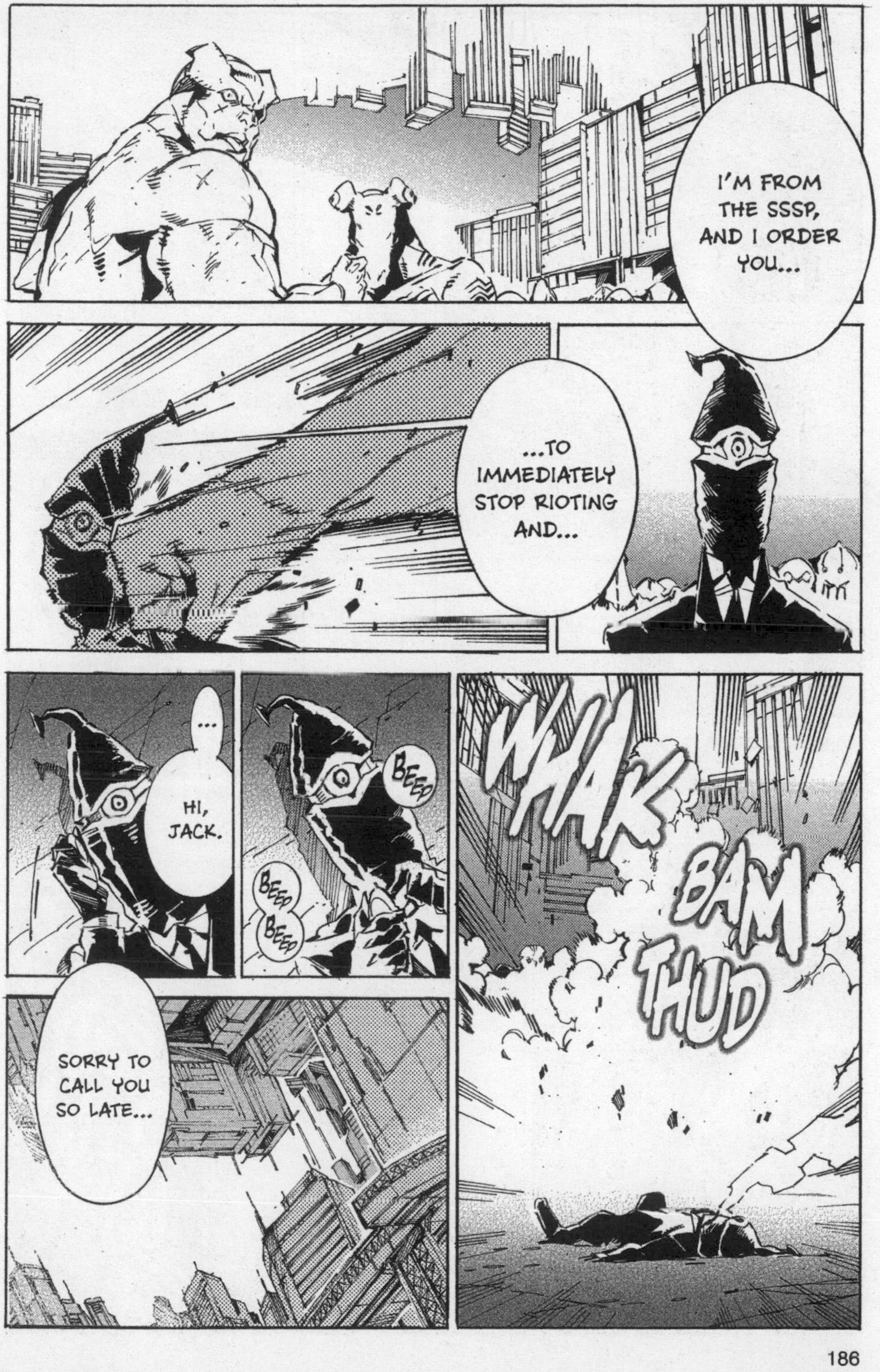
I'M FROM THE SSSP, AND I ORDER YOU...
...TO IMMEDIATELY STOP RIOTING AND...
WHAK
BAM
THUD
BEEP
BEEP
BEEP
...
HI, JACK.
SORRY TO CALL YOU SO LATE...

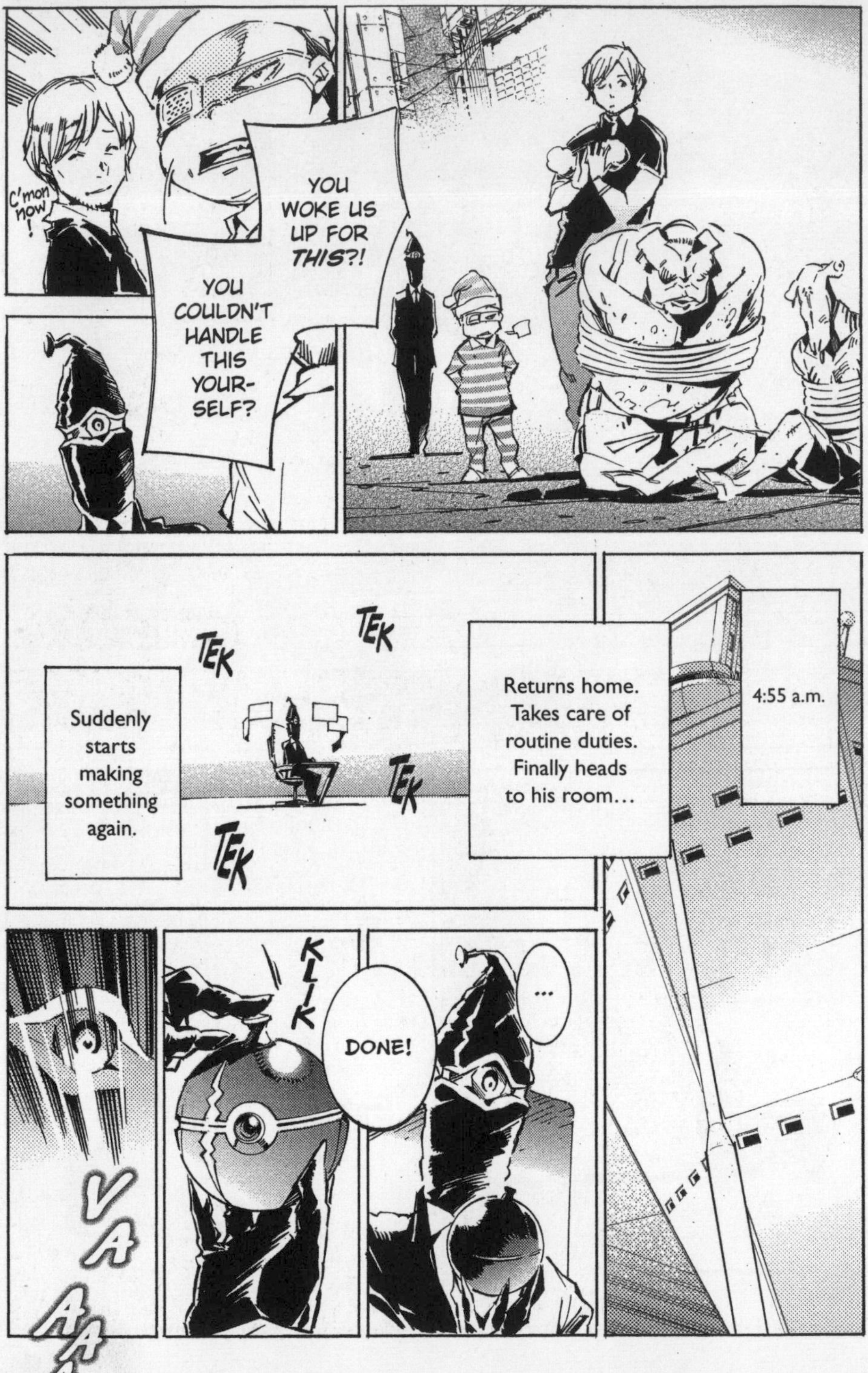
YOU WOKE US UP FOR *THIS*?!
C'mon now!
YOU COULDN'T HANDLE THIS YOUR-SELF?
4:55 a.m.
Returns home. Takes care of routine duties. Finally heads to his room…
TEK
TEK
TEK
TEK
Suddenly starts making something again.
...
DONE!
KLIK
VAAAA

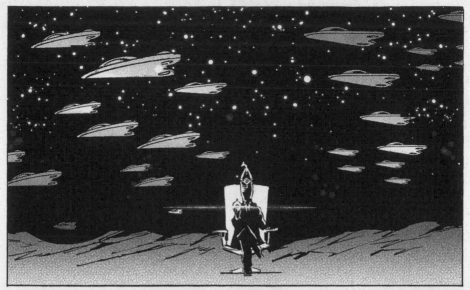

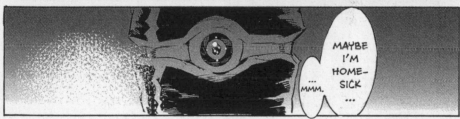

...MMM. MAYBE I'M HOME- SICK ...

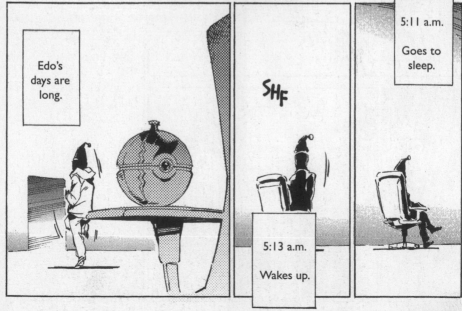

Edo's days are long.

SHF

5:13 a.m.

Wakes up.

5:11 a.m.

Goes to sleep.

THIS IS THE BEGINNING OF A NEW AGE

■ Seiji Hokuto's exo-armor, built by the genius alien engineer Yapool. Hokuto calls it his "Ace Suit." He chose a word beginning with the letter "A" to indicate that it is of "Alien" manufacture. The rest is his own self-aggrandizing flair.

FRONT

REAR

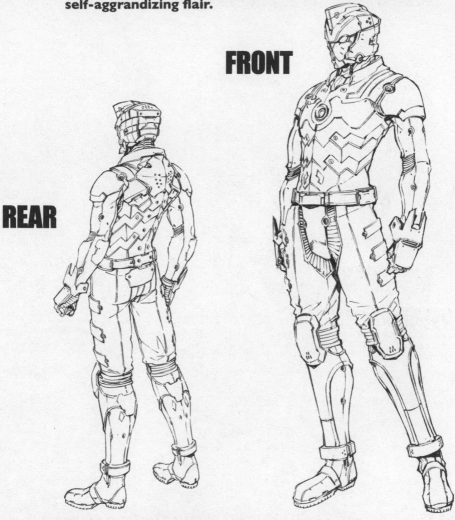

■ The thrusters—stored around the shoulder blades and deployed by opening and closing the covers—are designed for sudden leaps and high-speed movement. They are not meant for flight.

■ Including prosthetic arms and legs designed with built-in laser weapons for combat, the suit itself is loaded with multiple features to protect and support Hokuto. However, Hokuto himself has not yet discovered all the features (which Yapool included because of his parental affection for the boy).

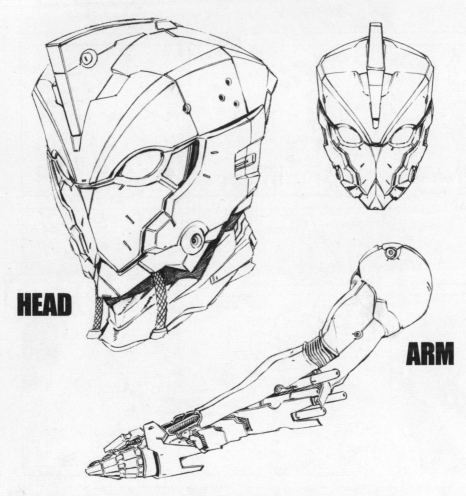

HEAD

ARM

■ Sliding the suit's wrist along the hand protector activates laser weapons embedded in the prosthetic arms. Both arms have this equipment, but one of them is designed to receive the emitted laser. The principle is the same as Shinjiro's Spacium Blade, but its combat use is very different due to its large size.

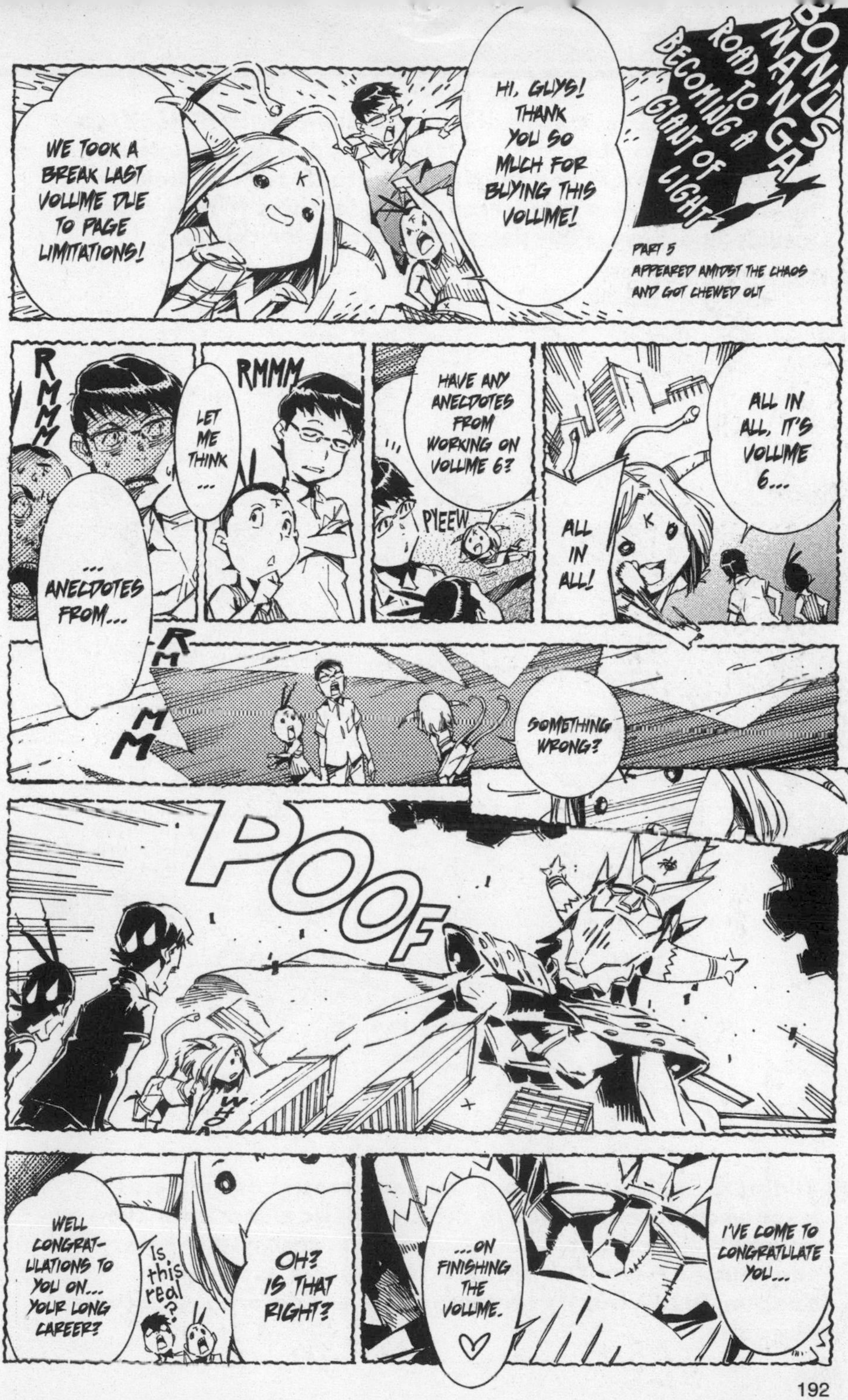
BONUS MANGA ROAD TO BECOMING A GIANT OF LIGHT
PART 5 APPEARED AMIDST THE CHAOS AND GOT CHEWED OUT
HI, GUYS! THANK YOU SO MUCH FOR BUYING THIS VOLUME!
WE TOOK A BREAK LAST VOLUME DUE TO PAGE LIMITATIONS!
ALL IN ALL, IT'S VOLUME 6...
ALL IN ALL!
HAVE ANY ANECDOTES FROM WORKING ON VOLUME 6?
PYEEW
RMMM
LET ME THINK ...
RMMM
... ANECDOTES FROM...
RMMM
SOMETHING WRONG?
POOF
WHOA
I'VE COME TO CONGRATULATE YOU...
...ON FINISHING THE VOLUME. ♡
OH? IS THAT RIGHT?
Is this real?
WELL CONGRAT-ULATIONS TO YOU ON... YOUR LONG CAREER?

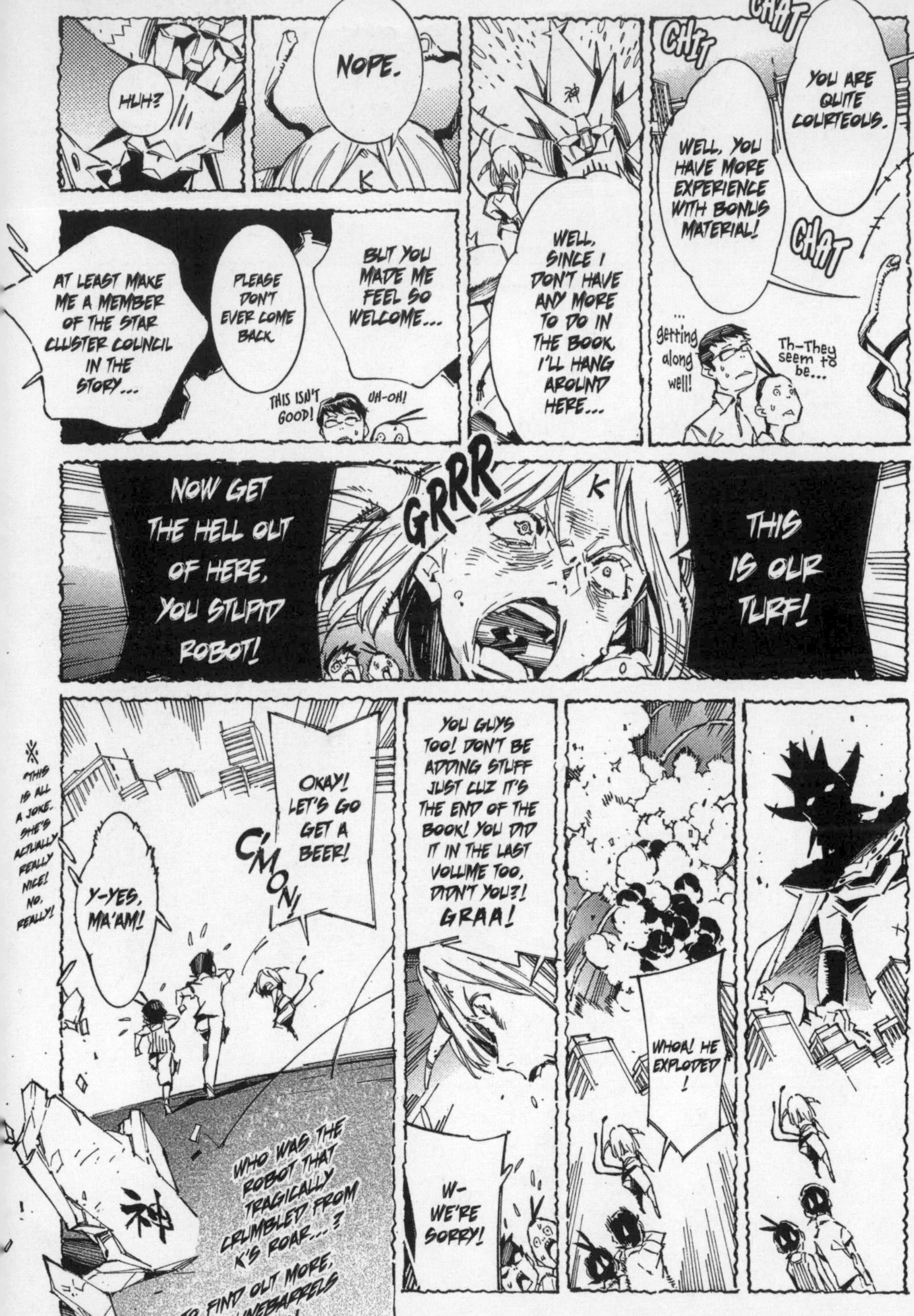
CHAT
CHIT
YOU ARE QUITE COURTEOUS.
WELL, YOU HAVE MORE EXPERIENCE WITH BONUS MATERIAL!
CHAT
Th-They seem to be...
...getting along well!
WELL, SINCE I DON'T HAVE ANY MORE TO DO IN THE BOOK I'LL HANG AROUND HERE...
NOPE.
HUH?
BUT YOU MADE ME FEEL SO WELCOME...
PLEASE DON'T EVER COME BACK.
AT LEAST MAKE ME A MEMBER OF THE STAR CLUSTER COUNCIL IN THE STORY...
UH-OH!
THIS ISN'T GOOD!
THIS IS OUR TURF!
GRRR
NOW GET THE HELL OUT OF HERE, YOU STUPID ROBOT!
WHOA! HE EXPLODED!
YOU GUYS TOO! DON'T BE ADDING STUFF JUST CUZ IT'S THE END OF THE BOOK! YOU DID IT IN THE LAST VOLUME TOO, DIDN'T YOU?! GRAA!
W-WE'RE SORRY!
OKAY! LET'S GO GET A BEER!
C'MON!
Y-YES, MA'AM!
WHO WAS THE ROBOT THAT TRAGICALLY CRUMBLED FROM K'S ROAR...?
TO FIND OUT MORE, READ LINEBARRELS OF IRON!
※ THIS IS ALL A JOKE. SHE'S ACTUALLY REALLY NICE! NO, REALLY!

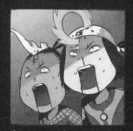

EIICHI SHIMIZU × TOMOHIRO SHIMOGUCHI

This might not matter to anyone, but there is a tiny
bit of info about Shimoguchi that I'd like to share
with those who bought this volume.

Every year, beginning around the middle of May,
Shimoguchi starts working in just his underpants.

According to him, this is "because it's hot."

That doesn't really matter to you, does it?

ULTRAMAN
VOLUME 6
VIZ SIGNATURE EDITION

STORY/ART BY **EIICHI SHIMIZU** AND **TOMOHIRO SHIMOGUCHI**

©2015 Eiichi Shimizu and Tomohiro Shimoguchi / TSUBURAYA PROD.
Originally published by HERO'S INC.

TRANSLATION **JOE YAMAZAKI**
ENGLISH ADAPTATION **STAN!**
TOUCH-UP ART & LETTERING **EVAN WALDINGER**
DESIGN **FAWN LAU**
EDITOR **MIKE MONTESA**

Printed in the U.S.A.

Published by VIZ Media, LLC
P.O. Box 77010
San Francisco, CA 94107

10 9 8 7 6 5 4 3 2 1
First printing, November 2016

VIZ SIGNATURE

www.viz.com

HEY! YOU'RE READING IN THE WRONG DIRECTION!

This is the END of the graphic novel

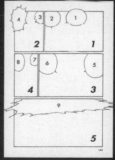

Follow the action this way.

To properly enjoy this VIZ graphic novel, please turn it around and begin reading from RIGHT TO LEFT. Unlike English, Japanese is read right to left, so Japanese comics are read in reverse order from the way English comics are typically read.

This book has been printed in the original Japanese format in order to preserve the orientation of the original artwork.

HAVE FUN WITH IT!